THE ELGAR COMPANION TO HYMAN MINSKY

The Elgar Companion to Hyman Minsky

Edited by

Dimitri B. Papadimitriou

Levy Economics Institute of Bard College, USA

and

L. Randall Wray

Levy Economics Institute of Bard College and University of Missouri at Kansas City, USA

Edward Elgar
Cheltenham, UK • Northampton, MA, USA

Published by
Edward Elgar Publishing Limited
The Lypiatts
15 Lansdown Road
Cheltenham
Glos GL50 2JA
UK

Edward Elgar Publishing, Inc.
William Pratt House
9 Dewey Court
Northampton
Massachusetts 01060
USA

A catalogue record for this book
is available from the British Library

Library of Congress Control Number: 2009941096

Mixed Sources
Product group from well-managed
forests and other controlled sources
www.fsc.org Cert no. SA-COC-1565
© 1996 Forest Stewardship Council

FSC

ISBN 978 1 84720 849 1 (cased)

Printed and bound by MPG Books Group, UK

Contents

Contributors

Tiziana Assenza, Catholic University of Milan, Istituto di Teoria Economica e Metodi Quantitativi (ITEMQ), Milan, Italy and University of Amsterdam, Center for Nonlinear Dynamics in Economics and Finance (CeNDEF), Amsterdam, The Netherlands.

Marshall Auerback, RAB Capital Plc, Global Portfolio Strategist, London, United Kingdom and Senior Fellow, Roosevelt Institute, New York, USA.

Robert J. Barbera, Chief Economist, ITG, Rye Brook, New York and Fellow, Johns Hopkins Economics Department, Baltimore, Maryland, USA.

Riccardo Bellofiore, Dipartimento di Scienze Economiche 'Hyman P. Minsky', University of Bergamo, Bergamo, Italy and Research Associate, History and Methodology of Economics Group, University of Amsterdam, Amsterdam, The Netherlands.

Domenico Delli Gatti, Catholic University of Milan, Istituto di Teoria Economica e Metodi Quantitativi (ITEMQ), Milan, Italy.

Sheila Dow, Emeritus Professor of Economics, University of Stirling, Scotland, UK.

Gary A. Dymski, Professor of Economics, University of California, Riverside, California, USA.

Piero Ferri, Professor of Economics, Hyman P. Minsky Department of Economic Studies, University of Bergamo, Bergamo, Italy.

Duncan K. Foley, Leo Model Professor of Economics, New School for Social Research, New York, and External Faculty, Santa Fe Institute, Santa Fe, New Mexico, USA.

James K. Galbraith, Lloyd M. Bentsen Jr. Chair in Government-Business Relations, Lyndon B. Johnson School of Public Affairs, The University of Texas at Austin, Austin, Texas and Senior Scholar, Levy Economics Institute of Bard College, Annandale-on-Hudson, New York, USA.

Mauro Gallegati, Università Politecnica delle Marche, Dipartimento di Economia, Ancona, Italy.

Joseph Halevi, Department of Political Economy, University of Sydney, Sydney, Australia, International University College of Turin, Torino, Italy and CRIISEA, Université de Picardie, Amiens, France.

Jan Kregel, Senior Scholar, Levy Economics Institute of Bard College, Annandale-on-Hudson, New York and Professor of Finance and Development, Tallinn University of Technology, Tallinn, Estonia.

Paul McCulley, Managing Director, PIMCO, Newport Beach, California, USA.

Eric Nasica, Associate Professor of Economics, University of Nice Sophia Antipolis and CNRS-GREDEG, Nice and Valbonne, France.

Dimitri B. Papadimitriou, President, Levy Economics Institute of Bard College, Executive Vice President and Jerome Levy Professor of Economics, Bard College, Annandale-on-Hudson, New York, USA.

Robert W. Parenteau, CFA, MacroStrategy Edge, Berkeley, California, USA, Editor, *The Richebächer Letter*, Agora Financial, Baltimore, Maryland and Research Associate, Levy Economics Institute of Bard College, Annandale-on-Hudson, New York.

Marco Passarella, Dipartimento di Scienze Economiche 'Hyman P. Minsky', University of Bergamo, Bergamo, Italy.

Daniel Munevar Sastre, of Colombia, a graduate of the University of Pinar del Rio, is a student at the LBJ School of Public Affairs, the University of Texas at Austin, Austin, Texas, USA.

Martin Shubik, Seymour Knox Professor Emeritus of Mathematical Institutional Economics, Yale University, New Haven, Connecticut, USA.

Éric Tymoigne, Assistant Professor, Lewis & Clark College, Portland, Oregon, USA.

Charles L. Weise, Department of Economics, Gettysburg College, Gettysburg, Pennsylvania, USA.

L. Randall Wray, Senior Scholar, Levy Economics Institute of Bard College, Annandale-on-Hudson, New York and Professor of Economics and Research Director, Center for Full Employment and Price Stability, Department of Economics, University of Missouri-Kansas City, USA.

Acknowledgments

The contributions included in this volume were especially commissioned from economists whose ideas and research have been influenced by the work of Hyman P. Minsky. They were all very excited to participate and interested in each other's work. Sincere thanks are due to Alan Sturmer, our publishing editor, and our immense gratitude to Deborah C. Treadway for her invaluable research and other assistance in preparing the manuscript.

Dimitri B. Papadimitriou
L. Randall Wray

Abbreviations

ABCP	asset-backed commercial paper
Alt-A	alternative A-paper mortgage
ABS	asset-backed security
ARM	adjustable-rate mortgage
BEA	Bureau of Economic Analysis
BG	Bernanke and Gertler
BLS	Bureau of Labor Statistics
BNW	Brave New World
CD	certificate of deposit
CDO	collateralized debt obligation
CDS	credit default swap
CEA	Council of Economic Advisers
CEO	chief executive officer
CPI	consumer price index
ELR	employer of last resort
FAH	Financial Accelerator Hypothesis
FDI	Foreign Direct Investment
FDIC	Federal Deposit Insurance Corporation
FED	Federal Reserve System
FIH	Financial Instability Hypothesis
FOMC	Federal Open Market Committee
FSLIC	Federal Savings and Loan Insurance Corporation
GDP	gross domestic product
GE	general equilibrium theory
GNP	gross national product
GS	Greenwald and Stiglitz
GSE	government sponsored enterprise
HE	heterogeneous agents
HPM	high power money
IKE	Information and Knowledge Economy
IMF	International Monetary Fund
IRS	Internal Revenue Service
LTCM	Long-Term Capital Management
MBS	mortgage-backed security
MM	Modigliani-Miller
MWMTR	Minsky/Wicksell Modified Taylor Rule
NAIRU	Non-Accelerating Inflation Rate of Unemployment

NATO	North Atlantic Treaty Organization
NBER	National Bureau of Economic Research
NOW	negotiable order of withdrawal
NRPB	National Resources Planning Board
OECD	Organization for Economic Cooperation and Development
PDCF	Primary Dealer Credit Facility
RA	representative agent
RBC	real business cycle
S&P	Standard & Poor's
SEC	Securities and Exchange Commission
SIV	structured investment vehicle
SPV	special purpose vehicle
TIPS	Treasury Inflation Protected Securities
TSLF	Term Securities Lending Facility

1 Introduction: Minsky on money, banking and finance
Dimitri B. Papadimitriou and L. Randall Wray

The genesis of this *Companion to Minsky* was the republication, in 2008, of Minsky's two seminal books: *John Maynard Keynes* and *Stabilizing an Unstable Economy* first published in 1975 and 1986 respectively. Introducing Minsky to the wider world, the *Wall Street Journal* wrote: 'Hyman Minsky spent much of his career advancing the idea that financial systems are inherently susceptible to bouts of speculation that, if they last long enough, end in crises . . . Indeed, the Minsky Moment has become a catch phrase on Wall Street.' There is, then, hardly any need to comment on the relevance of Hyman Minsky's work to the global financial and economic crisis that began in 2007 in the US and quickly spread around the world. Several of the chapters in this volume explicitly take up that topic. Many more economists have, recently, discovered Minsky's Financial Instability Hypothesis (FIH) and widely applied it to the course of events in the US from 2004 until the real estate market went bust, and many commentators used his hedge, speculative, and Ponzi classification scheme to analyze the evolution of mortgage markets. Many of Minsky's favorite themes – 'stability is destabilizing', the role of the 'Big Government' and 'Big Bank' in constraining endogenous instability, banker's rationality, money non-neutrality, creative destruction and innovation by financial institutions – are taken up in the chapters especially written for this companion to Minsky. This introductory chapter does not summarize those that follow, but in a few sentences attempts to demonstrate how each chapter connects to Minsky's core ideas. The reader will need to go to each contribution to discover its individual message.

In an earlier period, Minsky wrote concerning the devastating consequences that would take place on the balance sheets of households and businesses, and especially on financial institutions carrying mortgage debt should the price of real estate assets fall sharply (Minsky 1964). As Jan Kregel points out in the next chapter, this concern was voiced in the 1960s, when Minsky analyzed the then fragile financial environment and offered clear policy prescriptions that should be implemented by the central bank and more crucially by the authorities responsible for managing fiscal policy. Little did he know how prescient his writings of more than four

1

decades would be in August 2007, when the housing markets meltdown began. Minsky's analysis of the 1960s and the policy suggestions he made are the focus of this chapter as are the lessons that can be drawn from that period and their applicability in responding to the challenges of the current financial and economic crisis. Apt fiscal policy was very important to Minsky's thinking and his writings over the years reflect it (Minsky 1986 [2008], 1992). As he put it, an economy, to prosper, needed not only a 'Big Bank,' acting as a lender of last resort, but also a 'Big Government.' He was particularly concerned with simple and erroneous interpretations of 'Big Government' being synonymous with Keynesian fine-tuning of aggregate demand rather than associated with a structuralist approach ensuring stability and full employment and interacting with the private sector. Éric Tymoigne explores these important Minskyan connections with considerable detail in Chapter 3 and places them in a US historical perspective. These issues are also discussed and analyzed further by Bellofiore, Halevi and Passarella from an alternative perspective in Chapter 4. The authors of this chapter contextualize and document the relevance of Minsky's ideas of 'Financial Keynesianism' and 'Wall Street Paradigm' in contemporary forms of capitalism. An analysis of the Minskyan banker is offered in Chapter 5 by Eric Nasica aiming at explaining bankers' rationality contributing to pro-cyclical financial fragility in concert with Minsky's FIH. The underlying theme is banks' entrepreneurial and innovative behaviors being the cause of institutional weakening and the transitioning of a financially overleveraged system to a state of financial crisis. This is Minsky's banking theory.

In Chapter 6, Auerback, McCulley and Parenteau attempt to answer the question 'What would Minsky do?' in the current crisis. Their answer is deep rooted in Minsky's work on financial instability as a function of ever increasing risk, the institutional structure, organization of regulation and supervision of institutions and markets and the policy responses as proposed by Minsky sometime ago.

Minsky was not comfortable with mainstream economics, especially with its emphasis and use of mathematics to analyze and establish elusive theoretical concepts such as general equilibrium. He was more interested in the structural, social and political aspects of the discipline as they were represented by the institutional design of an economy. Barbera and Weise, accepting Minsky's suspicions of mathematical formalization, attempt, nevertheless, to create a Minsky warning structure of asset inflation by modifying the standard Taylor rule of monetary policy determining the federal funds rate. In Chapter 7, they develop an expanded Taylor rule relationship they call Minsky/Wicksell Modified Taylor Rule (MWMTR) grounded on Minsky's insights of increasing leverage and risk that can detect undue asset price increases. Their aim is to make it easier for economists and central bankers to embrace a Minsky model they understand. Minsky was well aware of the importance of the link between innovation and finance, and how this relation affects stability in modern and financially guided economies. He understood that innovation processes emanating from financial institutions could not be explained very well by formal theory since they were the creation of human beings and uncontrolled markets, but he insisted that they be designed and managed in such a manner as to ensure economic stability. Martin Shubik, in Chapter 8, considers these connections and the 'mechanisms for the creation of money and credit, the selection of innovation' and the mix of institutional form and function using simple but detailed models. Duncan Foley, in Chapter 9, agrees to a large extent with Shubik echoing his assessment of Minsky's refusal to articulate his insights on financial instability inherent in the financial dynamics of a contemporary capitalist economy using the rigor of a mathematical model. As Foley points out, Minsky's dialectical investigation of his FIH is validated from historical patterns linked to detailed institutional reality and the unfolding of particular incidents of financial crisis. And even though his ideas and penetrating analysis provided no alternative to the contemporary economic method, they nevertheless, found resonance in the worlds of finance and policymaking.

Many of Minsky's followers have attempted to transform his vision in the language of mathematical and econometric modeling with varying success. The latest examples are found in the work of Assenza, Delli Gatti and Gallegati, and Ferri, the focus of Chapters 10 and 11 respectively. The authors of Chapter 10 construct a macrodynamic model of firm specific financial conditions including behavioral characteristics of financially constrained firms and households to determine instability. The derived dynamics from their model are dependent on the laws of motion emanating from particular financial conditions of individual heterogeneous agents and, using computer simulations, they analyze the evolution of micro and macro state variables. They also contrast their results with those of the Financial Accelerator research they consider to some extent akin to Minsky. Piero Ferri's goal, in Chapter 11, is also the formalization of Minsky's financial instability, but he wants to determine under what conditions of endogenously generated fluctuations the system can reach a breaking point. The mathematical narrative of his approach, much more advanced than previously (Ferri 1992), is the specification of a nonlinear dynamic model that tests and simulates debt dependent aggregate demand and supply subject to conditions of bounded rationality. The policy implications determined by the model are contrasted with historical episodes in the US and other countries, and further advances in this lineage of modeling research are suggested.

Booms and busts are spatial with high levels of uncertainty in exchange rate conditions impacting investment-financing processes across country borders. Indeed, the global imbalances since the 1980s, with the US being the chronic current account deficit economy financed by the current account surplus emerging market economies in Asia, most notably China, have had serious implications in the development of the current economic and financial crisis in the US and the global economy (Godley et al. 2006). Minsky's framework has been principally applied in an environment that assumes the financial cycle develops and affects a closed and homogeneous economy. Gary Dymski, in Chapter 12, extends the Minskyan core model to an open economy framework. Financial instability and crisis, as Dymski documents, can be dependent on the real and financial tensions inherent in capital flows across countries and can develop even in the absence of a typical Minsky cycle, which has implications for policy responses.

Behavioral finance was not specifically acknowledged in Minsky's writings, even though, as Sheila Dow suggests in Chapter 13, his uncertainty-based epistemology and method viewed from the lens of psychology can enhance our understanding of financial instability. There is a lot of psychological content in Minsky, since it is behavior that leads up to financial turmoil and market responses to it. In behavioral finance, however, she finds a lacuna relating to the motivation for action under uncertainty that plays a crucial part in Minsky's FIH and his mentor's (Keynes) treatment of financial behavior. Dow also explores the effects of uncertainty and emotion at the level of social structures and institutions as they are recognized in Minsky's structural approach.

This companion to Minsky ends with the essay by Galbraith and Munevar Sastre (Chapter 14), which departs from the other chapters, including this introduction, in that it considers a more 'generalized "Minsky Moment"' by applying it to other areas of social science, as for example, the sphere of international relations. What Galbraith and Munevar do quite brilliantly is to develop 'an analytical framework that may help describe the economic, political and military interactions of nation states' according to Minsky's taxonomy of financing profiles: hedge, speculative and Ponzi.

What we want to do in the remainder of this chapter is to take a longer-run perspective. Rather than addressing the evolution of financial positions over the course of a cycle, we will use Minsky's framework to examine how the financial system evolved over the entire post-war period, from one that promoted stability to one that was much more fragile. Of course, over those six decades, there were many business cycles and a number of (increasingly frequent and severe) financial crises. Each one of these is worthy of a Minskyan analysis. In what follows, we will look at a few of these (with more attention paid to the first postwar financial crisis – the municipal bond crisis of the mid-1960s – before turning in some detail to the current global financial crisis of 2007–10). Our purpose, however, is to take stock of the longer-term trend rather than to provide a close analysis of any particular cycle or crisis. Minsky took it for granted that the fundamental instability of the modern capitalist economy is upward – that is, toward a euphoric boom – however, each speculative frenzy is unique, and the events that bring a boom to an end are specific. In other words, Minsky's analysis was always institutional and historical. Still, there are common features involved: innovations, rising leverage, and – most significantly – changes to the 'model of the model' used by households, firms, banks, and even governments to form expectations. Decision-making always takes place in the context of fundamental uncertainty, so that the 'emotions' identified by Sheila Dow in Chapter 13 are important. These underlie the margins of safety built into financial arrangements. And because institutional 'ceilings and floors' contained the thrust toward depression (at least until the current crisis), there has been a long-term, endogenously induced trend toward closer concatenation of prospective income flows and contracted payments. Finally, those institutions that constrained instability have been seriously eroded by a combination of profit-seeking innovation plus relaxed regulation and supervision by governmental institutions. Thus, the current crisis was in some sense inevitable, although the precise timing and what triggered it could have been almost anything.

In this chapter, we analyze what Minsky (1964) referred to as a 'longer wave' – a long-term swing that is due to cumulative changes in the financial variables. The exact evolution of the financial variables over a longer wave depends on initial conditions and institutional arrangements (both market arrangements as well as legislated arrangements). The longer wave takes place over a succession of shorter, mild, recession cycles. Over the course of a long wave expansion, assets get revalued and financial layering rises. Debt grows relative to outside money – high power money (HPM), stretching liquidity; further, it grows relative to the income required to service it (so debt to gross domestic product (GDP) ratios grow on trend). In addition, stock prices and real estate prices will also grow on trend. As these grow, this generates (largely unrealized) capital gains that can be used for additional borrowing, increasing leveraging. Further, over the expansion, government debt (and HPM) tends to grow more slowly than GDP, increasing fragility. All of these characteristics apply to the long wave expansion of the post-war period. Minsky argued that as this long wave continues, the maximum combination of income shortfalls and defaults that can be safely handled falls. This is because more of the income flows are pre-committed, and layering of debt rises (so that default by one leads to a snowball of defaults). A panic can occur when income falls or defaults rise. Beyond some point, the 'Big Government' and 'Big Bank' stabilizers might not be sufficient to prevent 'It' (a debt deflation) from occurring. It is possible that the crisis that began in late 2007 will end the post-war long wave.

The chapter is organized as follows: first, we examine Schumpeter's profound influence on Minsky, while in the next section, we look at the nature of a system dominated by commercial banks, the emphasis that both Schumpeter and Minsky placed on them and their role in financial innovation and the capital development of an economy. We then move to analyze the first significant financial trauma since the 1930s, the Credit Crunch of 1966, which involved a run on a financial instrument or institution without a specific case of a failure or fraud. We next examine the great Monetarist Experiment and its long-term impact on the financial sector setting the stage for the current crisis. The practice of securitization as a new way of finance and the dominant role it played in the current global economic collapse is the focus of the subsequent section followed by a section on what form a Minskyan reconstitution of the financial system will take. In the concluding section, we draw lessons from Minsky that are applicable for the current crisis.

Schumpeterian finance and innovation
Minsky always insisted that any student who wanted to understand his views on finance would first have to master Schumpeter's theory of economic development. (Schumpeter was Minsky's original dissertation advisor.) According to Minsky, Schumpeter successfully integrated financial entrepreneurship and financial evolution into his analysis of economic development.

The nature of such a 'Schumpeterian' system is dominated by commercial banks. In Schumpeterian terms the banker was the 'ephor' of capitalism. Schumpeter begins with an economy operating in the neighborhood of a 'general' equilibrium in which all industries, firms, and households are individually in a state of equilibrium in the Walrasian sense (Schumpeter 1944). In this state, the economy can be analyzed as a circular flow, where purchases of the output flow are undertaken on the basis of sales of labor, products, or services, but the flow for purchases without sales or sales without purchases is ruled out. In this case, the circular flow could continue unchanging as 'the circulation of the blood' (Schumpeter 1934 [1949], p. 61). While money might be used in the circular flow economy, it would be used merely to facilitate exchange; it would function only as a veil. Within a circular flow, individuals can act promptly and rationally; behavior can be the result of cold calculation of probabilistic outcome. The capitalist is merely a manager, reacting to the 'data' ground out by the circular flow economy.

Of course, no society would in practice remain static. Some changes can be analyzed as continuous, infinitesimal shocks to the circular flow that lead to new points of equilibrium. Schumpeter's focus, however, is on 'that kind of change arising from within the system which so displaces its equilibrium point that the new one cannot be reached from the old one by infinitesimal steps' (Schumpeter 1934 [1949], p. 64), that is, spontaneous, discontinuous, and revolutionary changes to the circular flow that displace it so far from equilibrium that adaptation becomes impossible and routine must be abandoned. This is what he calls economic development, the result of innovation, characterized as the carrying out of new combinations of materials and forces or productive means.

Entrepreneurial innovation breaks the norm of the circular flow since it requires purchase without sale; it requires use of money as a 'claim ticket' on productive resources without use of money as a 'receipt voucher' for sale of commodities or services (Bellofiore 1985, 1992). Just as the circular flow is broken by innovation, the neutrality of money is broken by entrepreneurial activity; indeed, economic development requires non-neutrality of money.

Schumpeter believed that the strongest case could be made on the assumption that within a circular flow, all resources are fully utilized. This means that the innovator must draw already employed resources from the circular flow and direct them to a new and revolutionary activity (Schumpeter 1934 [1949], p. 68). This requires creation of new purchasing power, which can only come from credit creation. Innovation, then, requires a credit system, and the credit system is a result of this necessity. The banker is the 'capitalist par excellence', the 'ephor' of the capitalist system, as he/she produces 'the commodity "purchasing power"' that makes it possible to carry out the new combinations associated with innovation (Schumpeter 1934 [1949], p. 74).

Since credit allows purchase without sale (of previously produced goods and services), it can be inflationary as innovators outbid resources in order to use them in the new combinations. The 'old' firms will command fewer resources and their output may well fall. Purchases of resources by the innovators, however, maintain aggregate demand even as aggregate supply falls, resulting in what Schumpeter calls temporary credit inflation. After some period (which can take several years), the new combinations can finally put products into the market while at the same time the sales receipts of new firms enable them to retire the credit initially advanced to allow the innovation to proceed. As a result, loans and deposits ('money supply') contract toward the initial position, and spending power and prices also fall back toward initial levels (Schumpeter 1944, p. 9). Thus, the credit inflation is only temporary, and the innovation can even lead to a deflationary longer-term trend or bias as it reduces costs of production (Schumpeter 1934 [1949], p. 111).

Schumpeter calls 'primary wave' the period during which the economy first moves away from the circular flow in an expansion, but then contracts back toward the initial equilibrium of the circular flow even with no expectational errors. However, as firms are likely to react to rates of change, the initial expansion of purchasing power (and inflation of prices) can lead to a boom driven by 'mass psychology', while the contraction can degenerate to recession as the economy overshoots the circular flow on the way down. These 'secondary waves' increase the instability that is inherent in the capitalist economy (an often used theme in Minsky's work).

Innovation, itself, is endogenously generated by the apparent tranquility of the circular flow. That is, within a circular flow, the capitalist is sure of his ground and can adjust conduct in response to economic data. This confidence, however, raises entrepreneurial spirits, inducing experimentation and encouraging innovation (Bellofiore 1992). Innovation, in turn, generates expansion and disrupts conventional patterns of behavior; it becomes too difficult to make predictions and entrepreneurial spirit is depressed. As Schumpeter argues, the innovation 'changes social and economic situations for good' as it alters the data of the system and moves it away from equilibrium, and makes it impossible – even for the new entrepreneurs – to predict the outcome of actions (Schumpeter 1951, p. 217; Bellofiore 1992). All of these themes can also be found in Minsky's work – the importance of innovations as well as the role that apparent tranquility plays in generating them.

According to Schumpeter, when new innovations stop coming forward the economy turns downward; it eventually returns to a circular flow of reproduction. Schumpeter argues that lack of inventions is never the barrier to innovation; rather, it is the lack of entrepreneurial spirit that would put the inventions to use in innovative ways that is the barrier to economic development. Once a circular flow has operated near equilibrium for a sufficient period, confidence will be restored sufficiently that innovation may reappear.

Minsky, in concert with Schumpeter, maintained that economies with financial innovations are subject to booms and busts because these innovations allow debt to increase faster than ability to pay, and because they shift income to the rentier class with a lower propensity to spend (thus, lowering the aggregate demand that would be necessary to continue to generate the income necessary to service debt). The strong influence of Schumpeter's many theoretical elements are clearly evident in Minsky's approach: importance of finance; endogenously induced innovations; and cyclical behavior responding to outcomes even as it influences outcomes. Minsky paid a lot of attention to commercial banking, and to this we turn next. In the early post-war period, the commercial banker was, indeed, the 'ephor' of capitalism, but that position was systematically eroded as 'managed money' took on a dominant role.

Minsky on commercial banking: reserves, loans and deposits
Minsky used to argue that anyone can create money – the problem is to have it accepted. This statement makes it clear that he identified 'money' with an IOU, and what he meant was that anyone can issue an IOU denominated in the money of account (dollar in the US), but some find more 'takers' for their IOUs. Indeed, he recognized a 'hierarchical' or 'pyramid' of money IOUs ranked according to acceptability, with the government's own IOUs at the top, then those of commercial banks, next the liabilities of other types of financial institutions, and finally the IOUs of nonfinancial firms as well as households at the bottom. Further, the IOUs of those lower in the pyramid are normally 'redeemed' for those higher in the pyramid; another way of stating it is to say that one usually extinguishes one's liability by payment of a liability issued by an entity higher in the pyramid. In this section we will focus on the commercial bank sector because commercial banks traditionally played the most important role in providing finance for businesses, households, and even state and local government loans. Over time, as we discuss later, they were displaced by other types of financial institutions and instruments – what we used to call 'nonbank banks', although they are now frequently referred to as the 'shadow banking sector'. In this section, when we write 'bank', we mean 'commercial bank' as defined by the Glass-Steagall Act that separated commercial banking from investment banking – institutions that both accepted deposits and made loans. We will identify the essential characteristics to indicate why Schumpeter placed so much emphasis on them.

   Following Minsky, we too reject the old notion of a deposit multiplier in which banks wait until they have excess reserves to make loans and issue deposits. That view essentially regarded bank reserves as a sort of 'raw material' used by banks subject to fractional reserve laws to 'manufacture' loans and deposits. Thus, the bank would try to attract a deposit so that it could make a loan; or, it would look to the Fed to provide reserves so that the bank could lend any excess reserves – with the system as a whole creating a multiple expansion of deposits and loans. Even in his earliest writings, Minsky (1957) realized this was far too simplistic because banks actively innovate in order to throw off reserve constraints. He discussed how the creation of the federal funds market as well as other innovations allowed a given quantity of reserves to support more loans and deposits. Later, he explicitly adopted the view that banks 'endogenously' create loans and deposits and then seek reserves as necessary from the central bank. Here we will discuss how commercial banks actually operate.

First, it is critical to understand that bank deposits are liabilities; while this may seem too obvious to warrant mention, casual discussion of bank operations often neglects to consider that a deposit makes a bank liable for something. The bank is liable for high power money (HPM – reserves and cash). Deposits are simply a 'horizontal' leveraging of HPM – a promise to deliver HPM according to the contractual agreement (on demand in the case of demand deposits, on a specific future date in the case of a time deposit). Effectively, the bank is short of HPM, betting it will be able to obtain the necessary HPM in a timely manner at a not-too-prohibitive cost. Reserve requirements are simply minimum HPM balance requirements, much as many readers are forced to maintain a thousand dollars in their checking accounts. These in no direct way constrain the bank's ability to 'make loans', although they raise the bank cost of shorting HPM (much as compensating balance requirements raise the cost to a firm of taking out a bank loan – shorting bank money), thus, may increase the return that must be obtained on assets to make them desirable. When a bank fails to meet the minimum HPM balance required, the Fed automatically books the 'fail' as a loan of reserves (much as 'overdraft' facilities routinely protect depositors of United Kingdom banks; American depositors can usually purchase overdraft insurance). In any case, a bank 'makes a loan', that is, purchases an asset, by 'creating a deposit', that is, shorting HPM.

As deposits are liabilities, banks do not worry about retaining them. However, when a check is written on a demand deposit, or when a maturing time deposit is not rolled-over, the bank is subject to a reserve, HPM, clearing drain. Since banks do not keep significant excess HPM balances, a clearing drain will cause a bank to fall below minimum HPM balance requirements. An individual bank will thus try to take a number of actions: 'purchase' HPM balances from the Fed, 'borrow' federal funds, 'sell' certificates of deposit, or 'repo' government bonds to meet minimum balance requirements. In the aggregate, the only 'net' source of HPM is the government, either the treasury or the central bank. When the treasury buys goods or services or provides transfer payments, it writes a check on the Fed, which ends up as a bank deposit of HPM at the Fed; when the Fed buys assets (government bonds, foreign currency, or commercial bank

IOUs) it credits a bank deposit of HPM. In other words, any time when the treasury or central bank spends, HPM is created. On the other hand, tax payments work in reverse – destroy HPM as bank deposits at the Fed are debited. Furthermore, treasury or central bank sales of government bonds also drain HPM, thus reducing bank deposits at the Fed. The excess of government purchases over tax receipts (or 'deficit spending') generates an equivalent net injection of HPM.

All else equal, government deficit spending generates excess reserves (HPM deposits in excess of minimum balance requirements); bond sales by the government thus are required to offer an interest-earning alternative to non-interest-earning excess reserves. Over the very short run (for example, a day or two), the central bank ensures that the banking system as a whole has just the right amount of HPM to meet minimum balance requirements – mainly through open market sales and purchases of government bonds, although the discount window is also used – in order to maintain orderly overnight (federal funds) markets. In other words, regardless of its announced policy, the central bank always chooses a short-term (overnight) interest rate target and then ensures that the quantity of reserves is just sufficient to allow banks to meet minimum balance requirements. Over the longer run, it is primarily the treasury that supplies the right amount of bonds to drain excess reserves from the system. The treasury and central bank develop complex, coordinated operating procedures to ensure that the banking system is continuously supplied with the correct quantity of reserves (see Bell 1998 and Wray 1999).

Previous to the development of the federal funds market (created in the mid 1950s, but maturing in the early 1960s), individual banks used government bond sales or purchases to adjust HPM balances (Minsky 1957). A sale of a bond by a bank to a bond dealer would result in an HPM debit of the dealer's bank's reserves and a credit to the HPM reserves of the selling bank. Purchase of a bond would work in reverse – debit the bank's HPM reserves and lead to a credit of HPM to the bond dealer's bank. Thus, banks effectively used the bond dealers as 'middlemen' to shift bank reserves from those with excessive balances to those who were deficient. Apparently this is what has led to the widespread belief – in part shared by Minsky – that banks 'operated on assets', selling out bond positions in order to make loans.

With the development of the federal funds market, banks cut out the middlemen to market excess reserves, or HPM balances, directly. This transparency led many economists to believe that something of fundamental importance had changed – that banks had 'discovered' liability management, so that they would no longer need to sell bonds before making loans. While it is possible that many bankers may have believed themselves to be subject to reserve constraints such that they would, indeed, need to sell assets to obtain the reserves supposedly required to make loans, it is clear from balance sheet analysis that this was an imaginary constraint. Banks always 'operated on liabilities'. Rather than selling out positions in government bonds over the post-war boom, they instead 'leveraged' them.

From the perspective of the bank, loans to customers generate long positions in IOUs; similarly, its holdings of government bonds are long positions in securities. A bank is not forced to liquidate its long position in bonds to obtain a long position in customer IOUs. Rather, it simply needs to short HPM to go long in IOUs. There are many factors that may go into determining the willingness of a bank to take long positions in IOUs and short positions in HPM. Obviously, one of the most important factors is the existing differential between the interest rate it expects to earn on the IOUs and the rate it must pay to short HPM (equivalently, to get depositors to go long in 'bank money'). The bank, however, must also factor into the analysis other costs (minimum HPM balances that have to be maintained against some of its short positions; capital requirements against its long positions – which reduce the return on capital). More importantly, because the short positions commit the bank to deliver HPM in the future (for the most part, on uncertain dates), it must be concerned with the future terms on which HPM can be obtained. This is why the expected course of interest rates will be (perhaps imperfectly) reflected in today's quotes. A 'panic' or market break can occur when it is feared that HPM may not be obtainable on reasonable terms in the future – in which case banks won't go short to take long positions.

None of this should be interpreted to mean that the quantity of HPM acts as a constraint on banks' ability to lend. At the end, the Fed will supply exactly the quantity of reserves it requires banks to hold. The question is over the conditions that will be placed on obtaining HPM: what will be the cost of 'purchasing' HPM when reserves are needed, and what sorts of obstacles will the Fed impose on a bank to obtain them? A case in point is the credit crunch of 1966, which we analyze in the next section.

Significance of the Credit Crunch of 1966
Minsky argued that the Credit Crunch of 1966 was the first financial trauma since the 1930s that involved a run on a financial instrument or institution without a specific case of a failure or fraud (Minsky 1986, p. 87). Further, the financial crises that followed the 1966 crisis followed a similar pattern, with the crisis relieved by swift intervention by the 'Big Bank' Fed (plus a countercyclical 'Big Government' deficit in most cases).

According to Minsky, the long expansion of the 1960s progressed as spending by nonfinancial corporations grew rapidly, fueled in part by external funds provided by banks. As he showed, net external funds as a per cent of purchased physical assets grew from less than 4 per cent in 1961 to more than 20 per cent by 1966 (Minsky 1986, p. 88). Worried about inflation, the Fed began to raise interest rates. The discount rate was raised from 4 per cent to 4.5 per cent in December 1965 where it remained for the rest of 1966; the federal funds rate was also raised, but more rapidly throughout the year. In addition, the Fed raised reserve requirements on time deposits and lowered ceiling interest rates on small time deposits in July. The higher reserve requirements would effectively raise the cost of making loans (since reserves are a non-earning asset), while the lower ceiling rates would force banks to turn to higher-cost, non-regulated sources of funds (by inducing 'disintermediation' – as we discuss below). Finally, after April the Fed directed that reserve growth should be restricted and tried to discourage discount window borrowing; Minsky reports that by July and August, the 'window was so tightly administered that there was no increase in borrowing by member banks, and the money-market banks believed that the discount window was effectively closed to them' (Minsky 1986, p. 90). In sum, monetary policy was tightened significantly on the belief that banks could be pressured to reduce lending that was fueling the expansion.

When the Fed began to raise interest rates in 1966, market rates were quickly pushed above Regulation Q ceilings (maximum interest rates permitted on deposits). Market savvy 'depositors' liquidated their long positions in regulated deposits and searched for better returns. This hurt the large New York banks relatively more than it would hurt the mid-western thrifts that relied on small share accounts of mom-and-pop depositors. Deposits tended to 'flow out' of New York banks and into 'Eurodollar' accounts of foreign banks, or, more simply, into accounts of foreign branches of US banks. Eurodollar deposits were not covered by Regulation Q (thus, raised costs) but did not require minimum HPM balance requirements (legally required reserves) until 1969 (which offset some of the increased cost). In addition, banks innovated to provide Americans with deposit accounts that circumvented Regulation Q (negotiable order of withdrawal (NOW) accounts) but these, too, promised higher interest rates – especially in comparison with zero-interest-earning checking accounts.

Not only were costs higher, but there was no way to know how high the Fed would raise interest rates, and there was every indication that the Fed would impose more obstacles for the banks to overcome. Fiscal policy remained expansive and the administration's success at informal wage and price controls was, at best, questionable. As a result, it was reasonable for 'the market' to conclude that monetary policy, alone, would be responsible for fighting inflation and that meant that interest rates could rise sharply. In such an expectational environment, banks were reluctant to 'short' HPM to go long in IOUs and securities. Some banks might even have tried to liquidate long positions in securities to continue to service valued customers (providing additional loans) without increasing short positions. However, while sales of bonds by an individual bank could increase its own deposits of HPM, this could not increase system-wide HPM deposits unless the sales were to the Fed.

Under Regulation Q, tight money episodes tended to reduce bank willingness to buy bonds as occurred in 1957, 1960, 1966 and 1969 when the federal funds rate spiked, and in every case bank holdings of US government securities fell sharply. This probably has more to do with the uncertainty generated by tight policy over the terms on which HPM can be obtained, as well as with the unexpected capital losses that might accrue to bonds if the Fed should persist in raising interest rates. Thus, while banks do not have to sell bonds to make loans, during tight money periods they choose not to increase bond holdings, and, indeed, in such periods reduce bond holdings by several billion dollars. In 1966, this led to a disorganized municipal market that forced the Fed to intervene.

Minsky argued that the US economy emerged from World War II with a 'robust' financial system with a predominance of 'hedge' financing. Bank balance sheets were flush with US government securities – about 40 per cent of total banking credit in 1955. This was a consequence of conservative financial practices (due in part to supervision and regulation, but also to memories of the Great Depression and to 'evolutionary' forces that had eliminated risk-lovers during the 1930s), of the tremendous government deficits of World War II (and the consequent issue of government bonds), and of the lack of opportunity to lend to the private sector (due to war-time controls, temporary nationalization of industry, and large household savings). Gradually, as the private sector began to grow and as memories of the Great Crash faded, balance sheet leveraging increased. Nonfinancial firms increased borrowing, committing larger portions of expected income flows to debt service; financial firms, including banks, financed this activity by increasing the ratio of loans (and other riskier assets) to government securities. The major change to the composition of bank credit was the rapid, sustained decrease of the importance of US government securities and the similarly rapid and sustained increase of the importance of loans. US government securities fell to less than a fifth of bank credit by 1966; in contrast, bank loans (excluding mortgages and consumer credit) rose rapidly from 24 per cent of bank credit in 1955 to 33 per cent by 1966. Financial innovations allowed banks to increase HPM leverage ratios – that is, to issue more liabilities without increasing reserve requirements.

Furthermore, banks, especially, moved from reliance on relatively stable demand deposits (which, while payable on demand are actually quite predictable) to greater reliance on time deposits (which, except for passbook savings accounts, are unstable) – as Minsky shows, demand deposits made up approximately 70 per cent of total bank liabilities in 1952, but this had already fallen to about 40 per cent by 1966. As discussed, fear of inflation led the Fed to increase interest rates over the course of the expansion; the federal funds rate rose from less than 2 per cent in 1961 to 5.75 per cent in 1966, causing market rates to rise sharply (the six month certificate of deposit (CD) rate peaked at nearly 6.15 per cent in mid 1966). While banks can always eventually adjust to higher rates, rising rates reduce profitability because assets are generally longer-term than liabilities. This is particularly true of thrifts – whose problem in 1966 was not so much that Regulation Q limited the interest rate they could pay on deposits but rather that they could not 'afford' to pay market rates given their return on mortgage assets. Similarly, as noted above, the problem faced by commercial banks was not 'disintermediation' but rising costs of issuing liabilities and uncertainty regarding the future course of interest rates. Finally, while banks could continue to provide loans to their customers, the loans required higher interest rates and thus required that borrowers would devote ever-higher portions of expected income flows to debt service. Given all these factors, but especially uncertainty over exactly how high the Fed would push interest rates, banks reduced their demand for government bonds – including US treasuries as well as municipal bonds. Between the fourth quarter of 1965 and the third quarter of 1966, banks sold $6 billion of US government securities, in addition to the $440 million municipal securities sold between the third and fourth quarters of 1966. Banks also sold off $340 million of corporate and foreign bonds between mid 1965 and midyear 1966. By late August, the large New York banks had withdrawn altogether from the municipal new issues market (Minsky 1986, p. 89).

As Minsky argues '[b]y the end of August, the disorganization in the municipals market, rumors about the solvency and liquidity of savings institutions, and the frantic position-making efforts by money-market banks generated what can be characterized as a controlled panic. The situation clearly called for Federal Reserve action' (Minsky 1986, p. 90). There is no doubt that the Fed was concerned about a potential mass bank withdrawal from the municipal market. As Minsky (1986) and Wolfson (1994) note, the Fed sent a letter on September 1 to all member banks emphasizing that '[f]urther substantial adjustment through bank liquidation of municipal securities or other investments would add to pressures on financial markets' (quoted in Wolfson 1994, p. 38). Effectively, the Fed announced it would open the discount window to all banks that would continue to hold municipal bonds so long as they could show they were constraining business lending.

What we have, then, is a robust post-war expansion during which liquidity is stretched. Fearing inflation, the Fed tightens monetary policy to the point at which profitability of at least some financial institutions is threatened. Growing uncertainty causes a run out of a portion of the securities market. The Fed enters as lender of last resort to stop the run, and within a few months, it is forced to loosen monetary policy. The financial crisis is quickly relieved, although the conditions placed on the lender of last resort intervention (that borrowing banks must show they are attempting to reduce loans to private business) cause a sharp reduction of investment, 'gross private domestic investment decreased at an annual rate of 26 percent between the fourth quarter of 1966 and the second quarter of 1967' (Minsky 1986, p. 90). This was accompanied by a large decline of the rate of growth of bank credit, which had been growing at about 8 per cent per year from December 1965 through July 1966, but the rate of growth fell to 1.5 per cent per year between July and December 1966 (Minsky 1966, p. 89).

However, a recession did not result because government spending more than compensated for the fall of investment; 'Big Government' maintained aggregate demand. Thus, as Minsky always argued, the two most important roles for government ('Big Bank' intervention as lender of last resort, and 'Big Government' spending to provide a floor to aggregate demand) came into play to stop the 1966 'crunch' from generating a recession. The economy continued to expand, new financial practices emerged and were validated, leverage ratios increased, memories of the Great Depression faded, and markets came to expect that big government and the Fed would come to the rescue as needed. The 1966 credit crunch was followed by extremely tight money policy at the end of the 1960s, then by the 'liquidity squeeze' and commercial paper run of 1970, the bank failures of 1973–75, the silver crisis of 1980, the LDC debt crisis of 1982, the saving and loan fiasco of the mid-1980s (and similar banking problems throughout the world), the 1987 stock market crash, the bond market crash of 1994, the Asian meltdown of 1997–99, the stock market crash of 2000, the Russian default and hedge fund crisis of 1998, and the Great Recession of 2007–09. That 1966 crisis was only a minor speed bump on the road to Minskyan fragility, but in broad outline the central features and policy responses were similar in the crises to come later.

In the next section we examine Volcker's Great Monetarist Experiment and its long-term impact on the financial sector, which set the stage for the current crisis.

Monetarism, the rise of securitization, and the demise of commercial banking

After the Fed–Treasury Accord (1951), the Fed was 'freed' to use interest rate hikes to try to fight inflation and eventually to fine-tune the economy (Wray 2008). Over time, its interventions became increasingly aggressive – finally culminating in the Great Monetarist Experiment of 1979–82, during which Fed Chairman Volcker raised the overnight rate above 20 per cent. While interest rates were never pushed up so high again, the Fed continued with aggressive attempts at fine-tuning all the way to the present crisis. Indeed, it began to practice 'preemptive' interventions, arguing that due to lags between the time action was taken and impacts on inflation, it needed to fight inflation even before it appeared. This forced financial institutions to speed the transformation away from relationship banking and toward a 'market-based' approach.

Previously to the time of the Monetarist experiment, each rate hike to fight inflation caused problems for commercial banks and thrifts that were subject to Regulation Q interest rate ceilings, as well as usury laws that limited loan rates, causing them to suffer retail deposit withdrawals when market rates rose above legislated deposit rates. To retain reserves they had to substitute more costly wholesale deposits not subject to Regulation Q. At the same time, they had to raise interest rates on loans, causing their best customers to turn to other sources of funds, such as commercial paper markets. Thus the interest rate ceilings allowed the Fed to engineer 'credit crunches' by pushing market rates up. In addition, other rules and regulations that dated to the New Deal financial reforms also constrained bank practices to preserve safety and soundness.

However, as Minsky argued, financial institutions responded to each tight money episode by innovating, creating new practices and instruments – making the supply of credit ever more elastic. The development of secondary markets in mortgages as well as the creation of 'hot money' jumbo certificates of deposit in the 1980s were financial innovations directly responding to the high interest rate monetarist experiment used by Volcker to fight stagflation (Wray 1994). As time passed, the increasing tendency toward speculative booms became correspondingly more difficult to contain. Furthermore, the Fed and Congress gradually removed constraints; ultimately the Glass-Steagall Act that had separated commercial and investment banking was repealed in 1999, allowing commercial banks to engage in a wider range of practices so that they could better compete with their relatively unregulated Wall Street competitors. As Minsky argued, at each step, innovation and deregulation allowed increasingly risky practices to make the system more vulnerable.

Still, deregulation and legal recognition of new practices were not, by themselves, sufficient to bring on a global financial crisis. If these innovations had led to excessively risky behavior that generated huge losses, financial institutions would have been reluctant to retain them. According to Minsky, the remarkable thing about the post-war period is the absence of depressions. While recessions occur with regularity, they are constrained; while financial crises arise from time-to-time, the fall-out is also contained. This is due in part to the various reforms that date to the New Deal, but also to countercyclical movement of the 'Big Government' budget, to lender of last resort activity of the 'Big Bank' Fed, and to periodic bail-outs arranged by the Fed, Treasury, or Congress. As Minsky always argued, by preventing 'It' (a debt deflation on the order of the 1930s collapse) from happening again, new practices and instruments were validated.

In other words, the upside exuberance observed in each bubble is just the end result of long-term policy-induced, and in turn policy-validated, profit-seeking financial innovations that stretched liquidity and enabled prices of real estate, of equity, and of commodities to reach unjustified and unsustainable levels. Just as what was termed by Chairman Greenspan the irrational exuberance that developed in equity markets in the 1990s was based on the belief that a 'new economy' had created conditions in which dotcoms could only rise in value – validating exploding stock prices – the 2000s saw unprecedented real estate appreciation that validated increasingly Ponzi finance. Yet both bubbles were fueled by a combination of optimistic expectations developed over many years and the search for high returns by money fund managers of accumulated wealth over decades. In the case of the real estate boom, the argument was that real estate prices 'always go up', and, having entered the era of the 'great moderation' competent central bankers were firmly in control of the economy, so that there were few downside risks.

Over this period, growth of what Minsky called managed money competed with traditional bank lines of business, as pension funds, insurance funds, hedge funds, and so on, provided an alternative source of funds in competition with bank loans. Initially, bank funding had an advantage over market sources of funding because banks could diversify risks across a large number of borrowers with different income sources. Further, banks had access to insured deposits as well as to Fed lender of last resort intervention, ensuring they could issue liabilities without facing much chance of a run. However, by the early 1970s, firms were already turning in large numbers to the commercial paper market for short-term borrowing. As

Minsky (1986) noted, an early 1970s crisis in the commercial paper market led to the practice of obtaining back-up lines of credit with banks. On one hand, banks then could earn fee income for provision of the back-up facilities, but on the other, this practice reduced their competitive advantage in direct funding of business. Another market innovation allowed for diversification of risk by issuing securities collateralized by pooling loans – detailed below. Taken together, such innovations reduced the advantages banks had previously held.

Over time, new instruments continually eroded the bank share of assets and liabilities – which fell by half between the 1950s and the 1990s: the securities market share of private nonfinancial debt rose from 27 per cent in 1980 to 55 per cent in 2008 (Greenlaw et al. 2008). Banks were forced to become more market-oriented. They would settle for a smaller share of the financial system, and servicing Wall Street firms would replace some of the relationship banking they had lost. Minsky (1987) observed that banks appear to require a spread of about 450 basis points between interest rates earned on assets less that paid on liabilities. This spread covers the normal rate of return on capital, plus the required reserve 'tax' imposed on banks (reserves are non-earning assets), and the costs of servicing customers. By contrast, financial markets can operate with much lower spreads precisely because they are exempt from required reserve ratios, regulated capital requirements, and much of the costs of relationship banking.

Banks had to find a way to economize. To restore profitability, they would earn fee income for loan origination, but by moving loans such as mortgages off their books they could escape reserve and capital requirements. They could, however, continue to service the loans, earning additional fees. Investment banks would purchase and pool these loans, then sell them as securities to investors. As Minsky (1987) argued, investment banks would pay ratings agencies to bless the securities, and hire economists to develop models demonstrating that interest earnings would more than compensate for the assumed risks. Risk raters and economic modelers would certify that prospective defaults on the underlying assets would be low enough to justify the investment-grade rating required by insurance and pension funds. All told, these developments appeared to offer an alternative to relationship banking. There was no need to develop relationships with individual borrowers to assess credit worthiness because loan pools diversified risks, raters evaluated the risks of the overall pools, and insurers protected against possible losses. To replace lost income, banks began to take direct positions in the poolers, the securities, and the insurers. They also provided back-up liquidity guarantees to those involved in packaging and selling securities, and even gave money-back guarantees to holders of securities if the underlying loans went bad. Ironically, this meant that they were now exposed to default risk of borrowers they had never assessed. And, as it turned out, no one had assessed those risks.

Securitization and the current global collapse
Securitization is a 'market-oriented' financial practice in contrast to 'bank-based' transactions where activities are financed by loans held on bank balance sheets against deposits held in the banking system. Securitization has also been called the 'originate and distribute' model, which accurately captures a distinguishing feature of the process: the institution that arranges the finance of activities does not hold the loan. Lots of presumptions about these instruments and practices have been exploded by the crisis, including the belief that securitization shifted risks off bank balance sheets, that securitization allowed for diversification of risks while efficiently allowing investors to achieve the proper risk-return trade-off, and that securitization put risk into the portfolios of those best able to handle it.

Minsky (1987) argued that securitization was part and parcel of the globalization of finance, as securitization creates financial paper that is freed from national boundaries. German investors with no direct access to America's homeowners could buy a piece of the action in US real estate markets. As Minsky was fond of pointing out, the unparalleled post-World War II depression-free expansion in the developed world (and even in much of the developing world) has created a global sea of managed money seeking returns. Packaged securities with risk weightings assigned by respected credit rating agencies were appealing for global investors trying to achieve the desired proportion of dollar-denominated assets. It would be no surprise to Minsky to find that the value of securitized American mortgages exceeded by a large margin the value of the global market for federal government debt.

The problem is that the incentive structure in which mortgage originators operated was certain to create problems. In the aftermath of the 2000 equity market crash, investors looked for alternative sources of profits. Low interest rate policy by the Greenspan Fed meant that traditional money markets could not offer adequate returns. Investors lusted for higher risks, and mortgage originators offered sub-primes and other 'affordability products' with ever-lower underwriting standards. Brokers were richly rewarded for inducing borrowers to accept unfavorable terms, which increased the value of the securities. New and risky types of mortgages – hybrid adjustable rate mortgages (ARMs) (called '2/28' and '3/27') that offered low teaser rates for two or three years, with very high reset rates – were pushed, even by Fed Chairman Greenspan.

While the troubled instruments and institutions varied, many of today's problems can be traced back to securitization. While seemingly innocuous, securitization led to a dizzying array of extremely complex instruments that – quite literally – no one understands. Throughout the financial world, 'mark to model' or even 'mark to myth' substituted for 'mark to market' because markets could not value the instruments. The current financial crisis began in the market for mortgage-backed securities (MBS), especially in the sub-prime section of that market. It quickly spread to securities backed by 'Alt A' mortgages (less risky than sub-prime, but too risky to qualify for conventional loans), and then to more exotic markets including collateralized debt obligations (CDOs), asset-backed commercial paper (ABCP), and other asset-backed securities (ABS), including other types of consumer debt. Furthermore, problems spread beyond specific asset classes to institutions such as special purpose vehicles (SPVs), including structured investment vehicles (SIVs) – monoline insurers (that provide insurance for MBS), and to major financial institutions (including private banks as well as government sponsored enterprises like Fannie Mae). Still other financial instruments faced problems, such as municipal bonds and credit default swaps (CDS). Finally, the credibility of real estate agents, property appraisers, accountants, credit rating agencies, mortgage brokers, and financial institution officers was called into question because of practices developed over the decade preceding the collapse.

Thus, by 2007 we faced a systemic problem resulting from the notion that markets can properly assess risk based on complex, backward-looking models; that markets can hedge and shift risk to those best able to bear it; and that market forces will discipline decision-making. Alas, each of these presumptions proved to be woefully incorrect. The models were constructed based on data generated during an unusually stable period in which losses were small, and required that the structure of the financial system remain constant. But as Minsky (1986) argued, relative stability will necessarily encourage behavior that changes the financial structure (he used the terms hedge, speculative, and Ponzi to describe the transformation). This evolution, in turn, rendered the models increasingly useless even as they were used on a grander scale to justify falling interest rate spreads implying virtually no defaults would ever occur. Further, as is now recognized, the models could not account for growing interrelations among debtors increasing the systemic risk that insolvency by some would generate a snowball of defaults. This was another process that Minsky always emphasized, and one that is enhanced by the kind of leveraging that became common as margins of safety were reduced. Further, as we now know, neither was risk properly hedged nor was it necessarily shifted.

Much of it came back directly to banks through buy-back guarantees, back-up credit facilities, and bank purchases of securities.

Finally, markets did not discipline behavior but instead encouraged ever-riskier activities. For example, the increased competition coming from managed money narrowed interest rate spreads but because fund managers were in a desperate search for high returns they were forced to ignore risk where it was under-priced. Competition forced them to take excessive risk given returns. Many did not even pretend to understand the instruments they were buying, as they were content to either rely on credit rating agencies or to simply follow the leader down the inevitable path to destruction.

Where do we go from here? A Minskyan transformation of the financial system

Let us begin with four appropriate quotes from Minsky (1987) (with a few of our editorial comments in square brackets; original italics):

> Securitization throws light on the nature of money: *money is a financial instrument (debt) that develops out of the financing of activity and positions in assets and becomes generally accepted in an economic community as a means of payment for goods and services and as an instrument by which debts are discharged.*

> It is conceivable that in the not too distant future we could be using $100 interest bearing short-term securities as currency. Private money is a distinct possible future outcome of current developments.

> Securitization implies that there is no limit to bank initiative in *creating* credits for there is no recourse to bank capital, and because the credits do not absorb high-powered money [bank reserves]. Both capital and reserve absorption may occur at the initiating stage of the credit [before the securities can be created and sold]. This has led to the terminology of 'bridge financing.' [But once the securities are moved off the bank balance sheet, neither capital nor reserves are leveraged any longer.]

> Securitization lowers the weight of that part of the financing structure that the central bank (Federal Reserve in the United States) is committed to protect. A need by holders of securities who are committed to protect the market value of their assets (such as mutual or money market funds, or trustees for pension funds) may mean that a rise in interest rates will lead to a need by holders to make position by selling position, which can lead to a drastic fall in the price of the securities.

These statements, written in 1987, not only provide a concise summary of Minsky's views on money and finance but also a prescient overview of the evolution of financing that occurred over the next two decades as well as hints of the form the crisis would take. Let us return to his statement that 'anyone can create money' – a financial instrument that develops out of the financing of activity or asset purchases. Mortgage-backed securities were the instrument that financed the real estate boom; positions in these securities were taken through the issue of shorter-term IOUs such as commercial paper. As Minsky recognized, because banks quickly moved mortgages off their balance sheets, most of this activity absorbed neither reserves nor capital – this was an innovation capable of creating an infinite supply of finance, to support an infinite run-up of real estate prices. Of course, this could not go on forever – because at some point, real estate prices must be validated by the ability of the mortgagee to service debt. And, as mentioned earlier, any number of events might have triggered the crisis. Because the 'shadow banks' and their instruments were formally outside the protection of the Fed and Treasury, insolvency problems quickly led to a liquidity crisis. After some false steps, both Big Government and the Big Bank came to the rescue of the shadow banks – with a huge array of bail-outs, guarantees, arranged mergers, and loans. In addition, the few remaining investment banks were handed bank charters so they would have access to insured deposits as well as to the lender of last resort. In this manner, the liquidity crisis greatly expanded the protection and role of both branches of government. The result is an untenable socialization of risks to protect private profits. At the same time, economic power has been concentrated in a handful of hegemonic financial institutions that are already as we write resuming many of the practices that brought on the crisis.

What would Minsky suggest?

First let us address what kinds of financial services must be provided; then we turn to the reconstitution of the financial system to ensure these are provided but within the context of a more stable system.

Among the kinds of services that must be provided, Minsky listed the following:

1. Payments system: deposit banking, postal savings, debit cards
2. Secure outlet for savings: narrow banks, insured deposit accounts, postal savings
3. Finance for housing and consumers: mortgages, credit cards, consumer loans
4. Commercial banking services: commercial loans, credit cards, payments services, deposit accounts, business savings
5. Investment banking services: equity issues, take-out finance
6. Asset management advice and accounts: retail stock brokers
7. And to his list we add Insurance: home, auto, life, health, business

The New Deal provided functional separation, but that was gradually eroded and then eliminated with the repeal of the Glass–Steagall Act. Yet it is not clear that 'universal banking' has been a success. Minsky actually did advocate a form of universal banking, but only for small community development banks. These would have been for-profit but closely regulated and publicly subsidized so that they would operate in the public purpose. The goal was to use them to provide needed financial services to underserved low-income citizens, inner-city minorities, and entrepreneurs who seek modest financing for small businesses. The community development banks proposal was unique since it emphasized the need for the development of an equitable payments system for the bottom quintile of the population, which is generally denied access to checking accounts and other services (Minsky et al. 1992 [1996]). These institutions were neither to be viewed as a significant countercyclical force, nor as a major factor in the growth of the economy, but rather designed to fill a gap in the ongoing institutional structure. Further, they could very well provide part of the institutional setting in which a climate of opportunity replaced stagnation for many segments of the population.

The problem of the existing system and the consequent recent crisis is systemic and derived from a fundamentally flawed model that viewed the move to markets as something that would increase efficiency and lower interest rate spreads while spreading and reducing risk. This was accomplished by reducing reliance on relationship banking and letting markets take over much of the financial sector. Yet, as Minsky always argued, the fundamental banking activity is guaranteeing credit worthiness. This requires a skeptical loan officer who carefully evaluates borrowers, and who reduces probability of default by establishing a long-term relationship such that credit is renewable only if the borrower fulfills obligations. The shift to the market 'originate and distribute' model meant that individual creditworthiness was never assessed. However, banks guaranteed creditworthiness, anyway, through a wide variety of exceedingly complex and mostly hidden agreements with originators and holders of securities.

So the key to restoration of healthy banking is to recognize, as Minsky did, that banking is a profit-seeking business based on very high leverage ratios. Banks, also, serve an important public purpose and thus are rewarded with access to the Fed's lender of last resort function and to government guarantees. What this means is that as soon as capital ratios decline toward some minimum (zero in the case of an institution subject only to market discipline, or some positive number set by government supervisors as the point at which they take over the institution), management will 'bet the bank' by seeking the maximum, risky, return permitted by supervisors. In any event, there is always an incentive to increase leverage ratios to improve return on equity as Minsky (1986) showed. Given that banks can finance their positions in earning assets by issuing government-guaranteed liabilities, at a capital ratio of 5 per cent for every $100 they gamble, only $5 is their own and $95 is the government's. If subjected only to market forces, profit-seeking behavior would be subject to many, and frequently spectacular, bank failures. The odds are even more in their favor, if government adopts a 'too big to fail' strategy – although exactly how government chooses to rescue institutions will determine the value of that 'put' option to the bank's owners.

Given these considerations there are three alternative but complementary strategies for dealing with banks: (a) require very high capital ratios; (b) require very safe assets; or (c) provide restrictive regulations and close supervision. Considering the first strategy, at the extreme, a 100 per cent capital requirement would ensure that the bank's owners would suffer all of the loss (and receive all of the gain) incurred on assets. In theory, that is the idea behind Islamic Banking. Jimmy Stewart's thrifts that operated as mutuals were similar – the deposits were really shares, and interest paid out was a distribution of the earnings. These worked exceedingly well for a very long time, but as described above they required an implicit assurance that the Fed would not use aggressive interest rate hikes. Of course, there was also a guarantee on the value of deposits and close regulation of the types of assets that could be held. The combination of high interest rates plus relaxation of regulation (including ownership rules) devastated the thrifts. However, a number of different models based on the mutual form of ownership as well as a large increase of capital ratios might generate new financial institutions that could provide a variety of financial services.

Note that while the Basel agreements were supposed to increase capital requirements, the ratios were never high enough to make a real difference, and financial institutions were allowed to assess the riskiness of their assets for the purposes of calculating risk-adjusted capital ratios. In reality, the Basel agreements contributed to the financial fragility that resulted in the global collapse of the financial system. Effective capital requirements would have to be very much higher, and if they are risk-adjusted, the risk assessment must be done at arms-length by unaffiliated parties. We conclude that short of a return to the mutual form, or imposition of very high capital requirements, additional constraints will be required.

Taking the second strategy, an extreme would be '100 per cent money' – institutions with access to government guarantees could hold only federal government liabilities (reserves plus bonds). Minsky endorsed such a proposal put forward by Ronnie Phillips (1995). To ensure competitive space for such institutions, government would have to remove guarantees (including the implicit but vaguely defined 'too big to fail' guarantee) from other types of financial institutions. Obviously, this would be moving in the opposite direction to the decisions taken during this crisis to hand bank charters to investment banks such as Goldman Sachs, which extended access to the 'government's money' (insured deposits) to the riskiest activities. Thus, separation of financial institutions into a 100 per cent money segment and an unprotected segment would be radical and politically difficult. Further, it is not clear that the temptation to provide 'emergency' guarantees in a crisis to the unprotected sector could be avoided. The so-called 'systemically important' institutions would therefore benefit from a presumed government guarantee in 'normal' times, making it difficult for the 100 per cent money sector to compete for deposits.

For this reason it seems that the best course of action would be the third strategy of creating new rules and regulations, and strengthening supervision. Both are necessary because as bank chief executive officers (CEOs) as well as government supervisors have publicly recognized, the financial instruments and practices developed over the past decade are far too complex to understand, let alone to supervise. Regulations will need to prevent some classes of financial institutions from using financial instruments and practices – many of which have already failed a 'market test' – deemed too complex. Supervision is required, because it is impossible to write rules and regulations to cover innovations yet to be developed. For this reason, both supervision as well as regulation is required. Some have advocated an FDA-type approach – financial instruments and practices are prohibited until they have been specifically approved by regulators.

Policy should avoid promotion of financial institution consolidation – a natural result of financial crises that can be boosted by policy-arranged bailouts. Minsky always preferred policy that would promote small-to-medium sized financial institutions. Unfortunately, policymakers who are biased toward 'free markets' instinctively prefer to use public money to subsidize private institution takeovers of failing financial firms. President Roosevelt's alternative should be adopted: temporary 'nationalization' of failing institutions with a view to eventually return them to the private sector at a small profit to the US Treasury. This is what Minsky advocated during the thrift crisis of the 1980s, but the administration of the first President Bush chose industry consolidation and public assumption of bad assets that resulted in Treasury losses. Policy should instead foster competition, with a bias against consolidation. And, following Minsky, it should return to a bias toward market segmentation, with greater regulation of the banking, protected, sector. Minsky always advocated smaller financial institutions, but halting the trend to bigness will be difficult (Minsky 1986). Unless the largest institutions can be down sized it is difficult to believe that government regulators and supervisors will be successful:

large institutions capture regulators but more importantly they can buy political influence to intervene on their behalf (the Keating Five comes to mind). And, as mentioned above, those institutions that escape regulation and supervision (for example, because they are not classified as 'banks') still might enjoy the perception that they will be protected in the case of crisis – another reason for the bias against 'too big to fail' institutions. In an important sense, any institution that is too big to fail is probably too big to exist as a private for-profit institution; indeed it should probably be operated as a public institution (a government sponsored enterprise).

The 'originate and distribute' model has shown its weakness and is unlikely to survive in its present form. Risk raters, property appraisers, quant models, and broker's markets cannot substitute for relationship banking. Managers of money funds that are too big to fail must be constrained because they will again get caught up in the next financial fad. Market forces induce each to try to beat the market, but that requires ignoring greater risk to obtain the higher returns.

To be sure, there is nothing to be gained by preventing everyone from taking on excessive risk. However, there is a clear public interest in the management of pension and insurance funds, which is supposed to be biased toward safety and soundness. Hedge funds and private equity funds are a different matter, but even these need supervision and regulation because of the potential impacts they can have on the economy – as Long-Term Capital Management (LTCM), Enron, and other examples have demonstrated.

Conclusion: what we learned from Minsky
Minsky argued that the Great Depression represented a failure of the small-government, laissez-faire economic model, while the New Deal promoted a 'Big Government/Big Bank' highly successful model for financial capitalism. The current crisis just as convincingly represents a failure of the 'Big Government'/Neoconservative model that promotes deregulation, reduced supervision and oversight, privatization, and consolidation of market power in the hands of money manager capitalists. In the US, there has been a long run trend that favors 'markets' over 'banks', that has also played into the hands of neoconservatives. The current financial crisis is a prime example of the damage that can be done.

The New Deal reforms transformed housing finance into a very safe, protected, business based on (mostly) small, local financial institutions that knew their markets and their borrowers. Homeownership was promoted through long term, fixed rate, self-amortizing mortgages. Communities benefited, and households built wealth that provided a path toward middle class lifestyles (including college education for baby-boomers and secure retirement for their parents). This required oversight by regulators, Federal Deposit Insurance Corporation (FDIC) and Federal Savings and Loan Insurance Corporation (FSLIC) deposit insurance, and a commitment to relatively stable interest rates. Other policies identified by Minsky as 'paternalistic capitalism' also helped to build a robust economy: cooperation with unions to ensure rising wages and thus growing consumer demand; a social safety net that also encouraged consumption; student loans that enhanced earnings capacity; and a sense of shared responsibility to take care of the young, the old, and people with disabilities. Together, these policies reduced insecurity, enhanced trust, and promoted economic stability.

Over time, however, the economy gradually evolved toward fragility. The cold war favored investment in the leading industries, where wages were already high. Inequality grew as other sectors and workers with less education fell behind. Social programs were cut and trickle-down economics favored growth of inequality. Policy increasingly turned to promotion of investment in particular, and business in general, to fuel growth – rather than relying on growing consumption financed out of growing household incomes. Because a large portion of investment in our type of economy must be externally financed, this policy mix increased the importance of finance. At the same time, absence of a depression in the post-war period allowed financial wealth to accumulate, albeit increasingly in the hands of an elite. A formally 'anti-government' bias led to the erosion of many of the New Deal reforms. In practice, however, the rising conservative ideology never really embraced a return to the pre-war small government form of capitalism, but rather merely substituted a meaner big government for the paternalistic government of the early post-war period. Hence, the 'Big Government'/Neoconservative model replaced the New Deal reforms with self-supervision of markets, with greater reliance on 'personal responsibility' as safety nets were dismantled, and with monetary and fiscal policy that is biased against maintenance of full employment and adequate growth to generate rising living standards for most Americans. In short, the government was neither smaller nor less interventionist. The constituency had, however, changed away from America's middle class and toward Wall Street's money managers. We turned American home finance over to Wall Street, which operated the industry as if it were a casino.

Minsky insisted that 'the creation of new economic institutions which constrain the impact of uncertainty is necessary', arguing that the 'aim of policy is to assure that the economic prerequisites for sustaining the civilized standards of an open liberal society exist. If amplified uncertainty, extreme income maldistribution and social inequalities attenuate the economic underpinnings of democracy, then the market behavior that creates these conditions has to be constrained' (Minsky 1996, pp. 14, 15). It is time to take home finance back from the hands of Wall Street's casino operators.

We believe that the chapters in this book contribute to an understanding of the reformation that will be required, following the insights developed by Minsky over the first half-century of the post-war period. We hope that the growing recognition of the importance of Minsky's contributions will finally bring to the greatest 'financial Keynesian' the accolades he deserves.

References

Bell, S. (1998), 'Can taxes and bonds finance government spending?', Working Paper No. 244, Levy Economics Institute of Bard College, Annandale-on-Hudson, New York.

Bellofiore, R. (1985), 'Money and development in Schumpeter', *Review of Radical Political Economics*, 1–2, 21–40.

Bellofiore, R. (1992), 'Monetary macroeconomics before the General Theory. The circuit theory of money in Wicksell, Schumpeter and Keynes', *Social Concept*, 2, 47–89.

Ferri, P. (1992), 'From business cyles to the economics of instability', in S. Fazzari and D.B. Papadimitriou (eds), *Financial Conditions and Macroeconomic Performance: Essays in Honor of Hyman P. Minsky*, Armonk, NY: M.E. Sharpe, pp. 105–20.

Godley, W., D.B. Papadimitriou and G. Zezza (2006), 'America and her creditors: thinking the unthinkable', *Milken Institute Review*, Second Quarter.

Greenlaw, D., J. Hatzius, A. Kashyap and H.S. Shin (2008), 'Leveraged losses: lessons from the mortgage market meltdown', paper presented at the US Monetary Policy Forum Conference (February 29).

Minsky, H.P. (1957), 'Central banking and money market changes', *Quarterly Journal of Economics*, 71 (May), 171–87.

Minsky, H.P. (1964), 'Longer waves in financial relations: financial factors in the more severe depressions', *American Economic Association Papers and Proceedings*, 54 (May), 324–32.

Minsky, H.P. (1966), 'Tight full employment: let's heat up the economy', in H.P. Miller (ed.), *Poverty American Style*, Belmont, CA: Wadsworth Publishing Co., pp. 254–300.

Minsky, H.P. (1975 [2008]), *John Maynard Keynes*, New York: Columbia University Press, republished in D.B. Papadimitriou and L.R. Wray (eds), *Hyman P. Minsky's John Maynard Keynes*, New York, NY: McGraw-Hill.

Minsky, H.P. (1986 [2008]), *Stabilizing an Unstable Economy*, New Haven, CT.: Yale University Press, republished in D.B. Papadimitriou and L.R. Wray (eds), *Hyman P. Minsky's Stabilizing an Unstable Economy*, New York, NY: McGraw-Hill.

Minsky, H.P. (1987), 'Securitization,' Handout, Econ 335A, Fall, mimeo, Archives, Levy Economics Institute of Bard College, Annandale-on-Hudson, New York.

Minsky, H.P. (1992), 'Profits, deficits and instability: a policy discussion', in D.B. Papadimitriou (ed.), *Profits Deficits and Instability*, New York, NY: Macmillan and St. Martin's Press.

Minsky, H.P. (1996), 'Uncertainty and the institutional structure of capitalist economies', Working Paper No. 155, Levy Economics Institute of Bard College, Annandale-on-Hudson, New York.

Minsky, H.P., D.B. Papadimitriou, R.J. Phillips and L.R. Wray (1992 [1996]), 'Community development banks', Working Paper No. 83, Levy Economics Institute of Bard College, Annandale-on-Hudson, New York; republished in D.B. Papadimitriou (ed.) (1996), *Stability in the Financial System*, New York, NY: Macmillan and St. Martin's Press.

Phillips, R.J. (1995), *The Chicago Plan and New Deal Banking Reform*, Armonk, NY: M.E. Sharpe, Inc.

Schumpeter, J.A. (1944), 'The analysis of economic change', in *Readings in Business Cycle Theory*, The AEA, Philadelphia: The Blakiston Co.

Schumpeter, J.A. (1934 [1949]), *The Theory of Economic Development: An Inquiry into Profits, Capital, Credit, Interest, and the Business Cycle*, Cambridge, MA: Harvard University Press.

Schumpeter, J.A. (1951), 'The creative response in economic history', in R.V. Clemence (ed.), *Essays on Economic Topics of J.A. Schumpeter*, Port Washington, NY: Kenikat Press.

Wolfson, M.H. (1994), *Financial Crises: Understanding the Postwar U.S. Experience*, second edition, Armonk, NY: M.E. Sharpe.

Wray, L.R. (1994), 'The political economy of the current US financial crisis,' *International Papers in Political Economy*, **1**(3).

Wray, L.R. (1999), *Understanding Modern Money: The Key to Full Employment and Price Stability*, Cheltenham, UK: Edward Elgar.

Wray, L.R. (2005), 'The ownership society: Social Security is only the beginning . . .,' Public Policy Brief No. 82, Levy Economics Institute of Bard College, Annandale-on-Hudson, New York.

Wray, L.R. (2008), 'Lessons from the subprime meltdown', *Challenge*, March–April.

2 What would Minsky have thought of the mortgage crisis?
Jan Kregel

Introduction

Many financial commentators who anticipated the difficulties in subprime mortgage lending before the 2007 market meltdown have credited their insight to their knowledge of the work of Hyman Minsky. Many noted that what came to be called a 'Minsky Moment' could be understood by what he had called a 'Ponzi' financing scheme.

But how would Minsky himself have analyzed the developments in the mortgage market in the new millennium? And what would he have identified as the greatest potential source of financial instability going into 2006? We will never know for sure, but he might have written something like this:

> At present real estate assets seem to be a more important source of financial distress than stock exchange assets. . . . real estate assets are collateral for an extensive amount of debt, both of households and of business firms, owned by financial institutions. . . . If the price of real estate should fall very sharply, not only will the net worth of households and business firms be affected, but also defaults, repossessions, and losses by financial intermediaries would occur. (Minsky 1964, pp. 180–81)

Of course, this passage was not written in 2006, rather nearly 50 years earlier at the beginning (summer 1960) of the 'soaring sixties'. Nonetheless, his analysis of financial conditions in the early 1960s did leave some very clear, one might say prescient, markers as to how he would have interpreted the conditions that provided the increasing financial fragility that laid the basis for the current financial market turmoil. More importantly, in addition to analyzing the financial distress building in the mortgage market, he also left very clear suggestions concerning the policies that should be followed by the monetary authorities in dealing with it. In particular he noted that, while 'the Federal Reserve System should become the lender of last resort to and the regulator of the entire financial system' (Minsky 1964, p. 182), he also warned that 'The central bank's significance as a guide and director to the economy decreases while its significance as a lender of last resort to the financial system increases as the financial system becomes more complex' (Minsky 1964, p. 179), suggesting a more important role for fiscal policy to direct the economy. This is an issue the Federal Reserve has not faced as it attempts to deal with the continuation of financial instability into 2008 and the impact on inflation of rising food and energy prices.

The general nature of Minsky's 1960 analysis

The modern-day relevance of Minsky's analysis and policy recommendations are more than a lucky repetition of history since, writing in the 1960s, he could not have been aware of the financial innovations that have played a central role in the evolving mortgage crisis. Indeed, mortgage securitization would not become an important part of mortgage financing until over a decade later. The analysis that Minsky used must thus have been grounded in some more general principles that give policy suggestions of more general application than simply to deal with the problems caused by securitization of mortgage finance. His early analysis is also interesting because it represents his first formal statement (he called it a 'pilot investigation using a particular approach to monetary and financial relations' (Minsky 1964, p. 173)), and it provides the groundwork for what eventually became the more formal Financial Instability Hypothesis (FIH) now best known by its use of the distinctions between hedge, speculative, and Ponzi finance.

This early analysis of financial distress is based on what would be the keystone feature of all of Minsky's subsequent work on financial instability, that is, the creation of an analytical framework which integrates 'the possibility of a financial crisis occurring with the way in which the economy normally functions' (Minsky 1964, p. 177). This formulation was the result of a reaction to the then emerging view that 'Keynesian fine-tuning' would eliminate the traditional business cycle. Ever a contrarian he argued that even if a normal, steady expansion of the real economy could be assured by such policies, this would inevitably produce changes in the financial structure of the economy which would eventually produce financial distress and bring the expansion to an end. 'The broadest hypothesis is that the behavior of an economic system with respect to the real variables is not independent of the financial structure of the economy' (Minsky 1964, p. 175).

This integration of the real and financial required to show the continued existence of cyclical behavior in the economy was based on a definition of the financial system 'that is much broader in scope than the set of organizations called financial institutions; in particular both corporate finance and household portfolio management and the government guaranteeing and underwriting activity are a part of the financial system' (Minsky 1964, p. 178). Since this cyclical behavior is determined by the particular financial structure that evolves to finance normal expansion one should not expect one period of sustained growth to be just like another. In particular we expect that lessons are learned, that legislation exists and institutions have been created which protects the economy against the typical financial crises that have been observed. But this learning from the past can result in a type of 'Maginot line' mentality, in which the economy is left vulnerable to new kinds of destabilizing financial reactions. (Minsky 1964, p. 177)

Thus the particular type of financial structure may differ, but the basic principles leading to its instability remain the same.

The actors in financial distress

Minsky notes that while the 'ultimate natural economic unit is the household, it is customary to think of nonfinancial business firms as another natural unit' (Minsky 1964, p. 185). These two units are joined by financial intermediaries and the government to determine the structure and distribution of financial liabilities in the system. While both firms and households have to finance their activities and have accumulated assets, Minsky assumes 'in a simple nonfinancial business model we can think of business firms having to finance activity and households as the source of the financing' (Minsky 1964, p. 186). Thus firms will be issuing debt and equity liabilities that households acquire in order to obtain control of the real assets that they require for their activities. Financial intermediaries will play an intermediary role in ensuring the interface between the differing objectives of the two natural units.

In this framework normal expansion (that is, the expectation that income will continue to expand at the current rate) will require financing of increasing investment expenditures that is 'external to the unit doing the investment' and will leave in its wake an accumulation of 'old financial residue in the form of external private liabilities in the balance sheets of the economy' (Minsky 1964, p. 200). Some of these liabilities will be issued by financial intermediaries against the assets of households and firms. Government will also be engaging in economic activities that seek to influence the growth and employment of the system through fiscal policies that will change the amount of government liabilities in the system. If the government operates a countercyclical expenditure policy the share of government securities in total financial assets will be increasing and vice versa. It is the form and distribution of these liabilities held as assets on household balance sheets that determines the fragility of the financial system. It is the form and distribution of the accumulated liabilities of all issuers held as assets on balance sheets that determines the stability of the financial system.

Public versus private liabilities

In approaching the question of how financial structure has an impact on the real behavior of the economy Minsky first considers the differential impact of private liabilities – debt and equity – issued to finance normal expansion and public liabilities issued in connection with government expenditure policy. This is because, in difference to business firms, households and financial intermediaries, 'the national state can always create money for current spending and debt commitments. . . . To the households, business firms, and private financial sectors which make up the private economy, the debts and money issued by the national state stand as assets which are not the debt of any unit' (Minsky 1964, p. 198). Government debt can thus be characterized as external or outside liabilities, compared to the internal or inside liabilities issued by the private sector that cannot be validated by the issuer, but depend on the expenditure decisions of the government and the rest of the economy. Thus, an initial indicator of the potential financial fragility in the economy is the ratio of private to government debt. During a normal expansion it is thus normal for the share of private 'inside' liabilities to increase, thus increasing the potential for financial instability bringing the expansion to an end.

Public liabilities: uncertainty in the choice of debt versus equity
The second factor determining instability is the form of private liabilities used to finance a normal expansion. Minsky notes that for both the investing business firms and the financing households, the outcome of their decisions to finance expansion will be dominated by uncertainty over future outcomes. Each financing unit has to balance the expectation of favorable and unfavorable outcomes that will result from alternative investment, financing and ownership decisions. This can be simplified to the choice between debt and equity finance. The owners of debts are 'protected, as least to some extent, against some unfavorable outcomes,' but will not fully participate in all the benefits, whereas the payoff to equity or ownership interest is magnified by leverage, 'but sets the upper limit to the amount of protection a unit can offer other units, and hence can set a limit to the debt which can be issued' (Minsky 1964, p. 186). Thus, 'the equity interest is the protection offered the debt owners, for it measures the extent of the unfavorable outcomes that could take place without forcing losses on the debt owners' (ibid.). This implies a protected debt to equity or gearing ratio of 1:1. Beyond this, the protection declines. In more modern terminology we would say that the debt holders have bought this protection by granting the owners of the firm a put option to prepay the bondholders with the market value of their ownership interest whenever it falls below the value of the outstanding bonds through bankruptcy.[1] Thus bondholders have superior claim on income to meet interest payments and the partial protection of the value of their bond holdings.

Over a period of normal expansion, 'new private debts increase relative to the new issues of equities' (Minsky 1964, p. 212); there is an incentive to equity holders to increase leverage since they participate fully in the increased income during expansion. As the expansion proceeds 'this means that equity and real estate prices will rise relative to debt prices' (Minsky 1964, p. 213). In addition, 'As the expectation that growth will take place becomes more widely and firmly held as the sustained boom continues, the capitalization rate for assets which are expected to participate in the growth will increase' (Minsky 1964, p. 214). As a result, 'The longer a sustained boom has continued the larger the proportion of equity and real property assets whose current values reflect the expectation that growth will continue.' But, this process may lead to a more than normal expectation of expansion: 'If the rate of increase of asset values, which takes place when the expectations change to the expectation that growth will be maintained, becomes the rate at which asset values are expected to increase, then the price of assets can become very large compared to current income being earned.' And

> the resulting increase in market values can take place over a relatively short period of time, yielding a rate of growth of asset values that is much greater than the expected rate of growth of income . . . This means that an increasing portion of the equity and real assets have market value which would fall sharply if the expectation that growth would continue were abandoned. A sharp fall in asset values affects the net worth of economic units and the protection in existence against outstanding debts. (Minsky 1964, p. 217)

This relative overvaluation of the value of equities and real estate that results from continued expansion thus results in an effective reduction in the protection offered by debt assets.

This analysis reflects the fact that 'financial distress cannot be due to equity liabilities. No matter how regularized dividend payments may have become, no penalty, aside from a decrease in the market value of the liability and the possibility that management may suffer from the ire of stockholders, results from a business firm's missing a dividend' (Minsky 1964, p. 249).

The financial system

Minsky divides financial institutions into two classes,

> those whose liability is and those whose liability is not money. The non-monetary financial intermediaries can acquire money only by issuing or selling liabilities which other units willingly accept in exchange for money. The monetary financial intermediaries (the commercial banks, the central banks, and portions of the treasury) can create money in exchange of anything they accept as assets. (Minsky 1964, p. 209)

For Minsky money is

> something quite different from the other liquid assets and the monetary institu-
> tions quite different from other 'financial' intermediaries. The amount of money
> in existence is not determined by the public; it is determined within the monetary
> system. Given the reserves and the reserve ratio, the amount of money and also
> the value of the earning assets owned by the monetary system are in principle
> determined. The reserves and reserve ratio are both determined within the mone-
> tary system. Hence in a very significant way it is not true that the monetary system
> adjusts to the behavior of the economy; what happens is that within wide limits
> the economy adjusts to the behavior of the monetary system. Within an economy
> money is an 'indestructible' asset; there is nothing that can be done (ignoring the
> silly case of the physical destruction of currency or coin) by a household or a busi-
> ness firm to change the quantity of money. Money as a demand deposit liability of
> a particular commercial bank is of course destructible, but not money as a liability
> of the commercial banking and monetary system. (Minsky 1964, p. 209)

Assuming that the destruction of money such as occurred in the 1930s
will never again be allowed to occur, 'money is the most riskless of all
assets' and provides the riskless asset preferred in the portfolios of strong
risk averters. 'In part the entire complex financial structure can be said to
exist in order to lure "money" out of the portfolios of such risk averters'
(Minsky 1964, p. 191). This is the role of the savings institutions, and in
particular of the money and capital market institutions.

The rest of the financial system is characterized by savings institutions
and money and capital market institutions. Minsky identifies three main
types of savings intermediaries, mutual saving banks, savings and loan
organizations and the time deposit business of the commercial banking
system, but also lists pension funds, life insurers, and credit unions. These
institutions are characterized by their issuance of deposit liabilities fixed
in dollar terms that are de facto demand liabilities. For the first the stability depends on the existence of the Federal Home Loan Bank to provide
refinancing in the case of a cash deposit drain, a function that is met by the
Federal Reserve for the term deposits of commercial banks.

The money and capital market institutions are involved in underwriting and brokering, or making markets in assets. Minsky notes that these
'Financial institutions differ from other types of business organization in
that their balance sheets are composed of intangible assets representing
discounted expected streams of future commitments to be paid and their
liabilities are streams of future commitments to make payments' (Minsky
1964, p. 189). It is these institutions that play a major role in the evolution
of financial instability; in particular those who deal in debt:

> position takers in debt markets, dealing the assets indirectly owned through
> financial intermediaries by risk averters, are much more important than

position takers in equity markets. The specialist making a market in particular stocks on the major stock exchanges is a position taker whose financing is privately arranged. Unless a catastrophic general decline in equity values is imminent, there is no need to provide him with guaranteed financing in addition to his normal sources. Of course, if the market for equities becomes closely linked with debt holding and issuing organizations, then a need to guarantee the refinancing of the borrowers on debt (really of the lenders to the borrowers on debt) is necessary. (Minsky 1964, p. 194)

Private debts created by financial intermediation
The third dimension of the linkage between the real and financial sector results from the reason for the existence of debt finance. As noted, households will in general differ in their assessment of the likelihood of uncertain outcomes and thus differ in their degree of risk seeking or risk aversion, with the former preferring equity type assets that provide the protection sought by the risk averters who prefer money and debt securities. The issue of debt is also the result of equity owners' willingness to bear additional risk to earn additional income through leveraging.

> The financial system therefore has two 'natural' starting places: the optimum liability structure for a firm engaged in particular activities, which determines the kind of real and financial assets it must control, and the optimum asset structure for a household with its special responsibilities. Corporation finance and private portfolio management are the two anchors for the behavior of the financial system. (Minsky 1964, p. 187)

Thus, Minsky defines 'The study of finance is a special case of the behavior of economic units when confronted with specified types of uncertainty, and financial institutions and usages are ways in which the uncertainty borne by a unit can be adjusted to the unit preferences' (Minsky 1964, p. 188).

When there is no direct match of preferences, 'a set of financial intermediaries are "interposed" between the ultimate borrowers (in a simple world of this non-financial firms) and the ultimate wealth owners' (Minsky 1964, p. 187) in which

> The financial intermediary issues a liability which the saving unit accepts, and uses the funds so obtained to acquire the liabilities of investing units. If we want to look at this process in terms of the acceptability of the liability of investing units by saving units, the financial intermediary upgrades the liability of the investing unit. (Financial techniques exist in which this 'upgrading' role of the financial intermediary is made obvious; these are the various endorsing or accepting financial arrangements). (Minsky 1964, p. 209)

The intermediary will profit from this activity 'whenever there is a differential rate of return between relatively specialized or risky assets on the one hand and liabilities that would be acceptable to strong risk averters on the other' (Minsky 1964, p. 187).

Minsky notes that an important characteristics of many financial intermediaries is that their profitability depends on 'the institution being fully invested, that is, not having any idle cash. At the same time these institutions stand ready to exchange "cash" for their liabilities on demand . . . as a result they have to be able to withstand transitory and somewhat persistent drains. They do this if they can either sell or pledge some of their earning assets for cash' (Minsky 1964, pp. 192–3). The assets of a financial institution can thus be thought of

> as a position the institution has taken. This position is financed by 'borrowing' and the liabilities are the debts issued to finance this position. If there is a demand for cash by the liability owners, the financial institutions must refinance their position. Any unit, let alone a financial intermediary, is 'foolish' with respect to the chance it takes if it has demand or call or short liabilities and no guaranteed way in which it can refinance its position. One way in which it can have guaranteed refinancing is if it owns assets which can always be sold at a moment's notice at a price that does not change much. For such an asset to exist, there must be either a very active market in the asset or there must be some set of organizations which are willing to take a position in the asset under any circumstances. When these conditions are satisfied then the savings and monetary intermediaries can function well . . . the existence of a market makes 'risk averters' more willing to own the asset. (Minsky 1964, p. 193)

But, it is other financial institutions that serve as market makers, and provide the possibility to refinance positions at prices close to market value when necessary. This is the general definition of market liquidity. When there is no financial institution willing to serve as market maker by lending against secured collateral, liquidity disappears and financial intermediaries are unable to meet their commitments, leading to a general fall in asset values similar to that which would occur with a reduction in the rate of growth of income on the value of debts and equity.

With respect to real estate finance Minsky also notes the

> rather serious trend for the liquidity of the savings and loan organizations, which have almost all of their assets in mortgages, to have a decreasing proportion of their assets in guaranteed, and therefore more readily marketable securities. The liquidity of these organizations in time of developing financial distress may depend on their ability to realize enough on their guaranteed mortgages to withstand cash drains. (Minsky 1964, p. 326)

In this respect Minsky notes that

> A defect in the US money market as structured today is the absence of any well-defined market in conventional home mortgages. The uniqueness of the

underlying real estate is one of the reasons. However, accepting and endorsing organizations exist which transform other 'unknown and specialized' liabilities into generally acceptable assets. It may be that the costs involved in making conventional mortgages marketable and servicing them are too high for the falling yields that can be expected to occur if they were so marketable, so that no private organizations which tend to improve the marketability of mortgages can be expected to arise. (Minsky 1964, p. 194)

Again, this was written well before the real estate crisis caused by the collapse of the savings and loans following their deregulation which further reduced their guaranteed securities led to the real estate crisis of the late 1980s and before the introduction of securitization, which he clearly viewed as a possible solution.

Thus, just as the share of private to public assets and bonds to equity increase during a normal expansion, the share of financial institutions assets in private assets also increases. This is what Minsky would eventually call 'financial layering', representing an overall financial structure that becomes more vulnerable to any decline in the expectation of a continued constant rate of growth of income.

In Minsky's 1960 terminology a condition of 'financial distress' occurs when an individual economic unit 'cannot meet its obligations in its balance sheet liabilities'. This may evolve into a 'financial crisis' when 'a very significant subset of the economy is in financial distress and a trend is evident so that unless some "outside" event takes place so almost all private economic units will be in financial "distress"'. When '"a slight disturbance" in money flows', due to whatever cause (a simple decline in the growth rate would be sufficient), 'creates such widespread financial distress that financial crisis is threatened' the economy will exhibit 'financial instability' which will inevitably lead to a downturn (Minsky 1964, pp. 250–51).

At each stage in the evolution toward financial instability economic units become more reliant on financial intermediaries to meet any shortfall, just as intermediaries become more reliant on other institutions such as banks to refinance their liabilities. As Minsky notes, 'A key to the generation of financial crisis is whether the holders of marketable securities who have large scale debts outstanding can refinance or must liquidate their positions when they need cash' (Minsky 1964, p. 266).

The worst thing that could happen to the solvency of any financial institution is a forced sale of its assets in order to acquire cash. Imagine what would happen to asset values, if there were a need to liquidate government bond positions by the government bond dealers or if the sales finance companies were suddenly to try to sell their portfolios of consumer installment paper on some market. In order to prevent this type of forced liquidation of assets, the financial intermediaries protect themselves by having alternative financing sources, i.e., by having 'de facto' lenders of last resort. These de facto lenders of last resort must ultimately have access to the Federal Reserve System in times of potential crisis. (Minsky 1964, p. 376)

Minsky notes that this support is different for the three different classes that he identifies in the financial system. For commercial banks in the monetary system this access is automatic, 'The Federal Reserve System as it is organized and as it has functioned is a lender of last resort to the commercial banks' (Minsky 1964, p. 375). 'If a commercial bank is forced to borrow at the Federal Reserve Bank's discount window because a consumer credit house unexpectedly draws upon its line of credit, we can expect that the credit will be granted' (Minsky 1964, p. 377).

However, Minsky notes that the Federal Reserve System has been

unwilling to regularize the access to the discount window of so important a money market intermediary as the government bond dealers. As a government bond dealer must have a guaranteed refinancing source in case they are unable to borrow enough from their normal sources to maintain their position, the Federal Reserve System has agreed to a subterfuge by which one of the New York City banks guarantees financing to the government bond dealers and this bank in turn has access to the discount window on an unrestricted basis. (Minsky 1964, p. 375)

Thus, in effect 'both the consumer credit houses and the government bond dealers do have direct access to the discount window of the Federal Reserve System' (Minsky 1964, p. 377).

However, in order to avoid a financial crisis, should commercial banks refuse indirect accommodation to money and capital market institutions

such access will have to become direct. There is no reason why approved government bond dealers and approved finance houses should not have access to the Federal Reserve System, now, when no crisis threatens. In addition to the Federal Reserve System, there are number of other federal agencies that either insure the liabilities of financial intermediaries, guarantee the assets held by financial intermediaries, or act as a 'lender of last resort' to some class of financial intermediary. A number of these agencies center around the home mortgage market and the specialized home mortgage banks: the savings and loan associations in order to make these guarantees, insurance schemes, and specialized lenders of last resort function in time of emergency, money has to be available when needed. (Minsky 1964, pp. 377–8)

Thus, Minsky's basic recommendation in 1960, half a decade before the credit crunch that nearly bankrupted government bond dealers in the first financial crisis of the post-war period, was to extend access to the Fed's discount window to primary securities dealers and important financial intermediaries.

Minsky also notes that the Federal Reserve must also provide direct access to these other Federal agencies' guarantees and insurance schemes effectively.

> In order to get money these institutions either issue their own obligations, guaranteed by the federal government, or they borrow from the Treasury. But unless the Treasury resorts to printing money, the Treasury must obtain the money needed by these commitments by selling Treasury debt for cash. But the ability of the market to absorb large quantities of government debt for cash in a time of financial distress depends upon the willingness of the Federal Reserve System to furnish reserves to the market by engaging in open market operations in government debt. Hence the ability of the government's deposit insurance, . . . etc. to live up to their commitments depends upon the cooperation of the Federal Reserve System. As a matter of fact, the Federal Reserve System is the lender of last resort to the 'lenders of last resort' if not to the threatened institutions themselves. Is there any virtue in channeling all contacts between the Federal Reserve System and various non-bank financial intermediaries to the commercial banks or the government bond market? The Federal Reserve System seems to feel there is. The possible ill effects of a restricted responsibility by the Federal Reserve System for financial stability are obvious. In times of potential financial crisis, the commercial banks, which today must act as the middleman between some of the institutions and the Federal Reserve System may be unwilling to act. In a developing financial situation, a delay while the Federal Reserve System makes up its mind to aid the non-bank institutions in distress may result in what would have been a manageable sectoral distress developing into a full-fledged crisis. (Minsky 1964, p. 378)

The Fed as guarantor of financial stability and regulator of the economy through monetary policy

Minsky notes that there may be a conflict between the role of the central bank in providing financial stability through direct refinancing support to the financial system and

> the current emphasis upon the central bank as a regulator of the economy. Changes in discount rates, open market operations, and reserve requirements, as well as direct controls are used by the Federal Reserve System to affect the volume and direction of lending. The reason given for such acts is that they will affect the level of activity in the economy. (Minsky 1964, p. 371)

However, for Minsky, 'in a world where a complex structure of financial institutions exists and where a large volume of short-term government securities are outstanding . . . the demand for financing makes the central banks a relatively ineffective regulator of the economy' (ibid). Thus the use of monetary policy to restrict aggregate demand in a period in which there is a secular buoyancy to the economy will lead to an economizing of cash balances. In place of increased activity being financed in part by increases in the quantity of money, increased activity will be financed, almost entirely, by substituting debt assets of private units for money in portfolios (or the monetary system may sell government debt to private units and acquire private debt). At every level in the economy such substitutions imply that each unit is less well able to withstand an interruption in its cash receipts; a given interruption of cash flows, say on income account, will now lead to a larger amount of portfolio changes at all levels in the economy. (Minsky 1964, pp. 372)

The conclusion is that 'If the attempt is being made to restrain this growth in private demand by monetary policy, the possibility that a financial crisis takes place will increase.' There is thus a distinct tradeoff between regulating the economy and stabilizing the economy.

Neither of the alternatives, tight money and a relatively lax fiscal policy or a relatively easy money situation combined with a tight fiscal policy, which can be used to restrain excess demand in an inflationary situation due to private demand, is without side effects which adversely affect the stability of the financial system. As a result, the criterion, 'What are the effects of the alternative policies upon the stability of the economy?' does not result in a clear-cut choice between policies. The actual choice of policy must rest upon other secondary grounds. (Minsky 1964, p. 372)

Minsky's policy conclusions – as relevant today as they were in 1960

The Federal Reserve System should be reorganized to make clear its responsibility for the prevention of a liquidity crisis for the economy. Its domain of control should be extended to cover the entire financial system. Its primary responsibilities will be to assure monetary stability, to act as lender of last resort to the financial system, and to prevent fraud and misrepresentation. The Federal Reserve's directive to operate to achieve short-term stability of the economy should be replaced by a directive to keep stability in the financial markets and provide money for growth. The day-to-day open market operations in the money market should be replaced by easier and wider access to the discount window at posted rates to iron out temporary market difficulties. Open market operations should be undertaken in order to effect permanent increases in the money supply. Seasonal adjustments in the money supply should be the result of discount rather than open market operations. (Minsky 1964, pp. 379–80)

As long as the types of issues, the government emits can affect the operation of the economy, and as long as the Federal Reserve System engages in open market operations as a part of its control technique, it may be desirable to make the Federal Reserve System responsible for management of the government debt. This can be done by making the Federal Reserve System, the owner of the entire outstanding government debt and having the Federal Reserve System issue its own debt in order to absorb 'reserves'. The Federal Reserve would be managing the debt and engaging in open market operations when it issued its own debt. (Minsky 1964, p. 379)

To summarize, given the complex changing financial structure, the Federal Reserve System's role as a regulator of the economy should diminish while the Federal Reserve System's role as a lender of last resort to the financial system should increase. (Minsky 1964, p. 378)

What could we have learned to analyze the subprime crisis?
From this simplified level, an analyst using Minsky's early work would have noticed the increasing rate of growth and share of private debt in total financial assets. This in itself would have represented a sign of potential difficulty. At the same time the rise in mortgage assets as a share of private assets would have been noticed. An important factor would have been the difference between private corporate bonds and the fixed interest liabilities issued by structured financial entities. The liabilities of the collateralized mortgage obligations backed by residential mortgage backed securities were clearly not 'protected' by 'owner's equity interest' in the same way as corporate bonds. The equity in these structured vehicles was represented by the super-subordinated residual tranche or the credit enhancement provided by a liquidity put from the originating bank or a credit default swap from an insurance guarantee company. In most cases these represented as little as 4 per cent (monoline insurers held as little as 1 per cent backing against their exposure) and usually no more than 10 per cent of the total liabilities. This implied initial issue gearing of between 10:1 and 20:1 for the overall structure. The super senior and senior tranches that were constructed to receive investment grade ratings could reach as much as 80 per cent of the total issue, implying a gearing for the totality of the investment grade rated securities of 5:1 compared to the 1:1 gearing that was considered the limit in Minsky's analysis of corporate fixed income. This suggests that the level of protection provided to investors in structured financial instruments with investment grade credit ratings were substantially different from that of corporate debt. It might have also suggested that the ratings process for these structures should have been differentiated from those of corporate and municipal bonds. Indeed, there is some question whether the liabilities issued by these structures should have been considered as 'bonds' at all since their return is more similar to that of equity, being largely subject to the behavior of income and price growth.

As noted, Minsky would certainly have appreciated the creation of a market in mortgage securities, although he doubted the possibility of doing so profitably due to the decline in the intermediation margin that he suggested that this would produce. Minsky's interest in such a market was to provide a supplement to the decline in the guaranteed assets of savings institutions engaged in mortgage lending even before the savings and loan crisis. The securitization of mortgages certainly did provide a way for financial institutions to sell mortgages, but it did not function precisely when it was needed – when there was difficulty in meeting balance sheet commitments. Further, Minsky certainly would have enquired as to how these structured finance vehicles provided sufficient return. He was skeptical since this would reduce the return on mortgages. One of the ways in which returns were assured was by being fully invested, which meant the absence of any 'guaranteed' liabilities that could be quickly converted into cash. Another was the credit enhancement, which as already noted was also based on the extremely low level or virtual absence of any 'guaranteed' liabilities. Aside from the Government Sponsored Enterprise (GSE) structures that carried an explicit or implicit government guarantee, all other mortgage backed securities lacked even a de facto lender or indirect access to a lender of last resort. For the GSEs he would clearly have recognized the necessity of the Federal Reserve in participating in validating the Treasury guarantee, whether formal or implicit. Thus, as the share of mortgage assets in total financial assets increased, there was a clear increase in the importance of access to the financial system to refinance positions, but without any clear institution or mechanism.

In addition, the increased layering, the assets and liabilities of financial intermediaries held on the balance sheets of other financial liabilities would certainly have been noticed, but the fact that this layering occurred amongst structured investment vehicles, none of which maintained high ratios of owners equity and thus fell into the category of institutions that always keep 100 per cent fully invested, would have been a cause of major concern over who would provide the indirect lender of last resort in the case of a disruption in income flows from the underlying mortgages.

Finally, the existence of conditions in which the rate of increase in real estate prices that is based on the expectation that growth would be maintained, is transformed into the rate at which asset values are expected to increase, brought a rate of growth of real estate values that was much greater than the expected rate of growth of income. This would have indicated that real estate assets had a 'market value which would fall sharply if the expectation that growth would continue were abandoned and the subsequent sharp fall in asset values would reduce the net worth of economic units and the protection in existence against outstanding debts' (Minsky 1964, p. 217). Thus, even a decline in the rate of increase in house prices would have generated warning signals of potential financial instability.

Thus, all of the signs of an impending collapse that would inevitably transform financial crisis into financial instability, infecting the entire financial system, would have been clear to Minsky on the basis of his 1960 analysis. The remedy would also have been clear. Indeed, it is interesting that his call to extend the lender of last resort function through discount window access is precisely what the Federal Reserve eventually did with the Primary Dealer Credit Facility (PDCF) that provides overnight discounting to primary government security dealers in exchange for a specified range of eligible collateral, and the Term Securities Lending Facility (TSLF), that allows primary dealers to exchange eligible collateral for Treasury general collateral for a 28 day maturity. However, as Minsky predicted, the Federal Reserve waited until it was faced with the threat of a collapse of the government security dealer system before taking action, rather than introducing such measures before the crisis. Following Minsky's advice would have prevented the collapse of secured lending and the difficulty in refinancing guaranteed assets that led to the failure of Bear Stearns and the subsequent freezing of liquidity in financial markets that has been a major contributor to the decline in the availability of credit to the overall economy. Indeed, Minsky's proposal would have spread the safety net of discount support to a much wider range of financial institutions than just primary dealers.

In addition, Minsky noted that the Federal Reserve would have to take action to support the other types of government financial guarantees that exist to provide de facto lender of last resort support to other financial institutions. This also has been prescient, as the support granted to the government sponsored entities, has required joint support in the form of borrowing from the Treasury and support from the Federal Reserve.

Finally, the extension of Federal Reserve support to non-member financial institutions has raised the question of the degree of regulatory control that it should exercise over them. Many have suggested that they should be subject to the same regulations as member banks. However, this discussion misses the main point that Minsky raised of the potential conflict between an extension of the Fed's role as the agency responsible for financial stability and the policy actions appropriate to regulation of the economy. Minsky argues that an increased responsibility for financial stability should go hand in hand with a reduced reliance on monetary policy to regulate the behavior of the economy. This means an increased role, and increased integration between the fiscal actions of the Treasury and the Federal Reserve. To this end he recommended that debt management become the responsibility of the Federal Reserve.

The fact that Minsky's 1960 analysis provides not only a prescient analysis of the current crisis, but also the blue print for the policy response to be taken, and to some degree already adopted, supports the validity of his main theses, despite his contention that every financial crisis will be unique and inevitable.

Note

1. Since a short put has unlimited downside risk and the bondholder cannot lose more than
    the purchase price of the bond the position of the bondholders should be formally repre-
    sented as being long, a riskless bond equal to the value of the bonds (or a riskless credit
    default swap) and short, a put on the firm written at a strike of the value of the bonds.

Reference

Minsky, H.P. (1964), 'Financial crisis, financial systems, and the performance of the
economy', in Irwin Friend (ed.), *Private Capital Markets: A Series of Research Studies
Prepared for the Commission on Money and Credit*, Englewood Cliffs, NJ: Prentice-Hall,
pp. 173–380.

3 Minsky and economic policy: 'Keynesianism' all over again?
Éric Tymoigne

Introduction[1]

Minsky's analysis led him to conclude that there are different forms of capitalism each with pros and cons. Laissez-faire capitalism, where the government represents an insignificant proportion of the economy, promotes individual initiatives and creativity (what one may call entrepreneurship) but also generates depressions and unfair inequalities. On the contrary, big-government capitalism is more stable but also comes with its own problems like a lack of dynamism and inflationary tendencies. Following Keynes, Minsky stated that unfair distribution, economic instability and unemployment were structural problems of market mechanisms, and so he promoted a form of capitalism that significantly involves the government.

Many economists would associate Minsky's view with the Neoclassical Synthesis of the 1950s and 1960s, also known as 'Keynesianism,' when monetary and fiscal discretions were used to fine-tune the economy. In this case, most economists would brush away Minsky's proposal for the same reasons they rejected Keynesianism in the 1970s: lack of rationality (Lucas's critique), ignorance of credibility and reputation, and lack of consideration for lags and structural barriers to low unemployment.

However, Minsky was careful to note that there are different forms of big-government capitalism and that not all forms of government activism are consistent with Keynes's policy agenda. The Bastard Keynesianism of the mid-20th century, to take Joan Robinson's colorful characterization, tends to generate arbitrary inequalities, inflationary pressures and long-term unemployment by creating strong income disincentives to reenter the labor force and to hire, by not dealing properly with the chronic shortage of jobs and focusing mainly on retraining and fine-tuning, by limiting collective bargaining processes, and by limiting government involvement to unproductive activities. This form of big government capitalism also tends to promote moral hazard in the financial sector by putting most of the emphasis on sustaining investment while having a limited reactive regulatory and supervisory framework. On the contrary, Minsky put forward a form of big government that limits political discretion in daily socio-economic decisions, tames inflationary pressures, and promotes work habits and individual initiatives.

The first part of the chapter broadly reviews Minsky's theoretical framework and compares it to the New Consensus in order to understand his position regarding the role of government. The second part of the chapter presents some of the pros and cons of big-government capitalism and presents some of the solutions proposed by Minsky to deal with potential problems. The last part of the chapter studies the 'Keynesian' agenda of the Roosevelt and Kennedy/Johnson eras. Overall, the chapter concludes that a big government is needed but that it should neither take the form of a fine tuner, nor of massive state controller, but of a planner that complements, and interacts with, the private sector.

Minsky and mainstream: two views of capitalism

Real exchange economy versus monetary production economy
Today most economists assume that the study of barter provides a good proxy to understand all economic systems (tribal, command and capitalist systems). In a barter theoretical system, economic agents have a given amount of resources and market exchange allows them to better their positions by obtaining the goods desired. Money may be added to the story but it does not change substantially, or at all, the conclusions drawn from pure barter. Money is just a means to smooth exchange and is not sought for itself; individuals care only about the material gains and losses from exchange before making a decision so that 'prior to the introduction of informational asymmetries, . . . financial structure is irrelevant' (Gertler 1988, p. 581). Once those gains and losses have been determined in a set of complete markets, all exchanges are executed instantaneously for all present and future contingencies, and nothing changes unless 'shocks' affect the system. The future is known with certainty at least in the sense that all contingencies have been priced correctly and included in decisions. Moreover, if, as a result of a shock, someone decides to reverse a decision, this can be done easily and immediately.

Keynes called the previous system a real-exchange economy and argued that it does not apply to capitalism. Capitalism is a monetary-production economy. Commodities need to be produced before they can be exchanged, and production is undertaken with the expectations of selling output, needs to be financed, takes time to be implemented and completed, gathers groups with different economic interests, and involves irreversible decisions. All this is done in the context of a competitive environment that emulates monetary accumulation and imposes monetary return targets. Thus, capitalism has two salient features, it pushes individuals to anticipate an uncertain future in order to get an edge against competitors, and financial considerations are at the heart of the system. Consequently, 'money plays a part of its own and affects motives and decisions' (Keynes 1933a [1973], p. 408) and so influences the allocation, production and distribution processes (Veblen 1901, p. 214–15). Another consequence is that the system is highly dynamic and forever changing; stability is inconsistent with the principle of edging others through constant innovations.

All this is in sharp contrast with the barter system; money is not a patch that can be added at will to the theoretical framework, it must be at the heart of a theoretical framework that aims at understanding capitalism. In a capitalist economy, people focus on their liquidity and solvency and those financial concerns are inclusive of purchasing power concerns. Thus, more than the purchasing power of money, people care about the financial power of money, that is, the capacity to meet financial commitments when they come due. The central importance of those financial attributes, however, is not based on the existence of asymmetries of information but on the nature of capitalist economies. Unfortunately, those financial aspects, which are at the core of Keynes's analysis, were pushed aside and made irrelevant by Bastard Keynesianism (Patinkin 1956; Modigliani and Miller 1958); 'Keynesianism' was back to a Pigouvian world and the insights of Keynes and the late Fisher were ultimately lost.

Intrinsic stability versus intrinsic instability
In a real-exchange economy, under perfect competition, market forces help to stabilize economic activity; they do not generate by themselves economic instability. The latter is a rare event that is generated by external factors like government intervention and random shocks. Government intervention is thought to be intrinsically unstable for two reasons (Friedman and Schwartz 1963; Friedman 1968; Kydland and Prescott 1977; Barro and Gordon 1983). A first reason is the assumed incompetence of policymakers to deal with economic problems, as well as the lags involved in policymaking. This leads to economic mismanagement, instability, and suboptimal economic results. A second reason is political interests, which, even if policymakers are well intentioned, lead to time inconsistency.

Minsky's research led him to conclude that capitalism is a highly dynamic system permeated by dialectical forces and circularities (feedback loops) specific to this system. He argued that 'stability is destabilizing,' that is, prolonged economic growth generates financial fragility, and that relevant business cycles are mainly 'due to financial attributes that are essential to capitalism' (Minsky 1986, p. 173). He noted that periods of financial instability are not rare events, but that since World War II their effects have been contained by massive government interventions (albeit with large side effects). He and others criticized Monetarists for being too restrictive in their definition of financial crises by reducing them to bank panics (Schwartz 1988, 1998), and for brushing aside events that would have been catastrophic (potentially of the same magnitude as the Great Depression) if government had not intervened (Sinai 1976; Minsky 1986; Mishkin 1991; Wolfson 1994).

The dialectical nature of capitalism means that both market forces and the government, as well as their interactions, may promote stability and instability. In terms of market forces, Minsky emphasized, among others, the dialectical nature of competition, innovations, and banks. Competition promotes economic growth and entrepreneurship, but it also promotes short-termism and conformism, even though this may entail a great deal of risks. Innovations create new markets but also alter the structure of the economy, behaviors, and incentives. Banks, at least in the 'commitment' (or 'partnership') banking model, promote stability by selecting borrowers carefully, but banks also promote instability because of the structure of their balance sheet and because of competitive pressures to meet targeted returns. In terms of government intervention, Minsky noted that a big government, through its buffer programs and regulations, promotes economic stability but also tends to generate inflationary pressures and to promote moral hazard. In addition, competition pushes the private sector to try to evade, through innovations, the barriers put on profit accumulation by regulation. Thus, if the government is too slow to respond to changes in the economy, its regulations may become obsolete and may promote instability.

This dialectical aspect of capitalism has been observed by many economists, practitioners and casual observers:

> In the 1960s, commercial bank clients frequently inquired how far they could prudently go in breaching traditional standards of liquidity and capitalization that were clearly obsolescent. My advice was always the same – to stick with the majority. Anyone out front risked drawing the lightning of the Federal Reserve or other regulatory retribution. Anyone who lagged behind would lose their market share. But those in the middle had safety in numbers; they could not all be punished, for fear of the repercussion of the economy as a whole. . . . And if the problem grew too big for the Federal Reserve and the banking system were swamped, well then the world would be at an end anyhow and even the most cautious of banks would likely be dragged down with the rest. (Wojnilower 1977, p.235–36)

Regarding the financial troubles involving the hedge fund Long-Term Capital Management (LTCM), Schinasi noted that:

> Although it is easy in retrospect to question why LTCM's counterparties did not demand more information, in a competitive environment, cost considerations must have weighed heavily. Clearly, LTCM's counterparties thought the cost of more information was too high, and walking away from deals was not seen in their interest. (Schinasi 2006, p. 221)

However, even if the cost of information is low, it may not be in the interests of individuals to check the information: 'Above all, it is evident that the capacity of the financial community for ignoring evidence of accumulating trouble, even of wishing devoutly that it might go unmentioned, is as great as ever' (Galbraith 1961, p. xxi). Recently, in the mortgage industry, lenders did not bother to verify the stated income of borrowers with the Internal Revenue Service even though they had the means to do so quickly and at very low cost (Morgenson 2008). Overall, therefore, Minsky noted that there is nothing magical about market forces, and the same applies to government intervention; however, the government can help to stabilize the system.

Aside from proper regulation and supervision, stabilization comes through the cash-flow and balance-sheet impacts of governmental activities (including the central bank). In terms of cash flows, government expenditures and transfers provide some income to the private sector. In terms of balance-sheet, a sovereign government injects default-free liquid assets in the private sector. Government deficits also indirectly help to sustain asset prices because the latter depend on the discounted value of expected future profits (which partly depend on current profits). Finally, the government also directly helps to sustain asset prices by acting as a lender of last resort whenever necessary. The Keynesian multiplier is a common way to present the direct and indirect income impacts, but Kalecki's equation of profit is maybe more insightful to show the direct impact of government spending and taxing on the private sector. The macroeconomic monetary gross profit of firms is equal to (Kalecki 1971):

$$\Pi = I - S_W + DEF + NX$$

with Π the gross profit after taxes, S_W the saving of wage earners, I the gross private domestic investment, DEF the government fiscal deficit, and NX net exports. Thus, through its fiscal policy, the government sector helps to contain the destabilizing effect of the positive feedback loop that is present in the previous equation. Indeed, the gross profit of the business sector is sustained by its investment expenditure, which in turn depends on the profit expectation of entrepreneurs. This 'peculiar circularity of a capitalist economy' (Minsky 1986, p. 227) is part of the internal flaw of capitalism; however, entrepreneurs have usually no knowledge of this process, or do not take it into account, which has important implications for the dynamics of the Minskyan system (Tymoigne 2008).

Government: temporary and limited versus permanent and broad

Because Minsky and the New Consensus have a diametrically opposed view of capitalism, it is not surprising that their view of the role of the government differs greatly. In the New Consensus, it is only if there are market imperfections, like price rigidities or asymmetric information, that the government has a role to play. The government should apply temporary, quick and targeted policies in order to compensate for those imperfections and to put the economy back on its 'natural' path. Policy intervention, thus, may be good as long as the government does not try to push the economy above its natural path and the response is quick. The latter conditions are usually not verified; therefore, having policy institutions that are isolated from political influences, or constrained by rules, is important. Moreover, this short-term fine-tuning should be complemented by a long-term policy that aims at promoting competition so that market mechanisms can play fully.

On the contrary, Minsky viewed the government as a necessary complement to the profit-oriented sector (and more generally the individual sphere of the economy). Given that, according to Minsky's Financial Instability Hypothesis (FIH), market mechanisms tend to promote inflationary pressures and financial fragility as the economy tends toward full employment, a major role of the government is to promote stable full employment, that is, non-inflationary and financially sound full employment. This requires that the government intervenes continuously over the business cycle, rather than sporadically during downturns and upturns. Given the institutional context, specific financial developments always tend to generate stagflation and/or recession, and the point of policy is to prevent, or at least to constrain, their development independently of short-term profitability and short-term welfare gains.[2]

In order for the government to be able to intervene continuously over the cycle, structural macroeconomic[3] programs should be put in place to directly manage the labor force, pricing mechanisms, and investment projects, and constantly monitor financial developments. Because those programs would be permanent and structural, rather than discretionary and specific to one Administration, they would be highly isolated from the political cycle and political deliberations. In addition, they would manage the goal directly, rather than indirectly through interest-rate manipulations, tax incentives or indirect spending.[4] All this eliminates problems of lags, credibility, and time inconsistency. However, this does not mean that the government should apply a rule blindly when implementing its policy;

discretion is still possible within each program to make sure that it works best. For example, Social Security is a structural program but government employees still have large discretions to determine if someone qualifies for benefits. As shown below, the same applies to the programs put forward by Minsky, in which human discretion is still possible within the set of rules and structures.

In the end therefore, for Minsky, individual economic freedom and big government are not incompatible. On the contrary, a big government is necessary to have an economy 'where freedom to innovate and to finance is the rule' (Minsky 1993, p. 81). Entrepreneurs' creativity and imagination can thrive more fully and be more focused because of the higher stability of the system.

Government intervention in Minsky: stabilization policy

From small to big government
Without a doubt, a bigger government has helped to stabilize the growth process in the United States. As shown in Figure 3.1 and Table 3.1, the period between 1900 and 2009 can be divided into two parts with a dividing line set in 1946. The first period recorded more frequent, longer and deeper recessions. Upswings were also much faster and shorter, making the overall business cycle erratic and unstable. The post-1946 era recorded smoother growth and grew at about the same rate as the first period, with a rate of growth of real GNP of 3.356 per cent (against 3.364 per cent for the first period).

This much more stable economy is due to the much bigger size of the government. Figure 3.2 shows that the government has more than tripled in size from about 9 per cent of Gross Domestic Product (GDP) in 1929 to more than 30 per cent of GDP in 2009. Figure 3.3 shows that most of the contribution to this growth has come from the federal government, which has grown from about 2 per cent of GDP in 1929 to about 20 per cent of GDP in 2009. The state and local governments have also contributed to the growth but in a more moderate way as shown in Figure 3.4. After the mid 1950s, this growth of the government sector has taken the form of increased Social Security payments, welfare payments, interest payments and subsidies, while government consumption and investment have declined steadily relative to GDP especially for the federal government.

This increased capacity of the government to stabilize the system is easy to understand if one refers to the Kalecki equation. Knowing that gross private domestic investment is the most erratic component of the equation, in order for the government to be able to stabilize aggregate monetary profit, its expenditures and taxes should be at least as big as investment.

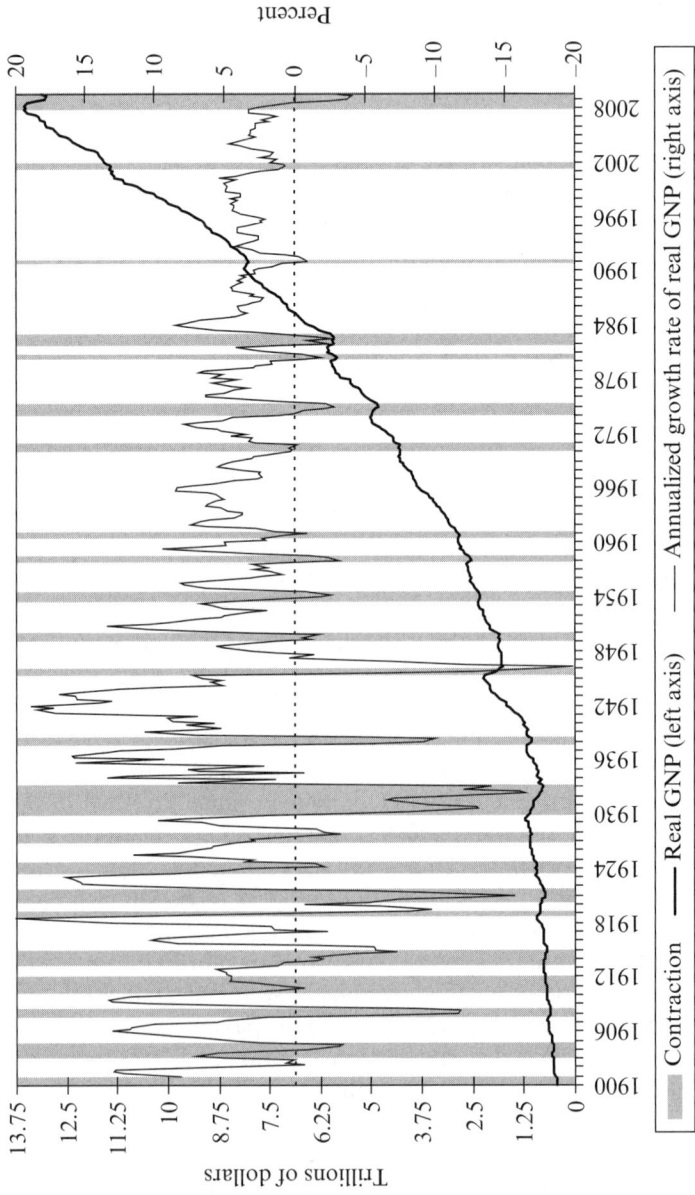

Sources: NBER, BEA and Gordon (1990). Calculation by the author.

Figure 3.1 US business cycle, 1900–2009 (base: 2005)

Table 3.1 Characteristics of recessions before and after World War II

	Number of contractions	Average Frequency	Average Length	Average Decline in real GNP
1900–46	12	3.9 years	18.1 months	6.8%
1947–2009	11	6.1 years	10.4 months	−1.7%

Note: The average decline in real GNP includes all quarters with a negative growth rate, even if there is no contraction at that time.

Sources: NBER, BEA and Gordon (1990).

Of particular relevance is the federal government because of its monetary sovereignty and the flexibility of its budgeting process. Figures 3.2 and 3.3 show that in the 1920s and 1930s the federal government was too small to be able to compensate for swings in investment. Leaving aside World War II, an adequate size was not reached until the early 1950s after which the federal government total expenditures always have been above 15 per cent of GDP which is approximately the size of investment in the US economy (post-1946 gross private domestic investment averaged 16 per cent of GDP). Thus, for the US economy, accounting for other fluctuations besides investment, a big government means a federal government that represents about 20 per cent of GDP. Judged with this criterion, the size of the federal government was too big in the 1980s and early 1990s.

However, since the mid 1980s some disturbing trends have appeared that have only been recently stopped by the Great Recession. As shown in Figures 3.3, 3.4, 3.5 and 3.6, not only has the size of federal government purchases been constantly declining, but there also has been a shift in responsibilities away from the federal government and toward state and local governments. This shift in the composition of government intervention is worrisome because state and local governments are not able to deal with macroeconomic issues, and because of the regressive nature of their tax structures. As shown below, one may also critique the composition of government spending. Minsky critiqued the ballooning role of transfer payments and the decline in regulation, which have respectively promoted inflationary tendencies and financial instability. In addition, given the shift toward transfers rather than purchases, the federal government has become less able to be proactive to stabilize the economy. One has to wait for a crisis to develop fully before government intervention kicks in meaningfully.

If a big government is able to stabilize the system – a desirable property that a small government does not have – it also creates new problems.

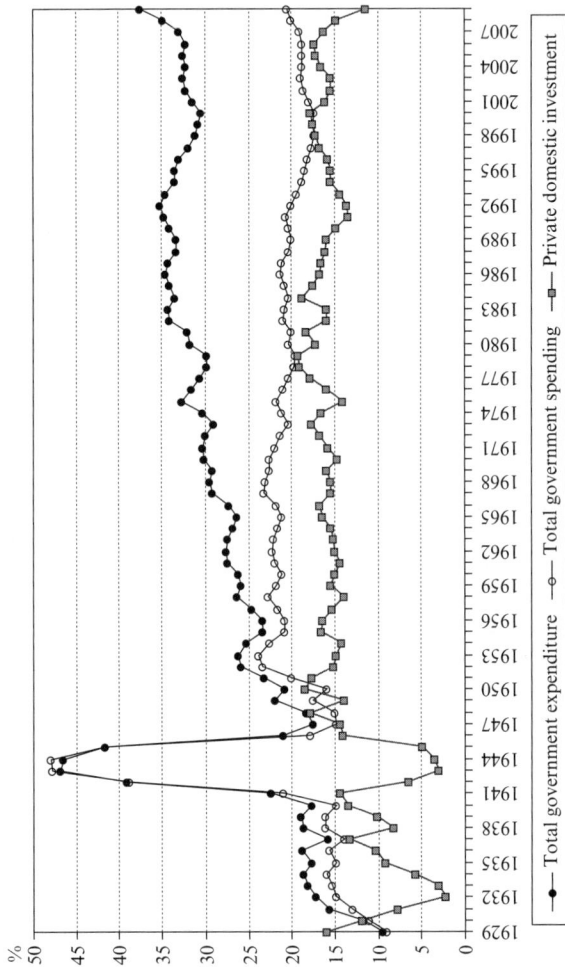

Note: Government gross purchases refer to the gross investment and consumption of the government. Government total net expenditures include government gross purchases net of consumption of fixed capital, plus all net payments to the private sector and the rest of the world.

To have a more accurate view of the capacity of government to inject funds in the domestic economy, one may want to exclude net payments to the rest of the world. In 2007, government total net expenditures represented 33.5 per cent of GDP out of which 1.4 percentage points constituted net payments to the rest of the world.

Source: BEA.

Figure 3.2   Size of government sector (%)

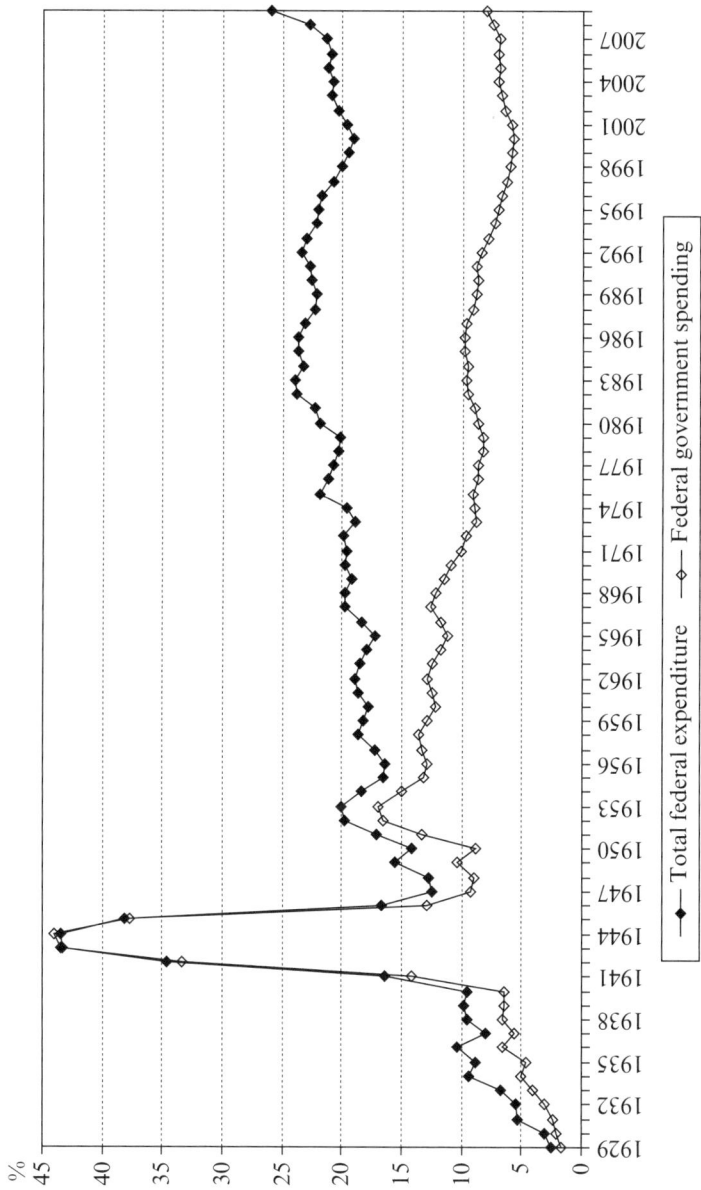

Source: BEA.

Figure 3.3 Size of the federal government (%)

57

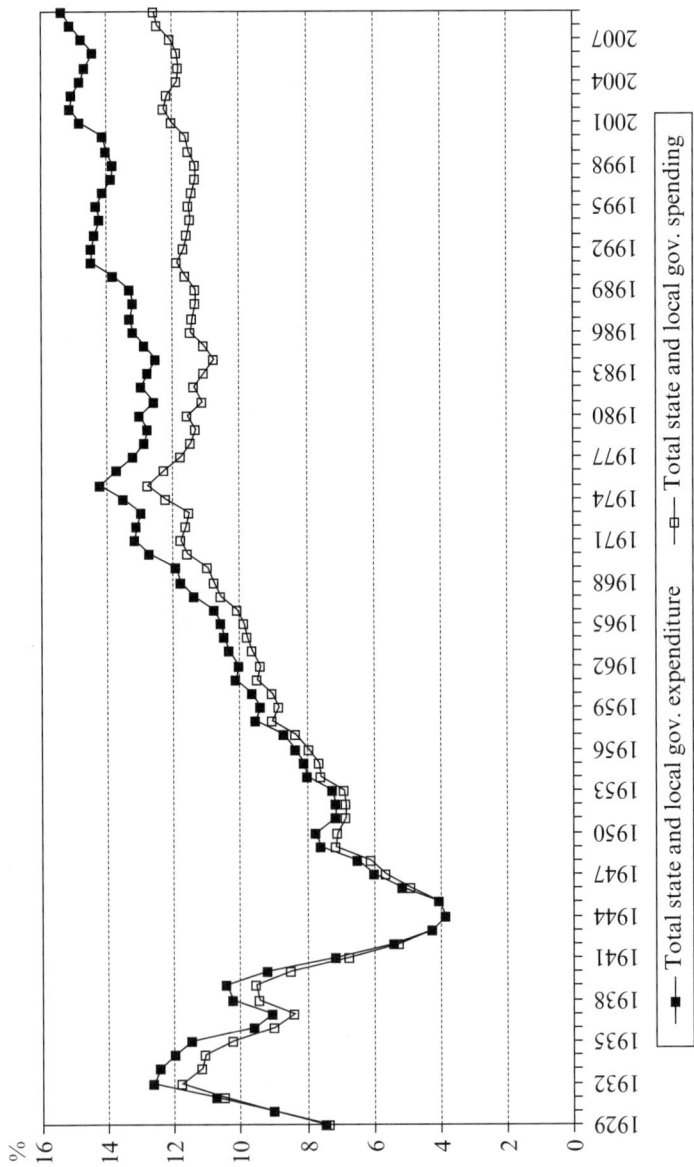

Source: BEA.

Figure 3.4 Size of the local and state governments (%)

Legend:
- Total state and local gov. expenditure
- Total state and local gov. spending

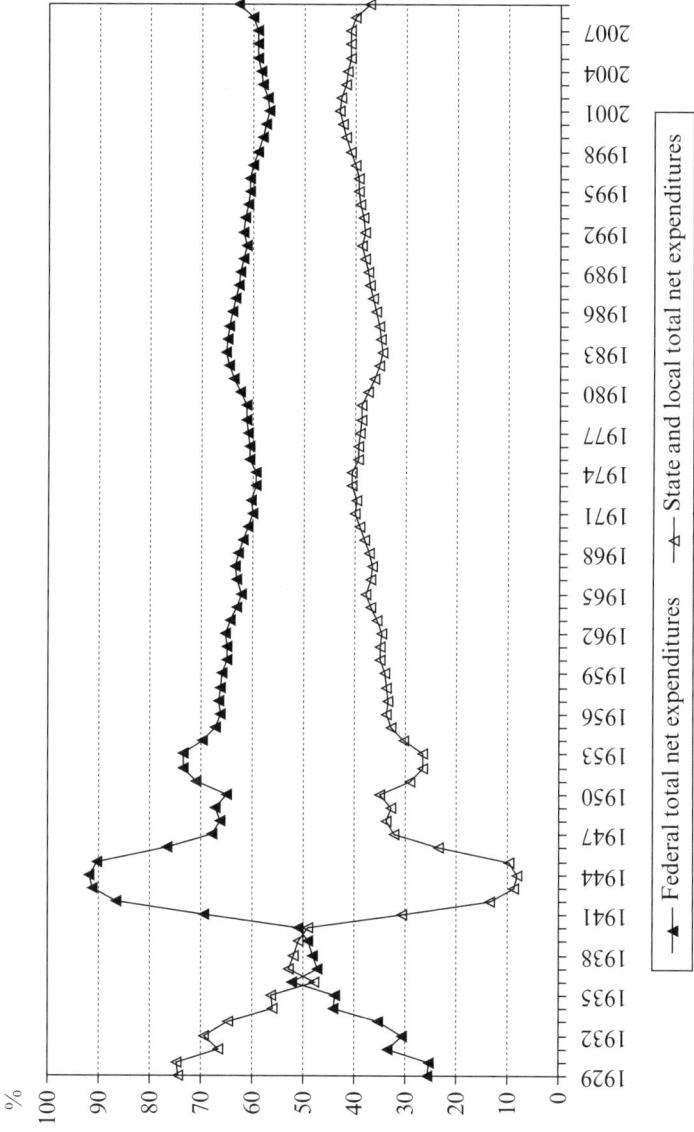

Source: BEA.

Figure 3.5 Size of the federal government relative to local and state governments (%)

Legend:
— Federal total net expenditures   — State and local total net expenditures

59

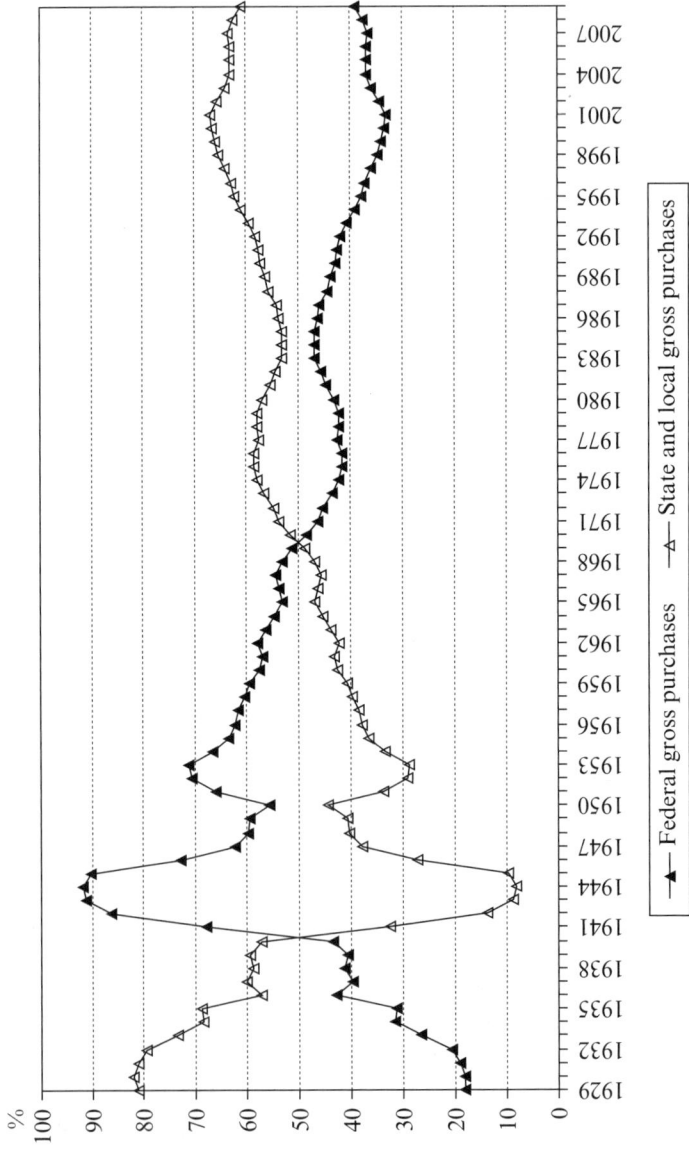

60

Source: BEA.

Figure 3.6 Size of the federal government relative to local and state government in the GDP (%)

Indeed, by becoming too big it may generate inflationary tendencies, promote moral hazard, and dampen entrepreneurship. In terms of inflationary potential, Figure 3.7 shows that, after 1946, there is a clear inflationary bias.

One may see the potential inflationary effect of big government by expressing in terms of relative growth the national income identity $PQ \equiv W + \Pi$ and the Kalecki equation of profit (Tymoigne 2009):

$$g_P \approx (g_w - g_{AP_L})s_W + (g_Z - g_Q)s_Z + (g_{C\Pi}s_{C\Pi} - g_{SH}s_{SH} + g_I s_I$$
$$+ g_G s_G - g_T s_T + g_X s_X - g_J s_J) - g_Q s_{\Pi nD} + (g_{T\Pi} - g_Q)s_{T\Pi}$$

with s_i the share of variable i in GDP and g_i the growth rate of variable i and, AP_L the average productivity of labor, w the average wage rate (including compensation and benefits), Π_{nD} the retained earnings of firms, S_H the saving level of households, and C_Π the consumption out of profit, I the level of gross investment, X exports, J imports, Z the non-wage incomes paid by firms (dividends, interests, rental income), and T_Π corporate income tax. This identity can be used to develop a theory of inflation by using, for example, the conflict-claim theory to explain g_w, the liquidity preference theory to explain g_Z, and the theory of effective demand to explain g_Q. g_{AP_L} can be assumed to behave differently depending on the structure of the labor market (very flexible in a sluggish labor market, close to constant in a free-market labor market). For the sake of argument, shares are given but could also be explained by using a monetary theory of distribution.

Thus, a big government, for which s_G, s_T and/or $s_{T\Pi}$ are big, can contribute to inflation by raising the wage of its employees too fast, by increasing spending too fast on goods and services, and by having a tax structure that contributes to a fast increase in corporate income taxes. Transfer payments may create additional inflationary pressures by growing disposable wage income and disposable net profit too fast. In addition, a big government in which political discretion in economic issues is high may prevent g_G and g_T from moving up or down when they need to in order to prevent inflation or recession. Finally, if the government mainly focuses its spending on defense and other unproductive expenditures, there is a greater chance that a big government will be inflationary (Han and Mulligan 2008).

In terms of potential moral hazard, by providing a safety net the government may achieve short-term stability at the expense of long-term instability. A first moral hazard is the tendency for businesses to take too many risks knowing that the government will rescue most of them in case of crisis. A second moral hazard is the potential decrease in labor force participation, especially if there are substantial income losses from going back

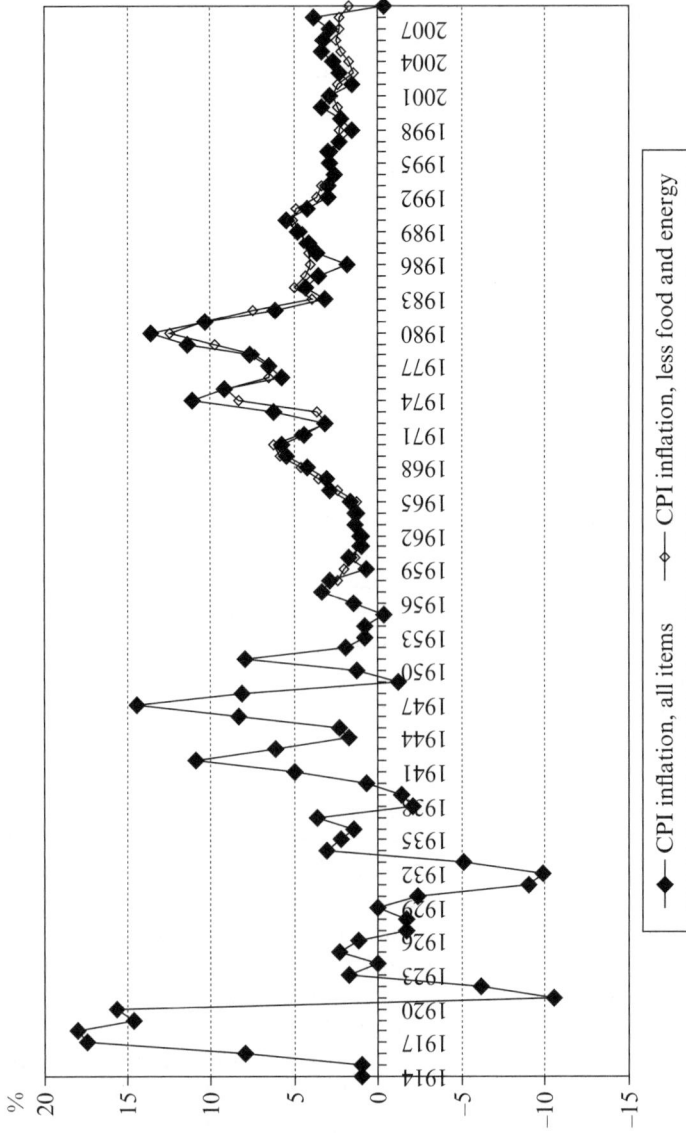

Source: BLS.

Figure 3.7 Changes in the CPI, 1914–2007 (%)

into the work force and giving up transfer payments, which may affect production capacities of a country and so may compound the potential inflationary pressures over the long term.

In terms of entrepreneurship, a too tight control of the economy may remove the fun from entrepreneurship by limiting choices and constraining possibilities. As Keynes noted, investment activity is highly uncertain and risky, but uncertainty is also a factor that promotes investment by leaving some space for human creativity and imagination. Minsky was aware of this and noted that:

> Federal Reserve policy therefore needs to continuously 'lean against' the use of speculative and Ponzi finance. But Ponzi finance is a usual way of debt-financing investment in process in a capitalist society. Consequently, capitalism without financial practices that lead to instability may be less innovative and expansionary; lessening the possibility of disaster might very well take part of the spark of creativity out of the capitalist system. (Minsky 1986, p. 328)

Overall, therefore, the government has to promote sound financing methods while also encouraging a dynamic economy that can respond to the needs of society.

In order to contain those problems, specific policies should be created that limit political interests in their implementation and that promote price stability as well as check for potential moral hazards. Politicians would have a way to influence long-term trends in government activities by influencing the existing structural programs and creating new ones. Minsky had a view of a big government that tries to respect those conditions.

Minsky's idea of a big government: the economics of control
In a controlled economy, to employ Abba Lerner's term, the government acts as a planner in order to prevent key elements of the economy from getting out of hand by applying neither fascism nor socialism, but by following a 'third course' which involves removing 'certain substantial spheres of activity from the hands of private enterprise' (Robinson 1943 [1966], p. 86).

> The policy problem is to devise institutional structures and measures that attenuate the thrust of inflation, unemployment, and slower improvements in the standard of life without increasing the likelihood of a deep depression. . . . The current strategy seeks to achieve full employment by way of subsidizing demand. The instruments are financing conditions, fiscal inducements to invest, government contracts, transfer payments, and taxes. This policy strategy now leads to chronic inflation and periodic investment booms that culminate in financial crises and serious instability. The policy problem is to develop a strategy for full employment that does not lead to instability, inflation, and unemployment. (Minsky 1986, p. 295, 308)

Minsky was aware that, given the dynamic nature of capitalism, there is no definitive solution to the control of the economy, and that the government must respond continuously to and, even better, anticipate changes in the institutional structure. New regulations lead to regulatory arbitrage, and the creativity of economic agents generates new economic structures and so a need to change regulations.

A first element that should not be determined by market mechanisms is the level of employment. Minsky promoted the creation of an 'employer of last resort' (ELR), that is, broad government employment programs similar to those of the 1930s. The programs would be permanent, decentralized and would employ at a uniform wage anybody willing and able to work but unable to find a job in the private sector, and would take individuals as they are, where they are. Recently, this program has attracted growing attention and it has been applied in a limited way in Argentina (Tcherneva and Wray 2007; Wray 2007; Kaboub 2008). There are several benefits to this program. First, by fixing the base wage at which one is employed, the program would help to keep in check the growth of the average wage rate, which can be a source of inflation. In addition, this program tends to eliminate the inflationary tendency of the existing welfare and unemployment insurance programs that provide an income even though no current economic contribution to society is made.[5] By contrast, ELR workers would contribute to the growth of the economy (g_Q) and an employment buffer program would help to sustain the productivity of workers by keeping them busy. Second, by acting as an income buffer to those who lost their job in the private sector, the program would act as an automatic stabilizer. This is a good way to eliminate lags and to limit political interests in fiscal activism because G and T would move automatically with the number of people employed in the ELR program. Third, this program would also contribute to a more harmonious society by decreasing income inequalities (the ELR wage would be a living wage), and by lowering crime and other negative consequences (most of them non-monetary) induced by unemployment.

A second element of the economy that should be controlled is the level and composition of investment. The government should socialize investment by fixing the reward received by entrepreneurs, and by allocating resources toward the most socially needed investment projects. This does not mean that all individual decisions would be removed because the government could just bring forward the areas that need investment and let the private companies propose solutions. The government (or special committees including government representatives) would select the most appropriate projects without necessarily undertaking their construction nor removing ownership from the private sector (Keynes 1936, p. 378ff).

The government could also leave frivolous investment projects (cell phones, and so on) to the private sector while housing, infrastructure and other social needs would be supervised by government.[6] Minsky's proposal for community development banks is part of this project. The goals of this policy are threefold. First, investment projects would be allocated to sectors that need them; this would help to homogenize society and so would contribute to its stability and well-being. Second, it would help to promote financial stability because the positive macroeconomic feedback loop between investment and profit would be mostly eliminated. Finally, given that the growth of investment may contribute to inflation, the socialization of investment would help to manage inflation.

A third element is the control of the growth of income through a generalized income policy. The ELR program and the socialization of investment would already help to control income growth by affecting the growth of wages and aggregate profit. Nevertheless, additional policies may be necessary that define general rules with respect to wage bargaining and the pay-out ratios of firms. For example, Minsky proposed that the pay-out ratio of banks be controlled by regulators so that the retained earnings of banks do not grow too fast, because this is a major cause of instability and inflation (Minsky 1975b, 1977, 1986, p. 234–38, 321). This policy has two essential benefits. The first one is to help to dampen inflationary pressures. As shown earlier, wage payments, interest payments, retained earnings and other income payments may have an effect on inflation if they grow too fast. The second benefit is to promote financial stability by limiting the demands that stockholders can put on rates of returns that firms and banks should generate.

A fourth element that should be controlled is the growth and distribution of assets and liabilities of all financial institutions. The main way this should be done is by a cash-flow oriented regulation and supervision while also using a flexible capital requirement policy. One may note, however, that focusing mainly on equity is not a good strategy because it does not provide a direct measure of the capacity of a financial institution to withstand liquidity shocks. Actually, it is not even a good measure of solvency because of the multiple adjustments to capital equity that do not necessarily reflect the capacity to have a profitable business. Current cash flows, future expected cash flows, and current amount of liquid assets provide a much better view of what the potential needs and costs of refinancing or liquidation are.

One may note that all these programs are coherently related and are meant to be permanent. They are not a patchwork of temporary discretionary policies. These programs are also largely independent of the political climate, and influence both production capacities and purchasing powers. Their implementation would be done by government employees who would have some discretion within the rules set up by the programs.[7] For example, an ELR worker may be fired if he or she does not perform, and, within the income policy, some sectors may be favored over others to encourage their development. Note also that the inflationary tendencies of a big government are constrained by controlling both public and private spending directly and indirectly. There is no doubt that all these programs will lead to changes in the behavior of individuals and that unpredicted and unintended adverse consequences will appear, but those have to be dealt with as we go *and* in conjunction with the changes in the structure of the economy. Again, there is no final solution to economic management of a society that is highly dynamic and that fosters individual decisions.

Past big government experiences in the United States
For most economists, 'Keynesianism' is synonymous to any type of 'fiscal activism.' Keynes's approach is usually summed up into a 45-degree-line diagram that seems to guarantee that any type of government expenditures and tax measures brings full employment, now and forever, without any problems. However, Minsky noted that this is a gross simplification and he was highly critical of what happened in the 1960s:

> Just as there never really was a Keynesian revolution in economic theory, there also never really was one in policy. . . . All that was assimilated from Keynes by the policy establishment and its clients was the analysis of an economy in deep depression and a policy tool of deficit financing. . . . Keynesian economics, even in the mind of the economics profession, but particularly in the view of politicians and the public, became a series of simple-minded guidelines to monetary and fiscal policy. . . . The institutional structure has not been adapted to reflect the knowledge that the collapse of aggregate demand and profits, such as occasionally occurred and often threatened to occur in pre-1933 small government capitalism, is never a clear and present danger in Big Government capitalism such as has ruled since World War II. (Minsky 1986, p. 291, 295)

In the last chapter of the *General Theory*, Keynes noted that the 'outstanding faults of the economic society in which we live are its failure to provide for full employment and its arbitrary and inequitable distribution of wealth and incomes' (Keynes 1936, p. 372) which 'may be considered dual aspects of a single basic trouble; for economists have long recognized a connection between unemployment and the maldistribution of purchasing power' (Keynes in Chew 1936). As a consequence, Keynes was for a direct participation of the government through specific fiscal and monetary measures, that included some form of planning via a cooperation between the private and public sector (socialization of investment), the maintenance of low policy rates so that market rates reward only risks and skills (euthanasia of rentiers), and a progressive tax policy that favors consumption. Let us look at past experiences and see how they conform to Keynes's view of government intervention.

The Roosevelt era

When campaigning in 1932, Roosevelt ran on the popular idea that the federal government should balance its budget. He blamed Hoover for his fiscal 'extravagance and . . . rashly pledged to reduce government expenditure by 25 per cent' (Badger 1989, p. 111). However, given that society was on the brink of collapse, once elected, Roosevelt decided to increase government intervention and to deficit spend. These dramatic changes were not based on the *General Theory*, which was not available, nor on the advice of Keynes, who had not provided any.[8]

From the end of 1933, Keynes had applauded most of the New Deal policies and he continued to do so over time:

> I accept the view that durable investment must come increasingly under state direction. I sympathise with Mr. Wallace's agricultural policies. I believe that the Securities and Exchange Commission (SEC) is doing splendid work. I regard the growth of collective bargaining as essential. I approve minimum wage and hours regulations. I was altogether on your side the other day, when you deprecated a policy of general wage reductions as useless in present circumstances. (Keynes 1938b [1982], p. 438–9)

However, he was also very critical of the lack of engagement of the Roosevelt Administration in recovery efforts. Keynes wanted it to go much further and at a much faster pace by deficit spending massively through large-scale government expenditures in housing,[9] unemployment relief programs, aid to farmers, public utilities, railroads and other public works (Keynes 1933d, 1934a, 1934b, 1938b). In addition to fiscal measures, he also pushed for a policy of cheap money that influences directly the whole yield curve:

> I put in the second place the maintenance of cheap and abundant credit, in particular the reduction of the long-term rate of interest. . . . I see no reason why you should not reduce the rate of interest on your long-term government bonds to 2 ½ per cent or less, . . .if only the Federal Reserve System would replace its present holdings of short-dated Treasury issues by purchasing long-dated issues in exchange. (Keynes 1933d [1982], p. 297)

Further, in 1936 he was able to present the core policy agenda of the *General Theory* to the Roosevelt Administration:

> The main defects in our present society are its failure to provide full employment, and its inequitable distribution of wealth and incomes. . . . In the

conditions that now exist the 'abstinence' of the rich impedes the growth of wealth, and action to remove great inequalities increases it. . . . It appears that effective saving depends on the scale of investment, which varies inversely with the rate of interest. Thus, it is socially advantageous to reduce the rate of interest . . . [so that it] would be possible to increase the stock of capital to a point at which the use of capital goods would cost little more than enough to cover wastage and obsolescence. This state of affairs, though it would leave scope for individual enterprise, would tend to eliminate the rentier, and to weaken the power of the capitalist to exploit the scarcity value of capital . . . and the functionless investor would have no place in the economy. (Keynes in Chew 1936)

Thus, the recommendations of Keynes's *General Theory*, chapter 24, mostly considered as obscure radical sidetracks unimportant for the whole book, were pushed forward by Keynes.

Overall, Keynes critiqued the Roosevelt Administration as 'unprepared' (Keynes 1938a [1982], p.432) and 'very slow to get moving' (Keynes 1934a [1982], p.308). He stated that the handling of some problems had been 'really wicked' (Keynes 1938b [1982], p.436) and that 'the attainment of the best results has been interfered with by certain fallacies of thought' (Keynes 1934d [1982], p.299). One of these fallacies[10] was the idea of 'sound finance' that pushed Roosevelt to limit the funding of New Deal programs and, especially during election years, to try to generate a budget surplus (Lee 1989):

Most New Dealers believed that recovery would come from the revival of private investment. . . . Similarly business advocates of spending in 1933 saw public spending as a 'quick fix' designed to 'start up' the economy, not a permanent crutch. Most supporters of government spending did not want to unbalance the budget. . . . Roosevelt's Secretary of the Treasury, Henry Morgenthau Jr., argued that in order to revive the private investment necessary for full recovery, the federal budget must be balanced so that business would have the confidence to invest. (Badger 1989, p.110–12)

As a consequence, as shown in Figure 3.8, the federal current budget deficit never accounted for more than 4 per cent of GDP in the 1930s. This is minuscule if one considers the size of the problem and that the minor recession of 2001 led to a deficit of about 3 per cent of GDP. In addition, after 1936, the Roosevelt Administration aimed at reaching surpluses as fast as possible, which led to a short but severe recession in 1937.

Given the constraint of sound finance, as shown in Figure 3.3, federal government spending grew very slowly. In fact, from 1933 to 1941 federal government spending mostly stagnated relative to GDP. In addition, in order to reach a surplus, Roosevelt suggested cutting New Deal programs:

He was embarrassed by Republican criticism of the budget deficits under the New Deal. He justified them by arguing that it was only extraordinary

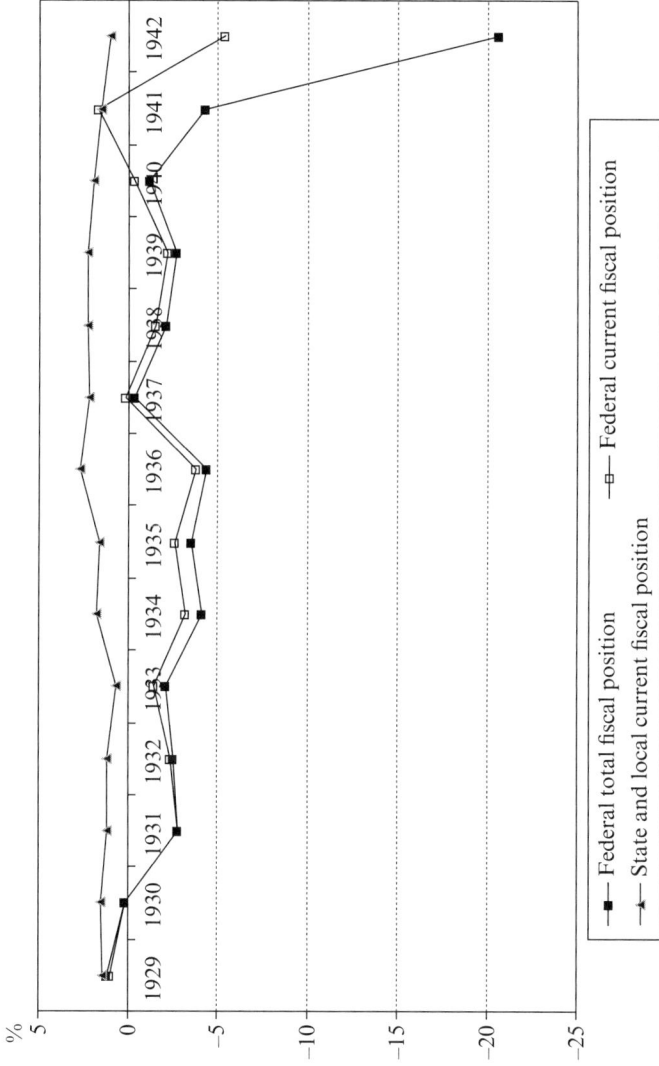

Note: Over the period, the total budget of state and local governments was balanced.

Source: BEA.

Figure 3.8 Fiscal positions relative to GDP (%)

> spending for humanitarian reasons that unbalanced the budget . . . . He looked
> for ways to show that deficits were being scaled down so that he could promise
> a balanced budget for fiscal 1938. . . . In 1936, an election year, he was even
> prepared to cut spending on the Civilian Conservation Corps . . . . (Badger
> 1989, p. 111)

Rather than a sound economic program, Roosevelt and Congress saw the
work programs as an emergency measure needed, if not for moral obligation, at least to avoid the destruction of capitalism altogether.[11]

By 1938, because of successful experimentations and through the influence of Hansen, Currie and Eccles,[12] the idea that government deficit
could be good to restore prosperity had gained some ground in the
Administration and the business community but, at least for the latter,
'only if it could be stripped of New Deal reformism' (Badger 1989, p. 116).
However, Roosevelt remained skeptical of fiscal-led stimulus. As a proportion of GDP, government spending and the federal deficit were lower
than in 1936 and the Administration went back to a surplus in 1941. This
surplus allowed Roosevelt to keep a good public appearance, but it did
not generate a recession because, due to national defense expenditures, the
total fiscal position of the government was now a deficit representing 4.9
per cent of GDP.

One has to wait until the entry of the US into World War II to see a
major government involvement in the economy and a commitment to let
the budget deficits grow as much as needed. Between 1942 and 1945, the
current deficit averaged 9.4 per cent of GDP and the total deficit averaged
22.1 per cent of GDP, which had the unintended (and probably unexpected) consequence of strongly putting the US economy back on its feet.
Since that time, as shown in Figure 3.9, defense spending has been the
main component of federal purchases. However, Keynes lamented that
this was not at all what he had in mind when he promoted government
intervention and complained that, 'Alas, your letter confirms the prevailing opinion that money is only available for what is useless' (Keynes in
Skidelsky 2000, p. 51). Similarly, the monetary measures (management of
the whole yield curve below 2.5 per cent) proposed by Keynes were only
implemented because of the war and were abandoned in 1953.

By the middle of World War II, the National Resources Planning Board
(NRPB), recognizing that the private sector cannot sustain full employment, took a giant step toward Keynes's position. It recognized that
deficits far greater than in the 1930s would be necessary to maintain full
employment, and that some private economic activities would have to be
partly implemented by the government in order to make sure to 'provide
work for adults who are willing and able to work, if private industry is
unable to do so' (NRPB in Barber 1996, p. 159). This was too radical

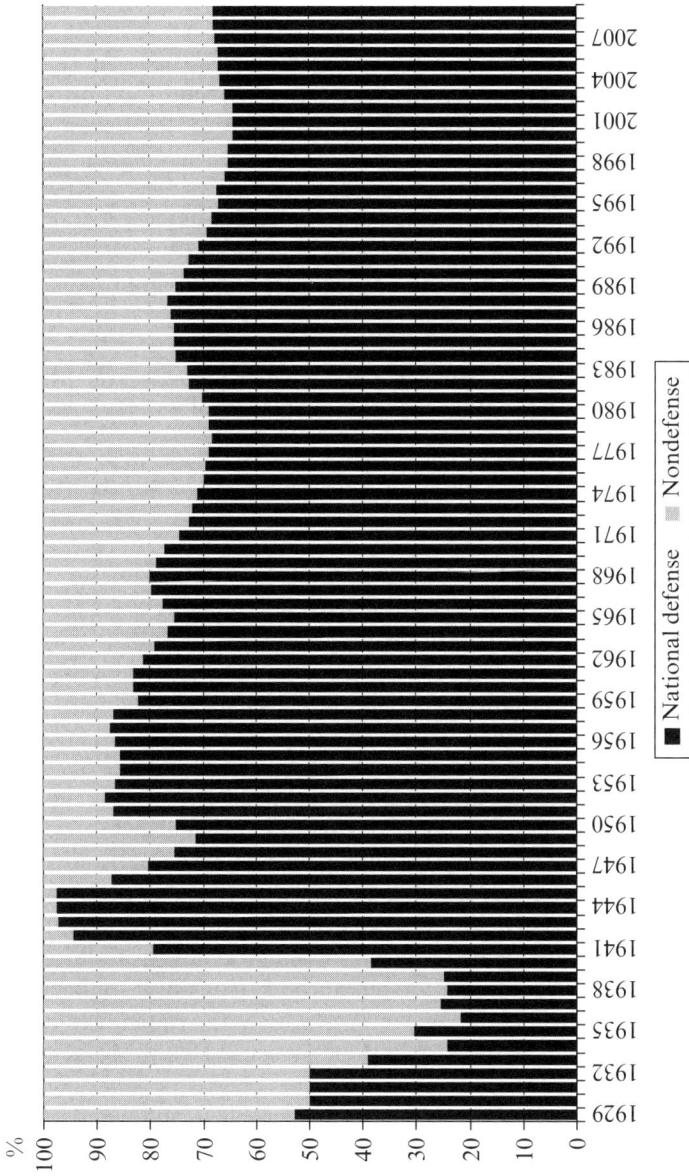

Source: BEA.

Figure 3.9 Composition of federal spending (%)

for Congress who stopped funding the NRPB in 1943. Another shot at government planning was attempted by the Full Employment Bill of 1945 which proposed to put in place a structural 'last resort . . . program of federal spending and investment' (Bailey 1950, p. 13–14) in order to make sure that 'all Americans able to work and seeking work have the right to useful, remunerative, regular, and full-time employment' (Section 2b of the Full Employment Bill of 1945 in Bailey (1950, p. 243)). However, the Bill did not pass the House and it was replaced by the Employment Act of 1946. Often, the Act is thought to represent the final victory of Keynes's ideas and the establishment of a long period of Keynesianism that culminated in Nixon's famous tirade 'we are all Keynesians now.' However, the Act was substantially different from the 1945 Bill (Santoni 1986) and Barber notes that:

> The legislative achievement represented by the Employment Act of 1946 has sometimes been treated as a triumph for a Keynesian point of view. It needs to be underscored that such a reading of that event is mistaken. . . . Even . . . the Council of Economic Advisers, owed less to their thinking than to the views presented by an economist hostile to Americanized Keynesianism. (Barber 1996, p. 169)

Rather than guaranteeing the right to employment, the 1946 Act transformed the US government into a full-fledged fine-tuner in order to make employment consistent with business interests. This paved the way for incoherent, discretionary programs, time inconsistency problems, and credibility problems that ultimately led to the incapacity to manage both price stability and employment.

If one must associate an economist to the policies of the 1930s, Irving Fisher is a much more appropriate candidate. At the end of 1932, he sent his *Booms and Depressions* to Raymond Moley (an original member of the Brain Trust who played a key role in shaping the first New Deal) and asked to meet with him (Barber 1996, p. 22). In 1933 and 1934, 'Fisher wrote to Roosevelt at least thirty-five times (receiving four replies) and visited him twice' (Allen 1993, p. 704) which is far more than Keynes. In addition, he had key allies in the Administration whom he personally recommended to the President (like George F. Warren), or who were sympathetic to the reflation approach such as the Secretary of Treasury Henry Morgenthau Jr. (Barber 1996, p. 15).

In order to solve what he saw as a monetary problem, and based on the quantity theory of money and the money multiplier, Fisher advocated a plan that emphasized reflating and then stabilizing prices by controlling the money supply and the velocity of money in order to manage aggregate spending[13] (Fisher 1932, p. 121ff, 212ff; Fisher 1935a). The control of the money supply would go through credit control (via large variations in nominal policy rates to affect real interest rates, enlarged open-market operations beyond real bills, manipulations of reserve requirements, and other means) and gold control (by forbidding gold coinage and by varying the bid and ask prices of gold at the Treasury desk). He also advocated temporary fiscal deficits during recessions (Fisher 1932, p. 104–5; Pavanelli 2004, p. 298) but was not very fond of public work programs and unemployment insurance. According to Fisher, the latter two were only 'palliative' policies because unemployment was only a consequence of the depression and because work programs were slow to implement and only effective on a very large scale, which goes against the private profit system. Beyond *Booms and Depressions*, additional influence can be seen through the correspondence between Fisher and the Roosevelt Administration, sometimes at its request, in which he advised a bank holiday (two days before Roosevelt declared it), going off the gold standard or at least devaluing the dollar by 50 per cent, the continuation of employment programs and government spending as long as they have a monetary component like subsidies and loans to private businesses (Barber 1996, p. 84–5; Allen 1977).

The Roosevelt Administration followed Fisher on most of these points, by running temporary deficits, by buying large amounts of gold in 1933 and 1934, by going off the gold standard within the US and by raising the trading price of gold at the Treasury desk in January 1934 (with the effect of devaluing the dollar relative to currencies still in the gold standard system), and by putting in place temporary working programs (Pavanelli 2004). Over time, however, his influence diminished. Against Fisher's advice, Roosevelt did not raise the value of gold above $35 (Barber 1996, p. 81) and, later, Roosevelt did not go for his 100 per cent money plan. In addition, Fisher vigorously opposed the New Deal measures to restrict supply and to institute economic planning.[14] In particular, 'he considered the initiatives to regulate wages and production as totally misguided' (Pavanelli, 2004, p. 298). In the end, only one of his secondary advices survived the trial period and this was the running of temporary fiscal deficits and temporary employment programs.

Thus, one does not have to look to Keynes for a justification of fiscal activism. However, Fisher's strategy is very different from Keynes's because for Fisher 'the depression does not indicate a general breakdown of capitalism . . . . It indicates almost solely a breakdown of our monetary system' (Fisher 1935b in Pavanelli 2004), whereas for Keynes the management of some aspects of economic life by the government is necessary to avoid 'the destruction of existing economic forms in their entirety, and [to guarantee] the successful functioning of individual initiative' (Keynes 1936, p. 380).

In the end, therefore, the Roosevelt Administration followed many different advices. As Roosevelt stated, it was time for 'bold and persistent experimentation' (Barber 1996, p. 19) and as Keynes noted:

> It must have been difficult for the President to know in what direction to turn for the best available advice. In practice he has shown himself extraordinarily accessible to anyone with new ideas to air whom he believed to be independent and disinterested. Naturally he had received a great deal of advice, some of it inconsistent with the rest and not all of it of equal quality. . . . [H]e has been happy to provide the political skill and the power of authority to give some sort of a run to all kinds of *ideas*, ready to judge by results . . . (Keynes 1934a [1982], p. 306–7)

This experimental approach can be seen within the structure of the Roosevelt Administration with the division between the Structuralists and the Monetarists. However, both favored sound finance and relied on price policies to bring a recovery (either through reflation or direct price manipulations) (Barber 1996, p. 80). Without the war, Roosevelt would have continued to muddle through, as any Administration has since, because there was no conversion to the Keynesian principles of submitting fiscal and monetary policies to the achievement of stable full employment. Overall, the fiscal and monetary strategies of the Roosevelt Administration were much closer to what Fisher had in mind.

The Kennedy–Johnson era
The Kennedy–Johnson era is thought to be the apex of 'Keynesianism.' Like the Roosevelt Administration, the Kennedy–Johnson Administration focused on stimulating investment and economic growth but it put more emphasis on tax incentives. In order to cope with poverty, Johnson, following Kennedy's initial preparations, also put in place his famous War on Poverty. The idea that public employment programs could help in the fight was advanced but Johnson was convinced by the Council of Economic Advisers (CEA) that pro-growth and pro-market policies would be more effective (Russel 2004). The idea that these policies allow everyone to benefit, reduce inequalities, and are a very effective means to reduce poverty has been a core assumption of the liberal program on poverty (Brady 2003).

All this again is far more consistent with Irving Fisher's idea of government intervention, and several authors have already criticized the Keynesian nature of this era (Kregel 1994; Wray 1994; Harvey 1999, 2000; Bell and Wray 2004; Russel 2004). Minsky, who by that time had become an accomplished economist, was very critical of the policy of the Administration.

In terms of the overall strategy, Minsky noted that the strong emphasis on investment and tax incentives is misplaced:

> Certainly there is an unwarranted emphasis on investment as the source of all good things: employment, income, growth, price stability. But in truth, inept and inappropriate investment and investment financing deters full employment, consumption, economic growth, and price stability. (Minsky 1986, p. 326)

One can understand why if one follows Minsky's apparatus. The Kalecki equation of profit creates a destabilizing feedback loop in which current investment is implemented on the expectation that investment will be done in the future. This creates long-term explosive patterns *à la* Harrod and Domar by increasing future production capacities without increasing future demand. The *General Theory* mainly focused on short-term demand problems, but Keynes was aware of long-term problems and demonstrated the need to emphasize consumption[15] and government spending, and the importance of managing investment in order to manage the supply side of the system (Keynes 1936, p. 105–6; Minsky 1975a). Consequently, an economic plan that aims at long-term full employment and price stability cannot be based on continuously promoting private investment because of the financial vicissitudes of investment projects, and because of their impact on future production capacities. Minsky also noted that the emphasis on investment creates inflationary pressures and income inequality (Minsky 1973, 1981, 1986).

In terms of tax incentives, this method of stimulating employment is highly indirect. Decreasing taxes (or providing subsidies) does not promote employment if businesses do not expect that there is a profitable demand.[16] Similarly, not all government expenditures are equally effective in promoting employment, not to say full employment, and just deficit spending will not do. As shown in Figure 3.10, the deficits run in the 1970s, 1980s and 2000s did not lead to unemployment rates below average. In fact, the correlation between the (current or total) fiscal position of the federal government and unemployment is about zero. The level of spending and taxing, if properly used, 'only' help to stabilize the economy. However, as Keynes said, there may be several slips between the cup and the lip, and promoting smoother economic activity will not translate automatically into a large increase in employment because of labor saving (productivity increases) and labor limiting (price increases) behaviors in the private sector. If one focuses on full employment, even over long periods of economic growth, the private sector was never able to employ everybody willing to work, so stimulating the private sector through government spending and incentives will never allow everybody to participate (Wray and Pigeon 2000; Harvey 2000). The only way to reach true full employment and shared prosperity

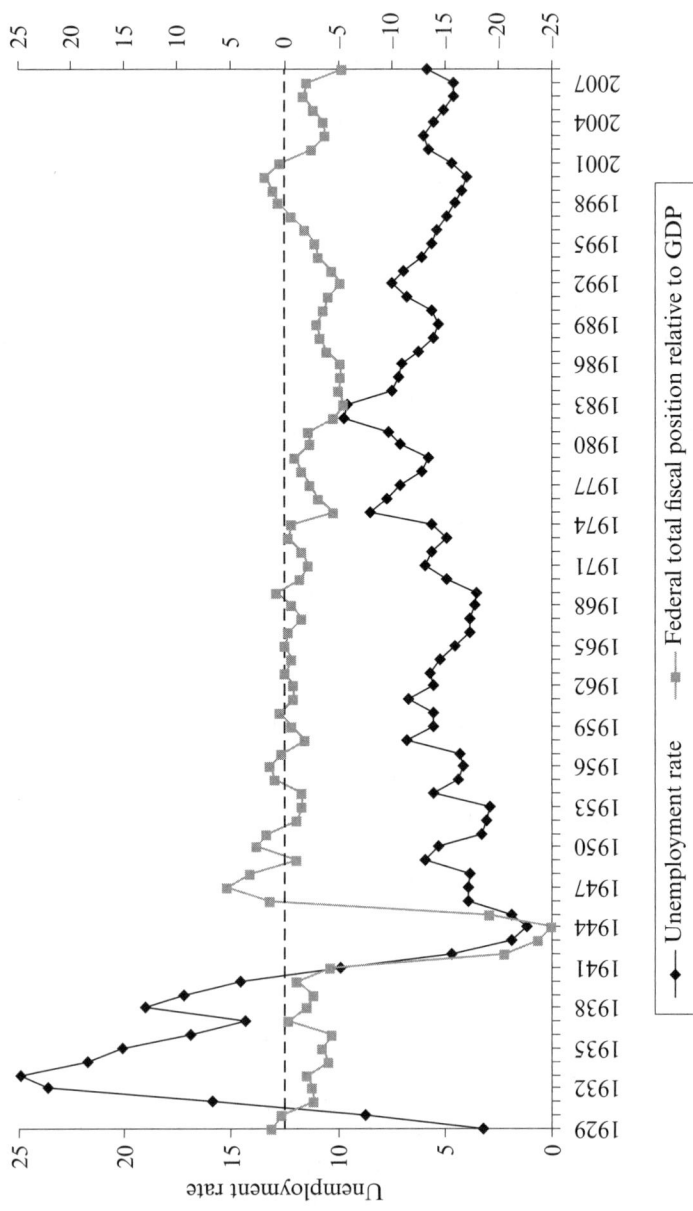

Source: BEA.

Figure 3.10   Total fiscal position of the federal government and unemployment (%)

is by orienting some government spending toward hiring the unemployed. The quality of government spending matters as much as the quantity of government spending (Tcherneva 2008).

In terms of War on Poverty, strong economic growth maintained the unemployment rate at about 5 per cent but the effects on poverty were limited. Again, the 'Keynesian' Administration chose a very indirect and market oriented way to solve a problem that cannot be eradicated by market mechanisms. The point was to train the low-skilled workers in order to make them competitive on the job market (Harvey 2000). But, as Minsky noted, if this strategy helps to homogenize the labor force and makes it more responsive to the needs of the business sector, it cannot deal with labor shortage. The implication is a redistribution of poverty not a diminution of poverty (Minsky 1965a, 1965b). Only providing enough jobs allows people to apply the skills they learned. Brady (2003) shows that the growth-market-productivity policy that has been applied in the second half of the twentieth century has had only limited success in reducing poverty in Western societies, even more so over the long-run, and has not been effective at all at removing entrenched pockets of poverty.

Finally, Kennedy and Johnson were both heavily influenced by the sound finance approach and were reluctant to put in place structural programs that would decrease control over the level of federal spending and taxing:

> Keynesianism has been frequently misrepresented in this country, and this was the case in the Kennedy Administration. Two general issues are involved in this misrepresentation. First, in the United States an incomplete kind of Keynesianism was practiced as understood and implemented by the [CEA] under Heller; thus, with no full commitment to planning and government deficit spending in place, the full impact of Keynesian measures has never been realized here. . . . Second, Kennedy and his political advisers . . . misunderstood and resisted the new economic practices. (Russel 2004, p. 145)

Kennedy and Johnson resisted government spending, tried to constrain it as much as possible, and refused any government employment program proposed by structuralists at the Labor Department, and instead favored the fine-tuning of economic growth by tax incentives proposed by the CEA (under the influence of Tobin and Samuelson).

Conclusion

The debate between structuralists (who think that market mechanisms are structurally flawed because they fail to provide full employment, fair inequalities and economic stability) and the fine-tuners (who think that discretionary temporary measures help to maintain the economy on its non-inflationary employment path, and that it is the only relevant thing a government can do) is likely to persist. The debate focuses not only on the goal to achieve, but also the fiscal *and* monetary macroeconomic strategies to reach the goal.

For structuralists, in the spirit of Lerner's functional finance, the size of the federal fiscal position should be determined by the needs of the economy given the structural programs in place. When dealing with socio-economic issues, politicians should not try to reduce deficits or to use surpluses through discretionary choices. What they should do instead is to promote programs that aim at price stability, financial strength and full employment. This should be complemented by low and stable policy rates so that market rates reward only competence and risk.

Keynes was a structuralist but Keynesianism has always been associated with the fine-tuners and has been reduced to any type of short-term fiscal activism to manage demand. This has allowed the economy to stabilize by producing smoother growth and shorter recessions. However, fine-tuning does not allow reaching full employment or reducing unfair inequalities, leaves aside the importance of supply management, and tends to create financial and upward price instabilities. In addition, the US government has limited its spending mostly to unproductive activities. Overall, fine-tuning is more consistent with Fisher's thought than with Keynes's, and, today, the former is still very influential, especially as a guide for modern monetary policy.

Like Keynes, Minsky was for a responsible big government, that is, a government that puts in place coherent structural programs that directly tackle socio-economic problems. Minsky was conscious, however, that big-government capitalism, while solving important problems, also creates new problems. Thus, rather than having a passive government that just reacts to economic problems through spending, taxing and manipulations of financial conditions, Minsky wanted a pro-active form of government that takes initiatives to direct the economy toward more stable and fair forms of capitalism. That would involve both monetary and fiscal measures and would influence both the supply and demand side of the economic system. That is what Keynesianism is all about, systematic decentralized planning rather than discretionary incoherent fine-tuning.

Notes

1.   The author thanks Yan Liang, John F. Henry, and John E. King for comments.
2.   Recently, innovative mortgage contracts and securities have been praised for allowing low-income households to become homeowners. However, given their structure, those financial innovations also led to the emergence of Ponzi home financing and frauds, and the welfare gains predictably were short-lived. Some of those financial innovations

should probably not have been allowed to exist and low-income homeownership may not be sustainable without government programs.

3. Micromanagement would be left to individual initiatives. The goal of the government is to control the overall direction of the system, not all prices and production processes (Minsky 1986, p. 293, 308).

4. Discretion could still be used to smooth the business cycle if needed, but the structural programs would already do most of the job. Tax incentives and subsidies should be used for long-term purposes in order to stir the economy in the direction that the government would prefer.

5. This does not mean that welfare and social security should be eliminated. Future contributors (children) and past contributors (retirees) to the economic welfare of developed societies deserve to be helped. However, an opportunity to work should be offered to those who are able and willing to contribute presently to the economic welfare of the society.

6. The 2007 bridge collapse in Minneapolis was a dreadful reminder that the US infrastructures are falling apart, mostly because their maintenance and expansion was not performed properly because of the lack of funding by state governments and private enterprises. The American Society of Civil Engineers (2005) gave a *D* average to American infrastructures and recommended a major overhaul and expansion. A government employment program like the Public Works Administration (which was responsible for the construction of many of the existing major infrastructures) would be very helpful.

7. These programs would be well funded and the government would try to attract the best and brightest individuals to manage them by paying a competitive wage. Too often, government programs are purposely under funded in order to limit their effectiveness and push for their abandonment.

8. As Lee (1989) notes, the idea that government deficit can be good had been advanced long before Keynes.

9. 'The best aid to recovery because of the large and continuing scale of potential demand, . . . the wide geographical distribution of this demand, and because the sources of its finance are largely independent of the stock exchange' (Keynes 1938b [1982], p. 436).

10. Another fallacy, promoted by Irving Fisher, was the idea that reflation was the best way to bring a recovery. Like Fisher, Keynes was for going off the gold standard and adopting a managed currency that gives the 'liberty to make your exchange policy subservient to the needs of your domestic policy' (Keynes 1933d (1982), p. 296; Keynes 1934e). However, contrary to quantity theoreticians, he thought that this was only a subsidiary policy. Output and employment should be stimulated directly through fiscal measures that affect spending and income, rather than indirectly by means of inflationary monetary measures (Keynes 1933d; Skidelsky 1994, p. 493).

11. This is illustrated by the name that the Administration gave to its first government work program. The Emergency Conservation Work Act of March 1933 created the Emergency Conservation Work program (officially renamed the Civilian Conservation Corps in June 1937).

12. However, this 'Currie Keynesianism' (Barber 1996) was of the fine-tuner type that 'shall exert such powers as it has toward promoting business stability and moderating fluctuations in production, employment and prices' (Eccles in Barber 1996, p. 94; Eccles 1937) and shall 'fluctuate the total expenditure . . . [and] income tax rates . . . as a means to regularize the flow of total expenditures and to promote economic stability' (Hansen in Barber 1996, p. 160).

13. In order to increase the velocity of money, Fisher proposed a 'stamped dollar' plan (Fisher 1932, p. 226ff) in which special dollar bills would be issued that would stay lawful only if their holders periodically apposed a postage stamp on the back of each bill. This would make hoarding costly and so would complement monetary growth in order to stimulate spending and so reflate the economy.

14.   Keynes too did not approve of price fixing and output limitations in most industries because this was too complex and arbitrary (Keynes 1934c [1982], p. 323).
15.   Keynes was aware that consumption-based growth should be managed carefully because a marginal propensity to consume equal to or above one leads to instability (Keynes 1936, p. 117). Since the 1970s, households in the US (and all over the world) have been encouraged by financial institutions to do precisely that, which has resulted in high instability.
16.   Fisher himself was aware of the need to stimulate spending before business incentives (subsidies, etc.) can have any positive effects on economic activity (Fisher 1932, p. 142).

References

Allen, W.R. (1977), 'Irving Fisher, F.D.R., and the Great Depression', *History of Political Economy*, **9**(4), 560–87.

Allen, W.R. (1993), 'Irving Fisher and the 100 percent reserve proposal', *Journal of Law and Economics*, **36**(2), 703–17.

American Society of Civil Engineers (2005), *2005 Report Card for America's Infrastructures*, Washington, DC: American Society of Civil Engineers.

Badger, A.J. (1989), *The New Deal: The Depression Years, 1933–1940*, Chicago: Ivan R. Dee.

Bailey, S.K. (1950), *Congress Makes a Law: The Story Behind the Employment Act of 1946*, New York: Columbia University Press.

Barber, W.J. (1996), *Designs with Disorder*, Cambridge: Cambridge University Press.

Barro, R.J. and D.B. Gordon (1983), 'A positive theory of monetary policy in a natural rate model', *Journal of Political Economy*, **91**(4), 589–610.

Bell, S.A. and L.R. Wray (2004), 'The war on poverty forty years on', *Challenge*, **47**(5), 6–29.

Brady, D. (2003), 'The poverty of liberal economics', *Socio-Economic Review*, **1**(3), 369–409.

Chew, A.P. (1936), 'Abstract of conversation with Mr. John Maynard Keynes', accessed August 1, 2008 on New Deal Network website (www.newdeal.feri.org).

Eccles, M.S. (1937), 'Controlling booms and depressions', in A.D. Gayer (ed.), *The Lessons of Monetary Experience: Essays in Honor of Irving Fisher*, New York: Farrar and Rinehart, Inc., pp. 3–22.

Fisher, I. (1932), *Booms and Depressions: Some First Principles*, New York: Adelphy.

Fisher, I. (1935a), 'Are booms and depressions transmitted internationally through monetary standards?', *Bulletin de l'Institut International de Statistique*, **28**(2), 609–37. Accessed August 12, 2008 on *Gallica* (http://gallica2.bnf.fr/?lang=en), the free digital library of the Bibliothèque Nationale de France. Reprinted in Dimand, R.W. (2003) 'Irving Fisher on the international transmission of booms and depressions through monetary standards,' *Journal of Money, Credit and Banking*, **35**(1), 49–90.

Fisher, I. (1935b), 'Government put deeply into business by debt', *Republican*, Waterbury, Conn., Sept. 30, 1935.

Friedman, M. (1968), 'The role of monetary policy', *American Economic Review*, **58**(1), 1–17.

Friedman, M. and A.J. Schwartz (1963), *A Monetary History of the United States, 1867–1960*, Princeton: Princeton University Press.

Galbraith, J.K. (1961), *The Great Crash*, 3rd edn, Cambridge, MA: The Riverside Press.

Gertler, M. (1988), 'Financial structure and aggregate economic activity: an overview', *Journal of Money, Credit and Banking*, **20**(3), Part 2, 559–88.

Gordon, R.J. (1990), *The American Business Cycle*, Chicago: University of Chicago Press.

Han, S. and C.B. Mulligan (2008), 'Inflation and the size of the government', *Federal Reserve Bank of St. Louis Review*, May/June, 245–67.

Harvey, P.L. (1999), 'Liberal strategies for combating joblessness in the twentieth century', *Journal of Economic Issues*, **33**(2), 497–503.

Harvey, P.L. (2000), 'Combating joblessness: an analysis of the principal strategies that have influenced the development of American employment and social welfare law during the 20th century', *Berkeley Journal of Employment and Labor Law*, **21**(2), 677–758.

Kaboub, F. (2008), 'Employment guarantee programs: a survey of theories and policy experiences', Working Paper No. 498, Levy Economics Institute of Bard College, Annandale-on-Hudson, New York.

Kalecki, M. (1971), 'The determinants of profits', in M. Kalecki (ed.), *Selected Essays on the Dynamics of the Capitalist Economy*, Cambridge: Cambridge University Press, pp. 78–92.

Keynes, J.M. (1933a), 'A monetary theory of production', reprinted in D.E. Moggridge (ed.) (1973), *The Collected Writings of John Maynard Keynes*, vol. 13, London: Macmillan, pp. 408–11.

Keynes, J.M. (1933b), 'The characteristics of an entrepreneur economy', reprinted in D.E. Moggridge (ed.) (1979), *The Collected Writings of John Maynard Keynes*, vol. 29, London: Macmillan, pp. 87–101.

Keynes, J.M. (1933c), 'The distinction between a co-operative economy and an entrepreneur economy', reprinted in D.E. Moggridge (ed.) (1979), *The Collected Writings of John Maynard Keynes*, vol. 29, London: Macmillan, pp. 76–87.

Keynes, J.M. (1933d), Open letter to President Roosevelt, December 30, 1933; reprinted in D.E. Moggridge (ed.) (1982), *The Collected Writings of John Maynard Keynes*, vol. 21, London: Macmillan, pp. 289–97.

Keynes, J.M. (1934a), 'Roosevelt's economic experiments', reprinted in D.E. Moggridge (ed.) (1982), *The Collected Writings of John Maynard Keynes*, vol. 21, London: Macmillan, pp. 305–9.

Keynes, J.M. (1934b), 'Can America spend its way into recovery?', reprinted in D.E. Moggridge (ed.) (1982), *The Collected Writings of John Maynard Keynes*, vol. 21, London: Macmillan, pp. 334–9.

Keynes, J.M. (1934c), 'Agenda for the President', reprinted in D.E. Moggridge (ed.) (1982), *The Collected Writings of John Maynard Keynes*, vol. 21, London: Macmillan, pp. 322–9.

Keynes, J.M. (1934d), 'Mr. Roosevelt's experiments', reprinted in D.E. Moggridge (ed.) (1982), *The Collected Writings of John Maynard Keynes*, vol. 21, London: Macmillan, pp. 297–304.

Keynes, J.M. (1934e), 'President Roosevelt's gold policy', reprinted in D.E. Moggridge (ed.) (1982), *The Collected Writings of John Maynard Keynes*, vol. 21, London: Macmillan, pp. 309–20.

Keynes, J.M. (1936), *The General Theory of Employment, Interest, and Money*, New York: Harcourt Brace.

Keynes, J.M. (1938a), Letter to the Editor of the *Times*, January 1, 1938; reprinted in D.E. Moggridge (ed.) (1982), *The Collected Writings of John Maynard Keynes*, vol. 21, London: Macmillan, pp. 432–4.

Keynes, J.M. (1938b), Letter to President Roosevelt, February 1, 1938; reprinted in D.E. Moggridge (ed.) (1982), *The Collected Writings of John Maynard Keynes*, vol. 21, London: Macmillan, pp. 434–9.

Kregel, J.A. (1994), 'The viability of economic policy and the priorities of economic policy', *Journal of Post Keynesian Economics*, **17**(2), 261–72.

Kydland, F.E. and Prescott, E.C. (1977), 'Rules rather than discretion: The inconsistency of optimal plans', *Journal of Political Economy*, **85**(3), 473–92.

Lee, B.A. (1989), 'The miscarriage of necessity and invention: Proto-Keynesianism and democratic states in the 1930s', in P.A. Hall (ed.), *The Political Power of Economic Ideas: Keynesianism across Nations*, Princeton: Princeton University Press, pp. 129–70.

Minsky, H.P. (1965a), 'The role of employment policy', in M.S. Gordon (ed.), *Poverty in America*, San Francisco: Chandler Publishing Company, pp. 175–200.

Minsky, H.P. (1965b), 'Poverty: the "aggregate demand" solution and other non-welfare approaches', report MR-41, Institute of Government and Public Affairs, Los Angeles: University of California.

Minsky, H.P. (1973), 'The strategy of economic policy and income distribution', in S. Weintraub (special ed.), *The Annals: Income Inequality*, Philadelphia: American Academy of Political and Social Science, pp. 92–101.

Minsky, H.P. (1975a), *John Maynard Keynes*, New York: Columbia University Press.

Minsky, H.P. (1975b), 'Financial instability, the current dilemma, and the structure of banking and finance', in Committee on Banking, Housing, and Urban Affairs (ed.), *Compendium of Major Issues in Bank Regulation*, Washington, DC: US Government Printing Office, pp. 310–53.

Minsky, H.P. (1977), 'Banking and a fragile financial environment', *Journal of Portfolio Management*, (Summer), 16–22.

Minsky, H.P. (1981), 'The breakdown of the 1960s policy synthesis', *Telos*, 50 (Winter), 49–58.

Minsky, H.P. (1986), *Stabilizing an Unstable Economy*, New Haven: Yale University Press.

Minsky, H.P. (1993), 'On the non-neutrality of money', *Federal Reserve Bank of New York Quarterly Review*, **18**(1), 77–82.

Mishkin, F.S. (1991), 'Asymmetric information and financial crises: a historical perspective', in R.G. Hubbard (ed.), *Financial Markets and Financial Crises*, Chicago: University of Chicago Press, pp. 69–108.

Modigliani, F. and M.H. Miller (1958), 'The cost of capital, corporation finance and the theory of investment', *American Economic Review*, **48**(3), 261–97.

Morgenson, G. (2008), 'A road not taken by lenders', *New York Times*, April 6, 2008.

Patinkin, D. (1956), *Money, Interest, and Prices: An Integration of Monetary and Value Theory*, Evanston: Row, Peterson.

Pavanelli, G. (2004), 'The Great Depression in Irving Fisher's thought', in I. Barens, V. Caspari, and B. Schefold (eds), *Political Events and Economic Ideas*, Cheltenham, UK and Northampton, MA, USA: Edward Elgar, pp. 289–305.

Robinson, J.V. (1943), 'Planning full employment', reprinted in J.V. Robinson (ed.) (1966), *Collected Economic Papers*, vol. 1, Oxford: Basil Blackwell, pp. 81–8.

Russel, J. (2004), *Economics, Bureaucracy, and Race*, New York: Columbia University Press.

Santoni, G.J. (1986), 'The Employment Act of 1946: some history notes', *Federal Reserve Bank of St. Louis Review*, (November), 5–16.

Schinasi, G.J. (2006), *Safeguarding Financial Stability: Theory and Practice*, Washington, DC: International Monetary Fund.

Schwartz, A.J. (1988), 'Financial stability and the federal safety net', in W.S. Haraf and R.M. Kushmeider (eds), *Restructuring Banking and Financial Services in America*, Washington, DC: American Enterprise Institute for Public Policy and Research, pp. 34–62.

Schwartz, A.J. (1998), 'Why financial stability depends on price stability', in G. Wood (ed.), *Money, Prices and the Real Economy*, Cheltenham, UK and Lyme, NH, USA: Edward Elgar, pp. 34–41.

Sinai, A. (1976), 'Credit crunches – an analysis of the postwar experience', in O. Eckstein (ed.), *Parameters and Policies in the U.S. Economy*, Amsterdam: North-Holland Publishing Co., pp. 244–74.

Skidelsky, R. (1994), *John Maynard Keynes, Vol. 2: The Economist as Savior, 1920–1937*, New York: Penguin Press.

Skidelsky, R. (2000), *John Maynard Keynes, Vol. 3: Fighting for Freedom, 1937–1946*, New York: Penguin Press.

Tcherneva, P.R. (2008), 'Keynes's approach to full employment: aggregate or targeted demand?', Working Paper No. 542, Levy Economics Institute of Bard College, Annandale-on-Hudson, New York.

Tcherneva, P.R. and L.R.Wray (2007), 'Public employment and women: the impact of

Argentina's *Jefes Program* on female heads of poor households', Working Paper No. 519, Levy Economics Institute of Bard College, Annandale-on-Hudson, New York.

Tymoigne, É. (2009), *Central Banking, Asset Prices, and Financial Fragility*, London: Routledge.

Veblen, T.B. (1901), 'Industrial and pecuniary employments', *Publications of the American Economic Association*, 3rd Series, **2**(1), 190–235.

Wojnilower, A.M. (1977), 'L'envoi', in E.I. Altman and A.W. Sametz (eds), *Financial Crises: Institutions and Markets in a Fragile Environment*, New York: Wiley, pp. 234–7.

Wolfson, M.H. (1994), *Financial Crises*, 2nd edn, Armonk, NY: M.E. Sharpe.

Wray, L.R. (1994), 'Is Keynesian policy dead after all these years?', *Journal of Post Keynesian Economics*, **17**(2), 285–306.

Wray, L.R. (2007), 'The employer of last resort programme: could it work for developing countries?, Economic and Labour Market Papers No. 2007/5, International Labour Office.

Wray, L.R. and M.A. Pigeon (2000), 'Can a rising tide raise all boats? Evidence from the Clinton-era expansion', *Journal of Economic Issues*, **34**(4), (December), 811–45.

4 Minsky in the 'new' capitalism: the new clothes of the financial instability hypothesis

Riccardo Bellofiore, Joseph Halevi and Marco Passarella

Introduction

Already in March 2007, George Magnus, Senior Economic Advisor of UBS, wrote that the US economy was approaching a 'Minsky moment' (Magnus 2007a; see also Magnus 2007b, 2007c, 2007d). The definition was actually coined by Paul McCulley, a bond fund director at Pacific Investment Management Company, during the 1998 Russian crisis (Whalen 2007). Magnus was commented in several financial blogs, and the expression found its way into authoritative newspapers all over the globe. This chapter investigates the meaning of a Minsky moment in the 'new' configuration of capitalism since the mid-1990s. Hence we shall, first, give a general outline of Minsky's thought and his Financial Instability Hypothesis (FIH). Then, we shall clarify what are the true novelties of the current stage of capitalism. Finally, we shall suggest a reading of the latter along the lines of a partially redefined FIH.

The basic core of Minsky's thought (Bellofiore and Ferri 2001; see also Fazzari and Papadimitriou 1992; Dimsky and Pollin 1994; Papadimitriou and Wray 1998) is centered around three interrelated topics: (1) an interpretation of Keynes's theory focusing on the role of financial markets, the endogeneity and non-neutrality of money, the systematic uncertainty surrounding the decisions made by units (banks, firms and other financial intermediaries), thereby integrating an investment theory of the business cycle with a financial theory of investment; (2) the FIH, according to which, after a period of 'tranquil' growth and robust finance, units' liability structures tend to shift towards fragility, so that the economic system is prone to financial crises; (3) the thesis according to which discretionary economic policies can smooth cyclical instability, creating ceilings and floors and constraining the dynamic behavior of the economy thanks to the intervention of the central bank as a lender of last resort and of the Government's budget deficits.

On these bases, Minsky built a cyclical theory of the capitalist economies marked by an alternation of speculative waves followed by a tendency towards debt deflation (Minsky 1975, 1982, 1986a, 1996). Keynes is Minsky's constant reference in his theoretical reconstruction of a modern capitalist economy with a multi-layered financial system. His 'Financial Keynesianism' is also influenced by Schumpeter's notion of 'creative destruction' extended to financial innovations (Minsky 1986b, 1990a, 1993). Minsky's implicit reference to Marx was reinforced by his use of Kalecki's macroeconomic profit equations, according to which 'capitalists' earn what they spend.

The Wall Street paradigm
Modern capitalism is characterized by expensive and long-lived capital assets coupled with a very articulated financial system. 'Real' equilibrium is primarily affected by the value of monetary variables and by the historical path of the economy. It follows that any approach that does not put money and finance at the very foundations of the theoretical building is bound to be irrelevant.

Minsky's original criticism is addressed against neoclassical (both neo-Keynesian and monetarist) economic orthodoxies. It is also directed against those heterodox approaches where money and finance are not considered essential from the very beginning of the analysis (Minsky 1990b). Indeed, capitalism may be accurately depicted as a monetary sequence of interrelated phases, involving the use of (bank) credit-money: a 'production of (more) money by means of money'. Accordingly, the analysis must include the following social (macro-)actors: (1) the banking and financial system (including the central bank, commercial banks and other financial intermediaries) which create endogenous credit-money and substitutes; (2) firms as a whole, which finance production and 'positions' in capital assets thanks to bank loans; and (3) wage-workers, selling their labor-power in exchange for the money wage bill, advanced by firms and financed by banks.

Money cannot be reduced either to a means of exchange just easing transactions, as in the quantity theory of money, or to liquid balances acting as store of value, as in traditional Keynesianism. On the contrary, money is, first of all, an 'access instrument to the market': a bond injected into the system to finance production and investment, or 'positions' in capital assets. Its supply is not 'given' once and for all, and it cannot but be endogenous. Indeed, both its definition and its magnitude change during the economic cycle: when the money supply in the strict sense, controlled by the banking system, begins to be too limited, the effective amount of money may increase thanks to the near-monies created by the intermediaries and their financial innovations. Although the effective quantity of money in circulation is demand-driven, it is not unbounded and it is positively related to the money rate of interest. Hence, the money supply is infinitely elastic for a while, and the resultant relation between interest rate and (effective) money supply can be depicted by a 'step' function.

Mainstream economics advocates a sort of 'village fair' paradigm. A barter, 'pure exchange' economy is the starting point, to which production activity, money and securities are later added to draw a more realistic picture. The essential features of a market economy are set in a basic model with no production process and where money comes into the economic system falling 'from a helicopter' (Lavoie 2006, p. 56). Minsky's vision is exactly the opposite. He offers a 'City' or 'Wall Street' paradigm where the role of banks and financial markets, together with the temporal irreversibility of the capitalist process, are considered from the start. Such a vision stresses the dynamics of cash flows (that is, wages to workers, salaries to clerks, sale proceeds to firms, interests or fees to banks, and so on) and the interdependence among balance sheets (registering the financial instruments feeding production, investment or other 'positions', which correspond to assets for some units and liabilities for others). The financing production and investment plans, as well as making 'positions', are affected by agents' expectations about an uncertain future. These decisions have to be validated by monetary returns in historical, and hence irreversible, time.

In the advanced capitalist economies, the intrinsic connection between banks and financial markets, on the one hand, and production processes, on the other hand, commits units to past decisions and makes present behavior dependent on monetary dynamics. Minsky's perspective appears entirely alternative to mainstream economics in the way it incorporates: (1) money (as a mere social symbol) into finance; (2) finance (as a condition to start economic activity) into income distribution; (3) the determination of total gross profits, as well as the volume and composition of aggregate demand, into relative price-setting. On this basis, Minsky puts forward a picture of capitalist economies where the tendency towards equilibrium is regularly overcome by the internal drive towards structural change.

Opposing mainstream economics, for which equilibrium can be broken only by policy errors, exogenous shocks, or market imperfections, Minsky stresses the endogenous evolutionary course leading from stability to instability. The economic cycle, evolving from 'tranquil' growth to speculative boom and ultra-speculative mania, and then falling into panics and financial crisis, is nothing but the necessary result of the monetary nature of capitalism, and of the connection between investment and finance.

The Financial Instability Hypothesis (FIH)
Although the vision Minsky put forward was simple and powerful, reconstructing his theory is not a trivial matter. Minsky, following Keynes, considers investment in fixed capital goods as the basic determinant of income and employment levels. The purchase of new capital goods has financial grounds, while the stock exchange is subject to cyclical speculative (but not merely irrational) waves. The key point in modern capitalism is rather that 'stability is destabilizing'. In effect, it is common to describe the process leading to systemic financial fragility as one of 'bubble' mania. As Kregel (2008) reminds us, in Minsky the endogenous reduction in the safety margins must be based on something more than euphoria or excessively optimistic expectations.

To bring out the contradiction inherent in the stability of the economic system, let us start, like Minsky does, from a generic economy characterized by a 'tranquil' expansion and a 'robust' financial system (with 'sound' liability structures of economic units). Initially mindful of past crises, firms, banks and financial intermediaries behave in a risk-averse manner. Monetary interest rates are low and stable, the supply of credit-money is potentially limitless. Borrowers (as a whole) are capable of settling, with their regular flow of money-proceeds, both the money interest and the stipulated part of the principal. If everything goes as expected, there will be enough profits to validate the previous financial commitments. This is what Minsky called a 'hedge' financial structure. According to Minsky, the spread between uncertain (income) cash inflows, subject to sharp and sudden revaluation, and certain (balance sheets) cash outflows is the key factor in assessing the liability structure of economic units. The 'hedge-financing' units are those units where the prospective income cash flows (expected quasi-rents), ensuing from their own economic activity, are greater than cash payment contractual commitments for every period. The expected present value of business is positive for all likely rates of interest, so that the debt volume tends to fall from one period to another. A hedge-financing unit faces up an 'economic risk' (in the commodities market as well as in the labor market), yet it is safe relative to the 'financial risk'.

The presence of profit opportunity drives units to embark on new activities, further stimulating economic growth. Since business does go well for a while, and units' profits exceed their expected level, entrepreneurs, bankers and financiers becomes less risk-averse, involving a greater disposition to take on additional debt. The process cannot be stopped even by a possible reluctance of the central bank to raise the supply of money. Indeed, the financial operators invent new payment instruments (which are substituted for fiat money), as well as new ways to use old instruments. The interest rates remain unchanged, while units' indebtedness grows, together with 'speculative' positions. Minsky labeled 'speculative-financing' units those where cash flow earnings allow for the servicing of the interest on debt, but no longer suffice to cover, in every period, the part of the principal which must be given back. Thus, for these units, the refinancing of debt positions becomes necessary, for some periods at least. Speculative units, which multiply with the boom phase, must face up not only the 'economic' risk but also a 'financial' risk due to a possible drop in the assets' value or to a sudden unexpected increase in the short-term interest rate fixed by the central bank. In either case, expected profits may turn into actual losses.

Speculative behavior is positive since it allows for a higher long term investment and growth. The problem is that it makes the whole economic system more fragile. The economic boom soon degenerates into a bubble where units prone to take 'ultra-speculative' positions tend to prevail. An ultra-speculative or 'Ponzi' financial structure is occurring when interest payments alone exceed the cash flow earnings for a significant number of periods, so that units must either liquidate part of assets (selling positions) or raise new funds (refinancing). An ultra-speculative position is held if the unit expects some 'bonanza', either exceptional profits or capital gains due to asset price inflation. In such a context, a small unexpected rise in the short-term interest rates, or a fall in asset prices, opens the door to the financial crisis. This may result in an economic recession coupled with debt deflation that – if not adequately opposed by an active counter-cyclical economic policy by means of government deficit spending and injections of liquidity – may lead to a chronic depression. The situation is worsened by the fact that, during the euphoric phase, all units (bankers, entrepreneurs and speculators) have been reducing their money balances and liquidity. When the crisis erupts, the liquidity preference starts rising again. The economic crisis is therefore the natural outcome of the fragility of the financial structure. This fragility is the upshot of the 'normal' working of the capitalist economy.

The FIH states that 'tranquil' growth and prosperity – in modern capitalist economies – naturally bring about changes in cash-flow interconnections, necessarily and endogenously leading from solidity to fragility. The 'normal' functioning of the economy may easily convert fragility into open financial crisis and finally into a credit crunch. With some provisos to be specified in the next sections, FIH is well adapted to the events that unfolded throughout 2007, that is, the so-called 'subprime mortgage loan crisis'.

Economic policy

Since the New Deal, government intervention was committed to prevent financial crisis from leading to a 'Big Crash', by raising the lower turning point of the cycle. Stabilization was pursued by means of government's budget deficits, backed by the central bank acting as a lender of last resort: the 'Big Government' and the 'Big Bank'. Minsky refers here to Kalecki's macroeconomic equations, where gross profits are positively related to the government deficit. An active anti-cyclical fiscal policy is necessary to avoid sinking into a never-ending depression because budget deficits increase the gross money profits for firms. However, gross money profits are vital not only because of the effective demand, but also because they support and validate the financial structure of units. Since the government pumps into the financial market State-securities, which are secure and readily marketable assets, the public's preference for liquidity is reduced and the 'robustness' of units' balance sheets increased. Hence, an expansionary fiscal policy allows units (firms and other market operators) to satisfy cash payment commitments on outstanding contractual loans, so that debt-deflation is kept under control. Since fiscal policy takes time before it has significant effects, it must also be associated with a prompt injection of liquidity (and contextual purchases of securities) from the central bank. This kind of intervention, which establishes a lower limit for the value of assets, must be coupled with the monitoring and the regulation of financial institutions and practices.

Government intervention imposes in this way new 'initial conditions' constraining the system's instability. The right policy mix needs however to be adapted to the given concrete situation. According to Minsky, economic policy is unable to abolish the fundamental drive to financial instability and hence to recurrent economic crises, even though it can avoid that 'it' (a 'Great Crash' like in the 1930s) happens again.

On the monetary policy side, the central bank cannot break off the increase in the volume of the payment instruments actually supplied by financial intermediaries in the upswing. It can regain control over the 'effective' quantity of money, but only if it is ready to risk the outbreak of a financial crisis (something which has been repeatedly rediscovered by Alan Greenspan, and lately by Ben Bernanke). When the upper turning point is reached, the central bank can limit the spread of the crisis by timely refinancing the economy, in order to prevent the bankruptcy of banks and financial intermediaries.

On the fiscal policy side, the issue is not just one concerning the nominal amount of expenditure: what matters most is the structural content of the State's active intervention. Minsky criticizes traditional Keynesian deficit spending, supporting either defense or private consumption, and which does not contribute to a more efficient productive structure. These policies, as well as a policy of money transfers, have reduced in time the degree of robustness of the financial structures, have shortened units' time-horizon, and have slowed down productivity growth. The price paid to prevent the economy from sinking into a prolonged depression has been that prosperity has become much shorter, and the next financial crisis much nearer. Low interest rates plus government's deficits originated stagflation, and facilitated the speculative behavior of banks and financial intermediaries. This accentuated cyclical fluctuations, producing spirals of euphoria and panic at ever-closer intervals of time.

On the other hand, *laissez faire*, with its myth of a 'small government' and a 'light State', is neither a leftwing or rightwing policy. It is just an illusory policy that will never be carried out again in practice, at least in a durable manner. Ever since the 1970s a formally anti-government bias, which can be named as 'neoconservative', has led to the zeroing of many of the New Deal former reforms. In practice, however, such an ideological attitude has never really turned into the pre-war non-interventionist policies (Wray 2008).

A 'perfect' economic policy, good in all possible times and places, does not exist: effective measures in a given situation are ineffective in another one. Moreover, entrepreneurs, bankers and gamblers (which are all profit-seeking agents) will periodically find new ways to circumvent the regulations in force. This does not mean that economic authorities can do nothing in order to reduce the cyclical instability of the economy. They must oppose debt deflation and depression risk, but they must also simplify financial structures, restoring the possibility of a lasting and moderate growth. Minsky suggests the following measures of economic policy: (1) an incentive to the production of consumption goods through less capital intensive techniques; (2) an indirect support to firms' productivity through public infrastructural expenditure and through R&D; (3) rules and limitations to units' liability structures; (4) an active anti-cyclical fiscal structure such that the government budget goes automatically into surplus (deficit) when investments, income and employment are high (low); (5) a restructuring of public expenditure reducing transfer payments and favoring employment plans (where the State plays the role of the 'employer of last resort'); (6) a privilege accorded to equity finance relative to debt finance; (7) measures promoting small and medium-sized units; (8) a shift in firm ownership from capital to labor.

Open issues

The use of Minsky's theoretical framework in order to interpret both the physiology of today's capitalism and the recent financial crises would require answering at least four problematic points.

The first is theoretical. The FIH, despite its strong intuitive content, presents some analytical difficulties (Lavoie and Seccareccia 2001). Minsky maintains that the 'leverage ratio' – that is, the ratio of debt to owned capital – increases as the economy grows. Yet, there is no compelling reason why an increase in leverage should necessarily materialize. During the growth phase, total money profits made by all units increase together with debt. While units taken individually do borrow, the debt ratio for the whole economic system may not change. For the sake of simplicity, let us consider a 'two-sector' model where firms supply either consumer or investment goods. The individual firm will spend the borrowed money on the market, in order to purchase the capital goods. The payments for investment orders made by the firms of the first sector are the monetary profits for the firms supplying the capital goods. That the global leverage may not necessarily increase is consistent with the core of Kalecki's analytical framework, endorsed by the same Minsky in the 1970s.

The other 'open issues' refer to more empirical conundrums. Though the increase in firms' leverage has been actually verified in past economic cycles, things seem to be different in the last years, at least in the US. After 2000–01, following the economic stagnation ended with the outbreak of the Iraq war, the overall leverage ratio of US firms has fallen. Their financial balance not only came out to be positive, but even in excess of the volume of real investment they undertook. So the industrial sector ended up providing capitals to the financial markets.

Moreover, Minsky's approach, as Keynes's, focused on investment demand and its financing. But, first, the boom of the 'new economy' cannot be fully explained referring to the demand for capital goods; and, second, private investments remained almost flat in the post-2003 recovery. As will be shown in the next sections, an account of the capitalist dynamics since the mid-1990s has to consider how the Federal Reserve, the banking system and the financial markets supported domestic consumption in a 'new' configuration of capitalism, thanks to an increase of households' financial wealth and an explosion of consumer debt.

Another difference to the original Minsky's train of thought is relative to 'stagflation'. The recent boom phases have not been marked by an increase in wages (the Phillips curve turned out to be flat), or in the commodity price level, at least in the old industrial countries. The spike in the prices of 'commodities' – like oil, raw materials, foodstuffs or agricultural goods – result from tendencies related to 'globalization', including world-wide financial speculation and geo-political factors.

A further element needs to be taken into account. According to Minsky, since banks cannot foresee the future, lending decisions are usually based on borrowers' credit history and on expectations about cash flows. Banks look backward rather than forward. As a consequence of a steady expansion, the borrowing experience becomes increasingly positive (Kregel

2008). As a consequence, economic growth itself, rather than any euphoric attitude or any variation in evaluation criteria on the part of banks, validates riskier behaviors. The banking system that has emerged from the reforms of the 1980s and the 1990s is very different. Now, banks seek to maximize their fees and commissions by issuing and managing assets in off-balance-sheet affiliate structures. In this context, bankers have no interest in credit evaluation, which is now made by rating agencies. The latter, however, have no direct knowledge of the borrowers, an aspect that no statistical procedure can replace. In effect, the 'subprime' crisis was announced from the very beginning: its outbreak has simply disclosed the fragility inherent in today's credit evaluation system.

This is due to the circumstance that 'those who bear the risk are no longer responsible for evaluating the creditworthiness of borrowers and correctly evaluating risk'. On the contrary, 'rating agency profits are correlated with the overestimation of creditworthiness and the undervaluation of risk'. So the subprime crisis has little to do with the housing market, 'but rather with the basic structure of a financial system that overestimates creditworthiness and under-prices risk' (Kregel 2008, p. 5).

In our opinion, the FIH has indeed come true. Yet, it happened with a different set of modalities and through a different concatenation of factors compared to Minsky's original formulation. Among the new factors, it is important to stress the role played by households' burgeoning debt to finance consumption as well as the increasing sway of merchant banks and financial intermediaries over savers. Today's fragile growth rests on the precarious condition of millions of wage earners that are, at the same time, 'manic-depressive' savers, 'indebted' consumers and – last but not least – 'traumatized' workers. They are 'terrorized' savers, subject to a bipolar syndrome. They are 'terrorized' by the uncertainties related to a new form taken by the financial system, that is, the 'money-manager' capitalism (Whalen 2007). They are also 'terrorized' by the progressive dismantling of the state retirement system together with the building up of a pension fund capitalism. Households are increasingly in debt to sustain their consumption, partially as a paradoxical side effect of assets' inflation together with the casualization of labor. They are 'traumatized', or 'scared', workers because of the transformations in the labor process and in the so-called 'labor market' after decades of restructuring, deregulation and globalization (Bellofiore and Halevi 2008a, 2008b).

The present capitalistic phase arose from the long wave of assault against wages and welfare provisions pursued, during the 1980s, by the then Chairman of the Federal Reserve, Paul Volcker, and by President Reagan. The primacy of financial markets gave way to a deep and permanent restructuring of the production processes. The utilization of the workforce nowadays occurs in increasingly 'flexible' occupations with a lengthening of labor time and an intensification of effort. More generally, what is going on is 'a centralization of capital without (technical) concentration' mainly through 'outsourcing', 'subcontracting' and 'in-house outsourcing' by hitherto integrated oligopolistic corporations. A global relocation of manufacturing fed upon the exponential increase of the disposable labor supply as well as upon the economic growth in China and in other Asian countries. The outcome has been a further, quite dramatic, fragmentation and disarticulation of the working class and its unions. It is also thanks to these factors that the expansionary monetary policy pursued after 1995 by the Federal Reserve has been accompanied by wage stagnation and comparatively low inflation in commodity prices. Liquidity rather pushed up the prices of financial assets, real estate activities, foodstuffs, oil and energy resources, in pursuit of speculative gains.

From the stagnationist tendency of the 1980s to the 'new economy'
The 1980s have been marked by a liberalization of capital movements, restrictive monetary policies, the progressive dismantling of the welfare state and an aggressive competition by new global players. The combination of all these factors set in motion a powerful and lasting stagnationist tendency in Western economies. As a result, there was a relative contraction of real investments and real wages. A support to effective demand came, however, from the Reagan Administration's military expenditure coupled with tax cuts for the wealthy people, financed by government debt. The US mix of restrictive monetary policies with expansionary fiscal policies, in marked contrast with the European countries, caused a substantial increase in the price of US financial activities. The differential in the level of international interest rates in favor of the United States led to capital inflows and to a revaluation of the US dollar. The US trade deficit grew out of all proportion, but it was not perceived as a real constraint in a country whose money was the main international reserve currency.

The real, monetary and currency shocks of the 1980s did not lead immediately to the emergence of a new capitalist phase. This latter emerged only in the mid-1990s, after a decade since the Plaza accords in New York on the 22nd of September 1985, which started a series of coordinated measures undertaken by the major industrialized nations' economic authorities to devalue the US dollar. Together with US dollar devaluation, lasting until 1995 and recurring after 2001, wage deflation became the permanent feature of both the United States (where real wages have been falling since the mid-1970s) and European countries. During the 1980s and 1990s, the capitalist labor processes have been heavily restructured. But the more novel feature after the mid-1990s can be aptly summarized, employing a

Marxian terminology, as the 'real subsumption' of labor to finance and debt. Households and workers are more and more 'included' into financial dynamics, and this 'inclusion' retroacts on firms' corporate governance and on working conditions within the immediate production process.

This qualitative change firstly materialized in the United States, with the so-called 'new economy' (1995–2000). In our perspective, the 'new' economy refers not so much to technological factors, but rather to the emergence of a delicate balance between a novel monetary policy, a stock exchange affected by 'irrational' euphoria, household increasing debt and higher autonomous consumption demand. Very active US policies, aimed at a 'strong' dollar and the central bank's expansion of liquidity, were able to sustain ever-increasing asset prices and a private sector going into a huge deficit. The leverage was more and more affecting households rather than firms, and consumption rather than investment.

As we have anticipated, this was all but spontaneous. In the summer of 1995 the US dollar was pushed up sharply by a joint operation carried out by the central banks of the United States, Japan and the Federal Republic of Germany, in order to avoid a collapse of the Japanese economy. The uninterrupted adoption of new financial tools, coupled with a shift from government bonds to private corporations' stocks, gave rise to a gigantic speculative bubble. The latter relied on completely unrealistic expectations regarding the profitability of newly born virtual firms (the so-called 'dotcom', that is, small concerns usually operating in data processing sectors) which were experiencing triple-digit rate of growth.

In the meantime, the centralization of international financial capital in Wall Street based assets has taken advantage of the prolonged Japanese economic recession, and the European stagnation as well. The outbreak of the Asian financial crisis of 1997–98, as well as the Russian and the Brazilian crisis of 1998, entailed a massive flight of capitals towards the United States. These factors, coupled with the worldwide spreading of pension funds (which enabled more capitals to flow to Wall Street), allowed the United States to sustain a widening external deficit. Financial markets' 'irrational' behavior reached a paroxysmal state, until the sudden rise in the benchmark interest rate, decided in 1999 by the then Chairman of the Fed, Alan Greenspan, which turned the boom into a slump. The bursting of the 1990s bubble materialized in early 2000. It was ultimately due to the fact that the financial assets boom tied to the 'new economy' was no longer sustainable (Godley 1999).

Shortly afterwards the Twin Towers attack occurred, and the US dollar started a new downward trend. In 2001–03, as Minsky would have expected, the 'floor' to debt deflation and recession was once again provided by government deficit spending (mainly because of higher military expenditure and tax cuts for the wealthy classes) and massive injections of liquidity. Under the administration of George W. Bush the twin deficit had been brought back. The Federal budget deficit reached, very rapidly, more than 7 per cent of the GDP, while the current account external deficit also neared 7 per cent. The 'dotcom' crisis was overcome only after 2003.

The new clothes of the Financial Instability Hypothesis (FIH)

The only way to keep the US economy growing after 2004 has been to bet on the renewal of a 'wealth effect' repeating, in a different context, the miracle of the 'new' stock-exchange economy. After the dotcom crisis, the Federal Reserve flooded the markets with cheap liquidity. The extremely low interest rates fueled the real estate market; the rise in house prices, in its turn, stimulated household consumption and debt. This time the growing leverage connected with the upswing was almost exclusively to be found in the household sector. These are the new clothes of the FIH, confirming the substance of Minsky's theory.

The renegotiation of mortgages with flexible interest rates coupled with rising real estate prices made houses a sort of 'cash dispensing machine' for wage earners. The role of the Federal Reserve, with its assuaging monetary policy, has been of fundamental importance here: it has supported effective demand both by inflating real estate prices and by backing the 'creative' finance of commercial banks and financial operators. Indeed, the banking system as a whole has provided firms indirectly with liquidity and market outlets for their production: finance to households' consumption was nothing but finance to firms. The sustainability of a 'paper pyramid' of this kind rests upon the willingness of the foreign holders of US dollars, amongst them to refinance the external deficit piled up by the United States.

In 2004, when the Federal Reserve started to raise the benchmark interest rate, the real estate market was almost immediately affected downward. The only way out of the mess in which commercial banks and financial companies had got themselves seemed to be dragging poor workers into the subprime loans market. Involving people with a high probability to be insolvent in loans business was a necessity dictated by the expanding circuit of capitals, without which the notion of 'expected future capital gains' itself becomes meaningless. Further steps in the 'real subsumption' of labor to debt and finance were offering negative equity loans (that is, loans greater than the value of the collaterals required by banks), or loans where the interest was to be paid in perpetuity without having to repay the principal, and the like, to an ever growing number of poor people. When poor households' revenues became insufficient to meet debt payments, the situation came to a head for the creditors. They could repossess the houses, but this happened in a market where (against their expectations) their prices were falling. The value of collaterals that banks packaged away to other financial operators turned out to be hollow. Through the risk distribution mechanism which was embodied in the so-called 'derivatives', lenders' losses traveled quickly through the financial channels all over the world, hitting hedge funds, investment banks, conduits and other financial companies. The stability of the financial system was at risk.

Minsky in the 'new' capitalism
The present stage of capitalism, seen as a new global order based on a 'new' stock market and financial economy, can be understood only within an overall macro-monetary framework. As we have argued above, its origin can be traced back to the attack against labor pursued by Western governments and central banks since the early 1980s. It is accompanied by an endogenous increase in the money supply (accepted nowadays even in mainstream macroeconomic models), originating speculative gains and an inflation in assets' prices. Asset inflation and the ensuing 'wealth effect' compensated the effects of wage deflation on aggregate consumption. The outcome has been a sequence of (policy manipulated) asset-bubbles sustaining for a while effective demand.

The US dynamics needs to be put in a wider context. Outside the Anglo-Saxon countries, which have a current account deficit (Canada is an exception), there exists an excess of aggregate income over aggregate expenditure. This is the outcome of a long standing 'neomercantilist' institutionalized policy which the same United States helped to shape in Asia and in Continental Europe for some decades after the Second World War (Halevi and Kriesler 2004, 2006). Since the stagnation of the mid-1970s the need of European and Asiatic manufacturers to find foreign markets has been permanent and acute. Against this background, the United States became more and more the catalyst of world effective demand. The question is whether, in the future, the United States could still sustain such a role.

According to the standard Keynesian macroeconomic accounting, in each national economy the level of aggregate demand is positively related to investment, consumption, net government spending and net exports. The US, however, must generate a chronic current account deficit because of their role of attracter of the world demand. Net government spending was negative in the 'new economy' period, because of the 'sound' fiscal policy of the Clinton Administration. As for private investment, its positive dynamics before the 'dotcom' crisis was not enough to close the monetary macro-circuit, and it has been depressed afterwards. It follows that, in recent years, the main support to US (and world) aggregate income had to be the private consumption of households.

Given the compression in real wages, the current account deficits and (for a while) the fiscal surpluses, effective demand could be created only by substituting private to public debt. In fact, the US and the world economy have been saved from stagnation thanks to wage earners' negative savings. This, in its turn, has been made possible by assets and real estate inflation. The core of the mechanism lies in the triad 'traumatized' workers – 'manic-depressive' savers – 'indebted' consumers. This amounts to what we have labeled the 'real subsumption of labor to finance'.

The real subsumption of labor to finance is actually nothing but the deepening of the 'money-manager' phase delineated by the late Minsky as a fourth stage after commercial, financial and managerial capitalism (Minsky 1996). As Charles Whalen puts it, after the 1980s money managers are the institutional investors (including pension and mutual funds, venture-capital funds, private-equity funds and hedge funds) which are the dominant players in the US, and now world, economy: 'Contemporary financial markets are not driven primarily by masses of individual investors or even by a few huge investment bankers, nor can today's corporate executives operate with the autonomy from shareholders and bankers that many of their counterparts had in the early days after World War II' (Whalen 2007, p. 100).

The inflation of financial assets gave rise to a discrepancy in price-earnings ratios. Earnings from assets did not rise as much as asset prices. In 'normal' conditions, this should have brought the system to a halt. The reason why it did not happen is that economic policy stimulated the speculative behavior, instead of discouraging it. Of course, this turned the system into a sort of 'casino' economy. Earnings expectations are linked not to the rate of return, but to the expected appreciation of assets, leading to mythical beliefs in the long-term nature of 'wealth effects'. Both commercial banks and financial intermediaries turned 'paper wealth' into a bottomless expenditure's flow, by means of an uninterrupted expansion in household debt, de-linking consumption from current disposable incomes, but on an unsustainable path.

As Minsky would have expected, an increasing leverage was also at the heart of the capitalist expansion in the 1990s and in the 2000s, with ultra-speculative behavior firmly entrenched in the 'manic' phase of the economy. Since the emergence of the 'new' economy, however, the leverage was dislocated from the firm sector to the household sector. The key factor in demand was no longer private investment nor defense plus public consumption, but rather private consumption. Monetary policy has thus been powerful in pushing up effective demand for a while, but its effectiveness is temporary and bound to reproduce an unstable and deeply flawed process.

All the theoretical and empirical 'open' issues of the FIH seem to find a clear answer when set against the morphological changes of contemporary capitalism and its economic policies. As Minsky would have argued, the way out from this paradoxical asset-bubble driven financial Keynesianism cannot but be based on a very different economic policy blueprint than the neoclassical or neo-Keynesian ones. Such a policy should embody a 'structural' intervention on demand and supply more akin to Roosevelt's New Deal or Keynes's 'socialization of investment' than to the standard Keynesianism of the 1960s and 1970s. In our view, Minsky's structural perspective should be reinforced, including: (1) an active government intervention, to determine the long run directions of investment; (2) an industrial policy, coupled with a selective credit policy; (3) a 'planning' of employment, taking into account social needs; (4) a reform of the welfare system, providing goods and services 'in kind' on an expanded basis. Not only the focus of monetary policy, but also of expansionary fiscal policy must be shifted, through the redefinition of the composition of government expenditure.

Such a perspective does not endorse a generic full employment, but stresses the quality of the output and of the employment. The only alternative is the deepening of the curse of financial instability, which produces, at best, a full under-employment of casualized workers.

References

Bellofiore, R. and P. Ferri (2001), 'Things fall apart, the centre cannot hold. Introduction to the economic legacy of Hyman Minsky', in R. Bellofiore and P. Ferri (eds), *Financial Fragility and Investment in the Capitalist Economy: The Economic Legacy of Hyman Minsky, vol. I*, Cheltenham, UK and Northampton, MA, USA: Edward Elgar, pp. 1–29.

Bellofiore, R. and J. Halevi (2008a), 'A Minsky moment? The 2007 subprime crisis and the "new" capitalism', in C. Gnos and L.P. Rochon (eds), *Employment, Growth and Development: A Post-Keynesian Approach*, Cheltenham, UK and Northampton, MA, USA: Edward Elgar (forthcoming).

Bellofiore, R. and J. Halevi (2008b), 'Deconstructing labour: What is "new" in contemporary capitalism and economic policies: a Marxian-Kaleckian perspective', in C. Gnos and L.P. Rochon (eds), *Credit, Money and Macroeconomic Policy: A Post-Keynesian Approach*, Cheltenham, UK and Northampton, MA, USA: Edward Elgar (forthcoming).

Dimsky, G. and R. Pollin (1994), *New Perspectives in Monetary Macroeconomics: Explorations in the Tradition of Hyman P. Minsky*, Ann Arbor, MI: The University of Michigan Press.

Fazzari, S. and D. Papadimitriou (1992), *Financial Conditions and Macroeconomic Performance*, Armonk, NY: M.E. Sharpe.

Godley, W. (1999), 'Seven unsustainable processes: medium-term prospects and policies for the United States and the world', Strategic Analysis, Levy Economics Institute of Bard College, Annandale-on-Hudson, New York, pp. 9–10.

Halevi, J. and P. Kriesler (2004), 'Stagnation and economic conflict in Europe', *International Journal of Political Economy*, Summer, 19–45.

Halevi, J. and P. Kriesler (2006), 'The changing patterns of accumulation and realization in East Asia since the 1990s', CAER Working Paper No. 9, University of New South Wales, Sydney, Australia.

Kregel, J.A. (2008), 'Minsky's cushions of safety: systemic risk and the crisis in the US subprime mortgage market', Public Policy Brief Highlights No. 93, Levy Economics Institute of Bard College, Annandale-on-Hudson, New York.

Lavoie, M. (2006), *Introduction to Post-Keynesian Economics*, Basingstoke: Palgrave Macmillan.

Lavoie, M. and M. Seccareccia (2001), 'Minsky's financial fragility hypothesis: a missing macroeconomic link?', in R. Bellofiore and P. Ferri (eds), *Financial Fragility and Investment in the Capitalist Economy: The Economic Legacy of Hyman Minsky, vol. I*, Cheltenham, UK and Northampton, MA, USA: Edward Elgar, pp. 76–96.

Magnus, G. (2007a), 'The credit cycle and liquidity: have we arrived at a Minsky moment?', *Economic Insights – By George*, 6 March, UBS Investment Research, London.

Magnus, G. (2007b), 'The credit cycle: getting closer to a Minsky moment?', *Economic Insights – By George*, 3 July, UBS Investment Research, London.

Magnus, G. (2007c), 'The credit cycle: beyond the Minsky moment: melt or muddle?', *Economic Insights – By George*, 12 September, UBS Investment Research, London.

Magnus, G. (2007d), 'Is the global monetary system starting to crack?', *Economic Insights – By George*, 12 November, UBS Investment Research, London.

Minsky, H.P. (1975), *John Maynard Keynes*, New York: Columbia University Press.

Minsky, H.P. (1982), *Can 'It' Happen Again: Essays on Instability and Finance*, Armonk, NY: M.E. Sharpe.

Minsky, H.P. (1986a), *Stabilizing an Unstable Economy*, New Haven: Yale University Press.

Minsky, H.P. (1986b), 'Money and crisis in Schumpeter and Keynes', in H.J. Wagener and J.W. Drukker (eds), *The Economic Law of Motion of Modern Society: A Marx-Keynes-Schumpeter Centennial*, Cambridge: Cambridge University Press, pp. 112–22.

Minsky, H.P. (1990a), 'Schumpeter and Keynes', in A. Heertje and M. Perlman (eds), *Evolving Technology and Market Structures: Studies in Schumpeterian Economics*, Ann Arbor, Michigan: The University of Michigan Press, pp. 51–74.

Minsky, H.P. (1990b), 'Sraffa and Keynes: effective demand in the long run', in K. Bharadway and B. Schefold (eds), *Essays on Piero Sraffa Critical Perspectives on the Revival of Theory*, London: Unwin, pp. 362–71.

Minsky, H.P. (1993), 'Schumpeter and finance', in S. Biasco, A. Roncaglia and M. Salvati (eds), *Market and Institutions in Economic Development: Essays in Honor of Paolo Sylos Labini*, London: Macmillan, pp. 103–15.

Minsky, H.P. (1996), 'The essential characteristics of post-Keynesian economics', in G. Deleplace and E. Nell (eds), *Money in Motion: The Post-Keynesian and Circulation Approaches*, New York: St. Martin's Press, pp. 70–88.

Papadimitriou, D. and L.R. Wray (1998), 'The economic contributions of Hyman Minsky: varieties of capitalism and institutional reform', *Review of Political Economy*, **10**(2), 199–225.

Whalen, C.J. (2007), 'The US credit crunch of 2007: a Minsky moment', Public Policy Brief No. 92, Levy Economics Institute of Bard College, Annandale-on-Hudson, New York.

Wray, L.R. (2008), 'Financial markets meltdown: what can we learn from Minsky?', Public Policy Brief No. 94, Levy Economics Institute of Bard College, Annandale-on-Hudson, New York.

5 Rational and innovative behaviors at the core of financial crises: banking in Minsky's theory

Eric Nasica

Introduction

The 2007 subprime mortgage crisis underlined the central role played by banks in generating a financial crisis. While this crisis surprised most economists and practitioners, a rereading of Hyman P. Minsky's writings on banking would have probably allowed anticipating a great part of the current dramatic events on money, credit and financial markets.

As is well known, starting in the middle of the 1950s, and for the next 40 years, Hyman P. Minsky developed an original business cycle theory based on a financial conception of economic fluctuations, and more specifically, on the 'Financial Instability Hypothesis (FIH)' (Minsky 1975, 1982 and 1986). This theory is mainly based on the succession of two phases during the business cycle: first, a process of transition toward greater financial fragility of the economy which builds up in the expansionary phase; second, the transition from a financially fragile situation to a situation of recession and then of large amplitude economic crisis.

The aim of this chapter is to specify the nature and the role played by the Minskyan banker in each of the phases of the business cycle. More precisely, we show that financial instability in the Minsky sense is a consequence of specific behaviors adopted by banks along the business cycle and neglected by other banking theories.

The chapter is organized as follows. First, the decision-making environment and the induced rationality of the Minskyan banker are highlighted. We show how the specific banks' rationality explains the process of pro-cyclical financial fragility characterizing the FIH. Second, the behavior of the Minskyan banker in the money market is studied. We show how entrepreneurial and innovative behaviors of commercial banks create an institutional instability and weaken monetary policy tools. These behaviors also explain the pro-cyclical rise in the money market rate. Finally, the behavior of the Minskyan banker in the credit market is analyzed. We focus on how banks' reactions to changes in the financial structure of economic agents (both firms and banks) help to explain the pro-cyclicity of the market credit interest rate and thus the transition from a financially fragile situation to a situation of financial crisis.

Banks' behavior under uncertainty and pro-cyclical financial fragility
In a general way, Minsky considers that simple observation of financially sophisticated economies shows that problems of imperfect and asymmetric information are essential and are empirically meaningful. In these economies agents (in particular entrepreneurs and bankers) specialize in the activities in which they have a specific informational advantage. The exception is then not asymmetry but rather symmetry of information. When asymmetric information prevails, lenders have access to complete information as to the projects that they finance only inasmuch as investors reveal it voluntarily. Thus, Minsky insists that in a world where 'each participant . . . has private information as well as its own market power' bankers never see a pro forma they do not like, since there is an incentive for borrowers to exaggerate the quality of their investment projects (Minsky 1989, p. 177). This observation suggests that there are points of similarity between Minsky's analysis of banking and the approach in terms of credit rationing under asymmetric information developed by new-Keynesian economists. By the way, Minsky himself suggested that 'a convergence between the new and the post-Keynesian economics can be expected, and the result is likely to be fruitful' (Ferri and Minsky 1989, p. 123).

There is no denying that both Minsky's banks and new-Keynesian lenders are 'rational skeptics' with regard to the information provided by borrowers. As expressed by Minsky, 'it is the duty of the "banker" . . . to be skeptic – to reveal the shaky or heroic assumptions and also the unwarranted inferences' (Minsky 1992, p. 23). In the two approaches skepticism leads to the emergence of a set of institutional arrangements whose purpose is to protect the interests of lenders: collateral (or net worth), restrictive covenants, interest rate increases and premiums on external finance that increase its price in proportion to the opportunity cost of self-finance (Minsky 1986, pp. 187–93). In this perspective asymmetric information cannot merely be considered as a minor imperfection of otherwise smoothly performing systems or as an arbitrary or ad hoc assumption. On the contrary, asymmetric information seems to be an inherent characteristic of market economies. Moreover, like in new-Keynesian models, the Minskyan banker limits the availability of finance once it has reached a certain level, thereby creating a form of rationing. As Minsky argues, 'although some risks faced by lenders are expressed in observable increases in interest rates, as leverage increases and the confidence in future cash flows decreases, this observed rise in interest rates is not the full picture of the rise in financing costs' (Minsky 1986, p. 123). Some agents will then be subject to quantitative constraints insofar as there will be no interest rate that will make banks more willing to grant them more loans.

However, the contributions made by new-Keynesian economists cannot entirely account for the way Minsky describes the behavior of agents, in particular their financial behavior. This is due to the differences in the decision-making environments within which the two approaches are embedded. Even if Minsky does consider problems that arise between agents in situations of asymmetric information, he also emphasizes that these problems occur in a world of fundamental uncertainty, one that has little to do with an environment of probabilistic risk used in new-Keynesian works. Indeed, the approach Minsky develops clearly fits in with Keynesian fundamentalism, as it considers that the concepts of expectations, uncertainty and ignorance are at the heart of Keynes's contribution to economic theory. That is why, in contrast to the new-Keynesians who extensively develop models that depart as little as possible from the premises of neoclassical theory, Minsky unambiguously rejects the axioms considered as fundamental features of new classical economics.

The first axiom he rejects is the one depicting an economic world oblivious of history and 'crucial decisions' (Shackle 1955). Instead Minsky's world is one of complex decision-making where fundamental uncertainty, in the sense of Keynes, dominates and where decisions, once taken, can exhibit over time a strong dose of indeterminacy. It is such an environment of strong uncertainty that must be considered, Minsky believes, in order to provide a relevant description of the way agents behave in the credit market: 'because both bankers and their borrowers are aware of time, they recognize that their current decisions are made in the face of uncertainty' (Minsky 1986, p. 118). This has obviously little to do with the exogenous uncertainty, the probabilistic risk favored by the new-Keynesians. Indeed like Knight for whom 'Uncertainty must be taken in a sense radically distinct from the familiar notion of Risk' (Knight 1921, p. 19), Minsky insists that 'the risks bankers carry are not objective probability phenomena; instead they are uncertainty relations that are subjectively valued' (Minsky 1986, p. 239).

Naturally the overruling character of strong uncertainty induces Minsky to reject a second axiom accepted by new-Keynesian economists, namely that the rationality of economic agents can be depicted by the standard hypothesis of rational expectations. In Minsky's model, considering strong uncertainty leads neither to Lucas's conclusion that we are in the presence of 'economic reasoning of no value', nor to radical indeterminacy of behavior. In line with the works developed by post-Keynesian authors in this area, Minsky's economic agent is driven by 'rational spirits' of a different nature.[1] This form of rationality finds strong theoretical underpinnings in Keynes's writings on probabilities (Keynes 1973a) and in the rationality of a conventional kind (Keynes 1973b). It is precisely this form of rationality that characterizes Minsky's analysis of the behavior of banks. Like Kregel for whom 'since expectations are partly formed on the basis of the operation of the economy and partly on the imagination of agents, they are composed both of endogenous and exogenous elements' (Kregel 1995, p. 218), Minsky describes the behavior of banks as based on 'objective' endogenous variables and on aspects determined in a conventional or 'subjective' fashion. As Minsky explains, 'an increase in debtors who find it difficult or impossible to fulfill their commitments on debts will induce bankers to be skeptical of new proposals for debt financing, even as nonfulfillment of debt contracts by business decreases available bankers' funds' (Minsky 1986, p. 118). To this objective factor influencing the formation of banks' expectations, there is an added subjective component. It implies that realized outcomes (for example, the quantity of loans that has been repaid) can induce banks to modify their decisions as to the amount of credit to be granted, independently of how these outcomes fit in with their expectations. This means in particular that, even if results merely confirm the banks' expectations, it is likely that, encouraged by increased confidence in their forecasting methods, they will make more loans. Accordingly, the longer the period during which the debt to equity ratio of the economy remains at a certain level without provoking a financial crisis, the more banks are likely to raise their estimates of the maximum level of indebtedness (in proportion to the value of assets both they and potential borrowers hold) to which it is prudent to agree.

This process of pro-cyclical fragility also affects banks' balance sheets. Indeed, competition among banks leads them to increase their indebtedness in proportion to the amount of their equity, reserves and safe assets (such as government securities). How banks undergo the process of balance sheet fragility is explained in Chapter 10 of *Stabilizing an Unstable Economy*, which Minsky devotes to banking (Minsky 1986, p. 223–53). He shows very simply that the profit-seeking behavior of banks leads them to reduce deliberately their equity-to-assets ratio when their activity is expanding. That is because even a small reduction in this ratio is likely to lead to large increases in the rate of profit as well as to a rapid increase in the size of the banks' total assets. Expansion thus encourages them to engage in financial operations involving high leverage.[2] Conversely, when the economy is slowing down, banks will seek to increase their equity-to-assets ratio in order to protect their shareholders against possible losses resulting from the default of borrowers. Thus, as a result of competition, the equity-to-assets ratio of commercial banks is subject to change during the business cycle, inasmuch as its evolution tends to be countercyclical.

Some authors claim to have detected a weakness or at least a certain looseness in this part of Minsky's theory. The question they raise is whether an increase in debt to equity ratios and thus in financial fragility is likely to occur. According to some commentators Minsky's model is inconsistent insofar as, while and even though agents might consider a depression or a financial crisis to be in the offing, the way they compose their portfolios actually tends to increase the likelihood of the crisis. In particular, for Friedman and Laibson, 'some element of myopia is a crucial ingredient here as well' (Friedman and Laibson 1989, p. 169). A similar point of view is voiced by Tobin who, commenting on Minsky's approach, writes 'rational expectations adherents will doubtless object that the alleged cycle would vanish as soon as borrowers and lenders understood it' (Tobin 1989, p. 106).

This argument hardly stands up because one variable remains unknown by banks and other economic agents, namely the exact moment at which the financial crisis will actually break out. Now this variable is a crucial one, inasmuch as today's market economies are characterized by an 'asymmetric reward structure' (Dymski and Pollin 1992). This means that for the individual financial or non-financial firm it is in no way profitable to engage in 'hedge' finance during an economic boom. In fact, a firm that would not make use of all available leverage would run the risk of seeing its market value drop (since, among other reasons, it would distribute fewer dividends than other, more indebted, firms). Moreover, in the long run, it would not be able to remain competitive. As a result, when prosperity wanes, aggressive managers will already have been rewarded, while hedge managers, if they have not been eliminated, will have made lower profits. In addition, during a crisis many aggressive managers default, so that the responsibility of financial distress falls on no one in particular, in sharp contrast to the situation prevailing during the boom where exaggeratedly cautious agents find themselves in an isolated position. The same idea was expressed by Keynes many years ago, in Chapter 12 of the *General Theory*: 'worldly wisdom teaches that it is better for reputation to fail conventionally than to succeed unconventionally' (Keynes 1973b, p. 158).

This discussion clearly establishes that Minsky's banker is neither irrational nor myopic. Simply, he or she must form expectations and make decisions in an uncertain decision-making environment characterized by an asymmetrical reward structure. As a result, financial fragility builds up endogenously in the expansionary phase because it is then individually rational for banks to make more loans (and for firms to issue more debt).[3] Notwithstanding the opinion of Friedman and Laibson, Minsky's idea that 'even as agents note the unfavourable objective circumstances, their significance for today is discounted' (Minsky 1989, p. 181) is not based upon 'behavioral underpinnings [that] have remained vague' (Friedman and Laibson 1989, p. 161). Minsky's banker is fully rational. He or she is, however, subject to a particular form of rationality.

Innovative bankers and the money market
We have just shown that banks' behavior under uncertainty generates the process of pro-cyclical financial fragility characterizing the first phase of the FIH. Let us see now how banks' behavior also explains the second phase of Minsky's theory of the business cycle, namely the transition from a financially fragile situation to a situation of financial and economic instability. The main determinant of this transition is an increase in interest rates in both money and credit markets that is likely to lead to present-value reversals when the weight of speculative and Ponzi finance is great. Increases in the interest rate also lead to less investment and thus to reductions in the aggregate flow of profits. A situation of this kind can lead to a liquidity run: firms that cannot meet their payment commitments either from their proceeds or through borrowings must sell off part of their assets (Minsky 1986, pp. 216–17 and 1988, pp. 22–8) Such sales cause asset prices to collapse, which might turn a recession into an economic depression.

In the following argument, we highlight how entrepreneurial and innovative behaviors of commercial banks explain the pro-cyclical rise in the money market rate. This part of Minsky's theory is inspired by several theoretical influences recalled below.

A 'Tobin–Schumpeter' view of banking
A key feature of Minsky's analysis is the fact that the behavior of banks is guided essentially by the permanent quest for profit opportunities. This view lessens to a great extent the distinction between banks, other financial institutions and non-financial agents. Indeed,

> the line between commercial banks, whose liabilities include checking deposits, other depository thrift institutions, miscellaneous managers of money (like insurance companies, pension funds and various investment trusts), and investment bankers is more reflective of the legal environment and institutional history than of the economic function of these financial institutions. (Minsky 1986, p. 223)

For similar reasons the distinction between financial institutions and non-financial agents does not seem crucial to him: 'banks and bankers are not passive managers of money to lend or to invest; they are in business to maximize profits. They actively solicit borrowing customers, undertake financing commitments, build connections with business and other bankers, and seek funds' (Minsky 1986, pp. 229–30).

Interestingly, this aspect of Minsky's theory is reminiscent of the approach developed in Tobin's article 'Commercial banks as creators of money' (1963), in which Tobin contrasts the 'old view' on banking with the 'new view'. Like Minsky, Tobin and the supporters of the new view make no clear distinction between banks and other financial institutions, or between what Gurley and Shaw call the 'monetary system' – comprising the commercial banks and the Fed – and the 'other financial intermediaries' (Gurley and Shaw 1956, pp. 260–61). All these financial agents are 'financial intermediaries' whose main and characteristic function is to 'satisfy simultaneously the portfolio preferences of . . . borrowers [and] lenders' (Tobin 1963, p. 274). Another important resemblance between banks and other financial institutions is related to the Marshallian behavior adopted by all financial intermediaries. As with 'nonfinancial industries', their supply will go on increasing as long as 'the marginal returns on lending and investing . . . will not exceed the marginal cost to banks of attracting and holding additional deposits' (Tobin 1963, p. 277, 281). Thus, in the absence of reserve requirements, 'expansion of credit and deposits by the commercial banking system would be limited by the availability of assets at yields sufficient to compensate banks for the costs of attracting and holding the corresponding deposits' (Tobin 1963, p. 279). Accordingly, it is the regulatory restrictions (reserve requirements and interest rate ceilings) imposed only upon banks rather than the monetary nature of their liabilities that underpin the relation between reserves and deposits, as determined by the customary money multiplier. However, as noted by Tobin, even in presence of such regulatory constraints, the simple money multiplier does not necessarily apply to all increases of reserves: the level of deposits and of bank assets is in fact also influenced by 'depositor preferences' as well as by the 'lending and investing opportunities' offered to banks (Tobin 1963, pp. 279–81).

Thus, Minsky's analysis of banking, by attenuating the distinction between commercial banks and other financial intermediaries, and between money and other financial assets, but also by underscoring the entrepreneurial behavior of banks, is akin to the one developed by the new view. However, the two approaches also display differences. Even though Tobin argues that changes in depositors' preferences can affect the lending capacity of banks, he does not seem to fully size up the role played by banks' active management of assets and liabilities as a way of, first, untightening the regulatory quantitative constraints to which they are subjected and, second, simply carrying out their profit-seeking activity. On the contrary, Minsky insists that banks are entrepreneurial firms whose innovations

allow greater profits: new financial instruments, new financial procedures and new financial institutions are in particular created by innovative bankers who receive monopoly rents that disappear as innovations
diffuse (Minsky 1990, 1993). This view is akin to Schumpeter's analysis of
banking. According to the Austrian author, in a capitalist environment,
bankers perform an entrepreneurial function, which is by no means less
important than the one of business entrepreneurs for economic development. Clearly financial institutions and practices appear and disappear.
Thus, Schumpeterian creation and destruction occur also in the field
of finance, as well as innovation, whether it takes the form of product,
process or organizational innovation or whether it consists in incremental
or radical change. Moreover, new types of financing media may emerge
and thereby trigger further process and product innovation. Though not
often stressed by commentators, this feature of bankers was emphasized
by Schumpeter. He indeed noted that

> financial institutions and practices enter our circle of problems in three ways:
> they are 'auxiliary and conditioning'; banking may be the object of entrepre-
> neurial activity, that is to say, the introduction of new banking practices may
> constitute enterprise; and bankers (or other 'financiers') may use the means at
> their command in order to embark upon commercial and industrial enterprise
> themselves (for example John Law). (Schumpeter 1947 [1989], p. 153).

Like Schumpeter, Minsky perfectly understood that financial institutions are also entrepreneurial organizations striving to innovate in order
to generate capital gains. This implies that financial systems evolve not
only in response to demands of business firms and individual investors but
also as a result of the innovative activity of profit-seeking entrepreneurial
financial firms. As will be seen below, the innovative and entrepreneurial
behavior of commercial banks is at the core of Minsky's explanation of
endogenous macroeconomic instability.

Money policy and banking innovation
The elements central to Minsky's analysis of banking were defined some
fifty years ago, in his very first article, 'Central banking and money market
changes' (1957). This article offers a clear picture of Minsky's complex
analysis of endogenous money supply. It also highlights the entrepreneurial and innovative behavior of commercial banks, with the effects such
behavior has on the determination of the money market interest rate.
    In the article, Minsky analyzes the case where the central bank is imple-
menting a restrictive monetary policy (Minsky 1957, pp. 182–4). Monetary
authorities apply a policy of this kind when they fear that economic
expansion might generate inflation, a policy that causes an increase in the

interest rate, owing to 'a vigorous demand for financing relative to the available supply' (Minsky 1957, p. 172). Two possibilities are considered. The first consists in reasoning within a stable institutional environment, one where 'a tight money policy will be effective and the interest rate will rise to whatever extent is necessary in order to restrict the demand for financing to the essentially inelastic supply . . . This can be represented as a positively sloped curve between velocity and the interest rate' (Minsky 1957, p. 182). Institutional stability is not, however, Minsky's main focus. At the beginning of the 1950s changes began affecting the money market, as the markets for Federal funds and for repurchase agreements emerged and expanded. For Minsky these evolutions simply reflected the existence of a form of institutional instability governed by the profit-seeking and innovative behavior of commercial banks.

The process described in the 1957 article unfolds as follows. Rising interest rates act as a signal which private market operators interpret as new profit opportunities. Higher interest rates imply that greater opportunity costs affect the excess reserves held by commercial banks. Their incentive is therefore to lend these reserves to the Federal funds market. Besides, the Federal funds rate is always lower than the discount rate, Minsky observes (Minsky 1957, p. 174). This is a circumstance banks short of reserves will take advantage of, as will non-bank financial institutions, such as government bond houses, induced to make borrowings by issuing repurchase agreements that non-financial firms acquire. This is made all the easier because high interest rates will lead such firms to move away from non-interest-bearing demand deposits and seek more profitable ways of investing their money.[4] Thus the increase in interest rates creates an environment propitious to the emergence and the development of financial innovations.

An important outcome of such innovations is that they increase the velocity of money and thereby the quantity of money supplied to potential borrowers. Two main factors explain the relationship that develops between the rise in velocity and the increase in the quantity of money. In the first place, greater reliance by banks on the market for Federal funds allows a larger volume of demand deposits for a given amount of central bank money: 'a given volume of reserves now supports more deposits' (Minsky 1957, p. 181). In the second place, the innovative process described earlier implies that the assets held by commercial banks undergo two important changes: (1) the proportion invested in short-term government securities, such as Treasury bills, diminishes as higher rates persuade non-financial firms to increase their holdings of such assets; and (2) lending to government bond houses also declines as these agents now collect a large amount of funds from non-financial firms through issues of

Interest rate

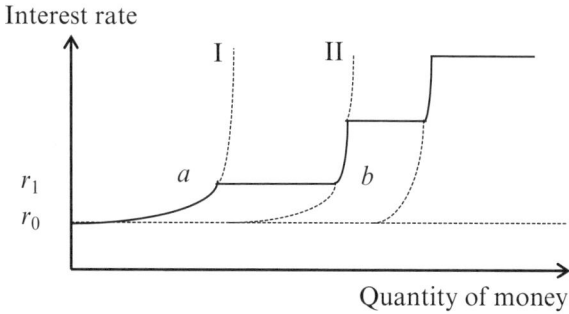

Figure 5.1   Banking innovation and the money market rate

repurchase agreements. As a result, for a determined volume of demand deposits, a larger amount of bank loans is granted to firms (Minsky 1957, p. 182). Why Minsky identifies these various changes, affecting the balance sheets of banks and brought about by the innovative process, with an increase in bank reserves thus becomes clear, as well as why both velocity and the quantity of money increase when economic activity expands (Minsky 1957, p. 182).

These changes that concern the money market thus create institutional instability, which gives rise to rightwards shifts in the interest rate–velocity curve. An upward-stepped money supply curve obtains, similar to the one represented in Figure 5.1. The increasing portions of the curve depict the effect of a restrictive monetary policy on the interest rate when the institutional environment remains stable. However, such increases do not last indefinitely, as an increase in the interest rate (for instance, from r_0 to r_1) creates profit opportunities, money market innovations and thus institutional instability, as described by the curve shift from I to II. A plateau, a–b, appears, which characterizes the period during which institutional innovation is spreading.

During this period the impact on the interest rate of a restrictive monetary policy is completely counteracted, while the velocity of circulation and the supply of money appear to be infinitely elastic. As stressed by Minsky, in such a context the effectiveness of monetary policy based on the surveillance of monetary aggregates weakens. As a result, in order to fight inflation, the central bank has no other choice than to act directly on the liquidity of commercial banks. It will therefore try to diminish reserves to an extent that is great enough to compensate for the increase in velocity. This reaction to the profit-seeking and innovating behavior of commercial banks will have the effect of pushing up interest rates even more, thus recreating the conditions for the whole process to recur. Hence the succession, over time, of the increasing and horizontal portions of the curves represented in the figure.

Moreover, the institutional innovative process also exerts a negative influence on the liquidity of the economy. In other words, the innovative process described earlier is likely to lead to a situation where the economy becomes less liquid although the quantity of money is rising. As Minsky writes, 'the reverse side of the coin to the increase in velocity is that every institutional innovation which results in both new ways to finance business and new substitutes for cash assets decreases the liquidity of the economy' (Minsky 1957, p. 184). This evolution is mainly due to the particular form of rationality that Minsky's banks exhibit when decisions are taken within an environment of Keynesian uncertainty.

As noted earlier, such rationality rests upon objective bases, but also on more conventional or subjective grounds. This means that, even if actual outcomes only confirm banks' expectations, it is likely that, on account of their increased confidence in the way they are forming their expectations, banks will augment their lending and contribute to making the economy less liquid. Reduced liquidity of the economy is in fact caused by the deterioration of the financial structure of borrowers and lenders, as manifested in the rise in the debt-to-net-worth ratio (Minsky 1957, p. 185). Moreover profit-seeking by both financial and non-financial agents implies decreased liquidity of holdings. On the one hand, it leads to the substitution in commercial banks' portfolios of private debt for government securities. It reflects, on the other hand, the replacement of deposits in firms' portfolios by government debt and, at a later stage, of government debt by repurchase agreements issued by government security houses.

It is interesting to stress here the particular features of the money supply curve. They afford a good understanding of the complexity of Minsky's reasoning and of its originality within post-Keynesian theory. In the latter, especially in the 'horizontalist' view (Moore 1988), the quantity of money is to a large extent determined by the demand for credit by entrepreneurs and is thus influenced by the level of effective demand. In other words it is the animal spirits of entrepreneurs that play the key role in the dynamics of money: any increase in the demand for money will increase the equilibrium amount of money, without any effect on the interest rate. The money supply is endogenous and adapts both completely and passively to the demand for money. On the contrary, interest rates are determined exogenously by the central bank. In short, one can qualify post-Keynesian horizontalism as an approach in which the money supply is endogenous and the interest rate exogenous.

There is thus a substantial divergence between Minsky and post-Keynesian horizontalists in the interpretation of the relationship between the central bank and the commercial banks. For Minsky the way commercial banks react to profit opportunities and to the policy conducted by the central bank prevents the latter from setting the interest rate at the level it deems desirable. The evolution of this rate depends strongly on the succession of phases of institutional stability and instability induced by the active and innovative behavior of the commercial banks. The horizontalist conception of the money supply is thus rejected in Minsky's interpretation, which makes room for an interest rate that is not entirely exogenous even though the money supply is endogenous. In addition, the money market interest rate behaves pro-cyclically: its increase simply reflects the dynamic process that takes place under the influence of the innovations of commercial banks confronting the restrictive reactions of the central bank when the economy expands.

Agents' financial structure and the credit market

Minskyan bankers' behavior explains not only the pro-cyclical rise in the money but also in the credit market rate. We underline below how banks' reactions to changes in the financial structure of economic agents explain the pro-cyclicity of the market credit interest rate and thus the transition from a financially fragile situation to a situation of financial crisis.

Banks' liquidity preference

With the effects of institutional innovation presented above the economy becomes subject to a greater risk of illiquidity, which in turn leads to greater liquidity preference. As stated by Minsky, 'economic units . . . desire more liquidity. A tendency to use savings to liquidate debt and hence to increase the ratio of net worth to debt will arise' (Minsky 1957, p. 186). To understand the impact of increased liquidity preference, it is necessary to observe that it is not equivalent to a larger demand for money. Reliance here on the distinction established by Wray (1992) is very helpful. According to Wray an increase in liquidity preference (the desire to exchange illiquid assets for more liquid ones) is actually the opposite of demanding more money, that is, demanding more funds because spending is expected to augment. Applied to Minsky's analysis of banking, this means that an increase in liquidity preference should be understood as not having the same effect on the interest rate as a greater demand for money. In fact, as seen previously, not only are banks eager (because of profit opportunities), they are also able (thanks to liability management) to respond to borrowers' larger demand for money. To the contrary, it is unlikely that banks will as easily agree to raise their supply of money in a context of enhanced liquidity preference. For Minsky, as for other post-Keynesian authors, such an increase in liquidity preference is associated with a reduction in anticipated profits, an environment that does not encourage commercial banks to develop their assets or to augment their supply of finance.[5] In fact, a situation of 'generalized liquidity preference' arises, since it concerns not only households and firms, but also banks. Although it might be assumed that borrowers would share the same expectations as banks and, as a result, would reduce their demand for money, Minsky reminds us that there is in fact an 'inelastic demand for finance', due in particular to the existence of investment projects displaying very long gestation periods and thereby requiring the roll-over of debt for the repayment of principal.[6]

The confrontation between a supply of money that is inclined to diminish under the influence of the preference by banks for greater liquidity and a demand for money that tends to become more inelastic during the ascending phase of the business cycle reinforces the pro-cyclicity of the interest rate.

Borrower's and lender's risk
Independent of any variation in liquidity preference, a second aspect, the indebtedness of the economy, also plays a fundamental role in the determination of the interest rate. In fact, as argued by Minsky as early as in 1957, the increase of the debt ratio is likely to exert an upward pressure on the financial conditions granted to borrowing agents (Minsky 1957, p.185). To understand this, account must be taken of the way the financial structures of both borrowers and lenders evolve.

In Minsky's analysis, the evolution of the borrower's financial structure affects the lender's as well as the borrower's risk. When he refers to the lender's risk, Minsky clearly alludes to Keynes's definition in Chapter 11 of *The General Theory*.[7] However, whereas Keynes relates the lender's risk to the decision to invest and to the comparative uncertainty of long-run expectations, Minsky also considers different types of financial structure. Indeed, notwithstanding the amount that can be self-financed, investment of whatever level involves issuing debt. The greater the size of its investments, the higher the risk that a business will default, which is reflected in the financial conditions applied by banks. To that effect 'some risks faced by lenders are expressed in observable increases in interest rates, as leverage increases and the confidence in cash-flows decreases' (Minsky 1986, p.193). Other effects of the increase in the lender's risk are that it can give rise to loans of shorter maturity, or loans of smaller amounts, or to restrictions in dividend payouts.

While the lender's risk can be clearly observed in loan contracts, Minsky notes that the relationship between financial structure and financial conditions also takes a more subjective appearance, in the form of the borrower's risk. Here again the author acknowledges his indebtedness to Keynes.[8] Yet, reference to the principle of increasing risk first brought to light by Kalecki (1937) is even clearer.[9] Indeed, in Minsky's approach the borrower's risk is the manifestation that, beyond the amount that can be self-financed, investment implies financial costs that are inescapable, whereas the cash flows generated by production are unquestionably uncertain. Therefore 'the borrower's risk will increase as the weight of external or liquidity diminishing financing increases' (Minsky 1986, p. 191). Then, because a bank loan is to a large extent granted on the basis of the debtor's expected profits, the bank's risk increases in line with the borrower's risk. It is therefore likely that an increase of the borrower's risk will lead, as with a greater lender's risk, to a rise in the interest rate charged on bank loans.

The relationship between the liability structure of borrowers and the financial conditions imposed upon them is an essential aspect of Minsky's explanation of interest rate determination. It is also one that is well known, as it underpins his financial theory of investment. Nonetheless, a second aspect of his analysis, one that is not quite so familiar, deserves to be examined. It concerns the effect on the interest rate of changes affecting the balance sheet structure of banks.

As mentioned before, competition among banks leads them to deteriorate their balance-sheets pro-cyclically. This has two implications. First, banks that have become financially more fragile because of high leverage may be confronted with steadily increasing refinancing costs, owing to the 'collegiate surveillance' exerted by banks and other institutions operating in the money market (Minsky 1986, p. 240). As is likely, banks that face growing borrowing costs in the money market will be inclined to pass them on to the rates they charge, thereby endogenously contributing to the higher interest rates on bank loans.

Second, increased leverage of banks is also at the heart of a second kind of upwards pressure exerted on bank loans. The reason, already noted by Minsky in 1957, is that 'the chances of insolvency and illiquidity [of commercial banks] increase simultaneously', which persuades them to demand higher interest rates in order to compensate for the increasing risk associated with the greater size of their assets (Minsky 1957, p. 185). Minsky thus proposes an enlarged view of the lender's risk since, in the present case, it no longer refers only to the borrower's financial structure, but also to the bank's.

Again, Minsky manifests his differences with other post-Keynesian theorists. Indeed, in the horizontalist approach commercial banks are extraordinarily passive, both in the money market where the interest rate is fixed exogenously by the central bank and in the market for loans where they respond automatically to borrowers' demands. In this approach commercial banks do not exert any significant influence on prices and quantities in the markets where they operate. In contrast, Minsky's commercial banks recover a more active role in the determination of prices and quantities both in the money market and, as has just been seen, in the loans market. In Minsky's view of banking, the endogeneity of the money supply is no longer synonymous with the passivity of commercial banks.

Conclusion
In this chapter we analyzed Minsky's theory of banking. This theory is somewhat an extension of the approach proposed by the new-Keynesians since Minsky believes that asymmetric information does exert some influence on the behavior of agents, in particular of those operating in capital markets. However the existence of this kind of imperfection cannot be considered as a necessary condition for there to be credit rationing or, more generally, constraints of some sort in the financial markets. The essential reason for this, as we have seen, is that, in Minsky's theory, financial arrangements are set up within a decision-making environment where asymmetric information and Keynesian uncertainty in fact coexist. Keynesian uncertainty, which has nothing to do with the probabilistic risk retained by the new-Keynesians, induces banks to adopt, independently of any effect of asymmetric information, a whole range of behaviors that go far beyond the rationing of the demand for loans in the credit market. Indeed, when Keynesian uncertainty prevails, the adoption of behaviors that are based upon a particular form of rationality, where conventions and animal spirits play an important role, implies that bankers, like other economic agents, do not act as do the robot-like decision-makers of the rational expectations theory. Other behaviors and other variables are to be considered: the level reached by the agents' indebtedness, the ratios of indebtedness that are judged acceptable, changes in the 'state of confidence', the liquidity preference of banks and the related appearance of financial and endogenous instability.

By focusing his analysis on active and innovative commercial banks, Minsky stands also clearly apart from the horizontalists whose positions are still widely shared by many post-Keynesian theorists of the endogenous money supply. This can be explained by the fact that numerous theoretical influences have inspired Minsky's analysis of banking. His ability to integrate the contributions of authors as different as Keynes, Schumpeter or Kalecki within a single consistent setting has allowed him to investigate certain aspects that are often lacking in even recent Keynesian analyses of banking: financial innovation, fundamental uncertainty, increasing risk, the financial structure and the liquidity preference of banks.

Finally, the pivotal role played by Minsky's analysis of banking within his theory of economic instability was highlighted. Taking banks and their behavior into account has enabled Minsky to lay down the foundations for an original approach of economic fluctuations. Organized around the study of the dynamics of financial relationships, his approach shows that the rational profit-seeking and innovative behavior of banks produces both financial fragility and financial instability. The behavior of banks, an aspect that is often neglected by commentators of Minsky's approach, thus appears to be one of the most important ingredients of the FIH. It is central to understand the complex financial relations that can trigger the kind of dramatic episode of financial crisis experienced in 2007 in 'financially sophisticated economies'. More generally, it deserves to be taken into account in all of its complexity by theorists interested in the relation between banking and economic instability.

Notes

1. See, in particular, Kregel (1987) and Davidson (1982–83). The phrase 'rational spirits' has been coined by Kregel (1987).
2. 'The impact of increased leverage on bank profits is impressive: if a bank that makes 0.75 per cent on assets decreases the ratio of capital to assets to 5 per cent from 6 per cent, the profit rate on book value will be 15.0 per cent rather than 12.5 per cent. If such an increase in leverage takes place over several years, the profit rate will rise each year. With a constant dividend on book value ratio, this implies that the growth rate mandated by retained earnings will rise from 7.5 to 10 per cent.' (Minsky 1986, p. 237).
3. Minsky proposed characterizing financial fragility by separating firms into three categories. He distinguished between 'hedge', 'speculative' and 'Ponzi' finance. Hedge finance is a situation where, in each period, debt repayments are smaller than expected profits. Firms that resort to speculative finance generate proceeds that allow for the payment of short-term interest charges, but which are sometimes lower than the corresponding total debt repayment costs (principal and interest). For businesses engaged in Ponzi finance, even repayment of interest is impossible without reliance on additional debt. The larger the proportion of agents engaged in speculative and Ponzi finance, the more fragile is the economy because it loses its shock-absorbing ability.
4. As Minsky explains, non-financial firms became the main source of finance for government bond houses in the middle of 1956.
5. See for instance, Minsky (1975, p. 76, 123).
6. Minsky (1986, p. 195). Consequently, the demand for money will be less elastic inasmuch as the economy exhibits greater financial fragility.
7. '[The lender's risk] . . . may be due either to moral hazard, i.e. voluntary default or other means of escape, possibly lawful, from the fulfilment of the obligation, or to the possible insufficiency of the margin of security, i.e. unvoluntary default due to the disappointment of expectation' (Keynes 1973b, p. 144).
8. 'The entrepreneur's or borrower's risk . . . arises out of doubts in his own mind as to the probability of his actually earning the prospective yield for which he hopes' (Keynes 1973b, p. 144).
9. According to this principle, the marginal risk of investing in fixed capital goods increases with the size of their acquisition. Kalecki gives two reasons for this increase. First, the more he invests, the greater the risk of failure to which the entrepreneur's wealth is exposed. The second reason relates to the illiquidity risk that arises when increasing quantities of capital are invested in industrial facilities that cannot be readily reconverted into liquidity without generating capital losses.

References

Davidson, P. (1982–83), 'Rational expectations: a fallacious foundation for studying crucial decision-making processes', *Journal of Post Keynesian Economics*, **5**(2), 182–98.

Dymski, G. and R. Pollin (1992), 'Hyman Minsky as hedgehog: the power of the Wall Street paradigm' in S. Fazzari and D. Papadimitriou (eds), *Financial Conditions and Economic Performance: Essays in Honour of Hyman Minsky*, Armonk, New York: M.E. Sharpe.

Ferri, P. and H.P. Minsky (1989), 'The breakdown of the IS-LM Synthesis: implications for post-Keynesian economic theory', *Review of Political Economy*, **1**(2), 123–41.

Friedman, B. and D. Laibson (1989), 'Economic implications of extraordinary movements in stock prices', *Brookings Papers on Economic Activity*, 2, 137–71.

Gurley, J. and E. Shaw (1956), 'Financial intermediaries and the savings-investment process', *Journal of Finance*, **11**, May, 257–76.

Kalecki, M. (1937), 'The principle of increasing risk', *Economica*, **4**(16), 440–7.

Keynes, J.M. (1973a), *Treatise on Probability*, reprinted in *The Collected Writings of John Maynard Keynes*, vol. VIII, London: Macmillan.

Keynes, J.M. (1973b), *The General Theory and After, Part I: Preparation*, reprinted in *The Collected Writings of John Maynard Keynes*, vol. XIII, London: Macmillan.

Knight, F.H. (1921), *Risk, Uncertainty and Profit*, Boston: Houghton Mifflin Company.

Kregel, J.A. (1987), 'Rational spirits and the post keynesian macrotheory of microeconomics', *De Economist*, 4, 520–32.

Kregel, J.A. (1995), 'Keynes and the New Keynesian on the rôle of uncertainty and information', in P. Malgrange and L. Salvas-Bronsard (ed.), *Macroéconomie, Développements Récents*, Paris: Economica.

Minsky, H.P. (1957), 'Central banking and money market changes', *Quarterly Journal of Economics*, **71**(2), 171–87.

Minsky, H.P. (1975), *John Maynard Keynes*, New York: Columbia University Press.

Minsky, H.P. (1982), *Can 'It' Happen Again: Essays on Instability and Finance*, Armonk, New York: M.E. Sharpe.

Minsky, H.P. (1986), *Stabilizing An Unstable Economy*, New Haven: Yale University Press.

Minsky, H.P. (1988), 'Back from the brink', *Challenge*, (January–February), 22–8.

Minsky, H.P. (1989), 'Comments and Discussion' on B. Friedman and D. Laibson, *Brookings Papers on Economic Activity*, 2, 173–82.

Minsky, H.P. (1990), 'Schumpeter: Finance and Evolution', in A. Heertje and M. Perlman (eds), *Evolving Technology and Market Structures: Studies in Schumpeterian Economics*, The University of Michigan Press, pp. 51–74.

Minsky, H.P. (1992), 'The structure of financial institutions and the dynamic behavior of the economy', Nice (September), mimeo.

Minsky, H.P. (1993), 'Schumpeter and finance', in S. Biasco, A. Roncaglia and M. Salvati (eds), *Markets and Institutions in Economic Development : Essays in honour of Paolo Sylos Labini*, New York: St Martin's Press, pp. 103–15.

Moore, B. (1988), *Horizontalists and Verticalists : the Macroeconomics of Credit Money*, Cambridge: Cambridge university Press.

Schumpeter, J.A. (1947), 'The creative response in economic history', *Journal of Economic History*, (November), 149–59. Reprinted in R.V. Clemence (ed.), *Essays on Entrepreneurs, Innovations, Business Cycles and the Evolution of Capitalism*, New Brunswick and Oxford: Transaction Publishers, 1989, pp. 221–31. Originally published in 1951 by Addison-Wesley.

Shackle, G.L.S. (1955), *Uncertainty in Economics*, Cambridge: Cambridge University Press.

Tobin, J. (1963), 'Commercial banks as creators of money', reprinted in *Essays in Economics, Volume 1: Macroeconomics*, 1987, The MIT Press.

Tobin, J. (1989), 'Comments on "Stabilizing an unstable economy"', *Journal of Economic Literature*, **27**(1), 105–8.

Wray, L.R. (1992), 'Commercial banks, the central bank, and endogenous money', *Journal of Post Keynesian Economics*, **14**(3), 297–310.

6 What would Minsky do?

Marshall Auerback, Paul McCulley and Robert W. Parenteau

Hy Minsky's framework has a very simple core thesis. Stability is destabilizing, because market participants, or economic agents, behaving as
human beings do in the face of fundamental uncertainty, will tend to
extrapolate stability well into the future. And, if stability is extrapolated
into the future, then there will be a tendency for economic agents to
assume ever more risky debt structures. In this sense, the world of financial
and economic decision making is inherently momentum-driven – human
beings are inherently reflexive. Intellectually, we know we are supposed to
buy low and sell high. Emotionally, we can't bring ourselves to do that.
Rather, we tend to do the exact opposite, which imparts an intense procyclical character to capitalism. Perhaps even worse, it imparts procyclicality
to regulatory structures.

While in the financial press, reference to the 'Minsky Moment' – the
dramatic point when a financial crisis erupts – has become increasingly
popular, it is important to understand that Minsky described financial fragility as an inherent process that builds over time, and not just a random
event.

For the past several years, we have traversed an economic expansion
fueled by debt and accompanied by leveraged speculation of unprecedented proportions. While some central banks expressed concern, we
have witnessed the development of a parallel, largely unregulated financial
system dominated by hedge funds, private equity funds, and investment
banks employing derivatives and structured finance vehicles. The concern
was rooted in the knowledge that throughout history, when debt financed
speculation runs amok, bad things can happen. As early as 2004, PIMCO's
Bill Gross warned:

> We are hooked on debt; we are a finance-based economy. And so? Why not
> just keep on going. So far so good the New Agers would claim. What's wrong
> with 400% of GDP or 500% of GDP? What's wrong with dropping it from
> helicopters if we have to as good Ben Bernanke has suggested? Well, let me tell
> you what's wrong. Debt levels and debt ratios have limits. When and if interest
> rates do go up, the servicing costs of an accelerating debt economy eventually
> bite the hand of its master.
>   My point is that at some point on this seemingly never ending ascent of debt/

GDP, someone will say *no más* . . . Maybe it'll be PIMCO and PIMCO think-alikes; maybe it'll be foreign holders of bond grown tired of currency/inflationary erosion of principal; maybe it'll be risk takers in high yield/emerging market/levered hedge funds scared to death from a future LTCM crisis. Hard to tell, but I'm telling you it'll happen, helicopter or no helicopter and with it will come an economic slowdown/recession unseen since at least the early 1980s when Volcker began his vigil. High Noon. (Gross 2004)

It took a while longer than many of us expected, but High Noon, or the so-called 'Minsky Moment' has clearly arrived. As mentioned above, a Minsky moment is the point in a credit cycle or business cycle when investors face cash flow problems due to spiraling debt they have incurred in order to finance speculative investments. As cash flows fail to meet expectations, and as debt service charges become less bearable, investors begin to question the assumptions they had been using in valuing tangible and financial assets. At this point, as conventional views are thrown into question by recurring cash flow shortfalls and increasing evidence of debt delinquency, a major sell-off in asset prices can begin. As the perception of a reversal of the previous asset price trend spreads, prospective buyers turn cautious, uncertainty spreads, existing owners seek to preserve prior unrealized gains, and a sudden and precipitous collapse in market clearing asset prices, as well as a sharp drop in market liquidity, can result. Declining asset values erode the net worth and collateral positions of households, businesses, and investment institutions, leading to further attempts to reduce risk exposures in portfolios, or in the extreme, margin calls and forced sales. Deleveraging can lead to a self-reinforcing cycle of contagion and cascade effects, with eventual repercussions on the capacity of an economy to keep growing.

In the following section, we will examine some of the unique characteristics of this episode of financial instability – one that as of this writing appears to be the most severe incident since the Great Depression. We will outline the forward journey to the Minsky moment, and argue that a new stage, known as 'Ponzi-squared', was introduced this time around. Next, we will explore the implications of this new stage for the nature of the reverse journey away from the Minsky moment. Finally, we will explore possible policy responses consistent with a Minsky framework – both those that might be brought to bear to contain the current financial crisis, as well as those that may set a foundation for a more robust financial system.

Minsky for more than a moment
In the early 1980s, when most economists were extolling the virtues of financial deregulation and innovation, a little known economist, Hyman P. Minsky, maintained a more critical view of Wall Street. Minsky argued

that 'capitalism is inherently flawed, being prone to booms, crises and depressions. This instability, in my view, is due to characteristics the financial system must possess if it is to be consistent with full-blown capitalism' (Minsky 1982). The process, which Minsky outlined in his Financial Instability Hypothesis (FIH), begins with the initial profitability of investment activity, but ultimately ends with unrealistically high asset prices and buildups of household and business leverage based on momentum effects, myopic expectations and competition between creditor and investors. When asset prices collapse, the negative wealth effect on aggregate demand is amplified by a 'financial accelerator'; that is, collapsing credit feeds on falling aggregate demand credit. A severe economic decline can be the outcome when credit is withdrawn from an overleveraged private sector.

Now known as the man who colorfully described this form of financial fragility as 'Ponzi finance', Minsky's analysis is actually more profound and encompassing: Stability in the economic system, he argued, begins to generate behavior that produces fragility; the longer benign conditions last, the more risks borrowers will inevitably take. The resultant increase in financial fragility makes the system more prone to an unstable outcome as adverse changes in financial circumstances impact negatively on the return on investment projects. In his words: 'Tranquility and success are not self-sustaining states. They induce increases in capital asset prices relative to current output prices and a rise in acceptable debts for any prospective income flow, investment, and profits. These concurrent increases lead to a transformation over time of an initially robust financial structure into a fragile structure' (Minsky 1982). Minsky expressed this idea in terms of a declining 'margin' or 'cushion' of safety in financial transactions, which is exacerbated through an increasingly reckless use of financial leverage. Equally germane as we examine today's environment, Minsky pointed to the integral role played by Wall Street in encouraging businesses and individuals to take on too much risk, generating ruinous boom-and-bust cycles.

Many of Minsky's colleagues regarded his FIH, which he first developed in the 1960s, as radical, and hardly relevant in a post-Cold War environment in which neo-liberal capitalism was viewed as the apogee of economic progress. In particular, it became commonplace to refer to the 1982 to 2005 period as the Great Moderation. Central bankers in particular took credit for successfully reducing inflation levels and inflation's variability, which in turn they believed led to longer, lower amplitude business cycles.

Today, with the subprime crisis metastasizing into what some, notably George Soros, have described as the greatest financial crisis since the Great

Depression, references to Minsky have become commonplace on financial websites and in the reports of Wall Street analysts. Such has been the reappraisal of Minsky, that his hypothesis is now considered an acceptable point of view when it comes to analyzing the recent macrofinancial meltdown.

The Minsky forward journey

Minsky described the three stages on the forward journey to an episode of financial instability. Initially, the majority of the actors in the economy are operating as hedge units. They are able to service principal and interest payments on debt out of current and future cash flows. As the expansion proceeds, more actors become speculative units. Current and expected future cash flows are sufficient to service interest expense, but the principal must be rolled over or refinanced. Finally, in the terminal stage, more agents take on the characteristics of Ponzi units. New debt is required to service prior interest and principal payment commitments. As more and more agents progress from hedge to speculative to Ponzi units, their purchasing power goes up. More goods and services are produced and purchased, and prices of existing tangible and financial assets are bid up. As cash flows to households and businesses beat expectations, the very act of moving from one stage to the next drives up asset prices and therefore validates the risk seeking behavior. In a sense, rising asset prices cover all sins.

In the housing market that the US traversed through the middle of the 2000s, there were actually three intertwined bubbles along the forward Minsky journey. The three bubbles were property valuation, mortgage finance, and the expansion of the 'shadow banking system', each interacting synergistically to feed the explosion in home prices and construction activity.

In the middle of these three bubbles were the mortgage originators, who were operating on the originate-to-distribute model. They had no skin in the game – no capital at risk, and so no active interest in serious credit analysis – because they simply originated the loans and then repackaged them. These rebundled mortgages were sold to what may be called the shadow banking system. A shadow bank is a levered-up intermediary that does not have a form of liquidity protection. In contrast, for commercial banks, the two key forms of liquidity protection are access to FDIC deposit insurance and access to the Federal Reserve's discount window as lender-of-last-resort support.

The most important of the shadow banking structures are investment banks, hedge funds, collateralized debt obligations (CDOs), and the whole alphabet soup of structured finance vehicles. The shadow banking system was demanding product to slice and dice into its own fee generating investment vehicles. From the ultimate investors' point of view (pension funds, university endowments, and so on), these vehicles were engineered to offer more attractive yields, often without having to drop down to lower quality rated debt. The fees to be earned by engineering such free lunches, and the apparently compelling risk reward trade-off they delivered, made for a voracious appetite in the shadow banking system for new debt issuance that they could repackage. One way to meet this demand for new debt issuance was to engage in a systematic degradation in underwriting standards. Of course, for the mortgage originator, this also meant a higher stream of fee income as mortgage debt was originated.

As underwriting standards decayed and debt became more available, residential property prices were bid higher, and default rate remained low. In some cases, homeowners became Ponzi units by extracting home equity in refinancings along the way, and using part of the proceeds to service the loan. As long as new debt was easily accessible, lenders and investors were able to conclude that what initially appeared to be junk borrowers weren't really junk borrowers. They were not defaulting as long as they could continue to leverage the equity building in their homes as home prices kited higher – in part as easier lending standards allowed more housing speculation to spread.

A second crucial reason this system worked was because it had the blessing of the credit-rating agencies. The shadow banking system did not have access to a lender of last resort (a role played by the Federal Reserve for commercial banks) but it could issue asset-backed commercial paper. Moody's and the Standard & Poor's (S&P) would compete to put an A-1/P-1 rating on the commercial paper issued by the shadow banking system, and this commercial paper was in turn purchased by money market funds. In essence, long duration, relatively illiquid assets held by the shadow banking system were being positioned with short duration, highly liquid liabilities in the form of commercial paper. Such a structure is inherently unstable, and is subject to runs in the form of refinancing risk. Once holders of the commercial paper begin to question the true value of the assets in the structured finance vehicle, or even the liquidity of those assets, they may refuse to rollover their existing commercial paper financing. At that point, the assets held in the structured finance vehicle must be sold outright, or they are forced onto the balance sheet of the originating institution.

Degradation of underwriting standards generally is not easily revealed during the bull market cycle, but it will be revealed over a full economic cycle. However, S&P and Fitch and Moody's put their stamp of approval on the securitization of junk mortgages by looking at only one period of a bull market, not a complete cycle. There exists an inherent problem in establishing ratings on new credit products – they have not had a chance to season, and they need to be observed over a full business cycle before any reasonable assessment can be made. Crucially, these three bubbles were prolonged because the rating agencies thought the full cycle default rates would be low, since they had been observed to be low for the existing lifetime on the shelf. But they had been low because the degradation of underwriting standards was making credit easier to access, and thereby driving up asset prices. This reflexive condition appears to have escaped the attention of the rating agencies, as well as the attention of the investors in structured finance vehicles.

The emergence of the Ponzi-squared phase
The evolution of this latest episode of financial excess suggests there are more than three stages in the forward Minsky progression of hedge, speculative, and Ponzi finance. The fourth stage that arose may be called 'Ponzi-squared', and it delays the arrival of the Minsky moment. To understand the Ponzi-squared stage, we need to turn to the mortgage market in 2005–06 and early 2007. During this period, the marginal loan or debt unit was not an actual loan. The marginal loan unit was a no money down mortgage, with no documentation of the borrower's ability to pay, with a teaser rate, and with the capacity to forego payments and accrue negative amortization. These four characteristics amount to an at-the-money call option (to buy the house at the current market price) and an at-the-money put option (to sell the house back to the lender at that price) – for free!

As mentioned above, the definition of a Ponzi unit is when a firm or a household borrows money to buy an asset, and the income from the asset is not only insufficient to amortize the principal but also insufficient to pay the interest in full. A zero down payment creates the next step beyond Ponzi. A unit is Ponzi-squared if it has all the characteristics of a Ponzi unit and no capital at risk in the transaction. Essentially, the shadow banking system was giving away that package of options – long-dated options struck at the money – to marginal borrowers. If you ran those options through a Black–Scholes option pricing model, you'd find they were very, very valuable.

For the marginal borrower holding this Ponzi-squared package, if the value of his house went up, the value of the call option went up, and he had to make a token interest payment at a teaser rate to stay in the game. By paying the interest expense, the borrower is protecting a position where the call option has gone 'in the money'. The put option arises because, in most states, the lender can either go after the collateral or after the borrower, but not both. Subprime buyers had no additional assets, so essentially they had a free put option to sell the house back to the lender. To exercise the put, they simply had to mail the keys back to the lender. The put is valuable, because if the price of the house falls, and the borrower exercises the put, the borrower can discharge debt that's greater than the value of the asset that was 'borrowed against.'

By the first quarter of 2007, the Ponzi-squared unit was more often than not the marginal borrowing unit. Right before we had the blowup of the hedge funds at Bear Stearns, early-payment delinquencies started to mount. An early-payment delinquency occurs when someone misses a payment *in the first three months* of their mortgage. Early-payment delinquency was a clear sign that financial excesses had reached beyond the Ponzi stage, into the Ponzi-squared phase. The debt unit isn't a loan, but a package of options given away for free.

The reverse Minsky journey

The reverse Minsky journey is all about reversing what happened on the forward Minsky journey. On the forward journey, rising home prices cover all the sins of rising leverage. On the reverse journey, falling home prices reveal all sins, as most economic agents are trying to deleverage at the same time.

Of course, mainstream price theory suggests lower prices are the cure to a situation of excess supply. This, however, may not always hold true in the case of durable goods or tangible assets that are owned with a high degree of leverage. While it is true the flow of newly constructed homes will dry up as existing and new home prices fall, there is an additional source of supply to consider with long-lived assets. Should prices fall far enough for a sustained period of time, existing homeowners may change their opinions about future values of their homes, and hence the expected return of owning a home. In addition, with a leveraged durable asset, as the existing home price falls, the net worth or the equity of the homeowner diminishes. Especially in the wake of an asset price bubble, it is possible for the homeowner to end up 'upside down', or owing more on the house than it is worth. In either case – where expected returns fall, or where equity in the home is erased – falling existing home prices can lead to more existing homeowners trying to sell their houses. Perversely, for durable assets like homes, falling prices can lead to more excess supply on the market. This flaw in the market adjustment mechanism for durable assets was recognized by Fisher, Keynes and Minsky, and it is one of the elements that can contribute to debt deflation dynamics, which can seriously undermine an economy.

When the tide went out on home prices, the inherent liquidity risk of the shadow banking system was revealed. In a period of three months in 2007, starting in August, the shadow banking system could not roll or refinance $350 billion of asset-backed commercial paper. There was a run on the shadow system, forcing it to deleverage, driving down asset prices, eroding equity or capital positions of financial institutions, which in turn forced it to deleverage again in a self-reinforcing cycle. Like the regulatory response, this deleveraging process is also incredibly procyclical. In the case of regulation, there is a rush to laxity on the way up, and you have a rush to stringency on the way back down. In the case of the shadow banking system, on the way back down, you have the equivalent of Keynes's paradox of thrift in the form of Fisher's paradox of deleveraging.

Keynes's paradox of thrift suggested that if households try to raise their rate of saving out of income, they may find their income falls short, as shortfalls in retailer revenues feed back through the economic system in the form of production, employment, and household income reductions. Without a commensurate increase in investment, net exports, or fiscal stimulus, the attempt to raise household savings could be thwarted. To break the paradox of thrift, Keynes suggested using the public's balance sheet by running fiscal deficits. But how do you break the paradox of deleveraging?

Addressing the paradox of deleveraging
One possible solution is to use the sovereign's balance sheet. On a reverse Minsky journey, the private sector wants to shrink and lower the risk on its balance sheet. Someone has to take the other side of the trade, or asset prices will collapse, raising the risk of a depression. That someone is the public sector, the sovereign.

We pretend that the Federal Reserve's balance sheet and Treasury's balance sheet are entirely separate, but from the standpoint of providing balance sheet support to buffer a reverse Minsky journey, there's no difference between the Treasury's balance sheet and the Federal Reserve's balance sheet. The Federal Reserve issues notes or reserves with zero interest as their liabilities, and they buy Treasury securities that pay interest – the ultimate in spread banking. The Federal Reserve kicks back the $32 billion in seignorage revenue each year to the Treasury as a result of this spread banking activity. If the Federal Reserve takes risky assets onto its balance sheet and loses money, then it simply reduces the rebate to the Treasury. The Treasury's balance sheet and the Federal Reserve's balance sheet are not so separate on a reverse Minsky journey. In fact, in the extreme, the monetary authority can effectively subordinate itself to the fiscal policy authority, as happened in Japan when they went to quantitative easing a number of years ago.

The reverse Minsky journey comes to an end when the full faith and credit of the sovereign's balance sheet is brought into play to effectively take the other side of the private sector's trade. The Federal Reserve took a giant leap in this direction on March 16, 2008 when it opened the discount window to the primary dealers. That created a firebreak, because the biggest shadow banks are the investment banks. This action brought investment banks under the Federal Reserve's liquidity umbrella. However, access to a public good – the discount window and hence the Federal Reserve's balance sheet – generally comes with obligations and responsibilities, like submitting to regulatory oversight.

In effect, in the years ahead, the shadow banking system will be reintermediated into a more bank-centric system, backstopped by the sovereign through access to the Federal Reserve's discount window, and regulated in a countercyclical way, to check financial excess. Financial controls will be tightened as economic growth accelerates, and relaxed as the economy slows – just the opposite of what we've got now.

The next big step is to have the government's balance sheet take on the mortgages at a 'haircut' price, below face value – to nationalize, in some respects, the subprime mortgage business, while making the shadow banking system and the real banking system that sold all of these free puts take a loss. If you short a put and the underlying asset goes down, what happens? You lose money. Financial institutions that shorted the put deserve to lose money. The government can refinance it to the amount that the put is in the money, and gets to share in any upside on the mortgage.

The more the sovereign's balance sheet is brought in to offset the impact of the deleveraging, the closer is the day that private investors will once again become risk-seeking. Then high-quality assets that have been beaten to death in forced sales can be bought at a price that provides equity-like returns

Of course, if we had had a responsible, preemptive, prophylactic regulatory regime, we would not be here. But we are here. And since we're here, we've got to do things that we wouldn't otherwise do, and accept the consequences. There are two alternatives: we can accept a somewhat higher level of inflation, and a somewhat higher level of socialization in our economy, or we can accept a depression.

As long as we have reasonably deregulated markets and a financial system that has severe principal–agent problems, you will have Minsky journeys, forward and back, punctuated by Minsky moments.

Several ounces of prevention
Minsky has been deployed in the context of answering the question of what, if anything, can be done to mitigate the fallout from the current crisis. Less attention has been applied to the corollary point: what, if

anything, can Minsky teach us in order to prevent recurrence of such a situation in the future?

There is little question that he would question the whole deregulatory thrust after the 1970s, insofar as his work ultimately highlighted the inherent instability of capitalism itself and concomitant flaws inherent in the now prevalent notion that it can be self-regulating. Minsky would no doubt argue that the only way to break this pattern was for the government to step in and regulate financial institutions, not simply because the latter are prone to bouts of 'irrational exuberance', but more because it is in the very nature of a modern capitalist economy to move in the direction of speculative excess, which, if left unconstrained by external regulation, could have hugely deleterious consequences.

And this is now becoming recognized within the financial mainstream: groups such as the Financial Stability Forum, a committee of global regulators and supervisors, are currently seeking to force banks to rethink the business models they have used to repackage assets such as mortgages into complex financial securities. If one is going to talk about embracing Minsky from the regulatory perspective, the key is the discussion on restriction of leverage, given that the destabilizing passage from 'hedge' financing to 'Ponzi' (or even 'Ponzi-squared') financing is ultimately exacerbated through the use of excessive leverage.

Our assessment is that Minsky would be against using monetary policy per se to try to stop runaway asset prices, because conventional monetary tools, particularly the use of interest rate manipulation, are less appropriate in an environment characterized by insolvency (brought about by the collapse of Ponzi style financing), rather than illiquidity. 'The Fed cured the equity market bubbles in 1987, 1989, and 2000 with a quick injection of liquidity to ensure the solvency of institutions and to stabilize market-traded equity prices' (Kregel 2008). By contrast, the present crisis presents much greater difficulties, because banks are manifesting 'an extreme liquidity preference' as they attempt to rebuild capital in order to offset real losses. None of the new tools offered by the various liquidity facilities set up by the Federal Reserve can be used to rebuild bank capital.

Which is not to say that Minsky would have opposed the actions taken thus far by the Federal Reserve: he likely would have argued that 'a financial crisis is not the correct time to try to teach markets a lesson by allowing defaults to snowball until a generalized debt deflation and depression can "cleanse" the system' (Wray 2007). Minsky was not a liquidationist, in the Austrian School tradition of Rothbard, Hayek, Mises, and the early Robbins. He would concede that there is a fine line that must be walked when one 'stabilizes an unstable economy', between allowing the worst abusers (and especially the perpetrators of fraud) to lose while protecting the relatively innocent. . . . Because financial markets cannot be allowed to learn lessons 'the hard way,' regulations and oversight must be strengthened to slow the next stampede toward a speculative bubble. Inherent tendencies toward speculative excess and overleveraging could only be managed by maintaining a constantly evolving corridor of stability around market behavior. (Wray 2007)

Dealing with failing financial institutions

Assuming, then, that he was starting with a clean slate, Minsky would likely focus on two measures: 'far more tough-mindedness about leverage (if you are bigger than a certain size, no matter what you are, you are subject to capital constraints' and regulation), 'and an ability for authorities to seize control of on-the-brink institutions before they actually fail' (Smith 2008). Note that Minsky would be unlikely to advocate the current neo-liberal approach championed by those such as former Treasury Secretary Paulson, 'who are biased toward "free markets" instinctively, and therefore prefer to use public money to subsidize private institution take-overs of failing financial firms' (Wray 2007).

More likely, the Swedish alternative would be more consistent with a Minskyan approach: temporary 'nationalization' of failing institutions with a view to eventually returning them to the private sector at a small profit to the Treasury. Indeed, this is what Minsky advocated during the thrift crisis of the 1980s, but the administration of President George H.W. Bush chose industry consolidation and public assumption of bad assets that resulted in Treasury losses, as opposed to allowing the public to participate in any recovery through the assumption of equity and/ or warrants as a quid pro quo for the provision of public funds (Wray 2007).

The objective here would be twofold: If public funds are to be used to rescue a financial institution, it should also get paid back for them. During the New Deal, the Reconstruction Finance Corporation commonly took preferred stock in banks it rescued – and there is no reason why the federal government should not do the same as it bails out Wall Street this time. Minsky would no doubt agree that the Federal Reserve had to stop providing free lunches to people who have told us for years that there is no such thing as a free lunch. And he would likely advocate the establishment of a regulatory framework that creates to the maximum extent possible a situation in which the failure of an individual institution itself (for example, Bear Stearns, Long Term Capital Management), was itself not a source of systemic risk, thereby constraining the growth of moral hazard.

Regulatory reduction of systemic risk
In trying to revive the economy, the Bush Administration, Congress and the Bernanke Federal Reserve groped toward alleviating the worst aspects of the deleveraging phenomenon which invariably follows in the wake of the collapse of Ponzi-style financing, but understandably had less time to focus on preventing a recurrence of the malady in the future. One might argue that the best solution is to prevent manias from developing at all, but that requires vigilance. Since the 1980s, Congress and the executive branch have legislated to weaken federal supervision of Wall Street. The first major step in this journey came during the Clinton Administration, when then Federal Reserve Chairman Greenspan and Treasury Secretary Robert Rubin championed the abolition of the Glass–Steagall Act of 1933, which was meant to prevent a recurrence of the rampant speculation that preceded the Depression. Although the abolition of Glass–Steagall per se could not be said to be responsible for the subsequent growth and collapse of our shadow banking system, it set the philosophic tone for the next 25 years, in which external regulation was replaced with 'self-regulation', a phenomenon now recognized as deregulation. In the words of former Treasury Secretary Lawrence Summers, 'Allowing institutions to determine capital levels based on risk models of their own design is tantamount to letting them set their own capital levels' (Summers 2008).

We now recognize the flaws in this approach, but what is the alternative? Minsky argued that 'apt intervention and institutional structures are necessary for market economies to be successful' (Ferri and Minsky 1991). But those structures have to reflect current reality, not an abstract theoretical framework. Were he alive today, then, Minsky 'rather than waging old debates about tax cuts versus spending increases' would likely be 'discussing how to reform the financial system so that it serves' the broader interests of 'the rest of the economy, instead of feeding off it and destabilizing it. Among the problems at hand: . . . how . . . to discourage excessive risk-taking,' exacerbated through the use of substantial financial leverage; how to constrain 'irresponsible lending without shutting out creditworthy borrowers'; how to assist 'victims of predatory practices without bailing out irresponsible lenders; and hold ratings agencies accountable for their assessments. These are complex issues, with few easy solutions' (Cassidy 2008), but as Minsky argued, 'Economies evolve, and so too must economic policy' (Minsky and Whalen 1996).

Fundamentally, the 'key asymmetry' that has exacerbated the unstable underpinnings of the economy is that the authorities have been 'unable or unwilling, whether for good or bad reasons . . ., to let large leveraged financial institutions collapse' (Buiter 2008). This has been policy since the 1930s and is unlikely to change, certainly not in the current environment where such an abrupt shift would exacerbate current deflationary pressures in the credit system. The September 2008 Austrian School solution for Lehman Brothers has reminded contemporary policy makers and investors of the reason for choosing a containment strategy. On the other hand, there has not been any 'matching inclination to . . . restrain highly profitable financial institutions' that are often the enablers of financial excess (Buiter 2008). Minsky would almost certainly argue that this asymmetry had to be corrected.

Therefore, any large leveraged financial institution, commercial bank, investment bank, hedge fund, private equity fund, SIV, conduit or other legal form central to the creation and ownership of financial assets, would have to be regulated on the basis that the use of leverage should be strictly curtailed in order to minimize the potential recourse to Ponzi-style financing. As Charles Goodhart and Avinash Persaud have argued, these liquidity constraints ought to be imposed counter-cyclically through the implementation of 'contra-cyclical charges – capital charges that rise as the market price of risk falls as measured by financial market prices – and a good starting point for implementation of such charges is the Spanish system of dynamic provisioning' (Persaud 2008; see also, Goodhart and Persaud 2008). Such a measure would be consistent with a Minsky framework as it would undoubtedly mitigate the embrace of Ponzi-style financing or, at the very least, significantly increase the threshold at which it could be realistically adopted.

Minsky would likely note that such rules would not apply simply to banks, but a number of new institutions which have emerged from the deregulatory environment of the past 25 years – hedge funds, bond guarantors, mortgage institutions, and insurance companies. If anything, he would have started from the premise that one had to view the financial system as it was, and not its idealized version, as enunciated in Economics 101 textbooks. As he wrote in 1991, 'To create a worthy successor to the financial system that served us so well between the 1930s and 1980s requires a deeper look at our institutions than we have taken so far'. That is to say, as credit intermediation moved outside the strict confines of the banking system, Minsky would have noted the evolutionary role of the banks themselves: no longer were they primarily dependent on net interest margins for their income. Rather, the vast majority of banking profits were generated from their

proprietary trading desks to generate profits and on . . . affiliates to produce fee and commission income. A major reform of US banking regulation in 1999 – the Gramm–Leach–Bliley (Financial Services Modernization) Act – allowed the creation of bank-holding companies to carry out virtually all types of financial activities. At the same time, the extensive application of the Basel minimum capital standards in 2004 encouraged banks to continue to increase their fee and commission incomes by moving lending to unrelated affiliates, and off their balance sheets. (Kregel 2008)

Recognizing this institutional change, Minsky would likely argue that future regulation remain focused on

> systemically important distinctions, such as maturity mismatches and leverage, and not on out-dated distinctions between banks and non-banks. Institutions without leverage or mismatch should be lightly regulated – if at all – and in particular would not be required to adhere to short-term rules such as mark-to-market accounting or market-price risk sensitivity that contribute to market dislocation. (Persaud 2008)

Those leveraged institutions would no doubt argue against this, saying that it creates an unlevel playing field. Minsky, however, would likely contend that a dynamic financial system such as capitalism is based on diversity, not homogeneity. After all, Minsky often stated that 'capitalism comes in as many varieties as Heinz has pickles' (Papadimitriou and Wray 1998). Moreover, given the notion of the economy as an evolving system, he also stressed the dynamic nature of the institutional structure.

In this vein, Stephen Cecchetti (2007) made this comment on regulated versus OTC markets:

> In September 2006 Amaranth Advisors, a US-based hedge fund specialising in trading energy futures, lost roughly $6bn (£3bn) of the $9bn it was managing and was liquidated. With the exception of its shareholders, most people watched with detached amusement. Eight years earlier, reaction to the impending collapse of Long-Term Capital Management was very different: people were horrified and the financial community sprang into action. One big difference is that Amaranth was engaged in trading natural gas futures contracts on an organised exchange, while LTCM's exposures were concentrated in thousands of interest-rate swaps . . .
>   The difference between futures and swaps is that futures are standardised and exchange-traded through a clearing house. This distinction explains why Amaranth's failure provoked a yawn, while LTCM's triggered a crisis. It suggests that regulators, finance ministries and central bankers should be pushing as many securities on to clearing house-based exchanges as possible. This should be the standard structure in financial markets.

While Amaranth and LTCM were individual firms, Cecchetti's observations 'are generalizable to the behavior of their respective markets as well. Standardized contracts, exchanges, and clearinghouses are three of the primary institutions through which the government regulates and supervises futures trading. They have been successful in maintaining functional markets despite tremendous leverage and volatility' (Cecchetti 2007).

Aligning incentive structures

Minsky would further argue that incentivising long-term investors to behave long-term meant that there would be more buyers when the inevitable Minsky moment occurred, and over-indebted investors were forced to sell even their solid investments to make good on their loans. Without such a population of long-term investors, sharp declines in financial markets, and the consequent demand for cash in the wake of market crashes, will invariably force the hand of central bankers and perpetuate moral hazard.

Minsky always recognized that bankers were inherently skeptical of a borrower's ability to estimate future cash flows and, hence, demanded certain margins of safety. In classic conditions of steady expansion, 'the universe of borrowing experiences becomes increasingly positive', and rising cash flows often validate increasingly aggressive lending postures at declining margins of safety (Kregel 2008). But in a securitized world in which banks no longer primarily service business lending, it becomes increasingly difficult to assess the actual margin of safety inherent in the loan structure. Banking profits become a function of a more transaction-oriented financial system based on the ability of their proprietary desks to generate income through fees and commissions.

At the same time, as Jan Kregel (2008) has noted, 'the extensive application of the Basel minimum capital standards in 2004 encouraged banks to continue to increase their fee commission incomes by moving lending to unrelated affiliates, and off their balance sheets', The resultant 'originate and distribute' model has come apart at the seams, in part because the margin of safety demanded by bankers has become virtually impossible to monitor as it moved off balance sheet and the external credit agencies tasked to rate the paper lacked the accumulated knowledge of borrowers that invariably develops in a conventional long-term banking relationship. That, coupled with their inherent conflicts of interest (being paid by the party who was distributing the product), and consequent inability to rate the underlying products' creditworthiness properly, invariably meant that 'the ephemeral margins of safety built into these structures declined and their fragility increased' (Kregel 2008).

It would be naïve to assume that such practices will continue to the same degree in the future, but recognizing the existing structure, Minsky would no doubt incentivize the credit intermediaries to build in greater cushions of safety by

> requiring banks to pay an insurance premium to taxpayers against the risk the taxpayer will be required to bail them out. If such a market could be created, it would not only incentivize good banking and push the focus of regulation

away from process to outcomes, but it would provide an incentive for banks to be less of a systemic risk. Today, banks have an incentive to be 'too big to fail,' as a bailout is then guaranteed. The right response to Citibank's routine failure to anticipate its credit risks is not for it to keep on getting bigger so that it can remain too big to fail, but for it to wither away under rising insurance premiums paid to taxpayers [in the event that it continues to undertake credit practices that lead to greater financial fragility and systemic risk]. (Persaud 2008)

Conclusion

The financial system has been structured to make credit too cheap, and financing structures too prone to financial instability. There is nothing that can be done to eliminate the inevitability of financial risk; it is inherent in a market economy where large-scale durable assets must be financed, as Minsky noted on several occasions. But fragility must be mitigated by systemic policies that Minsky would identify as being outside the purview of the financial sector itself – external and independent regulatory bodies were required to constrain the ability of financial excesses to develop to the point of introducing systemic risk. In the wake of a serious outbreak of financial instability, Minsky was always clear that fiscal policy should play a central role to support income and employment so debt service disruptions could be reduced. Minsky also advocated a role for the central bank in stabilizing asset prices in order to avoid a debt deflation spiral. Lender of last resort, or even market maker of last resort, roles were also appropriate methods for central banks to short circuit debt deflation dynamics. In the extreme, if necessary, public take over of impaired financial institutions may also have a role in stabilizing the economy. Reorienting incentive structures to insure adequate credit analysis, sufficient margins of safety, and a longer term orientation of investors must also be a focus of the public and private sector. This is the challenge ahead which awaits policy makers as they confront the deficiencies in today's global financial system. Fortunately, we can stand on the shoulders of this particular economic giant to help navigate through the storms ahead.

References

Buiter, W. (2008), 'Restraining asset and credit booms', Maverecon Blog, May 25.
Cassidy, J. (2008), 'The Minsky moment', *The New Yorker*, February 4.
Cecchetti, S. (2007), 'A better way to organise securities markets', *Financial Times*, October 4.
Ferri, P. and H.P. Minsky (1991), 'Market processes and thwarting systems', Working Paper No. 64, Levy Economics Institute of Bard College, Annandale-on-Hudson, New York, November.
Goodhart, C.A. and A. Persaud (2008), 'How to avoid the next crash', *Financial Times*, January 30.
Gross, B. (2004), 'The last vigilante', Investment Outlook, PIMCO, Newport Beach, February.

Kregel, J. (2008), 'Minsky's cushions of safety', Public Policy Brief No. 93, Levy Economics Institute of Bard College, Annandale-on-Hudson, New York, January.

Minsky, H.P. (1982), 'The financial instability hypothesis: a restatement', in Minsky, *Can 'It' Happen Again? Essays on Instability and Finance*, Armonk, New York: M.E. Sharpe.

Minsky, H.P. (1991), 'The rationale for the conference: an agenda for the good financial economy', remarks prepared for delivery at Levy Economics Institute of Bard College, Annandale-on-Hudson, New York, November 21.

Minsky, H.P. and C.J. Whalen (1996), 'Economic insecurity and the institutional prerequisites for successful capitalism', Working Paper No. 165, Levy Economics Institute of Bard College, Annandale-on-Hudson, New York, May.

Papadimitriou, D.B. and L.R. Wray (1998), 'The economic contributions of Hyman Minsky: varieties of capitalism and institutional reform', *Review of Political Economy*, **10**(2), 199–225.

Persaud, A. (2008), 'Opinion: the unbearable unsuitability of financial regulation', *Financial Week*, May 12.

Smith, Y. (2008), 'Restraining asset and credit booms', Naked Capitalism Blog, May 26.

Summers, L. (2008), 'Six principles for a new regulatory order', *Financial Times*, June 2.

Wray, L.R. (2007), 'Lessons from the Subprime Meltdown', Working Paper No. 522, Levy Economics Institute of Bard College, Annandale-on-Hudson, New York, December.

7 It's the right moment to embrace the Minsky model

Robert J. Barbera and Charles L. Weise

Introduction

US monetary policy from 1979 through 2000 delivered the world an important victory. The Paul Volcker/Alan Greenspan eras broke the back of the wage-price inflation dynamic that crippled the global economy in the 1970s. That victory was, however, misunderstood by mainstream economists. The defeat of the *Great Inflation* led to proclamation that the US had achieved a *Great Moderation*. Trade cycle worries, the story went, had been substantially reduced. Intelligent policymakers, corporate heads and investors would do best if they focused on long term issues. Boom and bust cycles remained, but their amplitudes were small and their likely appearance rare – so stick to the long term and you were likely to be on the right road.

Excitement about the *Great Moderation* elevated the status of the Federal Reserve Board. At the White House conference on the new economy, held on 4 April 2000, Alan Greenspan sat alongside President Clinton. In the eyes of most conference participants Alan Greenspan, not President Clinton, was the celebrity – the Maestro, as Bob Woodward called him.

Times change. As the first decade of the new millennium winds down, Ben Bernanke, the new Fed Chairman, is under intense scrutiny. The Chairman and his colleagues from mid-2007 through fall-2008 have confronted clear evidence of substantial US economic retrenchment laid alongside building inflationary pressures. Most commentators acknowledge that 2008 will likely be labeled a recession once official arbiters have a complete picture of the year's economic performance.

The crisis has unfolded in the credit markets. Over the twelve months ending mid-2008 the Fed felt compelled to engineer a forced merger for Bear Sterns, and award all investment banks access to the discount window. In addition, the US treasury was forced to put Fannie Mae and Freddie Mac under Federal control. These extraordinary steps were taken in response to the metastasizing problems tied to lending practices in the US residential real estate market. With the benefit of hindsight, it became clear that many US financial services companies spent several years writing home mortgages that depended upon rising home prices. Once house prices reversed direction the colossal US real estate edifice began to crumble, taking financial markets along with it.

This chapter will make the case that Alan Greenspan and more generally US Fed policymakers failed to award asset prices their just due between 1998 and 2008. During quiescent moments Fed officials embraced the standard orthodoxy that market prices provide the best guess available about the future. Alan Greenspan, in particular, emphasized that the Fed *had no ability to out guess the market*.

During financial system mayhem, however, Fed policymakers were compelled to do just that. By their actions Fed policymakers revealed that they understood the dangers that arise during Minsky Moments. To calm financial waters, without acknowledging Minsky insights, Fed policymakers established a practice of treating such events as 'special circumstances'. They have been labeled 'liquidity crises' or 'confidence crises'. Fed policymakers were then free to treat these events as isolated developments requiring unusual, one-time, divergences from the normal conduct of monetary policy. Fed officials, in effect, only embraced Minsky insights 'in the moment'.

The Fed's ad hoc strategy introduced a fundamental asymmetry into monetary policy. This asymmetry contributed to the process that put the US financial system, mid-2008, on very shaky ground. An explicit focus on financial markets, both on the way up and on the way down, is long overdue. Monetary policy will improve if it treats asset markets symmetrically. In other words, the Fed must stop merely responding to Minsky Moments and begin to conduct monetary policy consistent with the Minsky model.

To make the case for thinking about Minsky notions throughout the business cycle, this chapter first documents the poor predictive powers of standard Taylor rule equations over the past 10 years. We then suggest three successive adjustments to Taylor's Equation. The final equation we offer up, a Minsky/Wicksell Modified Taylor Rule (MWMTR) captures important swings in monetary policy over the past 10 years. The MWMTR, however, fails to capture all monetary policy swings. Why? Because Fed policy, 1998–2008 was wildly asymmetric in its treatment of asset prices.

We introduce a macroeconomic framework that rationalizes the MWMTR. We argue that the right way to think about monetary policy involves mapping out the dynamics between a changing fed funds rate, shifting risky real rates and evolving expectations about real economy investment opportunities. Our critical conclusion? Changing risk appetites over the course of the business cycle materially affect borrowing costs for real economy investment, and Fed policy needs to take account of these shifts throughout the business cycle.

Rules are for fools?

H.L. Mencken once remarked that 'for every problem, there is a solution that is simple, neat, and wrong' (Mencken 1927). He could easily have been talking about economists' pursuit of a one size fits all rule to guide monetary policy. We all know the ideological motivation behind efforts to make monetary policy automatic. Free markets, mainstream economic theory insists, will get us where we need to go. Ergo, the less room for meddling by the central bank, the better. And we also know why central bankers speak respectfully about rules. When they judge that policy needs to move in a politically unpopular direction, they can find some cover by claiming that the decision was ordained by a rule.

Paul Volcker, a giant among central bankers, brilliantly exploited this trick. When Volcker took over in August of 1979 he announced that money supply growth targets would dictate open market operations. By declaring that the Fed was eschewing interest rate targets for money growth trajectories Volcker could claim, with a straight face peering out from a waft of cigar smoke, that the ensuing spectacular rise for interest rates was an unfortunate burden, but one that he had no immediate way to remedy – given his need to adhere to his self-imposed money target straitjacket.

After the collapse of any recognizable linkage between money stock growth rates and growth rates for nominal economy trajectories, Stanford's John Taylor came to the rescue. The Taylor Rule arrived in the early 1990s. Taken literally, it says that central bankers have a new way to put monetary policy on autopilot – the end of money stock targeting notwithstanding.

The Taylor Rule and headline versus core inflation

John Taylor's elegant equation roughly reproduced Fed policy decisions over the 1987-93 years with a bare minimum of explanatory variables. But as H.L. Mencken reminds us, life is never simple. And the Taylor Rule's record, from the late 1990s, has been very spotty.

The 1998–2008 track record for Taylor's original equation (we make one modification to Taylor's equation, replacing the potential/actual GDP deviations with the Non-Accelerating Inflation Rate of Unemployment (NAIRU)/actual unemployment divergences (see Appendix)) is presented in Figure 7.1. Clearly, the Taylor Rule had a tough 10 years. Part of the problem reflected the wild swings for energy prices registered from 1998 through 2008. Oil prices plunged, falling below $10 per barrel, in mid-

Figure 7.1   The Taylor rule fails, as surging and volatile energy prices implied volatile, and very high, federal funds rates

1998. This had the effect of driving headline inflation well below the core rate. Sharp leaps for oil prices, in contrast, were the rule over the first eight years of the new decade, with oil prices mid-2008 near $150 per barrel. This wild ride for energy prices put headline Consumer Price Index (CPI) changes into volatile territory. Taylor Rule calculations, as Figure 7.1 shows, called for volatile swings for fed funds despite more muted swings for underlying price pressures. Fed policymakers, in response, elevated the importance of core inflation. As a consequence, as Figure 7.1 makes obvious, an equation predicting the funds rate that depended upon headline inflation looked for more volatile swings for the funds rate. Moreover, on average it looked for substantially higher funds rate, over the last eight years.

Nonetheless, as Figure 7.2 reveals, a Taylor Rule federal funds trajectory using the core CPI also does a poor job of catching actual swings in the overnight rate. In particular, a core CPI generated Taylor Rule fails to anticipate the intensity of late 1990s tightening. It fails to predict aggressive Fed ease in 2001 to 2002. And quite spectacularly, both the core CPI Taylor Rule and a Taylor Rule using headline CPI, from fall 2007 through spring 2008, fail to anticipate the dramatic ease put in place by the Bernanke-led Fed.

Indeed, blind faith in the Taylor Rule, or a Core CPI modified Taylor rule, could lead one to the conclusion that Fed policymakers lost their minds in late 2007 early 2008. It is instructive, therefore, to reflect upon the fact that mainstream commentators in the world's financial markets came

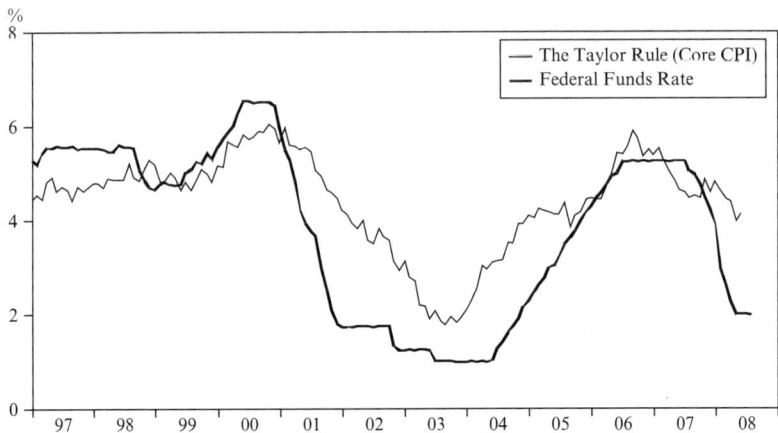

*Figure 7.2   A core CPI Taylor rule, in contrast, is slow to anticipate
moves to ease*

to a common explanation for the plunging fed funds rate through spring
2008. In the *Economist*, in the *Wall Street Journal*, the *New York Times*
and of all places the *New Yorker* (see Figure 7.3), it was acknowledged
that aggressive Fed ease was unfolding because the Minsky Moment had
arrived.

From rules are for fools to our rule is better than your rule
The power of the Minsky Moment, in the eyes of the many, to predict
Fed policy invites a simple question. Can we redefine the Taylor Rule in a
fashion that captures Minsky Moment insights and therefore does a better
job of tracking the funds rate over the past 10 years? After all, it is easy to
scoff at one line equations that purport to capture all essential information
needed to divine monetary policy moves. But in the current climate of retrospective thinking about the Greenspan years, reconstructing the Taylor
rule, imbuing it with Minsky-like insights, could well prove instructive.
Thus, as a vehicle for retrospective analysis, we offer up the MWMTR.
This equation, a reworking of Taylor's effort, does a much better job of
explaining the past 10 years of Fed funds movements. And it does so,
mostly, by including a term in the equation for Minsky Moments.

But the equation delivers more than that. It is our contention that the
MWMTR reveals that US monetary policy, for at least a decade, has
been clearly schizophrenic. Once we remind ourselves of Fed policymaker
justification for responding as they do during Minsky Moments, we lay
bare the Fed's conflicted stance toward financial markets. Simply put,

Source: Reproduced by kind permission of the artist.

Figure 7.3   *Illustration by Tom Bachtell, originally published in The New Yorker, 4 February 2008*

our equation confirms what many commentators have noted. Fed actions 1998 through 2008, responded to flights of anguish, but ignored flights of fancy. And part of the wreckage in place in 2008 can be laid at the doorstep of that unambiguous inconsistency, and the moral hazard that it helped to create.

What did we do to the Taylor rule to make it confess? We made two adjustments, one quite palatable to mainstream economic thinking, the other controversial. Our two adjustments look to market estimates for neutral real short rates and to market attitudes about tail risks. In combination they allow us to roughly reproduce 10 years of Fed policy and, at the same time to reveal one profound inconsistency.

From the number '2' to a Wicksellian neutral real short rate
Taylor's initial equation included a term for the neutral real short-term interest rate. In one of the grandest economic generalizations imaginable, Taylor embraced one value for this economic variable. The neutral real short rate, he decided, was '2'. How does '2' stand up to the past 100 years of US economic history? As Table 7.1 reveals, it has mostly been honored

Table 7.1   Real short rates: neighborhoods shift over time

	Inflation	Interest rate	Real rate
1920–29	1.0	3.8	2.8
1930–40	−5.0	0.6	5.6
1941–54	4.7	0.9	−3.8
1955–65	1.4	2.9	1.5
1966–74	5.6	5.6	0.0
1975–80	8.8	6.3	−2.5
1981–90	4.5	7.7	3.2
1991–2000	2.7	5.0	2.3
2000–07	2.7	3.0	0.3

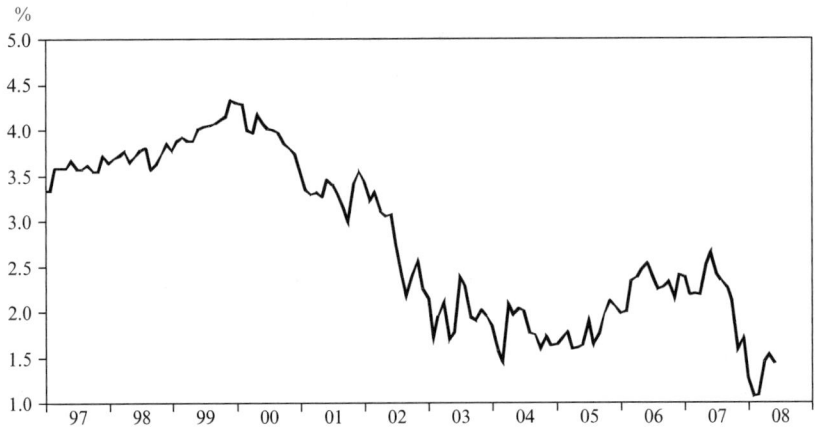

Figure 7.4   The long-term TIPS yield: a window on volatile real return expectations, clouded by monetary policy decisions (TIPS yield, 10-year)

in the breach. Attitudes about long-term trajectories for economic growth, long term real return opportunities for investors and regulatory regimes clearly change over time. In response, the average real short rate has changed, more times than not, from economic cycle to economic cycle.

With the advent of Treasury Inflation Protected Securities (TIPS) bonds we now have the ability to extract changing market opinion about long-term real return opportunities. The easiest way to get a fix on real return expectations is to look at the yield on 10-year TIPS (see Figure 7.4). We need to remind ourselves, however, that if we believe monetary policy matters, we must expect that it operates via financial markets. That, in turn means that the yield on 10-year TIPS is influenced by the Fed determined overnight interest rate. We can view the 10-year TIPS yield as a blend of expectations about Fed-engineered real short rates and the market's evolving sense of what constitutes an equilibrium real long-term interest rate.

Fed policymakers confront a similar issue when they look to TIPS instruments as indicators of long-term inflation expectations. The Fed's preferred long-term inflation indicator is teased out of TIPS bonds of different maturities. Taking a page out of the Fed's playbook, we infer the five-year forward real yield, by subtracting the five-year TIPS yield from the 10-year TIPS yield. We assert, further, that the five-year forward TIPS yield is largely free of short run Fed policy expectations.

The five-year forward TIPS yield gets us close to a market measure of the Wicksellian natural rate. We simply need to add a spread term to the inferred TIPS rate and we have a real time estimate of the Wicksellian long rate. Over the 1960 through 2008 period the spread between Baa corporate bonds and treasury 10-year notes has been 1.8 percentage points. We therefore add 1.8 percentage points to our five-year forward yield and we have an estimate at any moment for the Wicksellian neutral real long rate.

We posit that the neutral real risk free short rate relates directly to the capital market determined Wicksellian natural long rate. If the world comes to believe that the natural real long rate is 7 per cent, up from 5 per cent, clearly the neutral real fed funds rate will be higher in that world as well.

We propose that you can estimate the value for the neutral real short rate simply. Return to the implied equilibrium risk free real long rate – by subtracting the spread term from the Wicksellian rate – and subtract an estimate of the average term premium. This simply adjusts for the fact that the yield curve, historically, exhibits a positive slope. We use the average term premium from 1960 through 2008, 82 basis points.

We now have a capital markets determined assessment of the neutral real short-term interest rate. We use it to replace Taylor's static value of '2'. In symbolic terms, we replace '2' with '$W-(\tau+\sigma)$' (see Appendix). Figure 7.5 tracks the measured neutral real short rate over the 10 years.

What does invoking Wicksell and the natural rate notion afford us? Replay the late 1990s Brave New World euphoria. Greenspan and other members of the Federal Open Market Committee (FOMC) noted that the boom in technology investment had lifted notions of sustainable real growth, real investment opportunities, and equilibrium real risk free long rates. Accordingly, they went on, the neutral risk free rate had likely moved higher. By replacing the number '2' with '$W-(\tau+\sigma)$' we have a

%
5.0

4.0

3.0

2.0

1.0

98   99   00   01   02   03   04   05   06   07   08

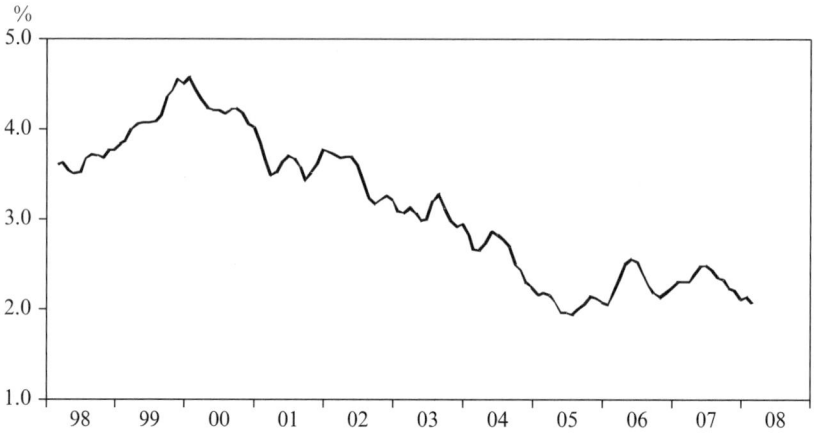

Figure 7.5   The forward TIPS yield: exuberant, amid the 1990s technology boom, plunging amid tech bust-cum 'global savings glut' (TIPS yield, 5-year forward)

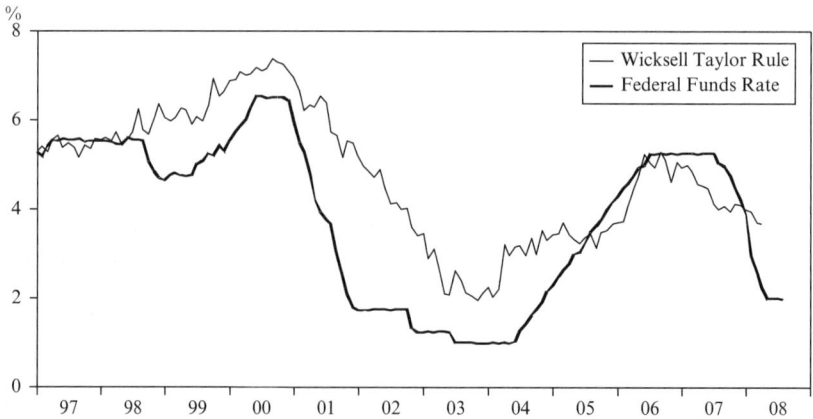

%
8

—— Wicksell Taylor Rule
—— Federal Funds Rate

6

4

2

0

97   98   99   00   01   02   03   04   05   06   07   08

Note: Wicksell rates. Jan.–July of 1997 are estimated. No TIPS existed, therefore interpolation was necessary.

Figure 7.6   The Wicksell modified Taylor rule anticipates late 1990s tightening, but systematically misses big ease

market driven measure of the neutral real short rate. A core CPI Taylor Rule with this adjustment tracks the tightening regime that unfolded in 1999 through 2000 more closely than does the traditional Taylor equation (see Figure 7.6).

Spread (%), 3-Month MA

Figure 7.7   *Risky–risk free credit spreads: a critical input for monetary policy, corporate bond yield, BAA minus 10-year treasury note yield*

What's missing? Minsky insights, compliments of risky/risk-free spreads

What remains to be explained, of course, are the moves to ease, in 1998, 2001 through 2002, and mid-2007 through mid-2008. What prompted the Fed to ease in each of these cases, in conflict with standard Taylor rule calculations? Panic in asset markets led Fed officials to conclude that risks to the financial system were large and growing. Attending these financial system risks were increasing concerns about the potential for extremely unfavorable real economy developments. Thus 'fat tails' in periods of mayhem, invite aggressive ease.

As a simple proxy for the state of fear in the system, we enter our Minsky term, credit spreads (see Figure 7.7). We compare treasury and BAA yields. We label 180 basis points a neutral credit spread. Deviations from the neutral spread justify changes in the target funds rate.

How does our MWMTR perform? As Figure 7.8 reveals, the revised formula does pretty well. It captures the tightening in 1999 through 2000, compliments of the Wicksell term. It looks for ease in 1998 and big ease, 2001 through 2002. Most tellingly, it does an excellent job of anticipating the 2007 through 2008 moves to easier money, a feat that the Wicksell modified Taylor Equation fails to perform.

As importantly, however, the MWMTR looks for the Fed to begin normalizing interest rates starting in the middle of 2003, a full year before

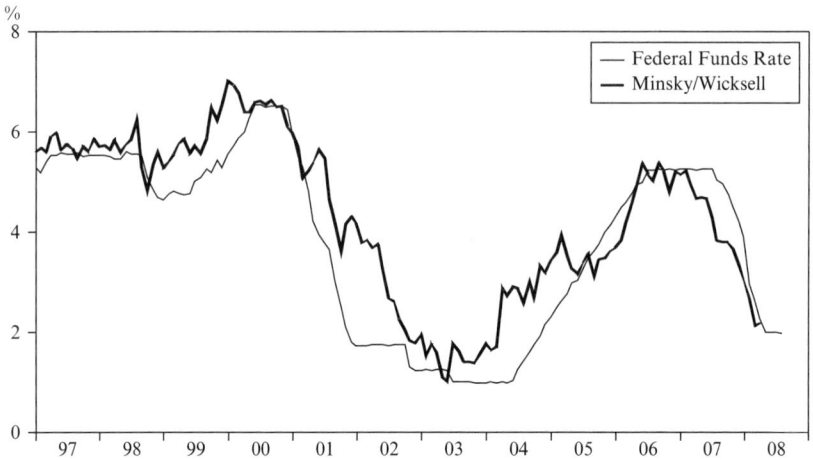

Note: Wicksell rates. Jan.–July of 1997 are estimated. No TIPS existed, therefore interpolation was necessary.

Figure 7.8   The Minsky/Wicksell Modified Taylor Rule: a better fit for the past two cycles

the Fed actually began raising rates. Does that mean the MWMTR is fundamentally flawed? We think not. Instead we think it is the conduct of monetary policy, over the ten-year period that has been flawed – a consequence of acknowledging Minsky Moments instead of embracing a Minsky model.

Replacing IS/LM curves with IS/TS curves
It is at this point in our story that we think it becomes important to tie some simple macro theory to swings in the Wicksell and Minsky terms. To that end we need to explicitly, if somewhat simplistically, describe the Fed's money transmission mechanism. The model we sketch out here is described in more detail in Weise (2007) and Weise and Barbera (2009).

We start by accepting the New Keynesian notion that the Fed sets the nominal short rate with an eye toward influencing the risky real long rate. The real risk-free long rate is a weighted average of the current federal funds rate adjusted to account for a term premium, and the Wicksellian natural risk-free rate of interest. This formulation, which is derived in the papers cited above, is consistent with the expectations theory of the term structure of interest rates:

$$R = \omega(f + \tau) + (1 - \omega)W$$

where *r* is the risk-free real long-term interest rate, *f* is the real federal funds rate, τ is a constant term premium, and *W* is the risk-free Wicksellian natural rate of interest. The real long-term interest rate is affected by the current federal funds rate through the first term. The second term embodies the assumption that in the long run the real long-term interest rate is expected to be equal to the Wicksellian rate, which anchors the long end of the term structure. Then ω is a weighting factor reflecting the length of time (relative to the term of the long-term bond) that interest rates are expected to depart from their long-run expected level. We define the neutral real federal funds rate to be the rate that corresponds to the Wicksellian rate.

$$f^* = W - \tau$$

According to the above equation, when $f = f^*$, $R = W$.

The real risky long-term interest rate is the risk-free rate plus a risk premium or credit spread term. Letting *S* be the spread term, we can write

$$S = \sigma + \eta$$

where σ is the mean value of *S* (assumed constant) and η is a stochastic credit spread 'shock' term with mean zero. Adding *S* to both sides of the equation for the risk-free rate and rearranging gives us an equation relating the real risky long-term rate of interest to the real federal funds rate and the Wicksellian natural risky rate of interest:

$$r = \omega(f + \tau + \sigma) + (1 - \omega)W^* + \eta$$

where $r = R + S$ is the real risky long-term interest rate and W^* is the real risky Wicksellian natural rate. We refer to this equation as the TS equation.

The second half of the model, the IS curve, is conventional: the output gap is negatively related to the difference between the real risky long-term interest rate and the (risky) Wicksellian natural rate:

$$y = a - b(r - W^*)$$

where *y* is the output gap, *a* is autonomous expenditures, and *b* represents the sensitivity of demand to changes in the interest rate.

We can use a graphical depiction to present, in stylized fashion, the events that transpired from 1999 through 2000. In 1999 much of the globe embraced the notion that the US had embarked upon a Brave New World

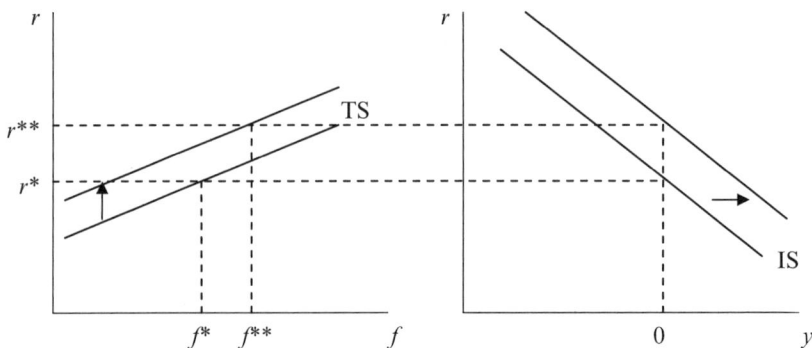

Figure 7.9   Brave new world

of technology driven boom. This Wicksellian event was reflected in a sharp shift to the right for the IS curve and an upward shift for the TS curve.

Again, the IS curve shifts to the right. This straightforwardly reflects a shift in expectations as people come to believe that the Brave New world (BNW) offers up substantially improved investment opportunities at a given interest rate.

Simultaneously, the TS curve shifts upward. How so? Refer back to Figure 7.5. The equilibrium Wicksellian rate climbs sharply, late in the 1990s, a function of the belief in expanded investment opportunities and higher real growth rates. This, directly, lifts the TS curve.

This BNW technology shock is captured by both our Taylor Rule equation and in our IS/TS graphical depiction (see Figure 7.9). IS shifts to the right. TS shifts upward reflecting rising W. Fed raises f from f^* to f^{**}. Both r^* and f^* are higher.

What does this imply for the Fed? The federal funds rate rises as the neutral real short rate climbs with the Wicksellian neutral rate. And much to the delight of efficient market theorists, the Fed does best by simply following the market's lead. Do what the TIPS yield tells you, in a Wicksell modified Taylor Rule, and you get to the right place (see Figure 7.6).

Now, however, we need to explain the swoon for federal funds, visible in 2001 through 2002 and again, mid-2007 through mid-2008. We begin with the 2001 through 2002 experience. When the BNW notion went bust financial markets began to violently re-price. What happened to the market's notion of equilibrium real interest rates? Look again at Figure 7.5, our imputed W falls reflecting newfound pessimism about investment opportunities. This drop for W can be interpreted as a shift left for the IS curve.

What about the TS curve? In a world in which central bankers had an

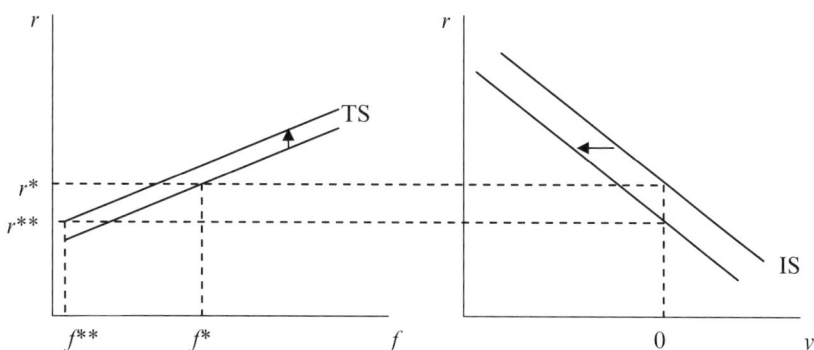

Figure 7.10   Minsky moment

easy life the TS curve would shift down sharply, lowering the risky real long rate and signaling to the Fed that the funds rate needs to fall commensurately. But we live in no such place. Instead we operate in a system where major disappointments, at business cycle turning points simultaneously drive real return expectations *and* risk appetites sharply lower. As a consequence, the risky real rate rises even as the conventional wisdom comes to believe that investment opportunities have fallen precipitously. In other words, the TS curve shifts upward just as the IS curve has shifted to the left compliments of surging risky/risk free spreads (see Figure 7.7). And that, of course sets the economy and the markets up for an adverse feedback loop that can end in catastrophe (see Figure 7.10).

Except, of course, that since the 1930s, 'It' hasn't. Why not? The answer, with all due respect to Mencken, is simple. The Fed understands its role as lender of last resort. In our diagram, the Fed recognizes that the sharp widening of spreads implies a sharp shift leftward for the IS curve, and it knows that it needs to ease with abandon to counter sharp spread widening and get risky real rates lower (see Figure 7.10). IS shifts left, TS shifts up because rise in spread exceeds fall in *W*. Fed recognizes fall for *W* has not lowered risky rate. Fed eases aggressively.

From macro theory to monetary policy critique
We like the fact that our MWMTR does a reasonable job of capturing the Fed's reactions during Minsky Moments. But the depiction tells us more. Greenspan's commentary, in both 1998 and 2001, amounts to labeling market moves as driven by 'unwarranted fears'. That sounds to our ears like an act of heresy for someone who embraces the wisdom of markets. And our simple diagram reveals that taking your cue from market implied neutral risk-free rates – a passive Wicksellian approach – is doomed

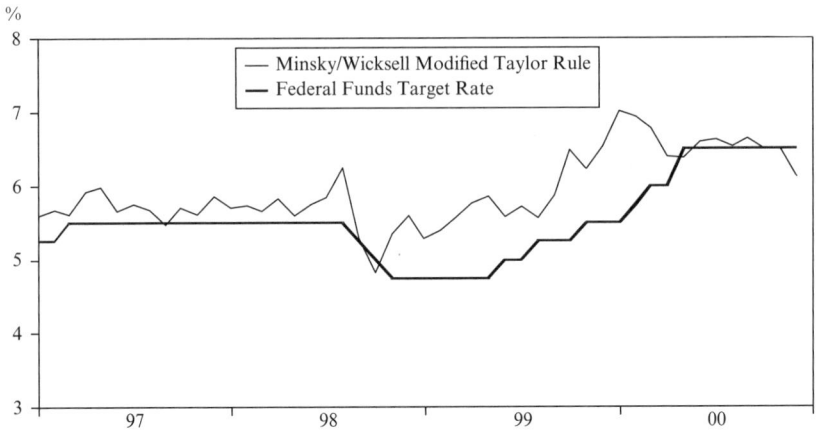

Note: Wicksell rates. Jan.–July of 1997 are estimated. No TIPS existed, therefore interpolation was necessary.

Figure 7.11   The Minsky/Wicksell Modified Taylor Rule judges 1997–99 as an easy money episode

to failure. At crucial moments like 1998, 2001 through 2002 and 2007 through 2008 the Fed needs to actively ease to counter system wide risks in an increasingly bearish backdrop.

This brings us back to Alan Greenspan and monetary policy over the decade. In both words and actions Alan Greenspan, in moments of crisis, made it clear that he was willing to reject market assessments. Unwarranted fears were met by aggressive ease. How, then, do we square these actions with Greenspan's oft articulated refusal to out think market judgments on the way up? Greenspan, with a straight face and no cigar smoke, insisted that the Fed had no tools available to judge whether markets were moving toward excesses.

It is at this juncture, we believe, that our MWMTR becomes most useful. By introducing spreads to the Taylor Rule we see that Minsky insight giveth and taketh away. From 1997 through 1999, super tight credit spreads implied higher fed funds than the rates that were in place (see Figure 7.11). Likewise, the pace of interest rate increase implied by the MWMTR, 2003 through 2005, was much quicker than the actual rise for Fed funds (see Figure 7.12).

What, then, does our MWMTR tell us? What most of us have known for some time. The Greenspan-led Fed had an asymmetric attitude toward efficient markets. It applied no resistance to markets when they wanted to go up. It countermanded market forces, when players' actions were

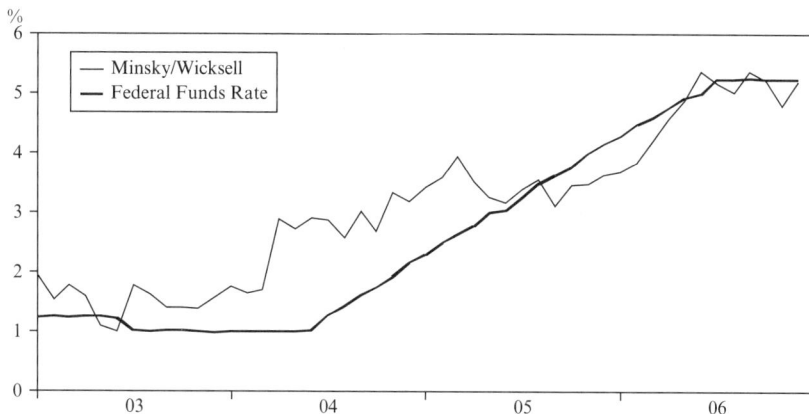

Figure 7.12   The Minsky/Wicksell Modified Taylor Rule suggests that Fed tightening, 2003–05, was delayed

pushing markets down. This asymmetry invited moral hazard. And some of the woes in place in 2008, no doubt were a consequence of this schizophrenia about rational markets.

Toward a more expansive definition of 'excess'
Stepping back from the particular dynamics of the decade 1998–2008 in the US we know history tells us that destabilizing imbalances in an economy can arise with little or no wage or price inflation. Wage and price pressures were absent in the US in the 1920s. In Japan, in the years leading up to 1990, inflation, excluding energy, remained moderate. Nonetheless, the US economy in the 1930s and the Japanese economy in the 1990s suffered extraordinary setbacks. In both cases spectacular asset price increases traveled hand in hand with inflation free booms. Subsequently, asset price implosions doomed each economy to a decade of economic contraction and price deflation.

A central bank exclusively focused upon wages and prices would have failed to react to the excesses that developed in the US in the late 1920s and in Japan in the late 1980s. Therefore, asset price excess, despite its devilishly hard identification, must be one of the excesses that a central bank pays attention to.

Alan Greenspan, to be sure, rejected this view during his tenure at the US Fed. And Ben Bernanke, during the 2003–06 run up for house prices, extended Greenspan's policy of refusing to outguess market judgments. Their collective refusal is completely consistent with mainstream economic theory. Financial markets set prices based upon investors' willingness to wager their own financial fortunes. As the saying goes, the forecasts embedded in financial markets 'are the best forecasts money can buy'.

But the Greenspan/Bernanke era, because it refused to respond to financial system excesses, until they revealed themselves in real economy pressures, oversaw a succession of asset market bubbles that required increasingly large financial system rescue operations. The blind spot in Federal Reserve Board thinking, unfortunately, reflects deep-seated economic ideology. Economists at the Fed, on Wall Street and in other economic policy jobs, embrace the idea that market forces lead us in the right direction. To acknowledge that the free flow of money in a capitalist system leads inexorably to excess and recession, on the face of it, sounds like a fantastic economic heresy. It need not be. How hard is it to say these words?

Capitalism is the best economic system. But it is not perfect. Its bias toward taking ever greater risks, as expansions age, requires Central Bank action, just as its periodic flight from risky endeavors also demands central bank action.

In simplest terms, Fed policymakers must be willing to take a pragmatic approach to asset markets, responding to giddy markets on the way up as well as despondent markets as prices come crashing down. Embracing essential Minsky insights across the business cycle, rather than only during crisis moments, makes good economic sense.

To suggest, however, that strict adherence to our MWMTR will prevent future episodes of financial system excess is, of course, absurd. Minsky's greatest insight was appreciation of the paradox of Goldilocks. Benign real economy circumstances invite financial innovation, increased leverage, and ultimately financial instability. But the amplitudes of asset market boom–bust cycles, may be tempered, somewhat, if Fed officials are willing to respond to financial system signals both on the way down and on the way up. It's the right moment to embrace the Minsky model.

Bibliography

Barbera, R.J. and Charles L. Weise (2008), 'Has Greenspan's conundrum morphed into Bernanke's calamity? A Minsky/Wicksell modified Taylor rule', in *Conference Proceedings: 17th Annual Hyman P. Minsky Conference on the State of the U.S. and World Economies*, Levy Economics Institute of Bard College, Annandale-on-Hudson, New York, April.
Greenspan, A. (2000), 'Technological innovation and the economy', Keynote Speech, The White House Conference on the New Economy, Washington DC.
Krugman, P. (2002), 'My economic plan', *New York Times* (October 4), p. 27.
Mehrling, P. (2000), 'Minsky and modern finance', *Journal of Portfolio Management*, (Winter), 81–8.
Mencken, H.L. (1927), *Selected Prejudices*, New York: A.A. Knopf.
Minsky, H.P. (1975), *John Maynard Keynes*, New York: Columbia University Press.
Minsky, H.P. (1986), *Stabilizing an Unstable Economy: A Twentieth Century Fund Report*, New Haven and London: Yale University Press.

Taylor, J.B. (1993), 'Discretion versus policy rules in practice', *Carnegie-Rochester Series on Public Policy*, **39**, 195–214.
Tymoigne, E. (2006), 'The Minskyan system, Part I', Working Paper No. 452, Levy Economics Institute of Bard College, Annandale-on-Hudson, New York.
Weise, C.L. (2007), 'A simple Wicksellian macroeconomic model', *The B.E. Journal of Macroeconomics*, **7**(1), 214–33.
Weise, C.L. and R.J. Barbera (2009) 'Minsky meet Wicksell: using the Wicksellian model to understand the twenty-first century business cycle', in G. Fontana and M. Setterfield (eds), *Macroeconomic Theory and Macroeconomic Pedagogy*, London and New York: Palgrave Macmillan, forthcoming.
Wray, L.R. (2007), 'Lessons from the subprime meltdown', Working Paper No. 522, Levy Economics Institute of Bard College, Annandale-on-Hudson, New York.

Appendix 7A: Taylor Rule equations

- Taylor's original formula (Taylor 1993):

$$f_t^{TR} = \pi_{t,12} + 0.5^* (\pi_{t,12} - 2) + 0.5^* (y^* - y_t) + 2 \qquad (7A.1)$$

- Taylor's equation modified using NAIRU, invoking Okun's Law (Figure 7.1):

$$f_t^{TR} = \pi_{t,12} + 0.5^* (\pi_{t,12} - 2) + (u^* - u_t) + 2 \qquad (7A.2)$$

- Taylor modified equation, using core CPI (Figure 7.2):

$$f_t^{TR} = \pi_{t,12}^c + 0.5 (\pi_{t,12}^c - 2) + (u^* - u_t) + 2 \qquad (7A.3)$$

- Taylor equation, additionally modified replacing '2' with Wicksellian natural rate (Figure 7.6):

$$f_t^{TR} = \pi_{t,12}^c + 0.5^* (\pi_{t,12}^c - 2) + (u^* - u_t) + w - (\tau + 0) \qquad (7A.4)$$

Taylor equation, finally modified, adding a Minsky 'risk' term (Figure 7.8):

$$f_t^{TR} = \pi_{t,12}^c + 0.5^* (\pi_{t,12}^c - 2) + (u^* - u_t) + w - (\tau + 0) - \eta \quad (7A.5)$$

(Where $\eta \equiv S - \sigma$)

where:
$f_t^{TR} \equiv$ Target rate for Fed funds in period t
$\pi_{t,12} \equiv$ Year-on-year change in CPI, in period t
$\pi_{t,12}^c \equiv$ Year-on-year change in core CPI, in period t

y^* $\equiv$ Potential GDP
y_t^* $\equiv$ GDP in period t
u^* *NAIRU*
u_t $\equiv$ Jobless rate, in period t
W $\equiv$ Wicksellian natural rate

$$W = (2(10\text{-year TIPS yield}) - 5\text{-year TIPS yield}) + \sigma$$
$$= 5\text{-year forward TIPS yield} + 1.8 \equiv \text{Neutral risky/risk free spread}$$

σ =   Average risk premium (Baa corporate bond rate – 10-year Treasury, 1960–2008) = 1.8

τ $\equiv$ Average term premium (10-year rate minus Fed funds rate, 1960–2008) = 0.8

S $\equiv$ BAA corporate minus 10-year Treasury rate

η $\equiv$ $S - \sigma$.

8   Innovation and equilibrium?
Martin Shubik

Introduction

This chapter is written in fond memory of Hyman Minsky whose writings on the possibilities for instability in a modern economy with many financial institutions have had considerable influence on the way economists view the strengths and weaknesses of our increasingly finance oriented economies (see Minsky 1986).

Hy had a considerable skepticism about the uses and abuses of mathematical economic theory, especially general equilibrium theory's emphasis on equilibrium. His skepticism has been shared by many macroeconomists of both left and right persuasion.

Starting as far back as Schumpeter in the early part of the twentieth century a provocative picture of the capitalist innovating economy was painted. Although the proponents of Schumpeter's approach have grown considerably over the last twenty to thirty years, primarily in Europe (see, for example, Nelson and Winter 1982 and Dosi et al. 1988), so, since the late 1950s, have the general equilibrium theorists. The thesis presented here is that the reconciliation of equilibrium microeconomics and disequilibrium financial economics and macroeconomics is both feasible and depends far less on correcting errors or misperceptions in either than on understanding the highly different questions being answered by each; and identifying the gaps in the models utilized by both that need to be filled if a reconciliation is to take place.

Keynes described and dealt with disequilibrium. Jim Tobin regarded the overall macroeconomic system as having a general equilibrium structure but with many changing parameters that needed to be re-estimated frequently. Lejonhufvud, Davidson and many others have stressed money, financial control and disequilibrium as the characteristics of the macroeconomic system. In all instances the stress is on process, in contrast with the general equilibrium stress on efficient static equilibrium.

Innovation, money, equilibrium or disequilibrium?

Much of economic activity involves the use of money and credit. The populist essays from the right may sing the virtues of the capitalist structure in promoting economic activity in general and innovation in particular. The

essays on the left suggest the evils of the system and the accrual of unwarranted power by the financiers.

The analysis of general equilibrium is carried out far more precisely and
mathematically than the literature on innovation. There are some simulations, but the predominant approach to innovation is via the essay. In spite
of its elegance and abstraction, as was noted by Koopmans (1977), general
equilibrium theory is pre-institutional. Because the economic world is
highly complex and multivariate, radical simplification is called for in the
mathematization of the models studied. Thus, considerable emphasis has
been placed on equilibrium conditions as the mathematics of processes in
disequilibrium is more or less intractable except in special cases. Even in
the low dimensional models of Lucas (1980), Shubik (1972) and Karatzas
et al. (1994) convergence to equilibrium from positions out of equilibrium
has not been proved.

Although originally written in 1911, Schumpeter's work on *The Theory
of Economic Development* (1934) provides an insightful description (in
essay form) of a plausible dynamic process involving the interaction
of the financial and physical processes of the economy intermixed with
the socio-psychological factors of optimism and pessimism. No formal
mathematical model was developed.

There is a growing literature involving the simulation of the dynamics
of competition as characterized by the early work of the Carnegie Institute
and the work of Nelson and Winter (1982) and others subsequently. This
essay is directed to considering the analysis among the mechanisms for
the creation of money and credit, the selection of innovation and the formation of price in an extremely simplified economy. In doing so a link is
formed between equilibrium analysis and the writings on the essentially
disequilibrium dynamics of innovation. It also becomes possible with this
approach to begin to examine precisely what is meant by the power or lack
of power to control innovation, of those who control the money and credit
supply in the financial system.

On simple well-defined models

The approach adopted here is to construct simple but detailed models
specifying every feasible move and all information conditions. Even with
the microeconomic detail of economic reality they represent a gross over-
simplification. Our approach is to try to construct the simplest mechanism
for which the phenomena of relevance appear. As they are well-defined
models they should either manifest the properties ascribed to 'more
realistic models' or otherwise they should serve to indicate why some
phenomena do not appear until a higher level of complexity is attained.

The stress is on process analysis. The economy is viewed as a game of strategy and an attempt is made to fully define a game in extensive form. This reductionist approach has many benefits, but as is noted below in attempting to describe innovation, at some point it may have its limitations.

The playable game test

> If after ten minutes at the Poker table you do not know who is the patsy, you are the patsy.

Although since the 1980s there has been an explosion of the uses of game theory in economics, even at the middlebrow level, nevertheless much of game theory writing is at a high level of abstraction with little attention paid to context. An important part of the approach here is based on the belief that many economic institutions and instruments are designed to be operated more or less efficiently by average, non-specialist individuals. There are some institutions and instruments such as the markets for sophisticated derivatives that require professionals, where PhDs in mathematics, physics or mathematical economics or finance may help. In these markets, the amateurs may be slaughtered. But for many institutions, if one wishes to gain insight into their operation it should be possible to build a playable experimental game whose rules can be explained with little difficulty to a student or a non-sophisticated owner of a small business.

Economic behavior and behavioral types

Much of the work in mathematical economics and in game theory has been based explicitly or implicitly on an abstract *homo economicus* or von Neumann man. This individual has perfect recall and an ability to compute everything. I suggest that for the development of economic dynamics it is probably worthwhile to recognize around eight different behavioral types. They are the:

- random player with the state space unknown;
- random player with the state space known;
- optimal response player with global scope;
- optimal response player with local scope;
- non-specialist human;
- specialist human;
- expert specialist human;
- von Neumann player

The lower and upper bounds on intelligence are usually the easiest to study and serve as useful benchmarks when studying behavior in experimental games. A market such as a one commodity double auction market provides an example of institutional design where the random player with state space known does approximately as well as the von Neumann player (see Huber et al. 2007).

The first player listed is the random player with the state space unknown. This is noted to point out that statement that a player chooses randomly, to be made precise requires the assumption that the player knows the domain over which she is randomizing. If the domain is not specified an individual must provide some subjective closure to take care of the uncertainty.

In experimental gaming considerable use has been made of the random player. This is seen in the work of Gode and Sunder (1993), and others.

Even the concept of a know-nothing cannot be modeled easily without taking some context into consideration. The know-nothing can be so ignorant that he/she does not even know the bounds on the choice to be made. Fortunately in many economic situations the bounds are given by context. Thus the economically naïve knows that she cannot bid a negative amount and cannot bid more than she has plus the amount she can borrow; and in spite of some mathematical economics theory, the amount that can be borrowed tends to be finite. Given these bounds the naïve may act randomly within these bounds.

Much of the study of repeated games has utilized an optimal response player with global response. The player bases her response on maximization given the belief that others will continue to do what they have recently done. There is a big picture and a small picture version of this behavioral assumption. Assuming that she has 'the big picture' implies that she is capable of searching over the whole domain of outcomes to select an optimal response.

In contrast with the global player the optimal response player with local scope has the ability to search only in a limited domain. This presupposes that there is some sort of metric, such as space, on the set of choices. A simple example is provided by a 5×5 matrix game where each individual can only see and move to adjacent squares. If the agents were at (10, 10) this is a local optimum and the local optimal response player would not be motivated to move, but the global optimal response player would move to the unique pure strategy non-cooperative equilibrium point at (20, 30). There are several local non-cooperative equilibria in this game.

The non-specialist human is what Keynes and many others in macroeconomic modeling consider the 'average' consumer to be. This individual is assumed to be more or less an economic agent, but is constrained by habit and limited by lack of expertise and detailed knowledge in many

Table 8.1   A 5 × 5 matrix game

	1	2	3	4	5
1	0,0	0,0	9,1	0,0	0,0
2	0,0	0,0	0,0	0,0	10,1
3	0,70	5,4	10,10	5,5	20,30
4	0,0	0,0	0,0	0,0	0,0
5	0,0	0,0	2,2	0,0	0,0

areas. Furthermore the same individual who as a consumer may be a creature of habit may also be a specialist in some body of knowledge such as production, engineering or medicine.

The specialist has been trained in some body of knowledge. He explicitly knows the rules of the game and if he is not a high expert will tend to operate with a high degree of conscious thought and calculation.

The high expert specialist, as chess studies have shown, appears to have routinized much of his knowledge, thus many of his moves do not require explicit calculation. Furthermore where the beginner or the ordinary player sees few alternatives, the expert sees many.

In specialized markets such as commodity hedging markets or various derivative markets the experts live with risk, but understand clearly how to perform and profit from the economically useful function of matching individuals with different risk profiles, thereby laying off much of the risk. Amateurs who wish to venture into this type of game are merely the welcome contributors to professional profits.

On institutions, innovation and analysis

> Like all men in Babylon, I have been proconsul; like all I have been a slave. I have known omnipotence, ignominy, imprisonment . . . I owe that almost monstrous variety to an institution – the Lottery – which is unknown in other nations, or at work in them imperfectly or secretly.
>
> (Jorge L. Borges, *The Lottery in Babylon*)

> His success may be great, but be it ever so great the Wheel of Fortune may turn again and bring him down into the dust.
>
> (Gautama Siddhartha)

The economic analysis of economies without exogenous uncertainty is far easier both conceptually and mathematically than the analysis of an economy with uncertainties. The presence of uncertainty can be made to disappear by waving the wand of complete markets; but this assumption useful for establishing an extreme bound on the class of economic market models, is far from economic reality. An economy with uncertainty is in constant flux.

In spite of the observations of Keynes (1921), Knight (1921), Savage (1954), Ellsberg (1961), De Finetti (1970), and others a completely satisfactory understanding of the distinction between risk and uncertainty still does not exist. The postulating of a priori numerical values to a subjective probability for any event provides a tidy way to set up a Bayesian updating analysis that has tucked away the fundamental difficulties in the model in the formulation of the initial conditions. The setting up of the betting odds market seems to be about as good a mechanism as we can propose at this time for eliciting subjective quantitative estimation of the unknown. The problem seems to lie more within the realms of the psychology of perception and in the social psychology of crowd behavior than in conventional economic theory.

The processes of innovation do not fit in a comfortable manner into either formal mathematical micro-economic theory, or into game theory. They fit more closely to the biological processes of mutation than into the economics of equilibrium.

Bankruptcy and dynamics
Highly associated with dynamics of the firm and individual are the bankruptcy and reorganization laws of a society. Money, debt and the bankruptcy laws are the three critical items required to break out of the static equilibrium framework of general equilibrium and to provide the flexibility to accommodate innovation and evolutionary processes.

The general equilibrium system calls for the mathematics of convex programming subject to linear constraints, where in equilibrium the constraints generically take the form of equality of the overall budget constraints. As soon as one attempts to model the system as a fully described strategic game it becomes necessary to specify both the cash flow conditions and what happens if, through error or intent, the conditions of equality are violated.

A supply equals demand equation can fail in two ways. There may be a gap between the two, or an overlap. If someone has sold more than she has bought, the balance can be settled in money. If someone has bought more than she has sold and is unable to settle the difference in money or credit, default and bankruptcy rules are required.

If the dynamic process is viewed as part of a game of strategy, bankruptcy laws are required to prevent strategic default. They are not just a happenstance institutional fact; they are a logical necessity. Bankruptcy laws are often accompanied with reorganization conditions, thus the death process of a firm is not like that of a human, as under reorganization it may have a rebirth like that of the Phoenix.

Innovation and mutation

It is one matter to understand the genesis of originality and the motivation for invention and innovation, and another matter to characterize the economic aspects of innovation. It is an error to attribute a sole economic goal to an inventor. Often it appears that the desire by the inventor to see 'the baby born' dominates the economic motive.

Probably through some biological process a given small percentage of the population may be potential innovators. Given the pool of talent, how are the innovators financed? The main aspects of the financing are considered below. Here only the role of default and bankruptcy is considered. Sweeping across the range from no penalty to a Draconian penalty such as death we observe that if there were no penalty for default there would be no lending as the lenders would have no protection against a non-paying borrower. If the penalty were enormous the borrowers would be afraid to borrow. If we assume continuity there should be a zone or a point with an optimal penalty. The interpretation of society's selection of the level of penalty is that it reflects the level of risk due to firm failure that society as a whole is willing to absorb. When a firm or venture fails, money and other assets are not destroyed, they are reassigned. Some credit may be annihilated.

As the bankruptcy penalty is relaxed more individuals are willing to risk financing new ventures and along with possibly more successful innovations, there are more failures. The analogy with mutation is that the bankruptcy penalty plays the role of the controlling device over the economic mutation rate, trading off the cost of failure against the value of success.

An aside on premarket and nonmarket innovation

> Necessity, who is the mother of invention.
>
> (Plato, *The Republic*)

Invention and discovery have existed long before markets and the elaborate mechanisms for financing invention in the modern economy. The first uses of fire are still not known with great accuracy. The wheel was possibly invented around 8000 years ago but no hard evidence appears to go back beyond Sumeria. The early inventions were probably by individuals and spread through families and tribes. Once social organization appeared it is a likely conjecture that government played a role.

It is probable that the talent for originality and invention is essentially exogenously given in any society. The difference that an organized society and economy can make is in the utilization of the idea generators, not the intrinsic generation of ideas. Searching for talent among the masses can increase the crop of innovators, but in a certain sense good ideas are cheap. It is the implementation of the ideas that counts.

With the market structure of medieval times it is likely that the prince or powerful families served as patrons. To this day the family and the private rich still play a role in the sponsorship of innovation.

Institutions' form and function
Part of the theme here is that even an elementary minimal model of innovation requires a complexity of organization far beyond that of General Equilibrium (GE) theory. A listing of the relevant institutions and their functions is noted. The primary functions are stated first. Then in parentheses some subfunctions are noted.

Form and function

- Markets: exchange (information aggregation and disaggregation)
- Firms: production (marketing, accounting, inventorying)
- Government: legislation and enforcement of the laws (standards, commercial code)
- Entrepreneurs: locating and promoting inventors, raising funds (evaluating markets and products)
- Inventors: invention
- Venture capitalists and investment banks: feasibility and profitability evaluation, assessment of management, financing
- Private banks: lending and accepting deposits (credit assessment)
- Central bank: management of money supply and interest rates
- Government other financial institutions: taxation subsidies and national debt
- Stock market: liquidity for extant stock and accommodation for new issues
- Bond market: a market for long term debt
- Money market: a market for short term debt
- Clearing house: clearing facility to maximize speed in exchange and minimize the need for monetary settlement.

The ultimate agents are real persons who are manifested in multiple roles as employees, consumers, owners and a variety of specialists generally attached to one of the organizations. The organizations are all legal persons owned in one form or another by the real persons. A loose biological analogy is that the real persons are the cells (who come in many manifestations) and the corporate persons are the organs of the body economic. For simplicity we refer only to corporations, rather than indulge in the other distinctions such as the various forms of partnership.

Among the more relevant rules are: corporate law, contract law, the commercial code, patent law, tax law, and accounting conventions.

An important evolutionary feature of financial and other economic institutions is that they are often created for a specific function and later may serve many different purposes that were not foreseen at the time of their creation.

Economic structures

Two types of agents have been noted, real persons and corporate persons, and around ten types of institutions have been listed. In this section three simple diagrams are given to suggest that there is a considerable difference in basic complexity between the pre-institutional static general equilibrium models and a structure complex enough to encompass a process model of the financing of innovation.

The first is the old textbook warhorse usually illustrated by the Edgeworth–Bowley diagram of barter exchange between two traders exchanging two commodities.

Figure 8.2 represents the simplest structure that can achieve a general equilibrium outcome for multilateral exchange with n individuals trading in m commodities. The x^i and y^i are to be interpreted as arrays of m goods offered and received in exchange. All individuals send their goods and bids denominated in their own credit money to a central clearing house that both clears goods and balances budgets by adjusting the relative prices of individual credit. No government money is called for. The work of Sahi and Yao (1989) and Sorin (1996) show that this is mathematically tractable, even though this perfect clearing house does not exist in practice. In Figure 8.2 the clearing house receives goods and messages from all individuals in the economy and ships the appropriate bundles of goods back.

Although mathematically elegant, the perfect clearing house and fiat moneyless central price calculating system exists primarily as a Soviet central planner's dream. Somewhat closer to reality is the institutional structure shown in Figure 8.3, although even here production and innovation institutions have not been made explicit.

In Figure 8.3 emphasis is on evaluation, enforcement and information aggregation, and disaggregation is presented by the explicit introduction of a credit evaluation agency, a clearing house and the courts. The consumers utilize both the clearing house and markets and, when needed, the

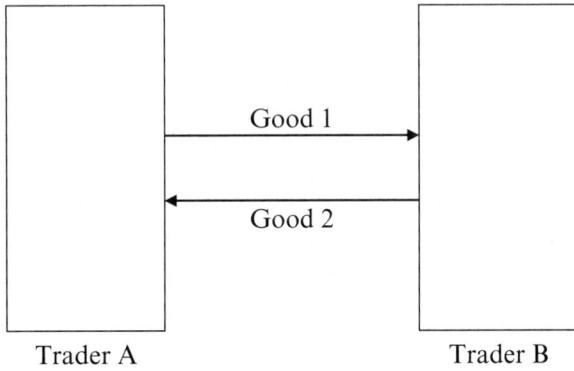

Figure 8.1   Bilateral exchange

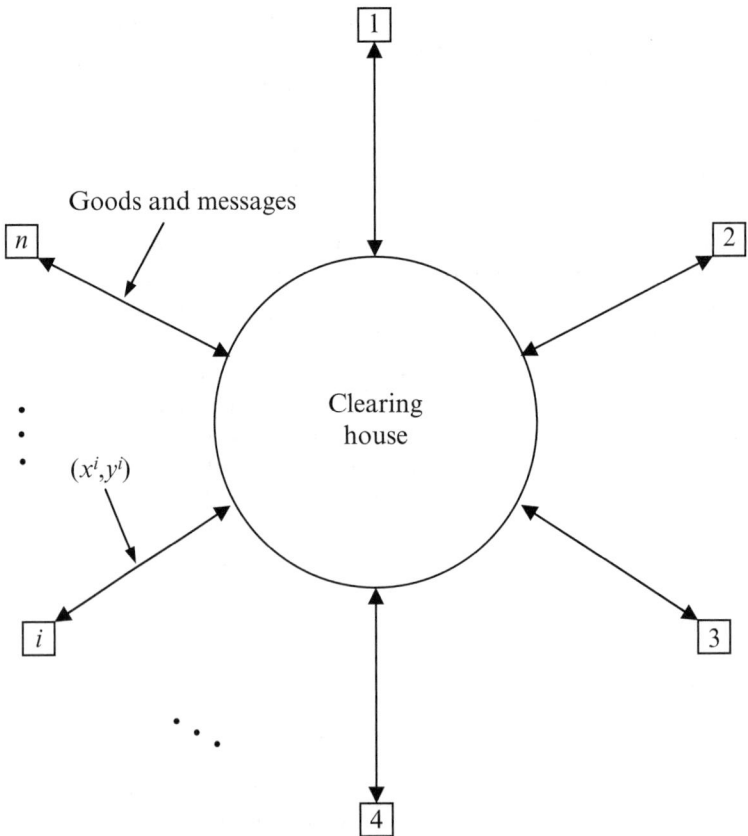

Figure 8.2   General equilibrium exchange with a clearing house

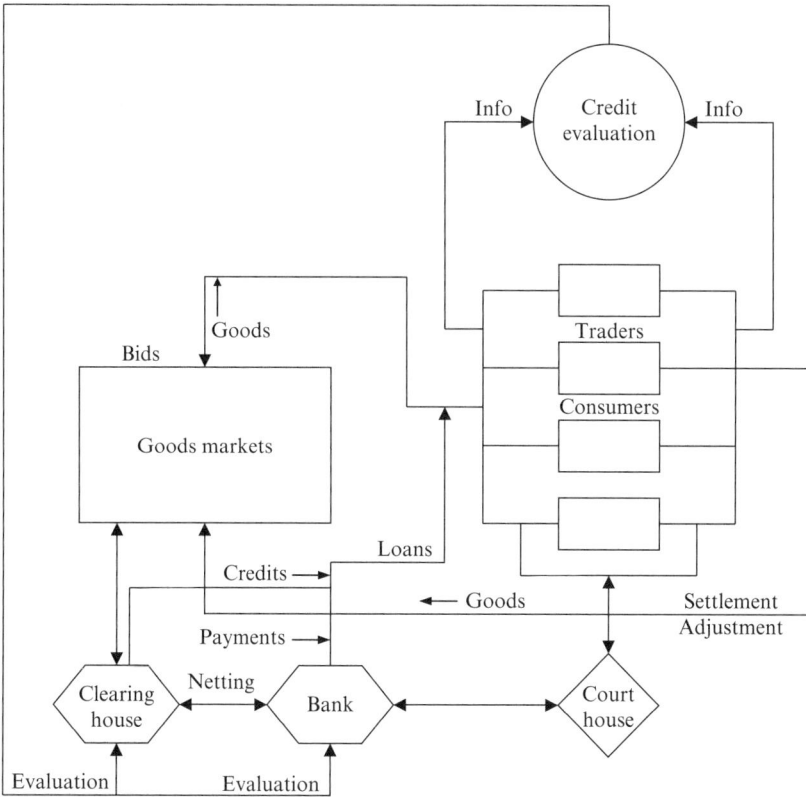

Figure 8.3   An economy with loans and credit evaluation

courts. The consumers both supply goods and services to the markets and obtain goods and services from them.

Types of innovation
There are at least three types of innovation that are worth considering independently. They are:

● Radically new product innovation
● Engineering variation of current product, and
● Cost, primarily organization or other process innovation.

In terms of uncertainty these are highly different. The most difficult to handle by conventional economic analysis is radical product innovation. Both the production procedures and the demand acceptance are unknown.

There is little, if any, precedence. The subjective probabilities, if any, may be cooked up by stretched analogy with other products that succeeded; and only quantified for the purpose of the construction of imaginary or *pro forma* financial statements used to persuade potential investors. An interesting discussion of the problems and approaches to managing innovation is given in Bechtel et al. (1996).

If a new product succeeds and there is a competing similar product then it is by no means clear who will capture the market. The insightful work of Brian Arthur (1989) develops a probabilistic increasing returns to scale model where chance determines who inherits the market and the best technology does not necessarily emerge.

More or less standard product variation fits reasonably well into the current theory of oligopolistic competition. The large firms selling, say, refrigerators have products that are close to being identical. It is the job of marketing and the production engineers to have a spice shelf full of technically known modifications or additions that can help to differentiate the product of firm A from that of firm B. Both costs and demand can be reasonably estimated for such innovations.

By far the most prevalent form of innovation in most modern economies is process innovation involving organization and most frequently costs. New inventions call for expensive prototypes. Even if the market for the new product clearly exists, there is a considerable focus on unit cost reduction over the first few years, especially with mass market possibilities. The prototype is highly expensive, and the first batch for sale, though cheaper than the prototype, is usually nowhere near the intended cost. The possibility to quantify a reasonable gaming experiment with cost innovation and to provide a reasonable scenario appears to be far easier than trying to construct an experimental game to illustrate basic product innovation.

Varieties in financing innovation

If economic activities are to be successful, they require that specific functions be performed; but these functions may be manifested in many different institutions. Thus there may be many configurations of institutions that are sufficient for the activity. So it is with the financing of innovation. Among the possibilities are:

- The folklore of family financing of the individual inventor in the garage
- The self-financed corporation
- Commercial bank financing
- Public or central bank/government sponsorship
- Financing via investment bankers, a private patron.

Any combination of these sources is also possibly dependent on the social and economic details of the society.

In spite of the brilliance of Schumpeter's general insights on innovation, the process he sketched may have been more relevant to Austria of 1900 than to the United States or China of 2000. The same functional requirements are more or less still in place but the institutions supplying them have changed.

A comment on circular flow and innovation

Key to all of the various methods is the need to break the circular flow established at a general economic equilibrium. Mathematically the circular flow is required by the equilibrium budget balancing conditions and robs the overall system of n degrees of freedom, one for each budget constraint.

The introduction of money, be it gold or fiat, provides a system that in equilibrium preserves the circular flow and gives the illusion that money is irrelevant; but this is an artifact of the equilibrium conditions. In disequilibrium money and bankruptcy conditions permit the violation of circular flow and the institutions created to control the availability of money and to enforce the laws of default.

Money and financial institutions open the general equilibrium structure to dynamics. The natural way to describe a dynamic exchange and production economy is via a strategic market game with money, and private and government financial institutions. In equilibrium the money and financial institutions disappear but in disequilibrium they are available to play their role in control.

The financial institutions provide a control mechanism to guide the evolution of the economy. In particular they help to guide innovation. The basic assumption is that an attempt to innovate requires that resources are diverted from the current economy. Although we believe that the economy is always in a disequilibrium state, as a first crude approximation we assume that it is in equilibrium, it is disturbed from equilibrium by innovation and then resumes equilibrium after the innovation succeeds or fails. This enables us to concentrate on the violation of circular flow and on the redistribution of resources during and after the attempt at innovation. In a separate paper Shubik and Sudderth (2010) provide and study a simple mathematical model of innovation. For simplicity we limit the investigation to cost innovation and note that even with this simple form of innovation the form of financing may control the welfare consequences and the nature of the disturbance to the circular flow.

Innovation, evolution and complexity

The argument above suggests that to a certain extent the static and dynamic equilibrium models of general equilibrium are consistent with evolutionary models as implied in the works of Schumpeter (1934), Keynes (1936 [1957]), Boulding (1950), and many others, but basically at a different level of complexity. Implicitly all of these, essentially verbal, treatments discuss disequilibrium states. Although the observations on disequilibrium are attractive, they are not well defined. Currently they appear to defy adequate mathematization. This is so because there is no sufficiently formal, agreed-on representation of the new product processes from invention to execution. A small step towards this appropriate mathematization can be achieved by first studying the far easier condition of cost innovation which still permits a comparative statics study as a way out of studying the full dynamics.[1]

The value and limits of reductionism
Innovation, mutation and life itself are off-balance sheet assets.

The approach considered here is heavily reductionist. As soon as the masterful simplifications of general equilibrium theory are given up one can be lost in a welter of special cases and institutional forms. Thousands, if not millions of detailed institutional structures appear calling for micro-micro economic or operations research detail. This appears to go with the economic facts of life of a modern economy. The study of myriads of special cases is the price to be paid to be able to say much about the dynamic behavior of an economic institution.

The hortatory analogies between economics and biology are attractive and undoubtedly contain elements of truth. But to operationalize them is another matter. In the approach followed here the stress has been on reductionism. Finer and finer details over and above the general equilibrium structure are added to obtain minimal structure to carry economic processes. As we add the requirements of complex structures capable of the aggregation of information and the evaluation of risk, minimal versions of the basic economic and financial institutions appear. Yet, when we start to address subfunctions of functions it appears that reductionism has no bounds. Each level of detail may be perfectly adequate to answer some operational questions, yet at each level more questions appear that are not adequately answered. In particular, in spite of the spectacular growth of network theory we do not have a satisfactory representation of the organizational, morale and management aspects of the firm. This is why the accountant must deal with off-balance sheet assets and why the distinction between the firm as an ongoing entity and its liquidation value must be made. These are practical operational decisions but do not answer the basic distinction between organized life and a pile of assets.

Institutions, mathematics and Hy Minsky

In the chapter above a sketch has been presented of an approach aimed at producing mathematical models capable of connecting equilibrium and disequilibrium models of the economy. This required models capable of violating the circular flow; but to be able to demonstrate how to construct formal mechanisms to do so is not the same as being able to construct models immediately pertinent to the current economy. Nor do these models enable us to estimate the size of the potential instabilities the financial institutions may introduce, especially when they may be utilized by individuals who do not fit into the narrow mould of the rational economic agent.

The power of Hy Minsky was in his insightful analysis in being able to offer an overview utilizing essay combined with selected statistics and little formal mathematics to outline clearly the nature of the instabilities inherent in the modern financially guided economies. He understood that the financial institutions are a creation of human society and hence can be managed and redesigned to provide the economic stability needed.

The economic functions required by a healthy economy are more or less invariant, but the institutions that provide them are in constant flux as the society evolves. At some basic level possibly human behavior can be regarded as a given (although social structure, wealth and education impose different behavioral profiles). The operational challenge is to produce further insights to influence the evolution of stable and efficient institutions. Combined with this the role of the formal micro-economic theorist is to be able to extend our understanding of the formal structure of the financial control system and to try to characterize what functions and behavior may be regarded as invariant and how they can be reconciled with the disequilibrium of the evolving economies and societies we live in.

Note

1. Technically, it is modeled as a non-stochastic parallel dynamic program with one controlled stochastic move at the start. In reality there are many random variables with unknown distributions constantly bombarding the system.

References

Arthur, W.B. (1989), 'Competing technologies, increasing returns and lock-in by historical events', *Economic Journal*, 99, 106–31.
Bechtel, S.D. et al. (1996), 'Managing innovation', *Daedalus*, **125**(2).
Boulding, K.E. (1950), *A Reconstruction of Economics*, New York: Wiley.
De Finetti, B. (1970), *Teoria delle probabilita*, Torino: Guilio Einaudi.
Dosi, G., C. Freeman, R. Nelson, G. Silverberg and L. Soete (1988), *Technical Change and Economic Theory*, London and New York: Pinter.
Ellsberg, D. (1961), 'Risk, ambiguity, and the savage axioms', *Quarterly Journal of Economics*, **75**(4), 643–69.

168   *The Elgar companion to Hyman Minsky*

Gode, D.K. and S. Sunder (1993), 'Allocative efficiency of markets with zero intelligence traders: market as a partial substitute for individual rationality', *Journal of Political Economy*, 101, 119–37.
Huber, J., M. Shubik and S. Sunder (2007), 'Three minimal market games: theory and experimental evidence', Cowles Foundation Discussion Paper 1623, Yale University, New Haven.
Karatzas, I., M. Shubik and W. Sudderth (1994), 'Construction of stationary Markov equilibria in a strategic market game', *Mathematics of Operations Research*, 19(4), 975–1006.
Keynes, J.M. (1921), *Treatise on Probability*, London: MacMillan.
Keynes, J.M. (1936 [1957]), *The General Theory of Employment, Interest and Money*, London: MacMillan.
Knight, F.H. (1921), *Risk, Uncertainty and Profit*, Boston and New York: Houghton Mifflin.
Koopmans, T.C. (1977a), 'Concepts of optimality and their uses', *American Economic Review*, 67(3), 261–74.
Lucas, R.E. (1980), 'Equilibrium in a pure currency economy', *Economic Inquiry*, 18, 203–20.
Minsky, H.P. (1986), *Stabilizing An Unstable Economy*, New Haven: Yale University Press.
Nelson, R.R. and S.G. Winter (1982), *An Evolutionary Theory of Economic Change*, Cambridge: Harvard University Press.
Sahi, S. and S. Yao (1989), 'The noncooperative equilibria of a trading economy with complete markets and consistent prices', *Journal of Mathematical Economics*, 18, 325–46.
Savage, L.J. (1954), *The Foundations of Statistics*, New York: Wiley.
Schumpeter, J.A. (1934), *The Theory of Economic Development*, Cambridge: Harvard University Press.
Shubik, M. (1972), 'A theory of money and financial institutions: fiat money and noncooperative equilibrium in a closed economy', *International Journal of Game Theory*, 1(4), 243–68.
Shubik, M. and W. Sudderth (2010), *Product Innovation: Schumpeter and Equilibrium*, forthcoming.
Sorin, S. (1996), 'Strategic market games with exchange rates', *Journal of Economic Theory*, 68, 431–46.

9 Hyman Minsky and the dilemmas of contemporary economic method
Duncan K. Foley*

Introduction

Hyman Minsky's work on financial fragility and the political economy of instability in advanced capitalist economies has had more influence in the policy-making and financial communities than among academic economists. This fate of Minsky's thought raises some basic questions about contemporary economic methodology, particularly the relations between economic theory, mathematical models, and statistical estimation. Minsky, in pursuing seriously the project of understanding the dynamics of contemporary capitalist society, ran into fundamental limitations of contemporary economic modeling technique. Given Minsky's strong quantitative training and the nature of his early work in economics, his refusal, often remarked upon, to develop a rigorous mathematical model to express his ideas about financial instability is a sharp reminder of the limits of our current methods. The fertility of Minsky's insights and the resonance they met in the practical worlds of finance and policy-making suggest that the examination of Minsky's work offers a valuable critical perspective on modern economic method. Minsky himself was aware of these dilemmas, and refers to them from time to time in explicating his ideas (for example, Minsky 1989), but never, I think, systematically addressed the methodological crisis inherent in his work, nor did he put forward an explicit methodological alternative.

Contemporary economics is a distinctive branch of statistical social science. Statistical social science, in turn, is an attempt to adapt the methods of experimental and observational physical sciences to the analysis of data generated in the course of human social interactions. Both the general attempt to apply the methods of physical science to social data through the use of statistics, and the specific attempt of economists to provide a rigorous theoretical foundation for social statistical models raise subtle and unresolved philosophical questions, on which Minsky's work on financial dynamics shed a powerful, if harsh, light.

At their root these problems involve the limits of statistical analysis to data generated by repeated similar events and the difficulty of representing dialectical transformations of systems mathematically. The phenomenon of financial fragility and its impact on the political economy of contemporary capitalism raise these problems in a particularly poignant form. Finance mediates the inescapable gap between an imperfectly imagined future and an inadequately equilibrated present that is inherent in the reproduction of capitalist economic life. While this mediation as a general phenomenon is a predictably repeated event, it always takes place in historically specific circumstances of changing technology, mores and beliefs, so that the underlying process is in statistical terms inherently nonstationary. Historical financial data thus carries at best a limited amount of information about the present. Furthermore, financial institutions, markets, and instruments are historically highly fluid and adaptable. The financial response to disequilibrating shocks takes the form of transformation and innovation of institutions and instruments as often as it takes the form of the re-pricing of existing securities. The rapid evolution of US financial instruments and practices in the 1970s and 1980s, in response to the crises Minsky analyzed with such penetration, is a dramatic example. But contemporary techniques of mathematical economic modeling presuppose a stable framework of traders, tradable commodities and assets.

Thus the difficulties Minsky and his followers encounter in formalizing the Minskyan world view in mathematical and econometric models reflect not merely technical mathematical and econometric problems, but fundamental philosophical limitations. Since the problems of financial fragility and instability Minsky identified and worked on continue to grow in importance as they reappear on a global scale, and since Minsky's work has evident scientific value in organizing our understanding of these issues, these limits pose an important historical challenge to received economic method.

How it is out there
Economics studies the way human beings organize themselves to provide for their material needs and wants. As a human and social science, economics must inherently confront the existential conditions of human life, such as the unresolved puzzle we call the passage of time. As we experience it, the present, in which we have our consciousness and experience ourselves as acting, divides time curiously between a past about which we have limited information, but do not seem to be able to change by our present actions, and a future which our present actions seem to shape, but over which we have limited control. Broadly speaking, two philosophical attitudes underlie our thinking about the passage of time, deterministic and dialectical.

The determinist view, deeply entwined in physical science theory, sees the passage of time as the unfolding of a lawful progression of causally connected events, and attributes our human inability to predict and control the future to limitations in our understanding of the laws linking the past to the future and to our information about the current state of the world. In the determinist view the future and past are quite symmetrical, in that there 'is' a definite future, just as there 'is' a definite past; the quality of our uncertainty about the actual unfolding of the future is no different from the quality of our uncertainty about the specifics of the past, in that both are attributable to our limited information.

The dialectical view, on the other hand, sees the future as genuinely undetermined but always in the process of coming to be through the unfolding of the present, and particularly the unfolding of human action. In the dialectical perspective the past is fixed, despite our limited knowledge of it, in a way that the future is not. Our actions in the present can change our knowledge of the past, but not what actually happened, while these same actions actually constitute the process of shaping the future.

These general philosophical conundrums appear in economic life in recognizable, and even simplified, concrete guises. The past imposes on the present economically in the form of the stocks of concrete capital goods, knowledge, habits and information we inherit from the past. From an economic point of view it does not matter very much exactly what the history that led to this capital endowment is, since there's nothing we can do to change it (the doctrine of 'sunk costs'). The stubborn resistance of existing stocks to change spontaneously in accord with our present wishes reflects the determinate quality of the past. On the other hand, human action in the present clearly changes the stock of capital goods and information we pass on to the future. In market-oriented societies the actions that determine investment are mediated by valuing existing stocks of goods and information and speculating on the future valuation of various possible investments. This process is the immediate metabolism of economic life. The economic moments of finance and investment express the deepest existential dilemmas.

To those who devote their lives professionally to this process it has something of a sacred mystery, partaking equally of faith and fear. Savers accumulate wealth in the form of money, general purchasing power, which can command all the huge variety of present pleasures the world offers. Yet savers know that their only hope of perpetuating their wealth into the future lies in converting it into some concrete investment that may turn out to be worthless. Like college sophomores horrified at the prospect of 'limiting their options', savers twist and turn in this contradiction, and in the process evolve fantastically elaborate mediations to disguise the plain distastefulness of the act of concrete investment. So wealth, which could provide so much immediate and certain pleasure, goes instead to build the ninth or nineteenth shopping mall around Springfield, Massachusetts, or an impossibly expensive apartment building in Tokyo. Financiers take on the dangerous, if well-compensated, priestly role of consecrating this sacrificial activity, carving up the entrails of historical statistics for omens, and seeking auguries in the flocking and flights of politicians.

Yet this existentially fragile moment of investment drives forward the whole process of production through which we secure our survival and reproduction. When finance and investment are proceeding smoothly and with controlled optimism, production and reproduction also flourish; when the worlds of finance and investment degenerate into hysterical over-optimism or disheveled panic, as they inevitably do, they disorder and disrupt the systems of valuation on which production itself rests.

From one point of view, these are repeated phenomena, which might be likened to the motion of the planets, or the fluctuations of the seasons. All market-oriented societies exhibit the development of financial and investment sectors, and experience the turbulence associated with them. There are recognizable similarities between the financial booms and busts of different economies and different ages, between the South Sea Bubble, the Baring crisis and the Penn Central bankruptcy. But there are also crucial differences. Each generation of savers and investors has to place its bets on its own array of technological and organizational options, in its own historical context. From the subjective point of view, each individual act of investment is a unique existential crisis, not to speak of the unfolding of a systemic boom or bust. Contemplation of the follies and triumphs of the past can perhaps console the investor with the feeling of company, but the South Sea Bubble has limited practical information relevant to the unraveling of world capital markets in 1997 and 1998.

Hy Minsky understood that this is how it is (as did John Maynard Keynes), and had the unusual philosophical courage to insist on the relevance of the dialectical point of view to the understanding of financial economics. His theses on financial fragility and instability stem from his vision of the financial process as an essentially human confrontation of the present with the future, mediated by all the psychological baggage humans carry to major life decisions: their self-deception, opportunism, and insecurity as well as their faith, imagination, and steadfastness. From this vision Minsky drew genuine and valuable insight about real historical events, and gained some perspective on the deeper rhythms of financial life. This insight attracted to his work a constituency and an audience, a mixture of financial professionals and heterodox critics of market economies, who disagree on many aspects of capitalist society, but share a fascination with its financial spectacle.

How economics presents matters

The high road of twentieth-century economics has been the systematic combination of the methods of statistical inference and mathematical modeling. Economists' knowledge of the real world takes the form of simplified mathematical models, in which the relevant phenomena are represented by an unchanging set of quantitative variables. Mathematical models have the great conceptual advantage that they can easily be manipulated to generate counterfactual predictions by changing the parameters of the model. Since one of the main things we want to know about the world is how it would have been (or would be) if we took (or take) some alternative course of action, the predictions of mathematical models satisfy a pressing demand. There are, however, many mathematical models that can plausibly represent relevant aspects of economic reality. Contemporary economics proposes to choose among them by testing their explanatory power over actual observed data. To accomplish this, it is necessary to stipulate a set of rules for connecting the abstract variables of a mathematical model to observable data. Given these rules, the counterfactual predictions of a mathematical model can be interpreted as predicted correlations among observed variables. The underlying mathematical model is validated by econometric technique when at least some observed data can be shown to exhibit at least some of the correlations predicted by the model under at least one set of rules for connecting the mathematical variables to the observed data.

The methodological weaknesses of this procedure turn up every day in econometric practice. It is easy to quarrel over the rules connecting the abstract quantities of mathematical models to observed data (as in the case of measurement of the money supply, for example). Even with agreed-upon rules for operationalizing models, the available data may be compatible with a wide range of mathematical models that have contradictory counterfactual implications (as the debates over identification problems illustrate). As a result, econometric tests have limited power to dislodge economic models that reflect strongly and widely held prior prejudices. Models get into trouble only when they exhibit gross anomalies that show up under robust statistical procedures in a wide range of data (as in the case of the real business cycle attempts to explain fluctuations in unemployment).

Beyond these chronic methodological weaknesses in contemporary economic practice, however, lies a philosophical limitation. Both the practice of mathematical modeling and the procedures of statistical inference are strongly biased against a dialectical understanding of the unfolding of time.

In the case of mathematical models, this bias arises because they represent change only as the quantitative variation of a given set of variables.

A central feature of the dialectical vision, by contrast, is the emergence of qualitatively new phenomena as a systematic response to the contradictions of existing structures. In the field of financial economics, for example, the market responded to the rise in interest rates of the late 1960s and early 1970s not just through a reallocation of portfolios over the existing spectrum of assets, but also through the invention of new assets and intermediaries. In a purely formal sense it might be possible to shoehorn this phenomenon into a mathematical model by positing the latent existence of these assets and intermediaries, and treating their emergence as a quantitative change from zero levels of trading to positive levels. But this is at best an ex post rhetorical maneuver to save the methodology, not a serious scientific strategy, since no sane modeler would venture to include all possible evolutions of the commodity or asset space in a usable model.

The philosophical bedrock of statistical inference is the assumption that the future will be like the past, so that we can use repeated observations of past events to infer at least some features of the future. This essential assumption of statistical method disables it from dealing with qualitative change in interactions, and therefore from coming to grips with a dialectical understanding of the world. Contemporary econometric practice is fertile in devices to minimize or evade this problem. Once one recognizes the pervasiveness of qualitative change, for example, in macroeconomic or financial interactions, it is tempting to save the statistical point of view by retreating to a higher perspective, and segregating the data points into separate 'regimes', each of which has its own statistical order. There is nothing logically wrong with these maneuvers, but the complexity of economic and financial reality sharply tests their practical usefulness. Once regimes are allowed to multiply, they rapidly deplete the degrees of freedom necessary to draw strong statistical inferences.

Contemporary econometric practice is most comfortable with a representation of the passage of time as the unfolding of a determinate future governed by the same laws and statistical regularities as the past. This leads economists to represent the moments of finance and investment as problems in forward-looking statistical inference: investors appear in economic models as merely imperfectly informed decision makers. The results of their actions are represented as the potentially insurable consequences of statistical variation. The future in contemporary economics is knowable, though imperfectly known. In a formal sense this strategy can accommodate any degree of irregularity in the operation of financial markets, but its fidelity to the actual conditions in which financial and investment decisions take place is questionable. Financial professionals eagerly consume the information generated from econometric models, because, like all information, it is potentially valuable, but are restless with the contention that their work is to divine a determinate future rather than to create an undetermined one.

Minsky's methodological dilemma
Hy Minsky was an able mathematical economist with a mastery of modern statistical method. Yet his most influential work largely eschews sophisticated mathematical and econometric methods. There is much to be learned from contemplating the dilemma he faced and the practical resolution of it he accomplished in his scientific career.

Minsky recognized important repeated patterns in the evolution of financial markets. For example, he calls attention to the gradual shift during expansions from extreme caution (hedge finance) through boldness (speculative finance) to abandon (Ponzi finance). This gradual loosening of financial restraint is characteristic of all capitalist booms, and plays an important role in supporting and extending boom conditions. But the exact form the progression takes and the mechanisms that support it differ from one historical episode to the next. In one boom the speculative vehicle may be equities, in another real estate, in another speculation in high-profit margin foreign investment. Investors can work themselves into perilous positions by borrowing to buy stock on margin, or through derivatives trades, or by depending on political promises of exchange rate stability to hedge positions across different currencies. Minsky can call our attention with hindsight to the structural similarities of these episodes but cannot give us the power to recognize the next concrete form the progression will take. Awareness of these structural similarities is surely valuable knowledge, rooted in a scientific recognition of a kind of repeatable and therefore partly predictable phenomenon. But the qualitative metamorphoses of financial fragility are at a far remove from the apparent quantitative regularities of growth rates of GDP, or intertemporal correlations of business cycle indicators.

When Minsky's followers try to formulate his vision into mathematical models, they face a series of methodological riddles. It is not easy to formulate a single, generic, range of assets to represent the multifarious vehicles for the financial maneuvers that lie behind financial fragility. The model needs to be able to represent a shift in the average riskiness of position. This presents a challenge to conventional portfolio analysis, which largely analyzes the distribution of a given pattern of risk among asset holders, or its pricing by a single representative asset holder. It is not clear exactly where to locate a parameter to represent the financial boldness of investors. In Minsky's discourse, the shift toward more exposed financial positions is not simply a psychological phenomenon based in the increasing optimism or level of denial of investors (though that is surely part of the process), but involves strong competitive pressures on individual investors to conform to group norms that are themselves shifting. Surveying episodes of financial fragility from the perspective of the rubble left by the eventual meltdown, we are predictably shocked and amazed by the willingness of responsible and experienced bankers or portfolio managers to continue to pour money into already gorged emerging markets, or negotiate even more improbably enormous loans with insolvent states. But if all the other banks or funds are generating exciting levels of fees and initial returns from these commitments, the manager who swims against the tide frequently lands in a department far away from the hot action and big bonuses long before the crash reveals her or his wisdom in retrospect.

Most attempts to model financial fragility mathematically settle on the procedure of positing a quantitative variable representing the risk tolerance of investors that appears as a shift parameter in asset demand functions (see Taylor and O'Connell 1985 and Sethi 1992 for two closely argued examples and references to further literature in this vein.) This variable itself is assumed to evolve in response to the history of the modeled system. It is possible to create models of this kind in which the instability of positive feedback between rising asset prices and higher risk tolerance leads to catastrophes or cyclical or chaotic trajectories. These models give us some general insight into the possible consequences of shifting asset preferences, but inevitably lose most of the richness of Minsky's account in the translation to mathematical language.

Furthermore, it is inherently difficult to calibrate these models to statistical data because of the key role played by the unobservable variable representing the shift in asset demands. It is tempting to associate this variable empirically with some measure of financial market stress, such as the difference in yield between privately issued bonds subject to default risk and government issued bonds free of default risk. But from a conventional modeling point of view these market measures are themselves endogenous to the financial process, so that they are unsuitable representatives of exogenous shift factors in the underlying mathematical model.

Even without the complications introduced by the need to pass from a mathematical model to an operational and estimable econometric model, Minsky's work raises significant problems concerning the quantitative measurement of financial fragility. Many financial statistics, such as the flow of funds tables, are essentially the statistical means of variables aggregated across a population of institutions or markets. These averages show rather low variability over the business cycle, even in periods where qualitative evidence for financial fragility is quite persuasive. What seems to be happening is that the drift toward exposed financial positions the financial fragility hypothesis posits takes place through a shift in the statistical distribution of balance sheets which has a smaller impact on the center of the distribution than on its tails. When financial crisis or pressure begins to tell, it hits a few highly exposed firms or sectors first, and only gradually spreads through the whole system. Thus there may be some reason to think that a research program focused on the higher moments of the distributions of key financial variables may shed more quantitative light on financial fragility.

But there are limits to all balance sheet based data as reflections of Minskyan fragility, because some of the central characteristics of assets are not and perhaps cannot be reported on balance sheets. Take the issue of 'nonperforming loans' of banks, for example. Bank examiners require banks to set aside capital reserves to offset potentially worthless loan assets. (The failure of Asian bank examination systems to enforce this procedure consistently is one of the forms of 'non-transparency' on which some commentators blame the Asian crisis of 1997–98.) These reserves are a kind of quantitative measure of the qualitative status of the bank's loans. But the reserves and judgments of potential 'performance' of loans are administrative evaluations, not market-generated data. Bank examiners may tend to fall behind the curve of the evolution of the market, in either underestimating or overestimating the actual value of assets. In a serious financial crisis and panic, for example, when the chips are down on the question of financial fragility, it is almost certain that some loans, that examiners view as sound, will fail to perform as a result of disruptions spreading through the financial and production system.

In view of these problems, I am not surprised that Minsky largely eschewed the project of formalizing the financial fragility hypothesis as a mathematical and econometric model. The pursuit of this project would have diluted the powerful insights of the financial fragility hypothesis in a host of ways. The general hypothesis would have become identified with a particular mathematical model and procedure for operationalizing the relevant concepts, and its scientific status would become hostage to the performance of that particular instantiation of the ideas. Since the financial fragility hypothesis calls into question the laissez-faire dogma of the superior informational and resource-allocating performance of markets around which mainstream economics unifies itself, any particular operationalization would become a target of critical work searching out its weaknesses. Minsky may have been justifiably wary of pursuing this rocky road.

But I think the deeper reason for Minsky's reluctance to formalize his ideas in line with econometric fashion was his recognition that the formal, statistical methods adopted by contemporary economists are inherently hostile to critical and qualitative insights into the performance of markets as human and social institutions. In this sense Minsky was loyal to what he knew from his voracious reading of financial and economic history, from his experience as a bank director, and from his lifelong astute observation of the drama of financial market instability and policy reaction to it. If mathematical or econometric models failed to confirm these insights, so much the worse for the models. Why make hard-won insights hostage to methodologies that approach subtle questions with blunt instruments?

Minsky's challenge to economic method
And what about those blunt instruments? Is it possible to improve the traditional methods of mathematical modeling and econometrics to embrace some or all of the dialectical point of view? While there are some constructive steps to be taken in this direction, it is doubtful that technical improvement alone can address the deeper problems involved here.

Perhaps the most pressing shortcoming of current mathematical modeling and econometric practice is its excessive reliance on assumptions of linearity in the relations it studies. Since 1980 there has been tremendous progress in the introduction of nonlinear methods into economic and econometric models. We now understand better the interplay between local and global stability in economic models, and the mathematical modeling toolbox has been greatly enriched by the addition of the ideas of bifurcation analysis and nonlinear dynamical systems. Nonlinear models can come closer to reflecting dialectical insights. For example, the emergence of new equilibria in bifurcations bears some resemblance to the dialectical notion of the qualitative evolution of a system. The existence of multiple equilibria in nonlinear systems and the consequent division of the state space into multiple basins of attraction allow small shocks to have large global impacts. As I remarked, these tools have been the main route through which economists have tried to formalize the insights of Minsky's financial fragility hypothesis. Despite the fertility and beauty of nonlinear mathematics, it is doubtful that these techniques, which remain firmly rooted in the assumption of an unchanging underlying state space, can completely express the fluidity of human social interactions.

Nonlinear econometrics has also made important advances in recent years, with the salubrious effect of revealing how much of what we thought we knew from empirical studies reflects researchers' assumptions of linearity rather than the underlying structure of the data. One helpful effect of nonlinear perspectives is to make econometric investigation more cautious in its claims. The use of nonlinear and nonparametric methods has revealed important nonlinear structures in economic data. But nonlinear and nonparametric methods also underline how limited the empirical basis for identifying these structures actually is. The assumption of parametric linearity (as in linear regression models) tends to exaggerate the resolving power of data over hypotheses by averaging correlations over different domains. Thus relations which are well identified in a small region of the domain of independent variables appear to be equally well identified by linear methods over the whole domain. Nonlinear and nonparametric methods, on the other hand, limit their inferences from each subset of the domain to that local region. The nonlinear perspective in this respect helps to reconcile econometric approaches to financial and macroeconomic problems with the qualitative insights of financial fragility analysis. Linear econometric studies appear to identify robust and pervasive relations in the data that are incompatible with the dialectical insights of financial fragility, while nonlinear studies of the same phenomena lead to more modest empirical claims which are more compatible with qualitative insights.

Another important extension of traditional econometric techniques is the explicit study of the higher moments of distributions of financial and economic variables across populations. Traditional econometrics tends overwhelmingly to assume that relevant distributions are Gaussian, and that information about means and variances are thus sufficient to characterize the whole distribution. As I indicated, many of the effects of financial fragility are manifested in changes in the spreads of distributions that do not affect the mean much, or at all, and that escape methods that assume constant variance over the sample period. As in the case of nonlinear methods, the extension of econometric techniques to a wider class of parametrically defined distributions or to nonparametrically estimated distributions greatly widens the range of empirical phenomena that we can recognize. But the apparent success of Gaussian methods in identifying structure in empirical data rests heavily on the a priori assumption of normality of the underlying distributions. With the abandonment of this assumption, it becomes much more difficult to identify structure reliably in the relatively small samples of macroeconomic time series.

There is a long minority tradition in data analysis, with which Minsky's work has considerable affinity, which has regarded the methods of linear, Gaussian, statistical inference with skepticism. This tradition puts its money on accounting identities, which do not by definition need to be estimated, only measured. A great deal can be learned about the evolution of contemporary economies by a careful study of accounting data. Since accounting methods are constructed to reflect actual developments with as much fidelity as possible, they have no bias toward representing the economic system as regular or stable. Thus it is possible to go a considerable distance toward joining the dialectical and accounting approaches to economic analysis. There always remains, however, an unbridgeable gap: accounting methods are inherently limited to measuring the outcomes of the system ex post, that is, after the fact and the resolution of the contradictions implicit in its motion. The dialectical point of view, on the other hand, strives to represent the world with its contradictions and possible futures intact, and thus to allow a discussion of such inherently ex ante issues as the appropriateness of policy.

While the development of more sophisticated and more modest mathematical and econometric methods to attack problems of the type that preoccupied Minsky is surely worthwhile, it is unlikely that this path will lead to a satisfactory synthesis of the dialectical and mathematical/statistical points of view in the foreseeable future. Lacking such a synthesis, financial and economic analysis could still benefit from two changes in methodological style.

First, we could acknowledge more directly the limits of traditional mathematical and econometric modeling techniques in attacking inherently dialectical problems in social science. The point here is not to abandon these methods altogether, since their utility in organizing masses of statistical information and clarifying our thinking about a huge range of complex policy problems is unquestionable. But the power and utility of these traditional methods is restricted to answering a particular type and range of questions, and this fact needs to be more widely appreciated. Mathematical models are tools to clarify our understanding of simplified, imaginary systems that we hope represent coherent aspects of a complex economic reality. They are possibly the only reliable tool for exploring the response of such imaginary worlds to parametric changes. Since we depend heavily on simplified imaginary metaphors to grasp real complexity, mathematical modeling is an indispensable moment in the development of our economic knowledge. But the insights mathematical models offer should not be exaggerated into a parody of science that claims that roughly calibrated models are 'true', or recklessly proposes to extrapolate their implications far beyond the natural limits of the metaphor on which they are based. Similarly, statistical techniques can tell us whether a given data set can resolve the magnitude of an empirical effect on the basis of a particular operationalization of a theoretical concept and within the limits of a particular stipulated statistical methodology. This is also important information, especially in cases where the result is relatively robust against changes in the operationalization of the concept and the assumptions of the statistical model, and is thus relatively uncontroversial. But the ability of statistical studies to answer this important type of question does not authorize us to elevate statistical correlations into facts of nature or society that transcend particular time periods or institutional structures.

Second, it would be well for economic and financial scholars to recognize more generously the validity and importance of the insights won through dialectical investigation, like Minsky's financial fragility hypothesis. This is also real human knowledge, and people who understand its discoveries are in a better position to understand historical developments, to manage their personal affairs, and to make economic and financial policy. The dialectical tradition in economic analysis serves, in any case, as the (too often unacknowledged) seedbed of ideas out of which mathematical and econometric models are constructed. There are surely important methodological problems that need to be thought through on the dialectical side as well. Given the historically specific and institutionally fluid nature of the dialectical vision, what types of arguments can its practitioners offer to recommend their claims? Here the financial fragility hypothesis and Minsky's development of the discourse based on it offer some promising suggestions. Minsky had a lively sense of the importance of validating his insights with historical examples and parallels, and of linking general patterns to a detailed examination of institutional reality and the unfolding of particular episodes of financial life. Without this thick texture of well-informed argument, the financial fragility hypothesis would have been less persuasive and less well-crafted as a part of economic knowledge.

The real knowledge that resides in qualitative, dialectical insights is recognized in the practice of many successful contemporary policy-makers. Good central bankers, for example, supplement whatever they can glean from state-of-the-art econometrics and mathematical models with information about the details and specifics of institutional evolution and market fluctuations, and a strong sense of historical perspective, precedent, and timing. A stronger dialogue between dialectical and mathematical/statistical perspectives and methods would bring academic discussion closer to the norms of financial and policy-making practice, and provide a stronger base for informed decisions.

It would be well for economic and financial scholars to take Minsky's work and methodological dilemma seriously. The seeds of future economic knowledge most likely are to be found in the fields Minsky tilled.

Note

1. This chapter was written in 2001 and is published here as it appeared in Riccardo Bellofiore and Piero Ferri (eds), *Financial Keynesianism and Market Instability: The Legacy of Hyman P. Minsky, Volume I*, Cheltenham, UK and Northampton, MA, USA: Edward Elgar, pp. 47–59.

References

Minsky, H.P. (1989), 'Comments on Friedman and Laibson', *Brookings Papers on Economic Activity*, 2, 173–82.
Sethi, R. (1992), 'Dynamics of learning and the financial instability hypothesis', *Journal of Economics (Zeitschrift für Nationalökonomie)*, **56**(1), 39–70.
Taylor, L. and S.A. O'Connell (1985), 'A Minsky crisis', *Quarterly Journal of Economics*, 100, 871–86.

10 Financial instability and agents' heterogeneity: a post Minskyan research agenda

Tiziana Assenza, Domenico Delli Gatti and Mauro Gallegati

Introduction

Has the economics profession learned Hyman Minsky's lesson?

Ask a fellow economist brought up in the neoclassical tradition and the answer will be that there is no lesson to be learned because (i) the Financial Instability Hypothesis (FIH) was cast in purely aggregative old fashioned Keynesian terms and (ii) it yields extreme, catastrophic and therefore unrealistic predictions.[1]

Ask a fellow economist brought up in the post-Keynesian tradition and the answer will be that the profession has definitely not learned the Minskyan lesson and never will because there is no way for Minsky's insights on financially sophisticated capitalism to penetrate the protective shield of the neoclassical mainstream based on the 'village fair' paradigm.

Our impression is that the landscape of economics is much more rugged than these two apparently alternative answers would lead us to think. If, in fact, they were true, financial instability would not show up as a hot topic in the most thriving research agenda. But this, clearly, is not the case. The majority of economists either ignore Minsky or consider him plainly wrong; since the mid-80s, however, a few influential economists who have not embraced any unorthodox credo have grown more receptive to his ideas, and are eager to incorporate them in their models – even if diluted and sometimes disguised – in order to make them more palatable to the conventional 'representative' macroeconomist.

Due to the asymmetric information revolution in microeconomics, and the associated emphasis on capital market imperfections, Minsky's ideas have received renewed attention and a large literature has developed in which financial factors play a major role: Greenwald and Stiglitz (1988, 1990, 1993, 2003), Bernanke and Gertler (1989, 1990),[2] Kiyotaki and Moore (1997). For the sake of clarity, we will consider all these models under the general heading of the Financial Accelerator Hypothesis (FAH).

Starting from different cultural and methodological premises, this literature yields predictions which are in line with some of the insights one can get from Minsky's conceptual framework. In other words, the FAH and the FIH share some features as we try to show in the second section.

Does Minsky's legacy go beyond the emphasis on the role of financial factors and provide directions for research on new and unexplored territory? Our answer is a resounding yes. In our opinion the role of heterogeneous financial conditions is the specific piece of Minsky's intellectual heritage that has been so far underresearched and may be the cornerstone of a new research agenda. Minsky's theory of investment determination can be formulated without making explicit reference to heterogeneity, since, at a deeper level, Minsky develops his ideas in a setting of heterogeneous agents. His distinction among hedge, speculative and *Ponzi* units, is crucial for the FIH. On the other hand, the FAH literature is still mainly based on the Representative Agent (RA), while heterogeneity has been confined to an almost innocuous role. The increasing availability of computational power has allowed the implementation of multi-agent models so that we are at present equipped with the most straightforward framework for the analysis of the role of heterogeneous financial conditions in macroeconomics.

In this chapter we provide an example of a macrodynamic model in which firms are characterized by hcterogeneous financial conditions at the firm level. In the fourth section we describe the behavior of financially constrained firms. In the fifth section we analyze the behavior of households. In the sixth section we describe and discuss the macroeconomic equilibrium. Finally, in the seventh section, we derive the dynamics generated by the model which are described by a myriad laws of motion of the individual financial conditions. Since it is impossible to compute closed form solutions for such a system, we have to resort to computer simulations to analyze the evolution of micro state variables and macro variables. In the eighth section we draw our conclusions.[3]

Investment

The core of Minsky's analysis is a financial theory of investment according to which investment is essentially driven by: (i) the difference between the market price of capital goods in place and the current price of investments goods; (ii) the volume of internal finance.

As to the first factor, Minsky writes: 'Prices of capital assets depend upon current views of future profit flows and the current subjective value placed upon the insurance against uncertainty embodied in money or quick cash: these current views depend upon expectations that are held about the longer run development of the economy. The prices of current output are based upon current views of near term demand conditions and

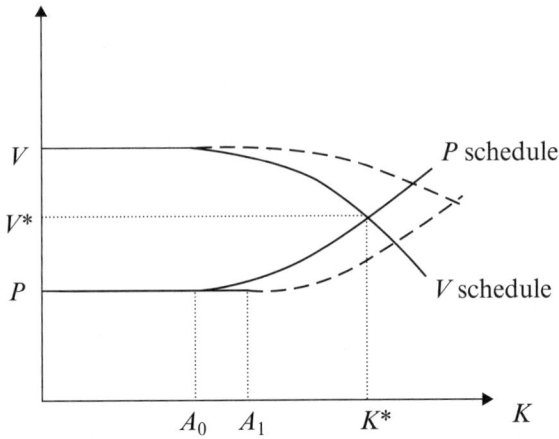

Figure 10.1   Minsky's theory of investment determination

current knowledge of money wage rates. Thus the prices of current output
. . . depend upon shorter run expectations. Capital-asset and current
output prices are based on expectations over quite different time horizons:
capital asset prices reflect long run expectations and current output prices
reflect short term expectations' (Minsky 1982, pp. 94–5).

As to the second factor, Minsky notes that the investment which can be
debt financed today depends on the cash flows expected by both borrowers
(firms) and lenders (banks) tomorrow. The higher the realized cash flow
relative to debt commitments, the higher the rate of fulfillment of contracts, which positively affects the state of confidence of both bankers and
business people and leads to a higher volume of investment being financed
and carried out.

Minsky's theory of investment determination can be illustrated with the
help of Figure 10.1. The quantity of capital[4] is measured on the x-axis and
the 'prices' of capital on the y-axis. Minsky draws a distinction between
the supply price of investment goods – which we assume for simplicity to
be equal to the average price level (P) – and the market price of capital
assets (V), which can be thought of as the present value of the stream of
expected quasi rent per unit of capital. By assumption, the latter coincides
with the stock price.

Investment can be financed in part by means of internally generated
funds, which coincide with net worth (A) and in part by external finance.[5]
For a given price of newly produced capital goods (say P_0) and a given
level of internal finance (say A_0), we can determine the maximum volume
of investment which can be financed by means of internal funds $K_0 = A_0$.

By assumption, the quasi rent is increasing with the volume of net worth. Hence we can compute the market price V_0 as an increasing function of A_0.

If the firm chooses a level of investment greater than K_0, it has to raise funds on the credit market. In this case banks have to be remunerated for the risk they assume *(lender's risk)*, so that the actual supply price of investment goods for the borrowing firm is higher than the price of newly produced capital goods P_0. The schedule of the actual price of investment goods *(P schedule)*, therefore, is flat at P_0 until the maximum volume of internally financed investment K_0 is reached and is increasing thereafter.[6]

Symmetrically, if the firm chooses a level of investment greater than K_0, the risk of bankruptcy for the firm *(borrower's risk)* increases and the expected quasi rent decreases so that the actual stock price is lower than the original one V_0. The schedule of the actual market price of investment goods *(V schedule)*, therefore, is flat at V_0 until the maximum volume of internally financed investment K_0 is reached and is decreasing thereafter.[7]

The equilibrium volume of investment (K^*) and the equilibrium price of investment goods (V^*) are determined at the intersection of the upward sloping schedule representing the supply price of investment augmented by lender's risk and the downward sloping schedule which describes the market price of capital goods augmented by borrower's risk. Equilibrium investment depends upon the volume of internal finance and on the degree of borrower's and lender's risk which affect the slopes of the V and P schedules: $K^* = K(A_0)$. An increase in the availability of internal funds from A_0 to A_1 brings about an outward shift of both the V and P schedules and an increase of investment as shown in the figure.

Figure 10.1 applies to the single firm. In principle, all the determinants of investment can be firm-specific. Let's assume for the moment, however, that the RA assumption holds true. In this case, aggregate investment is:

$$K = K(A) \qquad (10.1)$$

Equation (10.1) can be conceived of as the first building block of a skeletal Minskyan macroeconomic framework. It is an *investment equation* which links capital accumulation to net worth. This equation can be complemented by, for instance, a profit equation à la Kalecki. Aggregate output can be determined by means of Keynes's theory of effective demand. Most of the aggregative Keynesian-Minskyan models developed in the 1980s and early 1990s following the seminal paper by Taylor and O'Connell (1985) are based on this type of equation. We will not discuss their features here since our aim is to compare Minsky's theory with a more recent wave of models of financially driven fluctuations which essentially end up with a theory of investment determination reminiscent of Equation (10.1).

Minsky's FIH has represented the minority view in the profession until the mid-1980s when the asymmetric information revolution in microeconomics raised doubts about the plausibility of the Modigliani-Miller (MM) irrelevance proposition. Once one acknowledges that capital markets are imperfect due to informational asymmetries, the MM construct – according to which internal and external sources of funds are perfect substitutes so that the capital structure of the firm does not affect investment decisions – crumbles. Sources of finance are imperfect substitutes and can be ranked in a financing hierarchy in which internal finance comes first.

In this conceptual context, financial factors are indeed crucial for investment and, therefore, for business fluctuations. The tools to deal with this phenomenon, however, were not available to the representative neoclassical macroeconomist who had so far eagerly accepted the MM credo:

> How does one go about incorporating financial distress and similar concepts into macroeconomics? While it seems that there has always been an empirical case for including credit-market factors in the mainstream model, early writers found it difficult to bring such apparently diverse and chaotic phenomena into their formal analyses. As a result, advocacy of a role for these factors in aggregate dynamics fell for the most part to economists outside the US academic mainstream, such as Hyman Minsky, and to some forecasters and financial market practitioners. (Bernanke et al. 1999, p. 1344)

Since the late 1980s, a large and diversified literature has filled this void, incorporating financial factors in more or less mainstream – that is, microfounded – macroeconomic models, a line of research known as the FAH. At least three frameworks have been proposed by Greenwald and Stiglitz (GS) (1988, 1990, 1993, 2003), Bernanke and Gertler (BG) (1989, 1990) and Kiyotaki and Moore (1997, 2002).

Consider for instance investment determination in BG. In Figure 10.2 we measure capital on the x-axis and 'returns' on the y-axis. Internal finance has an opportunity cost equal to the return on a safe asset, that is, the risk-free interest rate. The cost of funds therefore is equal to the risk free interest rate r up until $K_0 = A_0$. If the firm chooses a level of investment greater than K_0, it has to raise funds on the credit market. In this case banks have to be remunerated for the risk they assume *(lender's risk)* so that the cost of funds for the borrowing firm – that is, the return on lending for the bank – is higher than the risk free interest rate, the difference being the *external finance premium*.[8] In other words, the cost of external finance

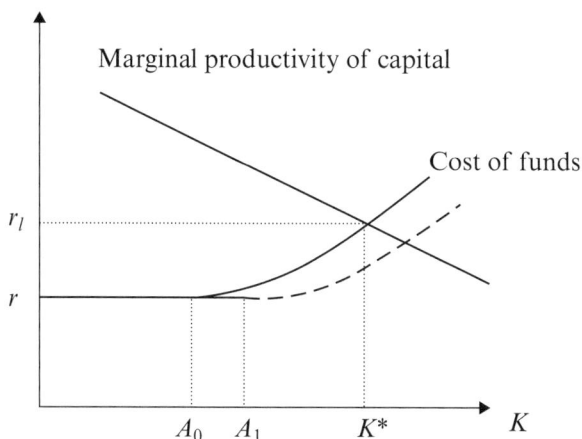

Figure 10.2 Investment determination in Bernanke and Gertler

is higher, due to imperfect substitutability between internal and external sources of funds. The schedule of the actual cost of funds is flat at r until the maximum volume of internally financed investment K_0 and increasing thereafter.

The equilibrium volume of investment (K^*) and the equilibrium interest rate on loans (r_l) are determined at the intersection of the upward sloping cost of funds schedule and the downward sloping schedule which describes the marginal productivity of capital. Equilibrium investment depends upon the volume of internal finance also in this context $K^* = K(A_0)$. An increase of net worth makes the external finance premium go down so that the cost of funds schedule shifts outward, investment goes up and the interest rate on loans goes down as shown in the figure.

Investment determination in a GS framework is shown in Figure 10.3.[9] The user cost of capital is equal to the interest rate r up to $K_0 = A_0$. If the firm chooses a level of investment greater than K_0, it has to raise funds on the credit market, running the risk of bankruptcy *(borrower's risk)*. Since bankruptcy is costly, the cost of funds for the indebted firm goes up. The schedule of the actual marginal cost of funds, therefore, is flat at r until the maximum volume of internally financed investment K_0 is reached and is increasing thereafter. The upward sloping portion of the marginal cost schedule incorporates the expected marginal bankruptcy cost, which in turn depends upon the probability of bankruptcy. GS show that this probability is decreasing with net worth.

The equilibrium volume of investment (K^*) is determined at the intersection of the upward sloping marginal cost of funds schedule and the

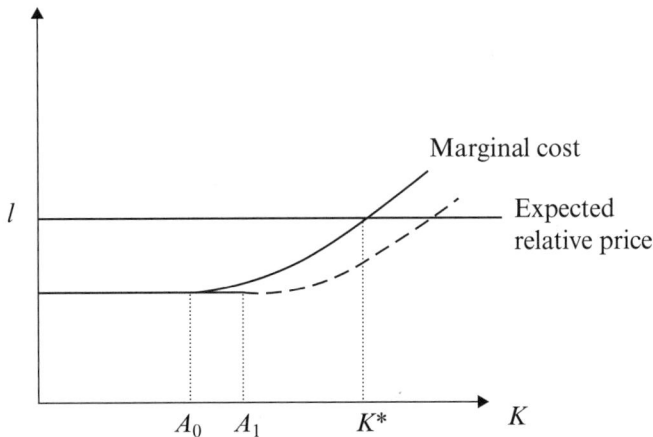

Figure 10.3   Investment determination in Greenwald and Stiglitz

expected relative price, that is, the mathematical expectation of the ratio of the individual price to the average price level. By construction, in a perfect competition setting, this expected relative price is equal to one.

Equilibrium investment therefore depends upon the volume of internal finance $K^* = K(A_0)$. An increase of net worth makes the marginal bankruptcy cost go down so that the cost of fund schedule shifts outward and investment goes up as shown in the figure.

It is clear therefore that in both GS and in BG we can reach qualitatively the same conclusion that Minsky already put forward on the importance of financial factors – namely internal finance or net worth – on investment determination (see equation (10.1)). The context, however, is different. The financial accelerator theories are generally derived from the solution of an optimization problem of a rational representative agent, often equipped with rational expectations or perfect foresight, while Minsky casts the FIH in a context of true Knightian uncertainty. This is clearly a major methodological divide and we don't want to underestimate the depth of the abyss between Post Keynesian and New Keynesian research strategies. In our opinion, however, Minsky's ideas have indeed penetrated the protective shield of mainstream macroeconomics. He's got a point, even if orthodox economists do not eagerly recognize it.

Heterogeneity

Minsky's theory of investment determination can be formulated without explicit reference to heterogeneity as shown above. At a deeper and more significant level, however, Minsky's ideas can be properly expressed only in an heterogeneous agents' setting. The FIH is based on the distinction among hedge, speculative and Ponzi units.

> For hedge financing units, the cash flows from participation in income production are expected to exceed the contractual payments on outstanding debts in every period. For speculative financing units, the total expected cash flows from participation in income production when totaled over the foreseeable future exceed the total cash payments on outstanding debt, but the near term payment commitments exceed the near term cash flow from participation in income production, even though the net income portion of the near term cash flows . . . exceeds the near term interest payments on debt. A Ponzi financing unit is a speculative financing unit for which the income component of the near term cash flow falls short of the near term interest payments on debt so that for some time in the future the outstanding debt will grow due to interest on existing debt. Both speculative and Ponzi units can fulfill their payment commitments on debts only by borrowing (or disposing of assets). (Minsky 1982, pp. 22–3)

In a 'tranquil era' ('prosperous times'), both borrowers and lenders expect future cash flows to be more than enough to validate debt. Asset prices, which incorporate these expectations, increase relative to the price of current output, stimulating investments which in turn drive up output, profits and employment. Banks are less cautious in extending credit and firms are less cautious in borrowing. As a consequence hedge units, that is, borrowers who are able to service debt in each and every period of the time horizon of their financial contracts, become speculative units. Borrowers who were speculative units, in turn, become Ponzi units, that is, they have to borrow in order to service outstanding debt. As the proportion of hedge units in the population of borrowers decreases, financial fragility increases:

> over a period in which the economy does well, views about acceptable debt structure change. In the deal-making that goes on between banks, investment bankers, and businessmen, the acceptable amount of debt to use in financing various types of activity and positions increases. This increase in the weight of debt financing raises the market price of capital assets and increases investment. As this continues the economy is transformed into a boom economy. (Minsky 1982, pp. 65–6)

In other words, in Minsky's heterogeneous agents setting, the increase of aggregate financial fragility during the expansion is due to the change of the structure of the economy, the weight of hedge units shrinking over time. When the perception spreads that in the aggregate cash flows do not validate debt any more – for instance because a stream of overextended borrowers goes bankrupt – the network of financial relations collapses and a financial crisis sets in.

Albeit very different, all of the financial accelerator theories consider economies characterized by imperfect and asymmetric information on financial markets. Implicitly or explicitly, therefore, they should be based upon the assumption of agents' heterogeneity. In the end, however, very few heterogeneous agents are dealt with in these models, basically one 'representative' for each group of agents (firms, households, banks, and so on). This shortcut allows us to resume the RA assumption, which allows us to simplify the analysis to a great extent.

The RA assumption is still the cornerstone of most of contemporary macroeconomics but the awareness of its limitations[10] is spreading well beyond the circle of more or less dissenting economists. Also in mainstream macroeconomics the RA is not as eagerly embraced as in the early years of the debate on microfoundations in the 1970s, but is still adopted mainly for lack of a workable alternative.

In this chapter, we try to cast the financial accelerator/financial instability story in a context of truly heterogeneous agents. True heterogeneity occurs when agents are different within the same group – in the present framework we will deal with heterogeneity of financial conditions across firms – so that we cannot rely upon the representative agent device even to describe the behavior of a class of agents. True heterogeneity is obviously appealing, but has a major disadvantage: we need an aggregation procedure to build the model from the bottom up. As it is well known from a large literature, aggregation is not an innocuous task in economics.

In order to take heterogeneity seriously in macroeconomic modeling, we should start with heterogeneous behavioral rules at the micro level and determine the aggregate (macroeconomic) quantity – such as GDP – by adding up the levels of a myriad individual quantities. The increasing availability of computational power has allowed the implementation of this bottom-up procedure in multi-agent models. Not surprisingly, in the last ten years or so, a proliferation of agent-based models has paralleled the diffusion of research on issues concerning heterogeneity.[11]

Multi-agent modeling is the most straightforward way of tackling the heterogeneity issue. In the profession at large, however, there is no agreement on the opportunity of following this methodology. While some unorthodox colleagues eagerly embrace the new research strategy, some others, mainly in the mainstream, are skeptical or even dismissive. There are at least three reasons for this skepticism: (i) a basic distrust for the output of computer simulations, which are generally very sensitive to the choice of initial conditions and parameter values; (ii) a critique of adaptive micro-behavioral rules which are often considered ad hoc; (iii) the difficulty and, sometimes, the impossibility of thinking in macroeconomic terms, that is, of using macro variables in the theoretical framework.

The first type of skepticism is rapidly fading away. After all, Real Business Cycle (RBC) models are too complicated to be solved by pen and paper and must be simulated. In order to do so RBC theorists have developed procedures to calibrate their models which, with the passing of time have become standard tools – we can even call them protocols – of macroeconomic research.The same is true of agent-based models: Calibration and validation are ranking high in the agenda of multi-agent models' implementation.

As to the behavioral rules at the micro level, it is true that multi-agent models allow the comparison of the impact of different behavioral rules of thumb, which are often traced back to bounded rationality and adaptive behavior. There is no reason, however, to assume that this is the only way of modeling individual choices. The multi-agent framework can also accommodate models of optimizing behavior of heterogeneous agents. In this chapter, for instance, we show that very similar behavioral rules concerning capital accumulation can be either assumed as a rule of thumb adopted by less than rational agents – according to the Keynesian-Minskyan approach – or derived from a constrained optimization exercise as in GS.

Finally, the difficulty of thinking in macroeconomic terms can be circumvented by means of an appropriate aggregation procedure. In this chapter, we adopt a stochastic aggregation procedure – labeled the *Modified-Representative Agent* – which allows us to resume macroeconomic thinking in a multi-agent framework.[12]

In this chapter we build a macrodynamic model starting from the assumption, well corroborated by the existing evidence, that firms differ from one another according to their financial conditions. The diversity of firms' financial conditions is the only type of heterogeneity in our framework. For the sake of analytical tractability, we keep the degree of heterogeneity at the lowest possible level, that is, only one type of heterogeneity for only one class of agents. Therefore, we will use the old-fashioned representative agent assumption as far as households are concerned.Within each household, however, we will distinguish between employed and unemployed family members.

Firms

We consider a closed economy populated by firms, households, financial intermediaries (banks) and the public sector (Government). Firms will be indexed by $i = 1, 2, ..., z$. Each firm is characterized by a certain degree of financial robustness, captured by the equity ratio that is the ratio of the equity base or net worth to the capital stock

$$a_{it} = \frac{A_{it}}{K_{it}}.$$

In other words, the equity ratio of the i-th firm at time t; a_{it} is a random variable with support $(0,1)$, whose distribution is characterized by expected value $E(a_{it}) = a_t$ and variance $E(a_{it} - a_t)^2 = V_t$. The expected value is the equity ratio of the average agent (average equity ratio for short). The variance measures the dispersion of the actual equity ratios around the average. The RA is a particular case of this framework: it coincides with the average agent when the variance is zero.

Banks extend credit to firms at an interest rate r which is uniform across firms and equal to the interest rate on bonds.

Each firm carries on production by means of a technology of the Leontief type and uniform across firms. The production function of the i-th firm therefore is $Y_i = \min(\lambda N_i, v K_i)$ where Y_i, N_i and K_i represent output, employment and capital (in the current period, that is, at time t), v and λ are positive parameters which measure the productivity of capital and labor respectively.

Assuming that labor is always abundant, we can write $Y_i = v K_i$ and $N_i = (v/\lambda) K_i = (Y_i/\lambda)$. v is the reciprocal of the capital/output ratio. v/λ is the reciprocal of the capital/labor ratio. Since these parameters are constant, by assumption output, capital and employment grow at the same rate. We will determine the rate of capital accumulation endogenously (see below) and will assume that output and employment grow at the same rate of the capital stock.

At this point we need a theory of *financially constrained capital accumulation*. We propose the following:

$$\tau_{it} = \pi - (r_t + f_{it}) \qquad (10.2)$$

where

$$\tau_{it} \equiv \frac{I_{it}}{\overline{K}_{t-1}}$$

is the investment ratio, that is, the ratio of individual investment to the average capital stock:

$$\overline{K}_{t-1} = \frac{\sum_{i=1}^{z} K_{it-1}}{z},$$

π represents earnings before interest – that is, revenue net of labor costs per unit of capital (in the following we will refer to π as the profit rate) – and

$$f_{it} = \frac{\phi}{a_{it-1}}$$

is the increase in cost due to the borrower and/or the lender risk which we will refer to as the *external finance premium*. In a nutshell, this theory states that (1) the cost of funds for each firm is equal to the interest rate (uniform across firms) augmented by the external finance premium and (2) the external finance premium is decreasing with the individual financial robustness captured by the individual equity ratio.

Equation (10.2) can be postulated as a convenient rule of thumb in a bounded rationality setting – as such, it is consistent with Minsky's theory of investment determination – or can be derived from the maximization of expected profit net of bankruptcy cost in a GS setting – as shown in detail in Assenza and Delli Gatti (2008). In this case and the parameter ϕ can be decomposed as follows $\phi = \beta\alpha$, where β captures the sensitivity of the bankruptcy cost to the scale of activity and α is the bankruptcy threshold, that is, the level of the equity ratio below which the firm goes bankrupt (a number very close to zero).

As we could expect, the investment ratio is increasing with the equity ratio. In fact

$$\frac{\partial \tau_{it}}{\partial a_{it-1}} = \frac{\phi}{a_{it-1}^2} > 0$$

In the case of the RA, we obtain:

$$\tau_t^R = \pi - (r_t + f_t^R) \tag{10.3}$$

where

$$\tau_t^R \equiv \frac{I_t}{K_{t-1}}$$

is the investment ratio of the RA and

$$f_t^R \equiv \frac{\phi}{a_{t-1}}$$

is the external finance premium in the RA case.

The first best can be defined as a situation in which there is no external finance premium, that is,

$$\tau_t^F = \pi - r_t \tag{10.4}$$

The average investment ratio τ is the average of individual investment ratios:

$$\tau_t = \frac{1}{z}\sum_{i=1}^{z}\tau_{it} = \pi - r_t - \frac{\phi}{z}\left[\frac{1}{a_{1t-1}} + \frac{1}{a_{2t-1}} + \ldots + \frac{1}{a_{zt-1}}\right]$$

Hence, it depends on π and r_t, which are uniform across firms, and on the entire *distribution* of the firms' degree of financial robustness $(a_{1t-1}, a_{2t-1}, \ldots, a_{zt-1})$.

Using Taylor's formula and computing the derivatives at the average equity ratio we can write:

$$\tau_{it} = \tau_t^R + \frac{\partial \tau_{it}}{\partial a_{it-1}}(a_{it-1} - a_{t-1}) + \frac{1}{2}\frac{\partial^2 \tau_{it}}{\partial a_{it-1}^2}(a_{it-1} - a_{t-1})^2 + \ldots$$

Taking the expected value of the expression above and recalling that, by definition, $E(a_{it-1} - a_{t-1}) = 0$ one gets:

$$\tau_t = E(\tau_{it}) = \tau_t^R + \frac{1}{2}\frac{\partial^2 \tau_{it}}{\partial a_{it-1}^2}E(a_{it-1} - a_{t-1})^2 + \ldots$$

where $E(a_{it-1} - a_{t-1})^2 = V_{t-1}$ is the variance of the distribution of the equity ratio. From the equation above, it is clear that the average investment ratio can be conceived as the investment ratio of the RA augmented by a weighted sum of all the moments of the distribution of the equity ratio. In the following, in order to keep the analysis as simple as possible, we will cut short the series above at the second term,[13] that is, we will approximate the average investment ratio as follows

$$\tau_t \approx \tau_t^R + \frac{1}{2}\frac{\partial^2 \tau_{it}}{\partial a_{it-1}^2}V_{t-1} \tag{10.5}$$

where

$$\frac{\partial^2 \tau_{it}}{\partial a_{it-1}^2} = -\frac{2\phi}{a_{t-1}^3} < 0$$

Therefore equation (10.5) boils down to:

$$\tau_t \approx \tau_t^R - \frac{\phi}{a_{t-1}^3}V_{t-1} = \pi - (r_t + f_t) \tag{10.6}$$

$$f_t \equiv \frac{\phi}{a_{t-1}}\left(1 + \frac{V_{t-1}}{a_{t-1}^2}\right) = f(a_{t-1}, V_{t-1}), f_{a_{t-1}} < 0, f_{V_{t-1}} > 0. \tag{10.7}$$

According to (10.6) the *average* investment ratio is the difference between the profit rate π and the interest rate r, 'augmented' by the *average* external finance premium f, which is decreasing with the average equity ratio and increasing with the variance of the equity ratio.

In the Keynesian–Minskyan macrodynamic aggregative literature pioneered by Taylor and O'Connell (1985), a formulation reminiscent of (10.6) is sometimes adopted. Taylor and O'Connell postulate the following theory of the growth rate of the capital stock:

$$\tau = g\left(\frac{\pi + \rho}{r}\right) \tag{10.8}$$

where $g(.)$ is an increasing function and ρ is the *expected incremental profit rate*, a proxy of the *state of confidence*. In an extension of the same framework, Franke and Semmler (1989) propose the following law governing expectational dynamics:

$$\dot{\rho} = \pi(a) - r(a) \tag{10.9}$$

where a dot on a variable is a shortcut for the time derivative. According to (10.9) euphoria sets in whenever the profit rate is higher than the interest rate. Both variables, in turn, depend on the equity ratio.[14] If the equity ratio for any reason goes up, the profit rate increases while the interest rate decreases, the gap between the two becomes wider and the expected incremental profit rate goes up, boosting investment. In the Franke-Semmler context, a stronger average financial condition positively affects capital accumulation through the state of profit expectations, which are procyclical. In the present context, on the other hand, an increase of financial robustness boosts investment through the external finance premium, which is anti-cyclical.

The Keynesian-Minskyan purely aggregative models quoted above, however, do not take heterogeneity into account. In the present context, on the contrary, heterogeneity plays a crucial role through the external finance premium.The average investment ratio in the presence of heterogeneity τ, in fact, is smaller than the investment ratio of the representative agent τ_t^R which in turn is smaller than the first best investment ratio τ_t^f. In other words we have the following hierarchy of investment ratios

$$\tau_t^F > \tau_t^R > \tau_t$$

To illustrate this point, in Figure 10.4 we represent equation (10.2). The investment ratio of the *i*-th firm τ_{it} is an increasing concave function of

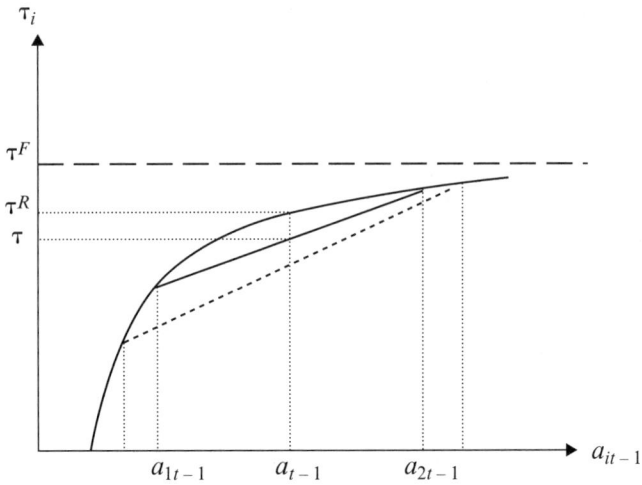

Figure 10.4   Individual investment ratio

the individual equity ratio a_{it-1} and tends asymptotically to the first best investment ratio τ_t^F.

For the sake of discussion, consider the simplest case of a corporate sector consisting of just two firms, indexed 1 and 2, whose equity ratios are a_{1t-1} and a_{2t-1}. Thanks to concavity of the investment ratio, by Jensen's inequality, the average investment ratio τ_t will be smaller than the investment ratio associated with the average equity ratio τ^R – that is, the investment ratio of the RA – which in turn will be smaller than first best. A mean preserving increase in dispersion will bring about a decrease of the average investment ratio.

Average investment will be $\bar{I}_t = \tau_t \bar{K}_{t-1}$ so that in the aggregate $I_t = \tau_t K_{t-1}$ and therefore $K_t = (1 + \tau_t) K_{t-1}$. The average investment ratio represents also the rate of growth of the aggregate capital stock: $\tau_t = g_t$. Due to the Leontief technology also employment and output grow at the same rate as the capital stock.

Households

As to households, for the sake of simplicity, we assume that they are homogeneous in every respect so that we can adopt the RA hypothesis. Households demand consumption goods, financial assets (bonds) and money balances. Money balances provide liquidity services which are necessary if transactions require a means of payment, as we will assume.

The household supplies inelastically one unit of labor. In period t

each member of the household may be employed with probability x_t or unemployed with probability $1 - x_t$. Assuming that the law of large numbers applies, x_t coincides with the fraction of household's members who are employed and can be thought of also as the employment rate economywide. Therefore $1 - x_t$ is the unemployment rate.

Since by assumption all the profits are retained within the firm, the only source of income for the household is the wage rate w if employed, the unemployment subsidy σ if unemployed, $w > \sigma$. Expected household's income therefore is $wx_t + \sigma(1 - x_t)$. For simplicity, both the real wage and the unemployment subsidy are constant. In the following we will keep the aggregate price level constant and normalize it to unity.

We can assume as a reasonable rule of thumb or derive under appropriate conditions – see again Assenza et al. (2007) for details – the following consumption and money demand functions for the representative household:

$$c_t = wx_t + \sigma(1 - x_t) \tag{10.10}$$

$$m_t = r_t^{-1}[wx_t + \sigma(1 - x_t)] \tag{10.11}$$

According to the first equation, per-capita consumption is equal to expected income while the demand for money is proportional to expected income (that is, consumption), the coefficient of proportionality being inversely related to the interest rate.

Equilibrium

In this economy there will be markets in goods, money and bonds. Due to real wage rigidity, the labor market can be characterized by under-employment even if both the money and goods markets are in equilibrium. Thanks to Walras' law, there will be also equilibrium on the market for bonds.

The goods market is in equilibrium (per-capita planned expenditure is equal to actual expenditure) if $c_t + \frac{I_t}{L_t} = \frac{Y_t}{L_t}$ where L_t is the number of households. Per-capita consumption c_t is defined as in (ct). Per-capita investment $\frac{I_t}{L_t}$ is equal to

$$\tau_t \frac{K_{t-1}}{L_t} = \tau_t \frac{K_{t-1}}{K_t} \frac{K_t}{N_t} \frac{N_t}{L_t} = \frac{\tau_t}{1 + \tau_t} \frac{\lambda}{v} x_t.$$

Per-capita income $\frac{Y_t}{L_t}$ is equal to

$$\frac{Y_t}{N_t} \frac{N_t}{L_t} = \lambda x_t.$$

Therefore, in equilibrium the following must hold true:

$$w + \sigma\left(\frac{1}{x_t} - 1\right) + \frac{\tau_t}{1 + \tau_t}\frac{\lambda}{v} = \lambda \qquad (10.12)$$

Thanks to the linearity of technology, x_t can be thought of also as a measure of *capacity utilization*. In fact, $N_t = Y_t/\lambda$ and $L_t = \hat{Y}_t/\lambda$ where $\hat{Y}_t$ is potential output so that $x_t = Y_t/\hat{Y}_t$. As a consequence, $1 - x_t$ – that is, the unemployment rate – can be thought of as the *output gap*.

In order to simplify matters, we linearize the term $1/x_t$ around full capacity (that is, $x_t = 1$) by means of the usual Taylor's procedure. Therefore $1/x_t - 1 \approx 1 - x_t$. Analogously, linearizing the term $(\tau_t)/(1 + \tau_t)$ around $\tau_t = 0$ we get $(\tau_t)/(1 + \tau_t) \approx \tau_t$. Hence equation (10.12) becomes $w + \sigma(1 - x_t) + \tau_t(\lambda/v) = \lambda$. Recalling that $\tau_t = \pi - r_t - f_t$ (see equation (10.6)) in the end we can write:

$$w + \sigma(1 - x_t) + (\pi - r_t - f_t)\frac{\lambda}{v} = \lambda$$

Notice now that $\lambda = w + \pi(\lambda/v)$. In fact $\pi(\lambda/v)$ represents profits per worker, being the product of the profit rate π times the capital/labor ratio λ/v. By definition, the sum of labor income per worker – that is, the wage rate – and non-labor income per worker is equal to income per worker.

Hence equation (10.12) becomes:

$$r_t = \sigma\frac{v}{\lambda}(1 - x_t) - f_t \qquad (10.13)$$

This relation between r_t and x_t represents the IS curve of our model. The average external finance premium is a shift parameter of the IS curve.

We now turn to the *money market*. Imposing the equilibrium condition $m_t = \overline{m}$ where $\overline{m} = M_t/L_t$ represents per-capita money supply we get

$$x_t = \frac{1}{w - \sigma}(r_t\overline{m} - \sigma) \qquad (10.14)$$

In the following we will assume that the rate of growth of money supply will be equal to the rate of growth of population so that per capita money supply will be constant over time. This relation between r_t and x_t represents the LM curve of our model.

The system (10.13)(10.14) can be solved for the equilibrium interest rate and capacity utilization. After some algebra we get the following reduced form

$$r_t = \Gamma\left[\sigma\frac{v}{\lambda}w - (w - \sigma)f_t\right] \qquad (10.15)$$

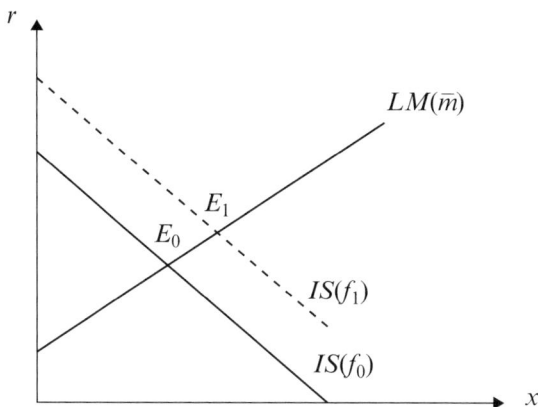

Figure 10.5 The macroeconomic equilibrium

$$x_t = \Gamma \frac{\overline{m}}{w - \sigma} \left[\sigma \frac{v}{\lambda} w - (w - \sigma) f_t \right] - \frac{\sigma}{w - \sigma} \qquad (10.16)$$

where

$$\Gamma = \left(w - \sigma + \sigma \frac{v}{\lambda} \overline{m} \right)^{-1}$$

is positive (since $w > \sigma$) and decreasing with per-capita money supply. We will assume

$$\sigma \frac{v}{\lambda} w - (w - \sigma) f_t > \frac{\sigma}{\Gamma \overline{m}}$$

in order to guarantee that both r_t and x_t are positive.

In Figure 10.5 we represent the macroeconomic equilibrium. Since

$$f_t \equiv \frac{\phi}{a_{t-1}} \left(1 + \frac{V_{t-1}}{a_{t-1}^2} \right)$$

(see (10.7)), the moments of the distribution of the equity ratio are shift parameters of the IS curve. For each level of the interest rate, the higher the mean and the lower the variance of the equity ratio, the higher will be employment and output.

If for example we consider a certain value of the mean (a_0) and of the variance (V_0) of the distribution, given the LM curve, the economy converges to the equilibrium E_0. At this point we consider the case in which the mean of the distribution increases while the variance decreases, the IS curve shifts up and the new macroeconomic equilibrium is represented by the point E_1 with a higher level of both capacity utilization and the real interest rate.

Dynamics

The moments of the distribution of financial conditions (incorporated in the external finance premium) show up in Figure 10.5 as exogenous variables. More precisely they are pre-determined variables. At this point we have to determine the law of motion of the moments because they are the driving force behind the model dynamics. In order to do so, first of all we have to establish the law of motion of the equity ratio.

In a model along GS lines we derive the following:

$$a_{it} = a_{it-1} \left(\frac{s_{it-1}}{s_{it-1} + \tau_{it}} \right) + u_i \nu - w\frac{\nu}{\lambda} - r_t - \frac{1}{2} \frac{\tau_{it}^2}{s_{it-1} + \tau_{it}} \quad (10.17)$$

where r_t is defined as in (rstar) and τ_{it} is defined as in (taui). u_i is a random shock, $s_{it} = K_{it}/\overline{K}_t$ is the relative size of the firm.

$$a_t = a_{t-1} \left(\frac{1}{1 + \tau_t} \right) + u_i \nu - w\frac{\nu}{\lambda} - r_t - \frac{1}{2} \frac{\tau_t^2}{1 + \tau_t} \quad (10.18)$$

Equation (10.17) is the *law of motion of the individual equity ratio*. In each period, given the real wage and technological parameters, the financial robustness of the i-th firm is a function of two individual variables, that is, the investment ratio – which is determined by the financial robustness of the past – and the relative size, one macro variable, that is, the interest rate, and a stochastic disturbance (u_{it}).

Notice that when the interest rate goes up, there will be a negative impact effect on a_{it}. This effect is uniform across firms. Moreover τ_{it} will go down, triggering also an indirect effect on a_{it}. This indirect effect shows up in the first and the last term of the equation above.

In a multi-agent setting, the dynamics of the model are described by a myriad laws of motion of the individual equity ratios, that is, a multi-dimensional system of non-linear difference equations subject to stochastic shocks. Since it is impossible to compute closed form solutions for such a system, we have to resort to computer simulations to analyze the evolution of micro state variables and macro variables. From the output of these simulations it is immediate to compute the moments of the distribution of financial conditions (that is, the cross-sectional mean and variance) for each time period.

The evolution over time of the individual equity ratio turns out to be

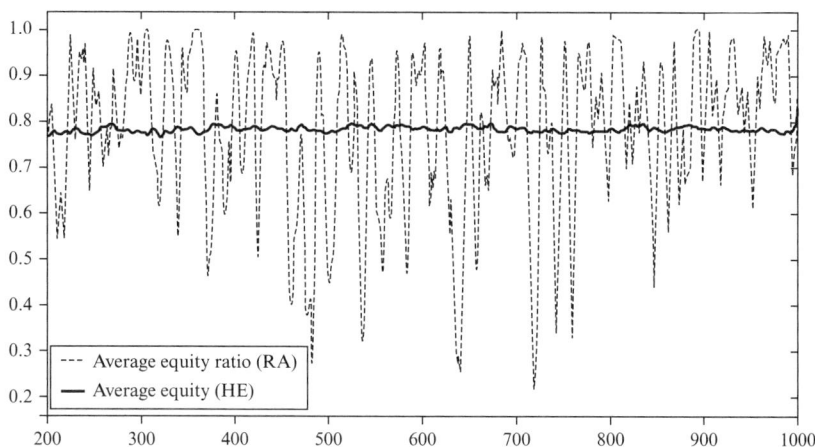

Figure 10.6 Average equity ratio

a function of the cross-sectional mean and variance of the equity ratios which shows up in the external finance premium and therefore affects the interest rate. This is the source of a macroeconomic externality whereby the economy-wide financial condition indirectly affects the individual financial condition.

We consider a virtual economy consisting of $I = 1000$ firms, over a time span of $T = 1000$ periods ('quarters'). There are six free parameters in the model – see Assenza and Delli Gatti (2008) for details – which are set as follows: $\phi = 0.004$, $v = 1/3$, $\lambda = 1$, $w = 0.7$, $\sigma = 0.2$, $\overline{m} = 200$. The configuration of parameters we have chosen will yield dynamic patterns of the main macroeconomic variables – that is, the interest rate, the output gap and the average equity ratio – roughly in line with the empirical evidence.

We compare the properties of this setting – which we label the Heterogeneous Agents (HE) case – with the benchmark, that is, the RA case, which can be simulated imposing the following restrictions:

$$z = 1, f_t = \frac{\phi}{a_t}, s_{it} = 1 \ \forall t.$$

In Figure 10.6 we plot the time series of the cross-sectional mean of the equity ratio in the HE and RA case respectively.[15] The average computed on the time series of the cross-sectional mean of the equity ratio in the HE case (0.7808) is higher than that of the RA case (0.7682). Volatility is much larger, on the other hand, in the latter case: the coefficient of variation, is 2.2 per cent in the HE case as against 39.3 per cent in the RA case.

Qualitatively the same result holds also in the case of the interest rate and the output gap (not reported). Summing up, in the HE case the average equity ratio, the interest rate and the output gap exhibit much less volatility over time than in the RA case. Heterogeneity, therefore, is a *dampening factor* in shaping the fluctuations emerging from the model.

Where does this dampening role come from? Our tentative answer is based upon an heuristic argument which goes as follows. Let's consider first the RA case. During an expansion the equity ratio of the RA goes up (along with capacity utilization). Being countercyclical, the external finance premium goes down. Notice now that the decrease of the external finance premium can be conceptualized as a positive demand shock. As shown in Figure 10.5 in our IS-LM framework the equilibrium interest rate goes up, for the usual reason: the increase in the demand for money due to the increased volume of transactions feeds back on the interest via sales of bonds that agents engineer to increase the liquidity of their portfolio. The increase of the interest rate, however, has a *dampening* role in the accumulation of the equity ratio, as shown by the law of motion of individual net worth (10.17).

Let's consider now the HE case. The same line of reasoning applied before to the equity ratio of the RA applies also to the cross-sectional mean of the equity ratio in the HE case. In this latter scenario, moreover, the change in the variance of the equity ratio and its correlation with the mean play a crucial role. As a matter of fact, the correlation between the mean and the variance of the equity ratio is *negative* (the coefficient of correlation is −0.74 in the data generated by the simulation). Therefore the reduction of the external finance premium due to the increase of the cross-sectional mean is strengthened by the decrease of the variance. Hence the increase of the interest rate is larger than in the RA case and consequently also its dampening role is strengthened. In the end the individual and the average equity ratio go up less than in the RA case.

Conclusion
This chapter provides answers, one tentative, one not, to the following two questions:

1. Has the economics profession learned Hyman Minsky's lesson?
2. Does Minsky's legacy provide directions for research on new and unexplored territory?

The answer to the first question is 'Not yet and not fully'. Starting from different methodological premises, the financial accelerator literature provides insights on business fluctuations which are convergent, in a sense, to those deriving from Minsky's conceptual framework as shown in the

Investment section above. In other words, the FAH and FIH hypotheses are at least relatives, even if not sisters and definitely not twins.

The answer to the second question is a resounding 'Yes'. The role of heterogeneous financial conditions is the part of Minsky's legacy that may be the cornerstone of a new research agenda. In this chapter we have embedded a theory of financially driven capital accumulation in a multi-agent model of an economy populated by firms characterized by heterogeneous financial conditions. We aggregate individual variables by means of a stochastic procedure which resorts to the first and second moments of the distribution of financial conditions. Through aggregation, the model boils down to a sort of IS-LM framework where the IS curve is augmented by the moments of the distribution of financial conditions. Therefore, in equilibrium, both the interest rate and capacity utilization are functions of the moments mentioned above.

We simulate the model to understand the statistical properties of the results. It turns out that the way in which we conceive of fluctuations of the major macroeconomic variables is deeply affected by the explicit consideration of heterogeneity. The adoption of the RA as a simplifying modeling device, therefore, is not at all innocuous. In particular, heterogeneity plays the role of a dampening factor in business fluctuations.

Notes

1. Incidentally, isn't objection (ii) itself patently unrealistic in the light of the subprime crisis?
2. For the most recent and encompassimg model along these lines, see Bernanke et al. (1999).
3. The third, fourth, fifth and sixth sections draw heavily on Assenza et al. (2007).
4. As a matter of precision, in Minsky's original framework, investment – that is, the *flow* of capital – is measured on the x-axis. Since the financial accelerator literature is cast in terms of the stock of capital, for the sake of comparison between similar but different conceptual frameworks, we will not emphasize this distinction here. The two notions coincide, of course, if the rate of capital depreciation is 100 per cent.
5. As a matter of fact, the flow of internal finance is represented by retained profits. Net worth is the stock of internal finance. This stock-flow distinction is somehow blurred in the financial accelerator literature. For the sake of comparison, we will not emphasize this distinction here and refer to internal balance as net worth without further specification.
6. In this theory of the price level one can recognize the so-called *cost channel* of the monetary transmission mechanism, which has raised a new wave of interest and a non negligible New Keynesian literature starting from the seminal paper by Ravenna and Walsh, 2006.
7. The concepts of borrower's and lender's risk have been discussed at length by Keynes in Chapter 11 of the General Theory.
8. As a matter of precision, in the original framework, BG assume that, due to ex post asymmetric information, the lender has to incur a monitoring cost to assess the return on the investment project he/she has financed (costly state verification). They show that in the optimal financial arrangement, the probability of monitoring is decreasing with the borrower's net worth. The probability of monitoring is the main ingredient of the external finance premium.
9. As a matter of fact, GS (1988, 1993) have developed a framework in which there is no

role for physical capital since the technology considered employs only labor. 'Capital' in their framework is meant to be a wage fund and the need for finance is due to a production lag so that wages must be anticipated by the employers to the employees. For the sake of comparison we discuss in this section a simplified model in which physical capital is the only input. For simplicity, we can assume a one to one technology: $Y = K$.

10. See Hartley (1997) for a detailed historical account of the development of the RA assumption and a thorough critique of its use and misuse.

11. See Tesfatsion (2006) for a survey of agent based models.

12. The procedure has already been used. See Agliari et al. (2000). It is thoroughly discussed and compared with other aggregation procedures in Gallegati et al. (2006) where it is labeled the Variant-Representative-Agent methodology, with a somewhat paradoxical touch.

13. The procedure adopted here is discussed at length in Gallegati et al. (2006).

14. As a matter of fact, Franke and Semmler adopt a different measure of the financial condition of firms, namely the leverage ratio $l = L/K$ where L stands for bank loans. They assume that the profit (interest) rate is decreasing (increasing) with leverage. Assuming that $K = L + A$, however, it turns out that $l = 1 - a$ where $a = A/K$. Their assumption therefore can be recast in different but equivalent terms as follows: the profit (interest) rate is increasing (decreasing) with the equity ratio as in (10.9).

15. In the figures we discarded the transient consisting of the first 200 periods. In order to reduce the noise, moreover, we reported five quarters moving averages.

References

Agliari, A., D. Delli Gatti, M. Gallegati and L. Gardini (2000), 'Global dynamics in a nonlinear model of the equity ratio', *Journal of Chaos, Solitons and Fractals*, 11, 961-85.

Assenza, T. and D. Delli Gatti (2008), 'Financially driven growth and fluctuations: does heterogeneity matter?', mimeo.

Assenza, T., D. Delli Gatti and M. Gallegati (2007), 'Heterogeneity and aggregation in a financial accelerator model', Working Paper 07-13, Center for Nonlinear Dynamics in Economics and Finance (CeNDEF), Amsterdam, The Netherlands, December.

Bernanke, B. and M. Gertler (1989), 'Agency costs, net worth and business fluctuations', *American Economic Review*, 79, 14-31.

Bernanke, B. and M. Gertler (1990), 'Financial fragility and economic performance', *Quarterly Journal of Economics*, 105, 87-114.

Bernanke, B., M. Gertler and S. Gilchrist (1999), 'The financial accelerator in a quantitative business cycle framework', in J. Taylor and M. Woodford (eds), *Handbook of Macroeconomics*, vol. 1, Amsterdam, The Netherlands: Elsevier, pp. 1341-93.

Franke, R. and W. Semmler (1989), 'Debt-financing of firms, stability and cycles in a dynamical macroeconomic growth model', in W. Semmler (ed.), *Financial Dynamics and Business Cycles: New Perspectives*, Armonk, NY: M.E. Sharpe, pp. 18-37.

Gallegati, M., A. Palestrini, D. Delli Gatti and E. Scalas (2006), 'Aggregation of heterogeneous interacting agents: the variant representative agent', *Journal of Economic Interaction and Coordination*, 1, 5-19.

Greenwald, B. and J. Stiglitz (1988), 'Imperfect information, finance constraints and business fluctuations', in M. Kohn and S.C. Tsiang (eds), *Finance Constraints, Expectations and Macroeconomics*, Oxford: Oxford University Press.

Greenwald, B. and J. Stiglitz (1990), 'Macroeconomic models with equity and credit rationing', in R.G. Hubbard (ed.), *Asymmetric Information, Corporate Finance and Investment*, Chicago: University of Chicago Press.

Greenwald, B. and J. Stiglitz (1993), 'Financial market imperfections and business cycles', *Quarterly Journal Of Economics*, 108, 77-114.

Greenwald, B. and J. Stiglitz (2003), *Towards a New Paradigm in Monetary Economics*, Cambridge, MA: Cambridge University Press.

Hartley, J. (1997), *The Representative Agent in Macroeconomics*, London: Routledge.

Kiyotaki, N. and J. Moore (1997), 'Credit cycles', *Journal of Political Economy*, 105, 211–48.
Kiyotaki, N. and J. Moore (2002), 'Balance-sheet contagion', *American Economic Review*, **92**, 46–50.
Minsky, H.P. (1982), *Can 'It' Happen Again? Essays on Instability and Finance*, Armonk NY: M.E. Sharpe.
Ravenna, F. and C. Walsh (2006), 'Optimal monetary policy with the cost channel', *Journal of Monetary Economics*, 53, 199–216.
Taylor, L. and T. O'Connell (1985), 'A Minsky crisis', *Quarterly Journal of Economics*, 100, 871–85.
Tesfatsion, L. (2006), *Handbook of Computational Economics: Volume 2, Agent-Based Computational Economics*, Handbooks in Economics Series, Amsterdam, The Netherlands: Elsevier.

11 Growth cycles and the Financial Instability Hypothesis (FIH)
Piero Ferri*

Introduction: Minsky and the economics of extreme events

There is a strict correlation between the presence of some kinds of turbulence in the economy and the rediscovery of Minsky's contributions. This anti-cyclical pattern between the state of the economy and Minsky's fame occurred when Minsky was still alive (for instance during the October, 1987, crisis, when the speed of the stock market decline took investors and market makers by surprise) and it has continued. Whether the crises hit individual firms (as in 1998 Long-Term Capital Management (LTCM) case), particular countries (Russia and Mexico in 1998), special markets (as the 2001 technological bubble) or pivotal sectors (as the sub-prime 2007 case), Minsky's analysis attracts attention in the most influential financial newspapers and academic journals. In other words, when some extreme events occur (using Barro's terminology, 2006), they become Minsky moments.

In such periods of time, a particular 'homo economicus' emerges that is more complex than the usual maximizer of the neo-classical tradition. Ponzi, the deus ex-machina agent, engages in some profitable activities by becoming indebted. What is more, for a not well-defined length of time, he pays interest by incurring additional debt in the hope that profits and capital gains will be available to repay the commitments when they become due. This behavior is not typical of a market economy, but it can emerge in particular environments that turn the financial system into a 'Ponzificating' mode (see the *Economist*, March 2007).

Minsky, despite his anti-cyclical popularity, was not a doomsayer: he simply did not believe that the invisible hand always works smoothly. This is why economic policy measures and the possibility of institutional changes are necessary devices to prevent these extreme phenomena from happening, or, at least, from degenerating the working of the system (Ferri and Minsky 1992). His background was Keynesian, and he intended his contribution to complete Keynes's research agenda.

A new edition of an important book by Minsky is an occasion to pursue three objectives: (i) to analyze the various contributions in time; (ii) to compare his work with those of other authors; (iii) to try to adapt it to a different economic environment. While, directly or indirectly, all these points will be considered, the objective of the present chapter is to focus on the last aspect. I consider an environment where financial instability phenomena can occur in order to continue the work initiated by Minsky in innovating Keynes. Furthermore, I try to advance Minsky's contributions in dealing with these issues by taking advantage of analytical techniques that have become available. Finally, I attempt to explain under what conditions endogenous fluctuations can degenerate into a process of crisis.

To develop these ideas, a dynamic Keynesian model is presented. Aggregate demand, where debts play an important role in the consumption function as in the current period, is integrated with supply aspects, while agents are boundedly rational and try to learn the values of the parameters. The nonlinearity of the model obliges to explore the dynamics by means of simulations. The resulting persistence of endogenous fluctuations constitutes a natural humus in which Ponzi phenomena can occur. From this perspective, an extreme event (see Gabaix 2008) characterized by Knightian uncertainty (Caballero and Krishnamurthy 2008) can become a dynamic possibility that is not excluded by definition, as it is in the rational expectation theory.

The structure of the chapter is as follows: the second and third sections deepen the relationship between Minsky and Keynes on the one hand, and Hicks's methodology on the other. The fourth section presents a medium-run, regime-switching growth cycle model, while the fifth section discusses the individual equations. The sixth section shows the steady states for the two regimes, and the seventh section illustrates expectations. The eighth section describes the overall dynamics. The ninth section introduces further developments where Ponzi phenomena can occur, and the tenth section concludes.

Minsky and Keynes

One has to wonder why the recurrent rehabilitation of Minsky does not imply a concomitant resurgence of the economics of Keynes, in view of the close relationship between the two analyses. The answer is complex; probably one explanation has to do with the discrediting of fiscal policy, a war horse in Keynes's analysis. Monetary policy has become the policy 'tout court,' and this has led many to strongly conclude that the aggregate demand problem has become obsolete (Phelps 2007).

Both conclusions seem to be too strong. First of all, Keynes's contribution cannot be reduced to fiscal policy. According to Skidelsky (2000),

> What survives today of Keynesian economics is not, I think, the "scientific" demonstration that under-employment equilibrium is possible, but Keynes's

intuition that a market economy is inherently unstable, and that the source of instability lies in the logic of financial markets. Market capitalism should be neither left alone nor abolished, but stabilized. (Skidelsky 2000, p. 112)

This is also the vision of Minsky, who tried to develop Keynes's analysis along three lines:

(i)   presence of uncertainty;
(ii) interdependence between real and monetary aspects;
(iii) dynamic processes.

These three dimensions, all present in Keynes's analysis, constitute an environment favorable to endogenous fluctuations, where there is interdependence between real and monetary aspects; uncertainty and risk coexist; and on certain occasions, the economics of extreme events becomes relevant. In Minsky's view, such fluctuations would be much larger were it not for policy measures: along with the lender-of-last-resort role of the Federal Reserve, there is a more direct role for the State.

Minsky, Hicks and the dynamics
Minsky tried to insert dynamics into Keynes's monetary economy of production. Economic analysis has invented many devices to overcome the difficulties that arise in such an undertaking. As stressed by Hicks (1989), Adam Smith referred to the invisible hand, Marshall invented tripartite periods of time, Edgeworth referred to recontracting, and for Walras the auctioneer is the deus ex machina. In this survey, one can also mention that Keynes referred to given money wages to anchor his monetary economy and that rational expectations analysis obliges razor's edge dynamics to avoid explosions (Cochrane 2007).

There is no doubt that the ceiling and floor methodology developed by Hicks (1950) is at the heart of Minsky's methodology to deal with dynamic problems (Ferri 1992). From an analytical point of view, this methodology implies piecewise linear relationships that generate acceleration in the dynamics within definite bounds. According to Minsky, this method is a perfect metaphor for the interplay between market forces and the role of policy and institutional changes. While the former tends to generate an explosive pattern, the latter introduces bounds.

This piecewise linear approach is a particular species of the more general genus of nonlinear models (Kuznetsov 2004). Regime-switching models belong to the same species and can therefore also be applied to dynamic problems (Ferri and Greenberg 1989). These regime-switching techniques can be applied either deterministically or stochastically (Ferri 2008). In the present chapter, both techniques are used. Deterministic regime switching is used to examine the behavior of a system characterized by a multiple equilibrium, while stochastic regime switching, where the threshold is stochastic, will be considered for formalizing the expectations process as a Markov regime-switching process.

The medium-run, growth cycles and the analytics of regime switching
Hicks (1989) stressed that Keynes's objection to Marshall's long period was valid and that Keynes's analysis needed to be amended to consider the impact of investment on supply. In this chapter, I shall follow both of these dicta by referring to a medium-run strategy. Solow (2000) has emphasized the importance of a medium-run approach (Blanchard 1997), where growth cycles are present.

When considering stylized facts in advanced industrialized economies, there is a tendency to concentrate on polar cases: either the short-run vibrations of the economy are considered, as happens in short-run forecasts of the economy, or very long-run spans of time are taken into account, as usually happens when dealing with technical change.

In a medium-run perspective, the stylized facts become particularly revealing. The US economy, for example, experienced sustained output growth during the 1960s. From the early 1970s to the early 1980s, however, output growth was low on average, and since the mid-1990s, there has been, for the most part, a return to strong growth.

Three points are worth stressing. The first is that these ups and downs pertain not only to the US economy, but also extend to such economies as those of Europe and Japan. Although the details differ, the experience of these two areas is characterized by similar ups and downs. In the second place, these ups and downs manifest themselves over a longer time span than expected for statistical business cycles. In the third place, these movements seem to be more consistent than those identified at shorter frequencies (Comin and Gertler 2006).

The hypothesis that the data can be interpreted by means of a multiple-equilibrium model, where some nonlinearities enriched by a regime switching imply this result,[1] is worth testing. Within this perspective, the 'ups' and 'downs' are reversible phenomena, while the state of indebtedness constitutes the threshold triggering differing policy reactions. It is assumed that the economy is characterized by a 'bad' state (state 2), with a high debt ratio, high rate of unemployment and possibly a lower growth rate, and by a 'good' state (state 1), marked by the opposite characteristics.

In order to implement this approach, one needs to consider three steps. First, a threshold must be identified. In the present case, a particular value of the consumers' debt ratio is chosen, so that Regime 1 is defined as the low-debt state of the economy, while Regime 2, which experiences a higher debt ratio than the threshold, is the more turbulent state of the economy. Second, one has to identify the equations that undergo changes when the threshold is reached.[2] In the present case, the focus will be on the policy equation that is represented by a Taylor equation of the following type:

$$R_t = R^* + \psi_{1j}(\overline{E}\pi_{t+1} - \pi_{0j}) + \psi_{2j}(\overline{E}g_{t+1} - g_{0j}) \qquad (11.1)$$

The monetary authorities are supposed to switch the nominal rate of interest, along with the inflation and the growth objectives, according to j, the prevailing regime, where $j = 1, 2$, and where a 0 subscript refers to a steady-state value of any variable.[3] Regime switching is represented by the following inequality:

$$d_{t-1} > d_{Th}$$

such that $j = 2$ when this inequality holds. As will be discussed later, this specification is a simple device that helps describe the dynamics. However, it is not the only factor responsible for the presence of fluctuations that are not policy driven but are the result of the working of the overall system of equations.

A demand and supply model
The model tries to integrate aggregate demand and supply aspects (Asada et al. 2006) in a medium-run perspective, where labor supply has been normalized. The equations try to maintain those nonneutralities that, according to Akerlof (2007), constitute the essential feature of a monetary economy. They are not strictly microfounded, even though they can be justified from both analytical (Ferri and Variato 2007) and econometric points of view (Fazzari et al. 2007).

The dynamics of the model are generated by a nonlinear system of equations supplemented by the regime-switching mechanism just described. Technically, one should present two systems of equations, one for each state. However, in order to economize space, only the meta system will be presented, indexed by $j = 1, 2$.

Let us start from the equilibrium condition that aggregate demand equals supply. In dynamic terms, this equality implies that 1 plus the rate of growth of output (g_t) must be equal to the sum of the investment ratio $(i_t = I_t / Y_{t-1})$ and the consumption ratio (in a closed economy without Government).

$$g_t = i_t + c_t - 1. \qquad (11.2)$$

The latter is a positive function of past and expected ($\overline{E}$) income growth and a negative function of the interest rate on accumulated debt ratio (deflated by expected inflation):

$$c_t = c_1(1 + \overline{E}_t g_{t+1}) + c_2 - c_3 \frac{R_t d_t}{1 + \overline{E}_t \pi_{t+1}} \tag{11.3}$$

where c_1 and c_2 represent the propensity to consume past and forecast income, while c_3 measures the impact of interest on past and new debt. In this formulation, debt for the worker-borrower increases from interest and consumption and diminishes because of wages received. The debt ratio

$$d_t = \frac{D_t}{P_{t-1} Y_{t-1}}$$

evolves according to

$$d_t = \frac{d_{t-1}(1 + R_{t-1})}{(1 + g_{t-1})(1 + \pi_{t-1})} - \frac{i_{t-1}}{(1 + g_{t-1})} + (1 - \omega^*) \tag{11.4}$$

where ω stands for the labor income share, assumed to be exogenous. Since debts contracts are predetermined in nominal terms, inflation can affect them. This is why π (the rate of inflation) appears in the denominator.[4]

The interdependence between real and financial aspects is mainly concentrated in the consumption function because a tribute to the 'zeitgeist' has been paid. Consequently, the investment function has been rather simplified; it depends on both the accelerator and the (simplified) cost of capital, r (Fazzari et al. 2008):

$$i_t = [\eta_1 + \eta_2 \overline{E}_t g_{t+1} - \eta_3 r_t] v_{t-1} \tag{11.5}$$

The presence of the capital-output ratio variable v_t transforms the investment ratio into the (gross) accumulation rate.

The real rate of interest is related to the nominal rate by the Fisher formula:

$$r_t = \frac{(1 + R_t)}{(1 + \overline{E}_t \pi_{t+1})} - 1 \tag{11.6}$$

Turning to the supply side of the model, we introduce the productivity equation.

$$\tau_t = \tau_1 + \tau_2 \frac{i_t}{v_{t-1}} \tag{11.7}$$

where i_t is the investment ratio (I_t/Y_{t-1}), and v is the capital output ratio. This formulation is compatible with different economic theories.[5] The capital-output ratio can be defined in the following way:

$$v_t = v_{t-1}\frac{1 + g_{k,t}}{1 + g_t} \tag{11.8}$$

where the rate of growth of capital (g_k) is given by

$$g_{k,t} = \frac{i_t}{v_{t-1}} - \delta \tag{11.9}$$

and δ represents the exogenous depreciation rate.

The product and the labor market are characterized by imperfect competition and by non-clearing situations. The inflation equation is due to Akerlof (2000):

$$\pi_t = (1 - \varphi_1)\overline{E}_t\pi_{t+1} - \sigma_1(u_t - u^*) \tag{11.10}$$

where φ_1 is the proportion of quasi-rational expectations people who, although making correct forecasts of inflation, do not use them for low values of inflation. While in Akerlof (2000) this variable is endogenized, in the present model it is treated as a parameter. Finally, u^* is the Non-Accelerating Inflation Rate of Unemployment (NAIRU) obtainable when this percentage is zero.

Labor demand is given by the following equation:

$$l_t = l_{t-1}\frac{(1 + g_t)}{(1 + \tau_t)} \tag{11.11}$$

where l_t represents the employment ratio, referred to a normalized labor supply. It follows that the dynamics of unemployment (u_t) are given by

$$u_t = 1 - l_t \tag{11.12}$$

For given expectations and labor income distribution, each regime contains the following 12 unknowns in 12 equations:[6] d_t, i_t, g_t, l_t, u_t, π_t, ω_t, R_t, r_t, g_k, v_t and τ_t

The steady states
The reason why the model presents multiple equilibria depends on the nonlinear relationship existing between the steady state values of g_0 and

r_0. In economic terms, its steady state is defined by the fulfillment of expectations,

$$\overline{Eg}_t = g_t$$
$$\overline{E\pi}_t = \pi_t$$

and by the constancy of growth and the main ratios. In this perspective, unemployment is constant and so are the debt ratio and the investment ratio. From equations (11.11), (11.7) and (11.5), one gets a relationship of type:

$$g_0 = \frac{\tau_{1j} + \tau_2\eta_1}{1 - \tau_2\eta_2} - \frac{\tau_2\eta_3}{1 - \tau_2\eta_2}r_0$$

while from equations (11.2), (11.3), (11.4) and (11.6), one gets a nonlinear relationship of the type:

$$Dg_0^2 + Fr_0g_0 + Gg_0 + Hr_0 + Ir_0^2 = L$$

where capital letters represent combinations of parameters. By solving the system, one obtains two roots for $r_{0,j}$, where 0 represents the steady state and 1 and 2 represent, respectively, Regime 1, the virtuous state, and Regime 2, where the debt ratio is higher and growth lower. And through the link between productivity growth and investment and the remaining part of the model, this dichotomy influences the remaining values. In particular, the steady state values of inflation are determined by the Fisher equation, given an exogenous value for R^*, while unemployment is given by equation 11.10.

Markovian expectations
In this multiple-equilibrium system, agents know that the economy experiences periods of 'low' growth, followed by periods of 'high' growth. However, the agents live in an Information and Knowledge Economy (IKE), according to the definition of Frydman and Goldberg (2007), and do not know the structure of the model or have complete information. The assumption is made that in forming their expectations they follow a two-state Markovian regime-switching process (Hamilton 1989; Jaimovich and Rebelo 2006). In more detail, at the end of period $t - 1$, agents believe that the growth rate in period t will be

$$g_{t+1}^e = \alpha_1 + \beta_1 s_t + (\rho_1 + \mu_1 s_t)g_{t-1}$$

where s_t is a random variable that assumes the value 0 in the low state and 1 in the high state. It evolves according to the following transition probabilities:

$$\Pr(s_t = 0|s_{t-1} = 0) = a_1$$
$$\Pr(s_t = 1|s_{t-1} = 0) = 1 - a_1$$
$$\Pr(s_t = 0|s_{t-1} = 1) = 1 - b_1$$
$$\Pr(s_t = 1|s_{t-1} = 1) = b_1$$

Since s_t is not known at time t, the expected value, conditioned on s_{t-1}, is taken as a forecast. If $s_{t-1} = 0$, the conditional forecasting rule is:

$$\overline{E}(g_{t+1}|s_{t-1} = 0) = \alpha_1 + (1 - a_1)\beta_1 + [\rho_1 + (1 - a_1)\mu_1]g_{t-1}$$

where the operator E is written with a bar to indicate its subjective character, which is different from rational expectations objective conditional expectation. For $s_{t-1} = 1$, the conditional forecasting rule is:

$$\overline{E}(g_{t+1}|s_{t-1} = 1) = \alpha_1 + b_1\beta_1 + [\rho_1 + b_1\mu_1]g_{t-1}$$

The general forecasting rule is given by:

$$\overline{E}g_{t+1} = E(g_{t+1}|s_{t-1}) = \alpha_1 + \beta_1[b_1s_{t-1} + (1 - a_1)(1 - s_{t-1})]$$
$$+ \{\rho_1 + \mu_1[(1 - a_1)(1 - s_{t-1}) + b_1s_{t-1}]\}g_{t-1}$$

With this formulation agents are supposed to form their expectations according to a particular form of bounded expectations. Hommes and Sorger (1998) argue that expectations must be consistent with data in the sense that agents do not make systematic errors. This criterion implies that, at least, the forecasts and the data should have the same means and autocorrelations.

A similar forecasting rule can be applied to inflation, where the random state variable is denoted by z. The forecast for this variable is

$$\overline{E}\pi_{t+1} = E(\pi_{t+1}|z_{t-1}) = \alpha_2 + \beta_2[b_2z_{t-1} + (1 - a_2)(1 - z_{t-1})]$$
$$+ \{\rho_2 + \mu_2[(1 - a_2)(1 - z_{t-1}) + b_2z_{t-1}]\}\pi_{t-1}$$

Although s and z are unobserved (latent) random variables that induce regime switching, this does not imply that they have no economic meaning. Regime switching is interpreted as a convenient device to apply to the problem of forecasting, and, in view of its popularity among forecasters, it may reflect their practices.

In the present model, we suppose that agents learn the value of these parameters by means of rolling regressions,[7] which is another source of dynamics in the model. The assumption that all agents have the same learning simplifies the coordination problem, as underlined by Howitt (2006).

Endogenous dynamics

The system of structural equations, along with the forecasting rule, is nonlinear and can be solved only by means of simulations. Our exercise is very close to the experiments suggested by Tesfatsion (2006). It differs in that the heterogeneity of agents is considered in a macro framework, and it is based upon a functional distinction (consumers, investors, firms, labor) rather than microeconomic heterogeneity.

The parameters of the simulations are presented in Table 11.1. In order to obtain overall results that mimic the main macroeconomic stylized facts, we have assumed values that are in agreement with econometric results (Fazzari et al. 2007).

The threshold is represented by the average of the two steady state values of the debt ratio. In particular, if

$$d_{t-1} > d_{Th} = \frac{d_{01} + d_{02}}{2} + \varepsilon_t$$

where ε_t represents a normally distributed stochastic variable, then the system enters Regime 2, so that $j=2$.

The results of the simulations (the last 50 runs over N=1000) are illustrated in Figure 11.1. The dynamics of the model show persistent fluctuations in growth and other related variables. These fluctuations, however, do not explode but remain bounded after 1000 simulations. In other words, the switching of the economy is a persistent phenomenon. This

Table 11.1   The parameters of the simulations

$u^* = 0.10$	$\varphi_1 = 0.40$	$\sigma_1 = 0.045$	$\tau_1 = 0.001$	$\tau_2 = 0.15$
$\eta_1 = 0.201$	$\eta_2 = 0.40$	$\eta_3 = 0.30$	$c_1 = 0.40$	$c_2 = 0.405$
$c_3 = 0.15$	$\psi_{11} = 1.50$	$\psi_2 = 0.6$	$\omega_0 = 0.77$	$R^* = 0.0051;$
	$\psi_{12} = 1.80$	$\psi_2 = 0.9$		

Variable	a_j	b_j	β_j	μ_j	ρ_j
$Eg_t\ (j=1)$	0.4	0.6	0.001	0.43	0.55
$E\pi_t\ (j=2)$	0.45	0.8	0.0002	0.48	0.48

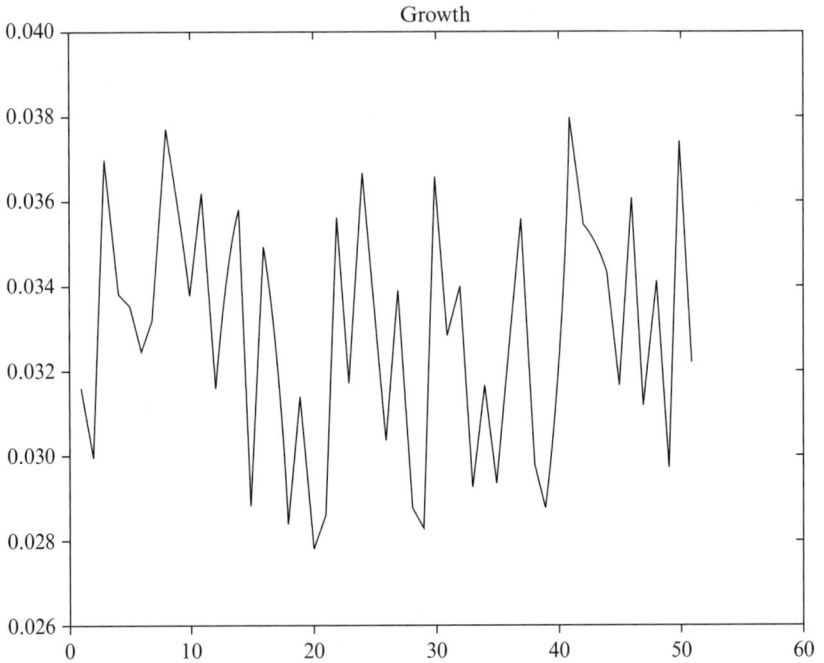

Figure 11.1   The dynamics of the model

Table 11.2   The steady state value of the two regimes

Regime	d	u	g	π
1	0.6	0.0103	0.034	0.007
2	0.9	0.0973	0.032	0.001

result[8] depends on many factors, some of which are worth considering. First of all, it depends on the presence and the nature of the two regimes. In the present case, the values of the parameters guarantee the existence of two steady states with the desired characteristics, as appears from Table 11.2.

In the second place, the dynamics are a function of the value of the threshold. If the threshold is changed, the relative time spent in the two regimes is different, and this affects the average rate of growth.[9] This implies that the medium-run behavior of *g* cannot be calculated simply by weighting the steady state values (of Table 11.2) by the ergodic probabilities of the Markov process (derivable from Table 11.1). In the third

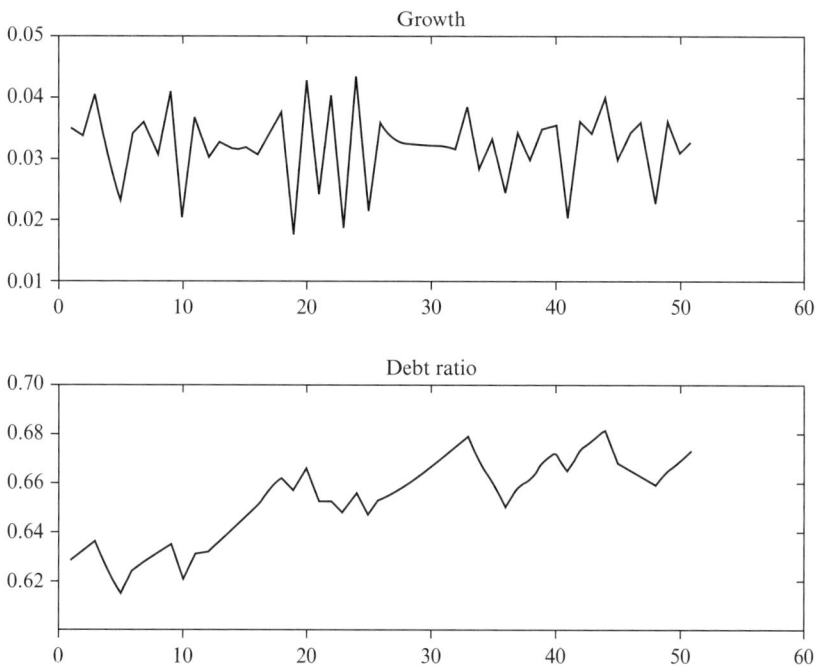

Figure 11.2 The financial instability

place, the dynamics are also a function of expectations. Since expected values are very close to the actual, the learning mechanism is working in a satisfactory way.[10]

The dynamics depend on the overall system of equations and cannot be attributed to a specific equation. In this perspective it cannot be exclusively attributed either to the expectations mechanism or to the policy pursued. The dynamics are robust to changes in the parameters of the Taylor equations, which implies that the model is not necessarily policy driven. The fact is that policy can constrain the fluctuations but not eliminate them. The mechanism based upon worker-borrowing is at the root of the results.[11]

The FIH
In order to test the robustness of the model, the consumption function has been modified in the following way:

$$c_t = c_1(1 + \overline{E}_t g_{t+1}) + c_2 - c_3 \frac{R_t d_t}{1 + \overline{E}_t \pi_{t+1}} + c_4(d_t - d_{t-1}) \qquad (11.3\text{bis})$$

where c_4 represents the propensity to consume from an increase in debt (Wright 2004). The dynamics depend on the values of c_4. For values of this parameters greater than 0.50, the system tends to explode, as Figure 11.2 shows (for N=200).[12]

In this case, the dynamics become unsustainable. Three aspects are worth stressing. First, the system is already experiencing fluctuations. Second, there is a situation where agents become more consumption prone through increase in debt. Finally, this does not necessarily mean that the system will eventually explode. In fact, changes in rules, institutions and policies can modify the dynamics, as Minsky has taught us (1986). He also reminded us that deflation may accompany this process, as Japan experienced in 1990, not to mention the famous 'It' as Minsky (1982) baptized the 1930 experience.

Concluding remarks
The chapter has tried to extend Minsky's analysis along two lines. On one hand, it has tried to put his analysis in a dynamic setting by referring to a regime-switching model that is very similar in its essence to the ceiling and floor approach employed by Minsky himself. It is important to stress that the dynamics depend on what happens: (i) within each state, (ii) between the two states and (iii) the time spent in each regime. In this case, history matters (Day and Walter 1989), and this is an important dimension to take into consideration in order to understand the various historical events. On the other hand, we considered the phenomenon of financial instability by means of a particular specification of the consumption function. The importance of consumer behavior in determining the US cycle is well known (Leamer 2007). And it is even more so considering the recent sub-prime crises.

In this environment, where the presence of the 'invisible hand' in coordinating markets is not omnipotent, the so-called extreme events find an appropriate environment. Three lines of extensions of the analysis become relevant. First, the justification of the equations should be pursued in a deeper way with the awareness that uncertainty must play an important role. Second, the financial sector must be deepened. In the context of the present chapter, the Taylor rule fixes the rate of interest, while money supply is endogenous. Furthermore, workers can borrow whatever they want at this price. A more sophisticated bank sector must be specified in order to understand the developments of the FIH. Finally, the mathematics of the model can be improved. For instance, the mathematics of heterogeneity (Di Guilmi et al. 2007) and of sudden stop (Mendoza 2006) must be developed.

Notes

* I am particularly grateful to S. Fazzari and E. Greenberg (Washington University) and AnnaMaria Variato (University of Bergamo) for stimulating suggestions. A financial contribution from the University of Bergamo is acknowledged.
1. In order to obtain multiple equilibria, nonlinear relationships are usually introduced (for this strategy, see for instance Evans et al., 1998). Alternatively, one might refer to a piecewise linear model, which assumes that certain functions change discontinuously when they reach a threshold. This is the strategy followed in this chapter (see also Ferri et al. 2001).
2. Changes can also be smooth as happens in the so-called STAR models. See Tong (1990) and Ferri (2008).
3. On a similar hypothesis, but based upon a different regime switching device, see Davig and Leeper (2007).
4. This formula for the borrower-worker is different when referred to firms.
5. On the relationship with a Kaldorian hypothesis, see Ferri (2007).
6. In the present formulation, it is more convenient to normalize the value of v. In this case, the depreciation rate becomes endogenous.
7. See Gilchrist and Saito (2006) for the use of a Kalman filter in the case of learning. It must be stressed that, in our model, agents do not learn the probabilities, but this option can be accommodated.
8. On the different asymptotic results in the case of nonlinear system, see Kuznetsov (2004).
9. The presence of the stochastic term, however, is not essential for the results.
10. The mean values of g and Eg are practically the same. The same holds true for π and $E\pi$.
11. The importance of investment in housing in the business cycle along with the financial mechanisms has been stressed by Leamer (2007).
12. In this case, the values of the other parameters are those indicated in Table 11.1, except that η_3 has been raised to 0.50.

References

Akerlof, G.A. (2000), 'Behavioral macroeconomics and macroeconomic behavior', *American Economic Review*, **92**, 411–33.
Akerlof, G.A. (2007), 'The missing motivation in macroeconomics', *American Economic Review*, **97**, 5–36.
Asada, T.P., C. Chen, C. Chiarella and P. Flaschel (2006), 'Keynesian dynamics and the wage-price spiral: a baseline disequilibrium model', *Journal of Macroeconomics*, **28**, 90–130.
Barro, R.J. (2006), 'Rare disasters and asset markets in the twentieth century', *Quarterly Journal of Economics*, **121**, 823–66.
Blanchard, O. (1997), 'The medium-run', *Brookings Papers on Economic Activity*, **2**, 89–158.
Caballero, R.J. and A. Krishnamurthy (2008), 'Collective risk management in a flight to quality episode', *Journal of Finance*, **63**(5), 2195–230.
Cochrane, J.H. (2007), 'Inflation determination with Taylor rules: a critical review', Working Paper 13409, National Bureau of Economic Research, Cambridge, MA, September.
Comin, D. and M. Gertler (2006), 'Medium-term business cycles', *American Economic Review*, **96**, 523–51.
Davig, T. and E.M. Leeper (2007), 'Generalizing the Taylor principle', *American Economic Review*, **97**, 607–34.
Day, R.H. and J.L. Walter (1989), 'Economic growth in the very long-run: on the multiple-phase interaction of population, technology and social infrastructure', in W.A. Barnett, J. Geweke and K. Shell (eds), *Economic Complexity*, Cambridge, MA: Cambridge University Press.

Di Guilmi, C., M. Gallegati and S. Landini (2007), 'Financial fragilità and the mean-field interaction as determinants of macroeconomic dynamics: a stochastic model', Working Paper, University of Ancona (Italy).

Evans, G.W., S. Honkapohja and P. Romer (1998), 'Growth cycles', *American Economic Review*, **88**, 495–515.

Fazzari, S., P. Ferri and E. Greenberg (2007), 'Aggregate demand and micro behavior: a new perspective on Keynesian macroeconomics', *Journal of Post Keynesian Economics*, **20**(4), 527–58.

Fazzari, S., P. Ferri and E. Greenberg (2008), 'Cash flow, investment and the Keynes-Minsky cycles', *Journal of Economic Behavior and Organization*, **63**, 555–72.

Ferri, P. (1992), 'From business cycles to the economics of instability', in S. Fazzari and D.B. Papadimitriou (eds), *Financial Conditions and Macroeconomic Performance: Essays in Honor of Hyman P. Minsky*, Armonk, NY: M.E. Sharpe, pp. 105–20.

Ferri, P. (2007), 'The labor market and technical change in endogenous cycles', *Metroeconomica*, **58**, 609–33.

Ferri, P. (2008), 'The economics of nonlinearity', in R. Scazzieri, A.K. Sen and S. Zamagni (eds), *Markets, Money and Capital: Hicksian Economics for the 21st Century*, Cambridge, MA: Cambridge University Press.

Ferri, P. and E. Greenberg (1989), *The Labor Market and Business Cycle Theories*, New York: Springer-Verlag.

Ferri, P. and H.P. Minsky (1992), 'Market processes and thwarting systems', *Structural Change and Economic Dynamics*, **3**(1), 79–91.

Ferri, P. and A.M. Variato (2007), 'Investment and the Taylor rule in a boundedly rational model', Quaderni del Dipartmento di Scienze Economiche, Università di Bergamo (Italy).

Ferri, P., E. Greenberg and R.H. Day (2001), 'The Phillips curve, regime switching, and the Nairu', *Journal of Economic Behavior and Organization*, **46**, 23–37.

Frydman, R. and M.D. Goldberg (2007), *Imperfect Knowledge Economics*, Princeton, NJ: Princeton University Press.

Gabaix, X. (2008), 'Variable rare disasters: an exactly solved framework for ten puzzles in macro-finance', Working Paper 13724, National Bureau of Economic Research, Cambridge, MA, January.

Gilchrist, S. and M. Saito (2006), 'Expectations, asset prices and monetary policy: the role of learning', Working paper 12442, National Bureau of Economic Research, Cambridge, MA, August.

Hamilton, J.D. (1989), 'A new approach to the economic analysis of non-stationary time series and business cycle', *Econometrica*, **57**, 357–84.

Hicks, J.R. (1950), *Trade Cycle*, Oxford: Clarendon Press.

Hicks, J. (1989), *A Market Theory of Money*, Oxford, UK: Oxford University Press.

Hommes, C. and G. Sorger (1998), 'Consistent expectations equilibria', *Macroeconomic Dynamics*, **2**, 287–321.

Howitt, P. (2006), 'Coordination issues in the long-run growth', in L. Tesfatsion and I. Judd (eds), *Handbook of Computational Economics, Vol. 2*, Amsterdam, The Netherlands: North Holland, pp. 1606–24.

Jaimovich, N. and S. Rebelo (2006), 'Can news about the future drive the business cycle', Working Paper 12537, National Bureau of Economic Research, Cambridge, MA, September.

Kuznetsov, Y.A. (2004), *Elements of Applied Bifurcation Theory*, New York: Springer-Verlag.

Leamer, E. (2007), 'Housing in the business cycle', Working Paper 13428, National Bureau of Economic Research, Cambridge, MA, September.

Mendoza, E.G. (2006), 'Endogenous sudden stops in a business cycle model with collateral constraint: a Fisherian deflation of Tobin's Q', Working Paper 12564, National Bureau of Economic Research, Cambridge, MA, October.

Minsky, H.P. (1982), *Can 'It' Happen Again? Essays on Instability and Finance*, Armonk, NY: M.E. Sharpe.

Minsky, H.P. (1986), *Stabilizing an Unstable Economy*, New Haven, CT: Yale University Press.

Phelps, E.S.(2007), 'Macroeconomics for a modern economy', *American Economic Review*, **97**, 543–61.

Skidelsky, R.M. (2000), 'Ideas and the world', *The Economist*, 25 November, 109–112.

Solow, R.M. (2000), 'Towards a macroeconomics of the medium run', *Journal of Economic Perspectives*, **14**, 151–58.

Tesfatsion, L. (2006), 'Agent-based computational economics: a constructive approach to economic theory', in L. Tesfatsion and I. Judd (eds), *Handbook of Computational Economics, Vol. 2,* Amsterdam, The Netherlands: North Holland, pp. 832–80.

Tong, H. (1990), *Non-Linear Time Series*, Oxford, UK: Oxford University Press.

Wright, S. (2004), 'Monetary stabilization with nominal asymmetries', *Economic Journal*, **114**, 196–222.

12 A spatialized approach to asset bubbles and Minsky crises

*Gary A. Dymski**

> The most significant economic event of the era since World War II is something that has not happened: there has not been a deep and long-lasting depression.
>
> (Hyman Minsky 1982)

Introduction

The succession of financial crises in the neoliberal era that began in 1980 initially titillated the economics profession. These crises posed a series of puzzles for theorists working with *au courent* banking models, all of which were premised on the idea that economic agents are rational and self-interested. Academic opinion leaders could come up with wrinkles in principal–agent models of credit markets: they competed to explain how design flaws in credit markets or in their regulation, in the presence of asymmetric information, could lead to loan non-payment or currency crisis (or both).

But then the 1997 Asian crisis jarred economists' confidence that economic outcomes must somehow reflect a rational (willed) outcome because economic agents are rational, and because asset prices respond to fundamentals. Ideas that allowed for irrational behavior in financial markets gained more currency. For example, economists affiliated with the market-oriented World Bank and IMF wrote numerous post-1997 working papers on how (expectationally arational, fundamentals-defying) contagion effects constituted an important dimension of the Asian crisis.[1] The subprime crisis has done even more damage to the old conceptual starting point. In this crisis, the ideas of Hyman P. Minsky about financial crises, long overlooked by mainstream financial economists, have come to the fore. Influential economists (Nouriel Roubini) and columnists (Martin Wolf) alike have turned to Minsky's ideas on financial instability to gain some insights on the emerging crises.[2]

This chapter acknowledges the force of Minsky's ideas about the role of asset bubbles in creating, transmitting, and resolving economy-wide financial crises. But there is a need to go further. For many of the contemporary references to Minsky reduce his Financial Instability Hypothesis (FIH) to a very small kernel – the notion that participants in financial markets, in the midst of speculative manias regarding asset prices, can take on too much debt relative to their income levels, creating widespread financial instability. In Minsky's fully developed account of his FIH, an economy-wide crisis of this sort was expected to recur on a regular basis, linked to the economy's macroeconomic dynamics. Minsky then conceptualized an appropriate response to such crises: lender-of-last-resort intervention and then what he termed 'big government' fiscal policy, both of which would eliminate pressures toward asset-price deflation and regenerate macroeconomic growth.

However, the patterns of financial instability and crisis observed in episodes such as the 1997 Asian financial crisis and the 2007–08 subprime crisis have not followed Minsky's form: their initial impacts were not linked to turning points in domestic macroeconomies, and their eruptions were taken as adverse 'surprises.' There is no doubt such surprises can undermine confidence and erode expectations. But the dynamic of financial instability is likely to be subject to other forces than just these two, economic units' expectations and endogenous macro-fluctuations.

This chapter explores the implications of 'spatializing' Minsky's core framework. Minsky's core financial boom-bust model is aspatial – it implicitly assumes that the financial cycle plays itself out in a closed, homogeneous economy. This analysis examines how Minsky's core ideas are impacted when we insert Minsky's model into an open-economy framework. Gray and Gray (1994) opened up this line of inquiry, and found that exchange-rate uncertainty increases the dimensionality of uncertainty in financial processes. Here we go further, by taking explicit account of the implications of investment-financing processes that cross spatial economic borders. This leads us to suggest some modifications of Minsky's core ideas about the emergence and resolution of asset bubbles and boom-bust financial cycles.

Once we have allowed for trade imbalances and factor flows across borders, it is easy to see that cross-border imbalances in capital movements can contribute to a build-up of financial fragility, independent of any impact on financial fragility of the economy's cyclical momentum. Ironically, Minsky himself suggested the building blocks of a spatially aware approach in work predating most of his writing on financial instability per se; in effect this chapter unites two strands of thought that Minsky left unconnected.

In sum, financial fragility and instability in an economy depend not just on the business cycle factors emphasized by Minsky, but also on the real/financial-sector tensions inherent in flows of capital across its borders. Whether asset bubbles and tendencies toward financial crisis emerge depends in part on any economy's institutional mechanisms for chan-neling inflows of capital into investment outlets.

This 'spatialization' of Minsky's model permits us to more accurately explain post-1980 episodes of financial instability. There are important implications as well regarding Minsky's prescriptions for appropriate policy responses to financial crises.

The Minskyan approach to financial fragility and asset bubbles
The twin entry points for any model building on the work of Hyman Minsky are Keynesian uncertainty and real time. Keynesian uncertainty refers to the key methodological insight in Keynes's *General Theory* (1936): the future is uncertain because events that unfold in real time do not obey pre-given probability distributions. For example, there is no way to know 'objectively' whether asset prices are rising because the fundamentals are improving, or instead because the fundamentals are being evaluated differently. In a world with uncertainty, people cannot be fully rational because parametric information is not out there to be had. Real time, in turn, means that agents seeking to accumulate wealth must purchase and hold partially or wholly illiquid assets for a series of short periods, during which market conditions may change substantially. Because of these two characteristics of the lived environment, humans will fluctuate between being willing to make irreversible commitments, and instead seeking liquid assets that maximize flexibility and minimize exposure to risk. Uncertainty also has implications for how agents form expectations and make deci-sions: agents cannot formulate expectations of asset values that are time-invariant; they know this, and so will have some level of distrust about both their own estimates and any given consensus of market opinion.

An immediate implication of this dual entry point is that it becomes impossible to know when a given market is subject to a 'bubble.' For even the perceived line separating sound from unsound investments is incon-stant and shifting through time; and there are no objective grounds for deciding. As Grant observes, 'Every loan, even if fully secured, is a kind of speculation' (1992, p. 5) When decisions are made under uncertainty, the passage of time itself can undermine even carefully laid plans. We make our way through this world under a condition of fundamental uncertainty that denies us knowledge about those things we most need to know.

These dimensions of an uncertain economic environment immediately suggest the importance of institutional structures. As Crotty (1994) has emphasized, people construct rules of thumb to guide their behavior; when widely adopted, these conventions can create conditional stability for periods of time by channeling behaviors in a way that bounds the consequences of uncertainty. These conventions provide people with assurance that they are minimizing their exposure to mistakes and permit them to make longer-term commitments (such as purchases of land and fixed assets). Crotty goes on to observe that while conventions will bound uncertainty, they do not reduce it to probabilistic risk; indeed, the very conventions that generate conditional stability for a time eventually have behavioral consequences that undermine that apparent stability and bring us face to face again with the consequences of uncertainty.[3]

Minsky's Financial Instability Hypothesis (FIH)

But economic events are not only molded by behavioral conventions; they unfold within aggregate structural settings that both give shape to economic dynamics and set limits on feasible outcomes. Many theorists have followed Keynes and Kalecki in observing that the relation between investment and saving can give rise to business cycles. Further, Keynes's observation that economic agents will discount liquidity in periods of economic growth and rising asset values, but run to liquidity when these magnitudes turn down, suggests a financial source of cyclical fluctuation. This was exposited definitively by Hyman Minsky (1975). He showed that just as expectations vary with the state of the business cycle, balance-sheet relationships too evolve systematically during the cycle. Initially, balance sheets are robust because assets are conservatively priced and debt commitments modest; but during the course of an expansion phase, asset prices rise and debt burdens grow until finally liability commitments outpace asset returns and a downturn is induced. An economy becomes more financially fragile as an expansion proceeds, with the consequence that a period of financial instability is eventually reached: asset values fall, and a debt-deflation cycle may be unleashed.

In Minsky's model, the evolution of balance sheets over the cycle would be accompanied by a cyclical pattern in the relationship between the stock-market and production-cost prices of capital assets, which he terms P^K and P^I respectively. Minsky argues that as a boom period proceeds, an asset bubble emerges: specifically, the asset bubble arises when the ratio (P^K/P^I) exceeds one for an extended period of time. Figure 12.1 shows a stylized picture of a Minsky crisis, emphasizing the key role of asset bubbles in cyclical fluctuations. The rapid pace of output growth eventually exhausts industrial capacity and forces firms to take on debt to expand production. The combination of euphoric expectations and competitive pressure drives up debt/income ratios and asset prices simultaneously; leverage is rewarded. The collapse, when it comes, comes fast.

Note that two financial characteristics define the difference between prosperity and crash: the collapse of the (P^K/P^I) ratio and the collapse of asset prices relative to liabilities. Income flows too are low relative to debt

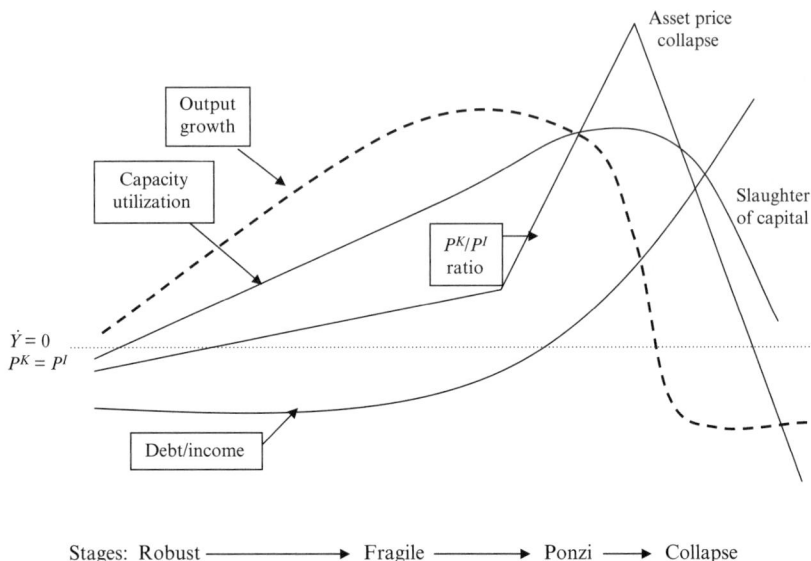

Figure 12.1   A stylized picture of a Minsky crisis

Note: The variables shown are measured against cyclical trend, with time elapsing from left to right in the diagram.

obligations. Defining L as liabilities, the crash period can be characterized as one in which $P^K < P^I = L$. In the debt-deflation state, the inability to service L leads to defaults, forcing the sale of assets on markets with few buyers, sinking P^K further. Note that a contraction in real prices (a fall in P^I) will only worsen the burden of debt. We denote this crash state herein as a *Minsky crisis*. Minsky's writings on financial dynamics suggest that a Minsky cycle (as described in Figure 12.1) precedes a Minsky crisis; implicitly, a Minsky crisis can be generated in Minsky's work by a prior Minsky cycle.

Responding to Minsky crises: big bank and big government
Minsky crises have devastating effects on advanced economies with sophisticated and interlinked financial markets. Consequently, recurring outbreaks of these crises lead to several systematic adaptations and institutional changes. Minsky (1975, 1986) described these adaptations in his 1970s and 1980s writing on financial instability; Kregel (1998) has suggested the colorful terms 'big bank' and 'big government' for the two central developments. 'Big bank' means the intervention of a central bank as a lender of last resort, providing liquidity to support banks' ability to

provide credit to businesses that would otherwise default on their loans and cease to function. To intervene in this way, the central bank must provide as much liquidity as is required to meet financially fragile cash-flow needs; and of equal importance, market participants must perceive the big bank as being willing to play this role.

The second adaptation is the rise of 'big government.' Minsky shows how countercyclical government spending by a public sector that constitutes a significant share of aggregate demand can check the tendency toward debt-deflation that emerges in the crisis. If liquidity provision by banks and the central bank in the face of a crisis is to stabilize cash flows, someone must spend it – that is, exchange liquidity for goods; and if business firms have little capacity to spend, and households are too scared to spend, then government can spend. This blocks the panic that otherwise emerges, and creates a floor on prices that prevents them from falling (as in the Great Depression) substantially below current levels. The importance of big government in economic dynamics was so fundamental that Minsky divided the performance of the US economy into two periods: a 'small government' era from the end of the Civil War to the Depression; and a 'big government' era dating from World War II. Indeed, US government share of spending in Gross Domestic Product (GDP) rose from about 5 per cent prior to World War II to 20 per cent or more thereafter.

Pollin and Dymski (1994) show that through the end of the 1970s, aggregate measures for the US economy do display very different cyclical behavior in the two eras. In particular, cyclical downturns in the 'small government' era were typically accompanied by falling prices, debt deflation, and high bankruptcy rates among banks and non-financial firms alike. Because of the deflationary trend of prices, the real cost of capital rose precipitously in the downturn. In the 'big government' era, cyclical downturns played out differently: price levels did not fall, the real interest rate fell dramatically, and the rise in the unemployment rate and the reduction in GDP growth were moderated: debt deflation did not occur. The average real cost of capital changed little in recessionary periods during the 1947–79 period. Non-financial business failure rates were vastly reduced, and bank failures almost nil.

It seemed that macroeconomic pain due to financial instability might recede into insignificance; it was a matter, as Minsky put it, of *Stabilizing An Unstable Economy* (1986). However, when Pollin and Dymski (1994) examined aggregate cyclical behavior for the 1980s, and Dymski (2009) for the 1990s and the first decade of the 2000s, many of these cyclical-response patterns changed: in effect, the macroeconomic benefits of 'big government' intervention weakened substantially after 1980.[4] Neither the rate of price inflation, the real interest rate, nor the unemployment rate has shown much cyclical variability in this time-period.

Pollin and Dymski (1994) explored why post-peak business cycle dynamics had changed after 1980. They speculated that 'big government/big bank' policies were no longer used solely in response to macroeconomic downturns, as had been the case in the 1960s and 1970s. In particular, tension began to emerge in the 1980s between the Federal Reserve's lender-of-last-resort role and its monetary-policy role. When pushed, the Federal Reserve's function as lender of last resort overrode its macroeconomic-policy commitments. In effect, the policy steps required to maintain financial stability became increasingly divorced from the policy steps required to maintain stable macroeconomic growth. This uncoupling was due in large part to the stresses placed on US banks and savings and loans by credit-market crises which could be traced to the effects of deregulation and to the globalization of US financial relations.

Pollin and Dymski (1994) concluded that these changes' cumulative effect was to reduce the ability of government decision-makers to call on 'big government/big bank' tools primarily in response to macroeconomic downturns. Episodes of financial turbulence were increasingly frequent, and less likely to coincide with fluctuation points in macroeconomic dynamics.

Spatializing Minsky's model 1: asset bubbles and spatiality
Here we propose another reason that Minsky's remedies have been increasingly disconnected from purely cyclical dynamics in the post-1970s world. That is, Minsky's model has to be explicitly opened, to expose the implicit setting of Minsky's model in a large, closed economy in which border relationships are insignificant. Minsky's mature model took a closed-economy approach because the US was, for him, the paradigm case of a large economy with mature financial markets. And Minsky focused on the US economy as a whole because he became increasingly interested in aggregate national dynamics, and in how national policy responses could limit the damage that might occur if those dynamics were left unchecked. Minsky excluded from analytical consideration the possibility of financial crises whose scale exceeded the response capacity of the authorities responsible for lender-of-last resort intervention. But unfortunately, financial-crisis episodes with this characteristic are becoming more and more common.

Because of his closed-economy approach, Minsky's core model does not analyze the possibly significant difficulties associated with current-account/capital-account imbalances. Experience in the 1990s, however, showed that financial crises are especially likely in open macroeconomies such as Malaysia, Mexico, and Korea, in which current-account/reserve relationships are crucial. Further, in the neoliberal era, asset-market booms and busts and episodes of financial instability have sometimes been characterized by extreme regional variability: some areas of a national economy may be subject to a speculative boom, while others are largely or wholly unaffected. One pertinent example is the California real-estate bubble which emerged in the mid-1980s and burst in 1991–92; another is the 2004–06 subprime-financed housing boom, which led to the subprime crisis of 2007–08.

What unites these situations of national and intra-national financial instability is the significance of cross-border relationships. Our objective here, then, is to point out the importance of spatiality, and of relations across spatial borders, in the emergence, outbreak, and resolution of asset-market booms and busts. That is, we consider how Minsky's core ideas about financial instability are altered by the explicit presence of financial flows and obligations across spatial borders.[5] This will lead us to see more clearly how Minsky crises depend crucially on the particularities of historical time and place that underlie financial flows.

We proceed in two steps. We first focus on some structural factors associated with the emergence of asset bubbles; second, we turn to factors associated with Minsky crises.

Asset bubbles and spatiality
The key structural feature of asset bubbles is that they are inherently spatial as well as temporal phenomena. Specifically, we want to understand economies as bordered spaces. The idea is very general: any contiguous enclosed spatial area can be treated analytically as a bordered economy. The term is intentionally plastic: a country is a bordered economy, but so is a city within a country; a neighborhood within a city; a street within a neighborhood; and even a home along a street. Every bordered economy has a current account balance which may be unstable due to the cross-border migration of factors of production and wealth. And even when wealth and labor don't flow across one border of an economy (such as the national boundary), these factors do flow across intra-national boundaries. It is highly unlikely that the incremental resources required to fuel a given region's economic growth can all be found within its borders. Interestingly, this idea originated with Minsky's own (1965) analysis of California's high growth rate relative to the rest of the US.[6]

The spatial segmentation that characterizes the division of income flows and asset and liability stocks gives rise to various structural complications for bordered economies, especially when flows across spatial borders are unbalanced. In neoclassical trade and finance theory, cross-border relationships are very simple – either a nation has an export surplus, and chooses between building up foreign exchange reserves or buying foreign assets; or it has an export deficit and must allow foreigners to acquire its assets. The country in question is viewed as passively adjusting to these flow equilibria. If movements of assets and goods are not impeded, regions with high consumption propensities will sell off their assets to support their spending habits; and vice versa. The countries in this simple story are just placeholders in a global consumption/saving-portfolio balance problem. The assets are out there and the right prices for them can be found as long as exchange rates and domestic asset prices are free to adjust. There is never a moment of crisis anticipated within the theory – only a period of adjustment to changed market circumstances.

But there is more to these processes than is allowed for in neoclassical theory. As Minsky always emphasized, asset accumulation requires liability growth. Further, assets and liabilities must balance on the flow and stock balance sheets of nations, as well as those of regions within nations. The nominal value of the capital assets emitted in a given region or nation may not – indeed is unlikely to – correspond precisely to these assets' production cost. This leads to the central point. There is no reason to expect nominal and real assets to correspond over time: hence asset bubbles and/ or asset collapses are omnipresent in bordered economies. Bubbles thus continually affect economic outcomes; their impact is a matter of degree, not kind.

This alternative approach to bubbles rests both on the idea of bordered economies and on the idea that cross-border wealth flows are not real flows, but nominal flows – abstract wealth claims chasing real assets. 'Wealth' itself is an inherently abstract concept, disembedded from the particular assets in which it is stored at any point in time. Capital mobility involves movement in the geographic ownership pattern of wealth claims, not a shift in the spatial locus of real capital itself. This applies whether the capital movement in question consists of a reserve shift due to household migration, of foreign direct investment (FDI), or of portfolio investment.

Several factors explain why asset bubbles arise in some bordered economies but not others. The first is the pattern of regional economic growth. We consider two scenarios vis-à-vis the growth rates of a bordered economy and of the region surrounding it: the bordered economy can grow faster than the surrounding region, or it can grow at the same pace. The faster-growth case here encompasses two cases: first, that the surrounding region is growing, but the bordered economy is growing faster; second, that the surrounding region is declining, in which case the bordered economy qualifies as a high-growth area even if it is declining

Table 12.1   Relationships between regional economic growth rates and asset bubbles

Patterns in regional economic growth rates	Is an asset bubble likely to form in one economy within a region?	
	No	Yes
Balanced regional growth	No wealth or labor transfers, dispersed technology and productivity	Moral hazard problems in banking, inadequate supervision
One economy grows faster in a growing region	Higher innovation rate or productivity in high-growth area	Faster wealth inflows into growing region: The 'boom' economy case
Balanced regional slowdown or stagnation	No capital flight, or offsetting capital outflows and inflows	Uneven economy-by-economy pace of capital flight from region
One region or nation grows faster (or declines less) than others in a stagnant or declining region	Higher innovation rate or productivity in high-growth area	Capital flight from the region, failure of overseas lenders to renew short-term loans

less quickly. These two cases of uneven economic growth can give rise to asset bubbles in the bordered economy.

Table 12.1 characterizes the possible relationships between asset bubbles and high-growth economies. The factors emphasized in other models – asset bubbles due to asymmetric-information problems and to unregulated banking markets – are independent of the uneven-growth case, as shown in the first row. Interest in Table 12.1 centers on the next three possibilities (rows). Note first that uneven growth could arise without asset bubbles in the faster-growing area, as long as its growth rate reflected superior productive capacity. An area with more skilled labor and more capital can generate more product and income than less well-endowed neighbors, all else equal; Japan in the 1970s is a case in point. Independent of productive capacity, however, an asset bubble may form in a bordered region due to its receiving wealth inflows at a higher rate than the surrounding region (of course, these inflows could originate within this surrounding region). This upward pressure on asset prices (relative to the real cost of producing assets) is evident, for example, in the virtually global rural-to-urban migration of the past four decades. Intra-national or international immigration, like that from foreign countries and other US states into California can also generate asset-price pressure of this type. We can define a *boom economy* as a high-growth economy whose rapid growth is attributable in part or whole to significant, sustained inflows of labor and wealth.

It is important to see – especially to encompass cases such as the 1997 Asian financial crisis – that the capital-inflow scenario can also work in reverse. Suppose, for example, that all economies in a given region experience capital flight, including the failure of overseas lenders to renew short-term credits. Suppose further that one bordered area within this region has less capital flight than the region as a whole. Unless this bordered economy has some other advantages in productivity or capacity, its asset prices may be viewed as too high – bubble prices – in the perverse sense that they have declined less than have other capital-asset prices in the region. And even when a bordered economy has avoided declines as large as those afflicting the remainder of the region, capital flight again can turn its asset prices into bubble prices. So the asset-bubble process works two ways, on the way up and on the way down.

As Table 12.2 illustrates, the cross-border wealth flows of interest here are typically both intra-national and inter-national. The vertical dimension of Table 12.2 shows that wealth (and/or population) can move into a 'boom' region from a 'hinterland' or 'rustbelt' region within a nation. This is equivalent, as Minsky (1965) points out, to a movement of funds across national borders under a strict gold standard. Every region is, of course, part of a nation that itself has a capital-account balance. If exports and imports balance, no wealth moves; and if exports are greater than imports, then either foreign exchange will build up or foreign assets will be purchased. In extreme cases – like those constituted by 1980s California, 1990s Seoul, and early-2000s areas of subprime-financed housing boom in the US – wealth enters the boom economy across both intra-national and inter-national borders. At the other extreme is a region systematically losing wealth to more rapidly-growing regions within a nation that is a net buyer of overseas assets – the case of rural Japan. Even when an economy has negative foreign savings, intra-national wealth shifts can create boom and hinterland economies within the nation – the case of Tokyo. The other ambiguous case combines a national trade deficit with regional capital outflow – the case of the US Midwestern 'rustbelt' in the 1980s.

There are important feedbacks between the pace of capital in- and outflows and the relative rate of regional economic growth. Indeed, Keynes's notion of a currency union can be understood as precisely an effort to resolve imbalances by forcing adjustments on the part of countries with trade surpluses (capital outflows). Apart from wealth flows and economic growth, other spatial factors can help generate or block

Table 12.2   Cross-border wealth flows and asset price pressures

Intra-national border condition	International border condition	
	Net foreign savings > 0 (wealth inflows)	Net foreign savings < 0 (wealth outflows)
Wealth inflows into this domestic region from other domestic regions	Strong upward asset-price pressure: More overseas and domestic claims on available real assets (1980s California,1990s Seoul, 2000s US subprime-financed housing boom)	Possible upward asset-price pressure: Net acquisition of foreign assets, more domestic claims on available real assets (1980s Tokyo)
Wealth outflows from this domestic region to other domestic regions	Indeterminate asset-price pressure: More overseas claims, but fewer domestic claims, on available real assets (1980s US Midwest)	Downward asset-price pressure: Net acquisition of foreign assets, fewer domestic claims on available real assets (other urban areas in Japan)

Note: The asset price pressures indicated here do not take into account other influences on asset prices, such as income growth.

asset bubbles. Table 12.3 focuses attention on two factors that can affect the rate of transformation of cross-border wealth flows into real capital assets. The cases of FDI and portfolio investment are differentiated. With FDI, financial inflows lead directly to the purchase or construction of real assets. Examples are overseas firms' construction of new factories and Midwesterners' purchases of Los Angeles homes.

Portfolio investment is more problematic than FDI because the claim is only on financial assets per se. One key factor identified here is the strength of the bordered economy's intermediation capacity: the lending capacity of its banks, the strength of borrower-lender relationships, and so on. A second key is pertinent to international capital flows: the presence or absence of controls or conditions for capital inflows and outflows. Inward capital controls and a strong intermediation sector can be used to improve the financial-real capital compression rate. Inflows, even when they take the form of portfolio investments, can be longer-term in nature, generating increases in the real-asset base and multiplier benefits for other companies. Conversely, with weak banks and no controls over capital movements, the

Table 12.3   Determinants of the pace of transformation of financial claims into net new real assets

	Type of capital inflows into domestic region	
	Foreign direct investment (domestic asset construction by overseas capital)	Portfolio investment (domestic asset purchase by overseas capital)
Intra-national lending and capital-emitting capacity		
Strong: robust banks, borrower–lender relations, and capital sources	High financial-to-real asset transformation with local multiplier effects	Strength of financial-to-real asset transformation depends on domestic allocation system
Weak: undercapitalized banks, fragile borrower–lender links, and few capital sources	High financial-to-real asset transformation with small multiplier effects	Low financial-to-real asset transformation
Cross-border capital-flow policies		
Active: ex ante policies encouraging long-term investment, punishing or preventing short-term flight	High and stable financial-to-real asset transformation	Enhanced financial-to-real asset transformation by discouraging short-termism
Passive: no conditions or controls on capital inflows or outflows	High sensitivity of local investment to external conditions, government policies	Low real-asset creation potential

amount of financial-real compression is likely to be small, all else equal. In this context, some problematic aspects of the subprime-financed housing boom in the US are readily seen: the financing of the new homes built in regions of subprime boom required long-term, FDI-like commitment; but it was viewed by the market more as a short-term portfolio play.

Our discussion has emphasized capital flows across borders; but movements of people across borders adds another dimension to boom-economy dynamics. While the interrelations between wealth and population movements deserve a lengthy discussion, here we make two points. First, a boom (capital-absorbing) economy like California grows seemingly without effort most of the time because it enjoys a steady stream of migrants who bring both their labor power and their wealth along with them. So California's productive capacity expands even as more nominal wealth pours in. Second, a boom economy that enjoys inward migration and hence labor-absorption is more capable of sustained growth than a boom economy with a stationary population. Both factors of production are expanding in the former case, but only capital – or actually, wealth claims on capital – in the latter case. A boom economy without labor in-migration must continually shift to a higher capital/labor ratio to avoid asset-bubbles or unused resources. This of course is the case of Japan in the 1960s, as it shifted its textile manufactures to Korea; it is the case of Japan in the 1970s, as it automated its factories; it is the case of Japan in the 1980s, as it built up productive capacity and office space too much, and suffered the collapse of a bubble.

Spatializing Minsky's model 2: financial fragility and spatiality
In his mature work on financial instability, Minsky argued that assets may often be overvalued in the late stages of a sustained period of cyclical expansion. Minsky asserts that the more powerful the boom, the greater the potential for an asset bubble; and the more rapid the growth of a bubble, the more certain are participants that the sky will not fall, the more likely a crash. So success breeds success, and this breeds fragility and eventually the reversal of the growth-generating conditions. At the core of this financial instability hypothesis is irreversibility. Agents in an over-heated economy are carrying forward asset positions acquired in the past, which tie them to balance sheet commitments in the present period. They must meet commitments in real time on those asset positions – and these units' viability depends on meeting these commitments in a timely manner. The downturn is driven by both the asset and the liability side.

The spatial conception developed here adds to Minsky's notions about financial fragility in two ways. First, it suggests a new source of financially fragile asset bubbles, independent of Minsky's cyclical conception. Combining uncertainty with a structural approach to bordered economies, recognizing that most economies have wealth and/or labor inflows or outflows, and acknowledging that asset-augmentation capacity varies widely, leads to the conclusion that asset bubbles arise everywhere. So boom economies are commonplace, not rare; and boom economies are very likely to become bubble economies; and boom economies are therefore likely to be financially fragile. Minsky himself recognized this in a 1965 volume predating his 1975 volume on Keynes and the financial instability hypothesis. Minsky wrote:

> California's growth . . . requires that capital be imported. The markedly greater growth rate of California proportional to the rest of the country has swamped,

and will continue to swamp, the export surplus that California would enjoy if the two grew at the same rate. The reserve base of the state's banks would tend to be dissipated unless it was supplemented by reserves acquired by way of capital imports. To import capital, California must either generate liabilities of the kind accepted throughout the country, or the migrants must carry with them sufficient capital to maintain the reserve base of the region's banks. (Minsky 1965, p. 99)

Because of uncertainty, the notion of an excessively high or low state of expectations cannot be well-defined, for there is no stable set of fundamentals to serve as a reference point. And even if one were to point to a set of firm characteristics as fundamentals, we have argued that border balances also matter. Indeed, there can be an asset bubble due to cross-border pressures even in the absence of expectational 'error' – that is, as a purely structural supply and demand phenomenon. So real/nominal imbalances occur all the time; they become quantitatively important when enough wealth seeks out assets in a particular place with inflexible labor supplies that this place's labor/capital wealth/asset relationships are disrupted. Then Minsky's point about the liability side comes into play – the liability structures that geniuses of leverage exploited in the high-growth days become nooses for aggressive-growth firms when low growth hits.

The second amendment to Minsky's financial instability framework involves the recognition that border constraints create broader possibilities for asset-price reversals and Minsky crisis. Table 12.4 summarizes the relationships developed here. The middle row of Table 12.4 presents the view of the Minsky cycle and crisis emphasized by Minsky himself. There are, however, two more rows. The top row illustrates the case of an economy that is in surplus vis-à-vis the rest of the world.[7] Such an economy is unlikely to have an asset bubble unless its asset prices are pulled up by an overseas asset bubble. This could occur if this economy's wealth-owners are consistently buying financial and other assets in overseas markets; if prices there are high, domestic securities prices may rise to attract wealth-owners' savings. The boom economy case occupies the bottom row. As noted, a boom economy can encourage the development of a domestic asset bubble independent of the Minsky cycle. This bubble can then be punctured, setting off a Minsky crisis, if wealth inflows slow gradually or are suddenly reversed in a capital-flight episode.

Implications for policy responses to financial instability
Spatializing the Minsky framework as we have done here creates complications due to cross-border relations that were largely unexplored by Minsky in his reflections on economic policy. He liked to say that 'the sky did not fall' after different episodes of financial disorder on Wall Street.

Table 12.4   Bordered economies, Minsky crises and Minsky cycles

	No asset bubble: financial prices and real prices are aligned	Asset bubble: financial asset prices rise above real asset prices in an expansion	Asset-price collapse: financial asset prices fall below real asset prices
Foreign savings <0: an asset-buying economy	Likely case if financial markets are tightly controlled	Possible if overseas financial-asset bubbles occur and pull domestic asset prices along	Minsky crisis if a collapse in overseas asset prices pulls down domestic asset prices
Closed economy case	Early stages of Minsky cycle: recovery from prior recession	Minsky cycle generates an asset bubble	Minsky cycle generates a Minsky crisis
Boom economy: foreign savings >0, a capital-absorbing economy	Boom without bubble	A 'bubble economy' can generate an asset bubble due to capital inflows	Reductions in capital inflows or sudden capital flight can generate Minsky crisis

Preventing the sky from falling was a Federal Reserve playing a lender-of-last-resort role with the world's reserve currency, the dollar. Such interventions would put a floor under macroeconomic growth (and hence a cap on the economy's unemployment rate), since financial instability was often correlated with the macroeconomy's cyclical dynamics.

The analysis in this chapter has emphasized how cross-border imbalances, which Minsky did not explicitly consider, can trigger asset booms or busts as well as financial crises. This section first considers the policy implications of managing financial instability in 'open macroeconomy' settings, and then the policy implications of financial instability linked to intra-national cross-border imbalances.

Financial instability in open economies
Lender-of-last resort interventions by the central bank, as noted in the first section, affect exchange-market equilibria. Increasing liquidity without limit also increases the relative supply of dollars. What happens depends

on whether a fixed or a flexible exchange-rate regime exists. If the former, then more dollars will end up offshore in foreign nations' reserve holdings, and the trade balance will worsen. This creates the possibility of devaluation and makes foreign governments more reluctant to hold the dollars. The ability of any central bank to play a lender-of-last-resort role is circumscribed if that central bank provides liquidity that overseas wealth-holders may not be willing to hold. If devaluation does occur, the domestic currency will tend to fall in value. In the longer run, this may improve the trade balance; but the larger point is that lender-of-last-resort interventions can generate complex and immediate reactions in foreign exchange markets, with numerous (and complex) implications for economic welfare.

This process works both ways. A government which issues a currency that is in demand by wealth-holders has a special advantage in seignorage. This has been the case for the US throughout most of the neoliberal period. In the savings-and-loan crisis of the 1980s, the US was able to rely on the special circumstance of the dollar, as well as the ability of the US government to credibly underwrite asset-market risks, to engineer a resolution that included a bailout of many actively and passively involved owners and depositors.

But this situation may be the exception that proves a more general rule. The developing world offers many cases of countries that have been unable to 'bail out' insolvent banks or firms – or even to implement lender-of-last-resort interventions – precisely because of the weakness of their currencies, which overseas portfolio managers were reluctant to hold. The US itself may be constrained in its efforts to respond to the effects of its subprime crisis due to reduced overseas willingness to hold dollars. Generally, the presence of overseas asset owners who can engage in flight reduces local authorities' room for maneuver. This flight, if large enough, can trigger (or re-kindle) debt-deflation and a Minsky crisis regardless of what domestic asset owners do, and regardless of the state of the domestic economic cycle.

Financial instability linked to intra-national cross-border imbalances
As Minsky himself recognized, intra-national cross-border imbalances in wealth flows can be a driving force leading toward an asset bubble and, ultimately, a build-up of financial fragility. We have pointed out that again and again, intra-national asset flows have tilted the investment/savings playing field toward certain winners: in Japan, capital flows to Tokyo; in Korea, to Seoul; and in the US, to California. This creates a challenge for regions such as these, which are chronically the recipients of net inflows of financial wealth: can real assets be created fast enough to 'attract' financial

wealth inflows, so as to avoid the sorts of real-asset bubbles (classically in housing) that can derail economic growth?

The case of Japan's post-1984 asset bubble deserves mention. This bubble involved both stock-market and land prices; this twin bubble was fed both by the return of offshore money to Japan, and by the centralization of population and capital in Japan's larger cities (especially Tokyo). The crash in stock-market prices in 1989 was dramatic and immediate, decimating the lending capacity and organizational resilience of Japan's banks. However, land prices did not fall for some time (see Figure 12.2). Since banks could not lend, and Japan's stretched homeowners were reluctant (or could not afford) to sell, the crisis persisted for nearly a decade. While incomes stagnated and declined (both on a per-worker basis and because of labor-force withdrawal), housing cost remained frozen. The average housing-price/income ratio in Japan drifted upward from just over 2.0 in the early 1970s to just under 3.5 in the mid-1990s.

The striking fact about the Japanese asset bubble of the 1990s, even after the asset-price crash was well under way, is its continuing grip on Japan's economy. Resolving this deeply rooted Minsky crisis would require measures either to stabilize and increase asset values and/or to reduce the effective weight of debt loads: both, for many years, were untenable due to their attendant political and economic costs. Seen in this light, the US subprime lending crisis has similar characteristics: and there is a risk that the US will be caught in a lingering, unresolved Minsky crisis like the one that has haunted Japan.

Managing national and intra-national cross-border financial imbalances: the case of Korea

The problem of establishing and maintaining policies that prevent the emergence of severe asset bubbles and, in turn, of financial instability is daunting. This is especially true in economies that are subject to substantial national and intra-national wealth-flow imbalances. There is substantial potential for financial fragility and then instability to emerge from the perverse interactions between these two-level flows – even when authorities undertake wise and far-seeing actions. Consider Korea's recent economic history. Korea was a classic boom economy in the early 1990s, as Seoul experienced a steady inflow of population and wealth from other areas in Korea – in addition to inflows of capital from abroad. As such, Korea's economy was certainly as susceptible to bubble and fragility problems.

Korea's trade balance has been generally negative in recent years. So Korea can be considered (in terminology developed herein) a boom economy, especially Seoul and its environs. As emphasized herein, one challenge confronting boom economies is to channel capital (and labor)

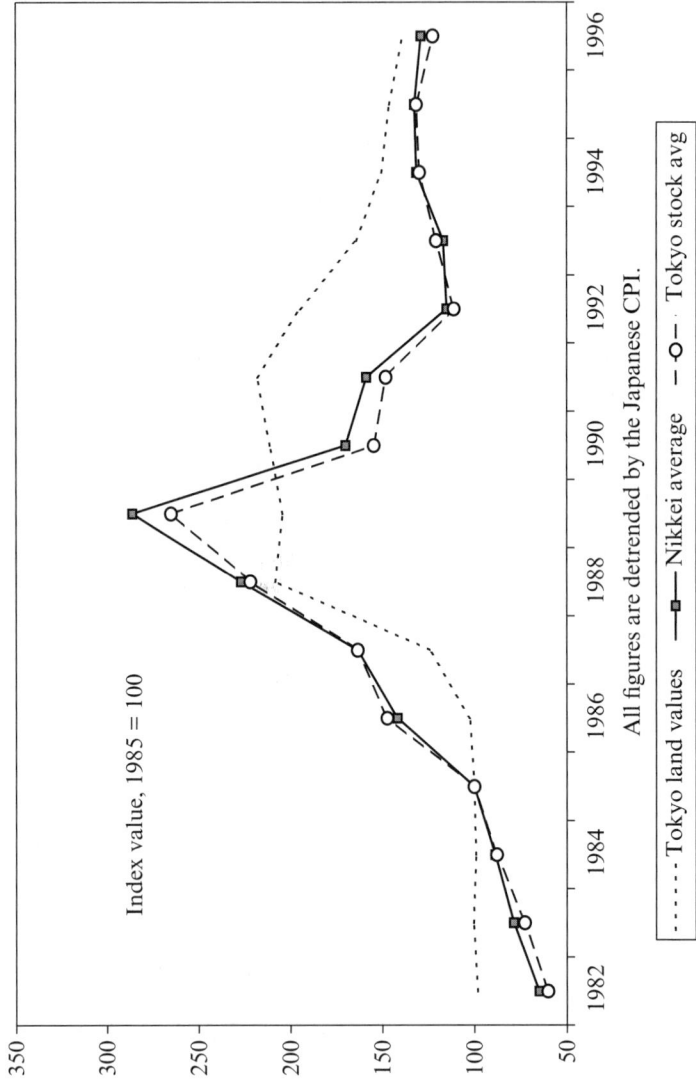

Index value, 1985 = 100

All figures are detrended by the Japanese CPI.

······ Tokyo land values   —■— Nikkei average   – O – Tokyo stock avg

Source: Akira Matsumoto, Ehime University.

Figure 12.2 Land and stock price index values, Japan

inflows so that they do not bid up the prices on existing capital assets and generate rent-seeking opportunities. Whereas California histori- cally relied on a set of powerful, California-owned commercial banks to convert financial claims into real capital, Korea became renowned for its public and corporate sectors' success in building a world-class industrial economy. In Table 12.1 terms, Korea had an efficient set of institutions for converting intra- and international wealth inflows into real asset accumulation. Part of Korea's fascination for outsiders was its ability to accomplish this nominal/real conversion and accomplish rapid or 'late' industrialization (Amsden 1989) with minimal use of arms-length market relations – to 'govern the market,' in Wade's (1998) phrase.

The land bubble of the early 1990s was one aspect of a profound chal- lenge for Korea – the shortage of affordable housing, health services, and other amenities for Korean families, especially the many lower- and middle-income families in the burgeoning urban areas. The very success of Korea's growth strategy, which had avoided extremes of wealth and poverty, became a threat to the widespread provision of adequate and affordable housing and other services, as Yoon (1994) and Kim (1997) describe in detail. Pushed in part by an energetic popular movement, Korea's government pursued an aggressive housing policy; a massive construction effort was begun, together with progressive taxes on thc sale of existing homes which socialized some of the gains from housing-price appreciation. Real government expenditures on housing and community development and on social welfare increased after the mid-1980s (admit- tedly no faster than did expenditures on economic services and defense). This effort to build homes and encourage ownership effectively countered the land (and housing) price bubble by putting new real assets in place (see Figure 12.3), in the form of thousands of new housing units.

However, the precarious balance between Korea's Seoul-focused intra- national financial flows and its increasing housing stock was upset by developments at the macro level. In the mid-1990s, Korea deregulated financial markets and took other steps to gain admission into the Organisation for Economic Co-operation and Development (OECD).[8] Banks remained under tight control; a new set of non-bank intermediaries (the merchant banks) arose. In part these intermediaries speculated on the arbitrage opportunities arising from regional interest-rate mismatches; in part these intermediaries channeled off-shore funds to chaebols seeking external finance to fuel their expansion plans. In any event, the Korean public sector lost control of the growth machine, and Korean dynam- ics flipped from boom-without-bubble to 'bubble economy.' The funds flowing into Korea were almost entirely short-term. Using short-term off- shore funds to support currency speculation and chaebol investment, since

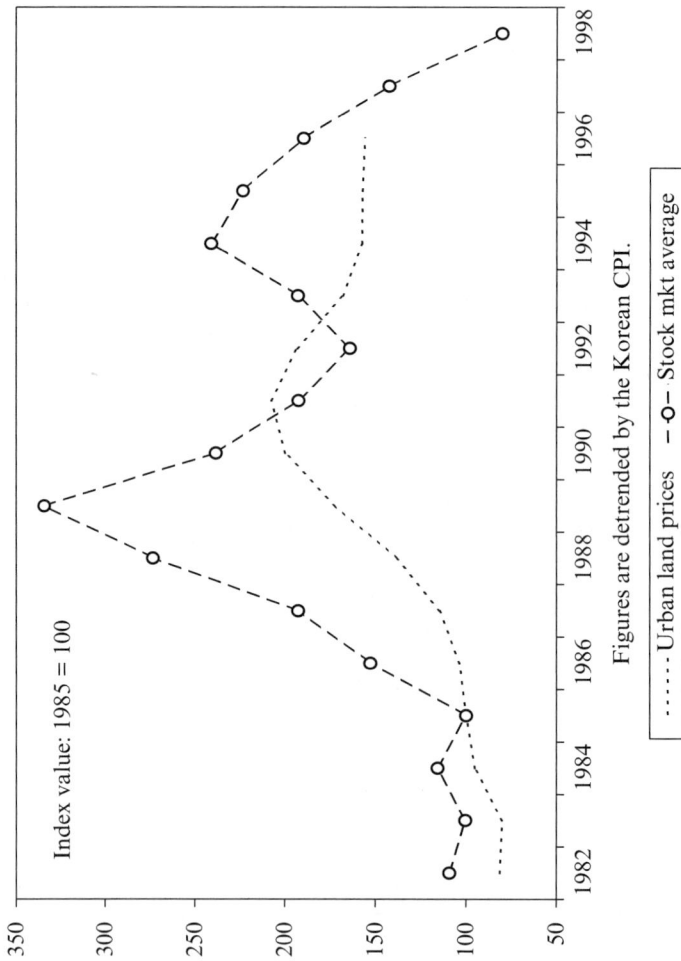

Index value: 1985 = 100

Figures are detrended by the Korean CPI.

······ Urban land prices   – O – Stock mkt average

Sources: Land prices, land taxation in Korea (Ro 1996); 1990–96 stock prices, Korean Stock Exchange; 1982–89 stock prices, author's calculations.

Figure 12.3 Land and stock price index values, Korea, 1982 to August 1998

these funds required continual roll-over, invited either a currency collapse, an attack on Korean industry, or – in the event – both.

After late 1997, the withdrawal of foreign investment and the collapse of asset and currency values created unsustainable debt burdens for many Korean businesses and households – that is, a Minsky crisis. Bankruptcies occurred at historically unprecedented levels, spurred by banks' need to reduce lending so as to build up capital-asset ratios. Firmly under the thumb of the International Monetary Fund (IMF), Korea's real money-supply growth turned sharply negative, and real domestic credit shrank as well. Thus, after Korea avoided a Minskyan fragility for years through careful economic management, a Minsky crisis arrived with a vengeance.

Conclusion

This chapter has considered how Minsky's core ideas about financial instability are altered by the explicit presence of financial flows and obligations across spatial borders. Our most significant finding is that a Minsky crisis may arise even if not preceded by a Minsky cycle. So there are more paths to a Minsky crisis than Minsky's own characteristic interpretation anticipates; and these depend crucially on the particularities of historical time and place that underlie financial flows.

Since the late 1970s, debates about the sources of the increasingly frequent financial crises have focused on a small set of factors: excessive or lax financial regulation; government interference in credit markets; moral-hazard lending problems due to unscrupulous borrowers; and contagion effects. This chapter has suggested a new contributing factor in Asian and other cross-border financial crises: imbalances between inflows of financial capital and the growth rate of real capital assets.

Far from being an unusual episode in economic dynamics, imbalances of this sort are a chronic tendency in boom economies – that is, in nations or regions that characteristically import capital and/or people from elsewhere. In a boom economy, what stands between stable asset prices and an asset-price collapse is an intermediation sector and/or a capital-controls policy dedicated to channeling inflows into appropriate real-asset accumulation. When these institutions are weakened, an asset price bubble and collapse become more likely. Indeed, we show that Minsky crises can be triggered by cross-border shifts of capital, not just by Minsky cycles. The interpretation of asset bubbles developed here spatializes Minsky's notion of financial fragility – that is, it shows the special balance-sheet tensions that emerge when financial positions extend across economic borders. Interestingly, this extension of Minsky's well-known financial-instability model makes use of Minsky's own earlier, neglected insights into the importance of cross-border relations in economic growth.

This expanded Minskyan perspective throws new light on recent experience in nations ranging from Japan and Korea to the US. There is no one asset-bubble story that is told and retold over the millennia, no one lesson that can immunize policy-makers from the pitfalls of asset bubbles. Quite the opposite point is made here: asset bubbles are a chronic tendency of boom economies, and boom economies are recurring structural phenomena. Neither an asset bubble nor a build-up of excessively fast macroeconomic growth is required for the emergence of a Minsky crisis, when they are fuelled by shifts in unbalanced cross-border financial flows. These shifts can occur for any number of reasons, including fear and ignorance.

Notes

*   Preliminary versions of this chapter were published in 1998, in the *Journal of Regional Studies*, Korea (pp. 135–59) and in Portuguese, in *Globalização Financieira: Ensaios de Macroeconomica Aberta (Financial Globalisation: Essays on Open Macroeconomics)*, edited by Fernando Ferrari-Filho and Luiz Fernando de Paula (Petrópolis: Editora Vozes 2004, pp. 402–48). The research reported here was supported by the Pacific Rim Research Program of the University of California and by the Center for Global Partnership. The author received helpful comments from Jim Crotty, Tokutaro Shibata, Fernando Carvalho, Fernando Costa, and Luiz Fernando de Paula, from participants in seminars at Seoul National University, Fukyong National University, Ehime University, Tokyo University, UNICAMP, the Federal University of Rio de Janeiro, and the University of California, Riverside.
1. For two examples, see respectively Martin and McKibbin (1999) and Zhang (2001).
2. Roubini entitled his July 30, 2007 on-line blog entry, 'Are we at the peak of a Minsky credit cycle?' Wolf entitled his December 23, 2008 article in the *Financial Times*, 'Keynes offers us the best way to think about the financial crisis.' In it, he referred to Minsky as Keynes's 'most interesting disciple.'
3. An example of a self-undermining rule of thumb is the notion that real estate in a given market area is at once the highest-return and safest asset one can hold.
4. These empirical measurements involve assessments of the trough and post-trough values of the variables mentioned here, measured on an annual basis. Using data measured at an annual time-scale permitted Pollin and Dymski (1994) to analyze data as far backward as the late 19th century. At the same time, using annual data suppresses some of these variables' shorter-term cyclical responses.
5. We do not explore the broader challenge of creating an open-economy macroeconomic model subject to Minskyan financial fragility. We abstract here from macroeconomic dynamics proper.
6. Minsky pointed out that 'one of the truisms of economics is that the current account balance balances' (1965).
7. Because of intra-national capital flows, an economy as a whole can occupy one row, while a region within it occupies another. Japan, for example, chronically sits in the top row, while Tokyo falls into the bottom row.
8. On Korea's liberalization and its consequences, see Wade and Veneroso (1998) and Crotty and Dymski (1998).

References

Amsden, A. (1989), *Asia's Next Giant,* Oxford and New York: Oxford University Press.
Crotty, J. (1994), 'Are Keynesian uncertainty and macrotheory compatible? Conventional decision making, institutional structures, and conditional stability in Keynesian

macromodels', in G. Dymski and R. Pollin (eds), *New Perspectives in Monetary Macroeconomics: Explorations in the Tradition of Hyman P. Minsky*, Ann Arbor, MI: University of Michigan Press, pp. 105–42.

Crotty, J. and G. Dymski (1998), 'Can the global neoliberal regime survive victory in Asia? The political economy of the Asian crisis', *International Papers in Political Economy*, 2.

Dymski, G. (2009), 'Heterodox Economics as crisis theory? From profit-squeeze to the global liquidity meltdown', in J. Goldstein and M. Hillard (eds), *Heterodox Macroeconomics: Keynes, Marx and Globalization*, New York: Routledge, pp 66–84.

Grant, J. (1992), *Money of the Mind: Borrowing and Lending in America from the Civil War to Michael Milke*, New York: Noonday.

Gray, H.P. and J.M. Gray (1994), 'Minskian fragility in the international financial system', in G. Dymski and R. Pollin (eds), *New Perspectives in Monetary Macroeconomics: Explorations in the Tradition of Hyman P. Minsky*, Ann Arbor, MI: University of Michigan Press, pp. 143–68.

Keynes, J.M. (1936), *The General Theory of Employment, Interest, and Prices*, London: Macmillan.

Kim, W.-J. (1997), *Economic Growth, Low Income, and Housing in South Korea*, London: Macmillan Press.

Kregel, J. (1998), 'Yes, "it" did happen again – a Minsky crisis happened in Asia', Working Paper No. 234, Levy Economics Institute of Bard College, Annandale-on-Hudson, New York.

Martin, W. and P. McKibbin (1999), 'The East Asian crisis: investigating causes and policy responses', Working Paper No. 2172, World Bank Policy Research, Washington, DC: World Bank.

Minsky, H.P. (1965), 'Commercial banking and rapid economic growth in California', in H.P. Minsky (ed.), *California Banking in a Growing Economy: 1946–75*, Berkeley, CA: Institute of Business and Economic Research, University of California, pp. 79–134.

Minsky, H.P. (1975), *John Maynard Keynes*, New York: Columbia University Press.

Minsky, H.P. (1982), *Can 'It' Happen Again?: Essays on Instability and Finance*, Armonk, NY: M.E. Sharpe.

Minsky, H.P. (1986), *Stabilizing An Unstable Economy*, New Haven: Yale University Press.

Pollin, R. and G. Dymski (1994), 'The costs and benefits of financial instability: big-government capitalism and the Minsky paradox', in R. Pollin and G. Dymski (eds), *New Perspectives in Monetary Macroeconomics: Essays in the Tradition of Hyman P. Minsky*, Ann Arbor, MI: The University of Michigan Press, pp. 369–401.

Ro, Y. (1996), '*Land Taxation in Korea: A Critical Review of Current Policies and Suggestions for Future Policy Direction*, Seoul: Korea Institute of Public Finance.

Roubini, N. (2007), 'Are we at the peak of a Minsky credit cycle?', *RGE Monitor*, July 30.

Wade, R. (1998), 'From "miracle" to "cronyism": explaining the great Asian slump', *Cambridge Journal of Economics*, **22**(6), pp. 693–706.

Wade, R. and F. Veneroso (1998), 'The Asian crisis: the high debt model vs. the Wall Street-Treasury-IMF complex', *New Left Review*, 228, March–April.

Wolf, M. (2008), 'Keynes offers us the best way to think about the financial crisis', *Financial Times*, December 23.

Yoon, Il-S. (1994), *Housing in a Newly Industrialized Economy: The Case of South Korea*, Brookfield, VT: Avebury Publishing Co.

Zhang, Z. (2001), 'Speculative attacks in the Asian crisis', Working Paper No. 01/189, International Monetary Fund, Washington, DC.

13 The psychology of financial markets: Keynes, Minsky and emotional finance
*Sheila Dow**

Introduction

Hyman Minsky's Financial Instability Hypothesis (FIH) has provided an influential explanation for the current phase of systemic instability, tying it into a cyclical pattern of asset valuation (Whalen 2007). For Minsky, boom periods result from a growing tendency to reduce expectation of risk and to expect an increasing appreciation of asset values, with consequent growth in credit and thus exposure to risk. This tendency increases the fragility of the financial system and thus its potential for reversals, as expectations are confounded and defaults increase. A key element of the process is that illiquidity problems, through knock-on effects on asset valuation, can create insolvency problems. The boom period is categorized as one of 'euphoria', which has a key role in the absence of the necessary conditions for objective quantitative risk assessment. While uncertainty diminishes with the general confidence in low risk during the boom period, the reversal increases uncertainty about future asset values, encouraging a rise in liquidity preference which continues as expectations become more firmly held of asset price deflation.

The concept of euphoria, and indeed of uncertainty in the absence of objective quantifiable risk, are redolent of psychology rather than rational economic man. Indeed the expression 'the psychology of the market' is often used in this context, and notably by Minsky's (1975) mentor Keynes. While Keynes explicitly discussed psychology in a variety of ways as an integral part of his economic analysis, Minsky did not actively explore it. Indeed, as Chick (2001, p.40) has pointed out, Minsky's theory demonstrated the structural nature of cycles in contrast to Keynes's 'ad hoc appeals to a collapse in expectations'. It is the financial fragility which builds up in the euphoric phase which accounts for the reversal, not any particular event (anything which breaks through the euphoria will do). For all Minsky explicitly adopted Keynes's theory of expectations under uncertainty, he appeared to distance himself further from psychological exploration by referring, for example, to 'the irrational fact of uncertainty' (Minsky 1982, p.118).

Indeed there was a long period of increased disciplinary separateness

(Hausman 1992), whereby economics was understood to be concerned with rationality and psychology with irrationality. But in recent years there has been an increasing focus on the scope for combining economics and psychology, from a variety of perspectives, particularly with reference to financial behavior. The purpose of this chapter is to consider the available ideas on economics and psychology in order to flesh out, in the spirit of Minsky, the psychological content of his theory.

We start by considering the recent emergence of importing psychology into economics in the 'new' behavioral finance literature, as a way of understanding how psychology can be used in economics, tying the chapter into some different approaches within psychology itself. We find that psychology is introduced as a 'separable' additive element, which does not affect the fundamental structure of theory. Further psychology enters theory in terms of either preferences or cognition, treated separately. But the 'old' behavioral economics, which focused on cognition issues, proposed a different approach to theorizing, employing a broader notion of rationality (see Sent 2004 for a chapter on the distinction between the 'new' and 'old' behavioral finance). We discuss this approach to cognitive problems in the second section, along with some of the subsequent thinking in neuroscience which raises questions about separability between issues of cognition and emotion. Indeed historically psychology evolved alongside economics in the eighteenth century within moral philosophy, allowing for more integration between the economic and the psychological, not least because of the integrated treatment of cognition and emotion. In the third section, we trace this approach to economics and psychology to Keynes, whose theories were a primary inspiration for Minsky. In the fourth section we consider some new work in the area of emotional finance with its emphasis on uncertainty as the crucial factor. This indicates how the Keynes/Minsky account of financial markets might be developed further.

Financial instability is a complex phenomenon, best explained as Minsky has done as a structural phenomenon which is natural to market economies. The intention here is not to argue that psychology alone can explain cycles. Within Minsky's structural framework, other important factors particular to context, such as institutional arrangements (both within public sector institutions and within banks), are an integral part of any account. The purpose here is to focus on the nature and role of the psychological element in cycles.

'New' behavioral finance

Identifying the psychological content of economics is not straightforward, in that the field of psychology itself has its own history and range of approaches. Indeed how we understand this context also depends fundamentally on the approach to economics within which we consider psychology (see Dow, forthcoming). We start with the traditional efficient market theory explanation for financial instability as a jumping-off point for the contributions of the new behavioral economics; this is the area of combining economics and psychology which perhaps currently has the highest profile.

In order to explain financial instability in efficient markets where behavior is rational in the standard axiomatic sense requires the importation of some market imperfection. This imperfection could take the form of imperfect information, or more logistical factors which limit the efficiency of market arbitrage. Once the market has deviated from equilibrium, rational behavior can initially amplify the deviation, although rational behavior then reverses the process, the whole process constituting a 'rational bubble'.

Given the traditional demarcation between economics and psychology, psychology can enter into the financial instability explanation in the form of a deviation from equilibrium caused by an element of irrationality in the market. Thus for example, the amplification of the deviation could be explained by herding behavior (an irrational overemphasis on past trends). Yet efforts have been made to explain such behavior as being rational given the extent of available information (Bikhchandani and Sharma 2001).

Alternatively, some heterogeneous agent models segment the market into rational players (primarily the professionals) and irrational players who allow sentiment to influence their choices (Baker and Wurgler 2007). Eventually the rational players drive the market back to equilibrium. Other heterogeneous agent models allow for disagreement in interpretation of market trends, but imperfect updating of inferences as to others' beliefs. These latter explanations have psychological content: sentiment/ irrationality and cognitive limitations.

Irrational behavior on the part of the representative agent too can explain financial instability. This kind of psychological input has tended in the past to be treated as exogenous (economics not being concerned with irrationality). But Kahneman and Tversky (1974, 1979) in particular have sought to explore further into the nature and content of this psychological input. The benchmark for them too is rational economic man, but their work has used experimental evidence to challenge the realism of the rationality assumptions in economics, since the outcomes were not those predicted by standard decision theory. Rational choice theory explains choice as the outcome of optimizing with respect to some objective function, subject to constraints, which generally yields an unambiguous best outcome. However, Kahneman and Tversky (1974; 1979) demonstrated that the choices actually made in experiments depend crucially on how the agent frames the choice problem (a matter of cognition) and preferences (a matter of sentiment or emotion, as in loss aversion, for example). The scope for different framings arises from cognitive limitations, which are addressed in practice by the adoption of heuristics. This is potentially of tremendous significance. From a psychological perspective, accepting different framings, there is no longer one best solution. For economists to model choice, there needs to be a model of framing. From an economics perspective, however, there is still the best rational choice, and any framing other than in terms of classical logic is deemed irrational.

Kahneman and Tversky's work has sparked off a large literature in behavioral theory, which addresses actual behavior as it appears from experimental evidence. However, this interest in behavioral economics builds on behavioral psychology. This approach to psychology does not inquire into the actual causal processes behind behavior, but rather seeks stable predictable relationships, which can be modeled, between stimulus and response. Behavioral psychology thus takes a 'black box' instrumentalist approach.

While a large gap remains between the pure, deductivist, theoretical literature and the inductivist applied literature drawing on experimental evidence, the goal is to combine the two, by achieving a much more complex specification of rational choice which takes on board the psychological elements taken to lie behind the experimental results. As Hong and Stein (2007, p. 126) put it:

> The enduring appeal of classical asset-pricing theory over the last several decades owes much to its success in forging a consensus around a foundational modeling platform. This platform consists of a core set of assumptions that have been widely-accepted by researchers working in the field as reasonable first-order descriptions of investor behavior, and that – just as importantly – lend themselves to elegant, powerful, and tractable theorizing.
>
> If behavioral finance is ever to approach the stature of classical asset pricing, it will have to move beyond a large collection of empirical facts and competing one-off models, and ultimately reach a similar sort of consensus.

We can summarize the psychological input to behavioral finance in a stylized way as follows, where D = decision, U = utility/preferences, S is the state, or context, within which the decision is taken and which constrains the decision, and f is the functional form of the decision-making process: $D = f(U|S)$.

Psychology enters first in the functional form, f. Rather than an optimizing structure, decision-making may follow a satisficing structure with its own decision rules (such as Maslow's hierarchy of needs). This is explained by human cognitive limitations as well as the nature of the subject matter. Cognition also enters into the perception of context, S; agents may apply their own particular frame to the situation, events may have triggered particular emotions, and social norms may enter into both the interpretation of the choice situation and the forming of expectations.

Psychology enters secondly in the preferences. The utility function may include arguments based on emotion or sentiment (e_1, e_2, e_3, . . .), such as loss aversion or the preference for particular classes of asset, as well as the conventional arguments, such as income and leisure: y and l: $U = U(e_1, e_2, e_3, . . . ; y, l)$.

The core framework therefore remains outcome-oriented rational optimizing behavior. As Kahneman (2003, p. 1469) put it, 'theories in behavioral economics have generally retained the basic architecture of the rational model, adding assumptions about cognitive limitations designed to account for specific anomalies'. Indeed Altman (2004) argues that Kahneman and Tversky focus on deviations from predictions of rationality models as error or irrationality. Their verbal analysis is broader ranging than what is modeled; see also Shiller's 2005 work on irrational exuberance. But the formal modeling of behavioral economics imposes restrictions on what can be incorporated. The modeling of heuristics (and framing) poses particular problems. As de Grauwe (2007 quoted by Goodhart 2008, p. 7) notes, 'The challenge when we try to model heuristics will be to introduce discipline in the selection of rules so as to avoid that "anything is possible"'. Further, while psychological factors can be incorporated as preferences, there is no obvious way of explaining the large changes in behavior associated with financial instability. This would appear to require some exploration of psychological motivation, that is, a theory of the mind.

'Old' behavioral finance and neuroscience
Long before the emergence of behavioral finance, Herbert Simon (1955) was exploring the significance for economic behavior of cognitive limitations. Rather than focusing just on outcomes, Simon was concerned to inquire into mental processes. Indeed Simon (1986) argued that the economic concept of rationality focused on choices, whereas in the other social sciences rationality was a matter of processes. He argued that the subject matter is such that we cannot have perfect information; indeed knowledge is generally inevitably held with uncertainty. This argument (shared by Keynes and Minsky, as we shall see below) did not attract the attention of mainstream economics. What did attract attention was his other argument that, in addition, our human cognitive capacities are limited. Both limitations in general rule out optimizing behavior. The informational and computing demands, for example, for a complete

indifference mapping of preferences over all possible choices, including all contingencies, are beyond human capabilities. Instead, we employ heuristics to guide decision-making. This was rational in a broader sense than the term is used in the rationality axioms. Further, Simon's approach emphasises induction over deduction, as the way in which economic agents build their knowledge and adopt heuristics, but also as the way in which the economist should build theory. Indeed Simon took a strong stand against deductivist reasoning and therefore formal equilibrium models (Sent 2004, p. 747).

One decision-making strategy is to follow others, which is efficient in many circumstances, but which also can have disastrous consequences in others. For example, Earl, Peng and Potts (2007) have used Simon's heuristics approach to analyze financial instability in terms of herd behavior, which can precipitate a crisis. The emphasis is on diversity of investment strategies rather than diversity of information. Drawing on Dopfer and Potts's (2008) analysis of rules as meso trajectories, they explore decision-rule cascades in speculative markets. Strategies are developed creatively (requiring their own analysis, drawing on Kelly 1963), but then these strategies cascade down through expert levels to households, and lose detail in the process. Thus a sophisticated strategy for buying real estate may degenerate into a simple 'buy-real-estate' rule for households regardless of capacity to finance the necessary mortgage loan. As the heuristic degenerates, speculative buying builds strength and the seeds of instability are sown.

Simon's work provided encouragement for the move within psychology from behavioral psychology to the development of neuroscience, which explored the source of behavior in the structure of the brain, opening up new possibilities for explaining apparent deviations from the predictions of the conventional rational optimizing agent model. As Camerer et al. (2005, p. 54) put it, 'there is no theoretical basis in finance for why attitudes towards risk would vary over time. Maybe neuroscience can supply one'.

First, adding to Kahneman and Tversky's argument about different possible framings, neuroscience demonstrated that behavior depends on the specific part of the brain triggered by an event, adding further to the conclusion that there was scope for a variety of outcomes (Martins 2008). Indeed it would be difficult in these terms to contemplate a unitary set of preferences, even for the individual (far less the representative agent). Second, behavior is in general dominated by affect (or emotion) rather than rational calculation. Affect is generally unconscious, as opposed to feelings, which are, in general, conscious; a common form of affect is the unconscious desire for system.

> The most important consideration in human decision-making and action is not how to optimize cost/benefit ratios, but how to maintain an emotional state in the person performing the action that is as stable as possible and free of contradiction within itself. (Gerhard 2003, p. 2)

Indeed it is argued that emotion is necessary for decision-making, citing evidence from individuals whose emotional capacity is limited (Damasio 1994; Gigerenzer and Selten 2001, p. 207). Yet behavior can be understood as the outcome of a struggle between different mental processes, such as reason and emotion.

There have been attempts within this literature to model decision-making taking account of emotion (that is, incorporating emotion into a model of rational choice). This is particularly the case in the artificial intelligence literature (see, for example, Marvin Minsky 2006). But the scope for these attempts to succeed has been challenged by Gigerenzer (2000, 2007), who argues that the evidence suggests that decision-making is based primarily on biological evolved heuristics and gut feelings, rather than calculative rationality. While this decision-making is rational in a broader sense than calculative rationality, it seriously undermines the meaningfulness of the idea in the economics literature that rational behavior (in the narrow sense) could drive out the irrational (see further Gigerenzer et al. 1989; Gigerenzer and Selten 2001). In particular it challenges the Kahneman and Tversky approach with its separation between calculative rationality and other (apparently irrational) bases for action. But this literature is continuing to evolve. There is now a growing literature in psychology on emotion theory, where there are competing strands of thought, for example, as to whether it is reason which generates emotion (as in fear as a self-preservation strategy) or whether emotion such as fear is rationalized afterwards as a mechanism for self-preservation.

The question remains as to what instigates activity in the brain, and thus behavior: whether it is always the result of an exogenous stimulus to given mental states. (There is a parallel with the theory of financial instability being caused by exogenous events, or, as in Minsky, by structural changes rather than the events as such.) Indeed there is a strand of thought in psychology which questions the validity of separating emotion and reason (something which is evident to a limited extent in Camerer et al.'s 2005 survey article). For example, individuals are depicted as generally ambivalent rather than single-goal directed (Berezin 2005). What is clear from the neuroscience literature is that deductive protocols themselves cannot stimulate action, particularly the kind of change in behavior patterns evident under financial instability; behavior itself requires inductive reasoning. As Klein and d'Esposito (2007) argue, there is a profound incompatibility between deductive reasoning and the inductive reasoning needed to address ill-defined, complex strategic situations. Indeed Camerer et al. (2005) argue that the rational protocols of rational choice models, as explored in neuroscience, have a better chance of illuminating animal behavior than the behavior of humans who are capable of deliberating about emotion and the consequences of emotional acts.

At issue is the presence or not of dualism, that is, the propensity to structure thought around all-encompassing, mutually exclusive categories with fixed meaning, which is characteristic of closed systems (Dow 1990). The duals at issue here are rationality/irrationality and reason/emotion, as well as (probabilistic) certainty/ignorance. If these duals do not adequately represent the psychological reality of decision-making, because of the nature both of the mind and of the environment, deductive calculation cannot explain behavior. It may then be that the standard finance approach, being deductivist, cannot provide a satisfactory explanation for behavior. We have seen that the standard theory imports psychology in separable form, into the preferences of agents, and their capacity to optimize. Further, behavioral economics represents decision-making within a goal-oriented framework, where the preferences can be understood as having emotional content. But changing emotional states not only change behavior but may also make it difficult to represent the behavior as addressed to goals, rather than, say, instincts, in a clearly-defined way. It may also be an insuperable problem to incorporate heterogeneous emotional states.

Bruni and Sugden (2007) trace the emphasis of economics on rationality back to Pareto, rather than the combination of economics with psychology, focusing on the pleasure/pain principle, as pursued by Edgeworth and Jevons. But we can trace the combination of economics with psychology much further back. Some of the issues explored above were addressed in the early days of the evolution of modern economics, as well as modern psychology, in the writings of key figures in the Scottish Enlightenment, notably Hume and Smith. Some of these ideas resurfaced (with further influence from Freud) in Keynes's writings. In both cases the significance of psychology followed from this epistemology. We now proceed to explore these ideas in order to inform our modern thinking on psychology and economics.

An integrated approach to psychology and economics

Modern psychology may be said to have stemmed from one of the same roots as modern economics: the Scottish Enlightenment. We find many of the features of the mind which are now being demonstrated by neuroscience. What is now referred to as 'psychological' was Adam Smith's (1795) explanation for the motivation for science and the spread of ideas. Scientists are motivated by the urge to set the mind at rest when it comes across disturbing instances which seem not to be explained by current theory; they also have a disposition to find particular pleasure in solving such puzzles. This urge was subconscious; as Foucault (1972) argues, this period saw the emergence of the unconscious mind. The real world was too complex to generate certain knowledge; knowledge was therefore built up provisionally through induction and the development of provisional principles through reason, on the foundation of sentiment. Further, ideas are spread by means of persuasion, in the absence of access to truth. Theories are more persuasive which are pleasing to the mind; they are simple, connect with something which is already thought to be known, and derive from first principles. Indeed the psychological factor of aesthetic sense was a central aspect of Smith's theory of knowledge (Comim 2006).

Central to Smith's work was the view that knowledge is the product of the mind (a view shared and developed later by Marshall and Hayek; see Loasby, 2009). Indeed the modern theory of mind found its origins in this period in the debates around common sense philosophy, which posited that the mind adds to the observations of the senses. The mind was the locus of ideas as well as the registering of experience, and reason. Reason was a faculty which came into play only after the sentiments established motivation, and also the grounding of belief (for example, in the existence of reality) which underpinned observation. As Hume (1739–40, p. 413) put it, 'reason alone can never be a motive to any action of the will; . . . it can never oppose passion in the direction of the will'.

Sentiment could also constrain action. Thus, the impartial spectator, understood through imagination, was the locus for moral sense which, along with self-command, constrained self-interest (Montes 2004). This interpretation is in marked contrast to Ashraf et al. (2005) who have interpreted the impartial spectator as imposing reason on irrational sentiment (consistent with our account of behavioral economics above). Yet the first interpretation accords well with the neuroscience analysis of deliberation limiting affect. Reason could also be applied perversely in that human beings are capable of self-deception. In the case of Smith's (1759, p. 181) poor man's son, for example, increased economic activity is the fortunate side-effect (as if arranged by the Invisible Hand) of an unreasonable expectation that riches will bring happiness.

Psychology then referred to the sentiments rather than reason, but the two were intertwined, for example, in the process of persuasion, or of the development of moral sense. While sentiments would be different, and manifested in different ways, in different contexts, there was a belief in the commonality in human nature, allowing general statements, for example, as to what is more persuasive in one theory than another. This interdependence of sentiment and reason followed from an epistemology which emphasized the limits to human knowledge.

It is not surprising, given the similarities between Keynes's epistemology and the epistemology of the Scottish Enlightenment, that psychology could enter similarly into his approach to economics. For Keynes too, psychology provided the subconscious motivation for behavior. Thus, drawing on Freud, Keynes argued that economic activity in a market economy is driven by the urge for financial accumulation. Like Smith, he saw this urge as involving self-deception, operating against individuals' best interests (Winslow 1995). This view of money as a good sought in itself, rather than as a veil, is also supported by the modern literature in neuroscience.

In the *Treatise on Probability*, Keynes (1921) explored how we establish reasonable grounds for belief as the basis for action. Given the limited scope for certain (or certain-equivalent) knowledge, most knowledge is held with uncertainty. In the absence of the ability to establish knowledge with reason alone, then, we use what direct knowledge we have, along with indirect (theoretical) knowledge, conventional knowledge, and expert advice. But, as he explained with respect to the valuation of assets and the investment decision, this knowledge is never enough to justify action. Rather it must be supplemented by instinct, and a psychological urge to action ('animal spirits'). As he argued in the *General Theory*, action in the form of investment could never be justified by rational calculation, since all knowledge with respect to the future was subject to fundamental uncertainty. 'A large proportion of our positive activities depend on spontaneous optimism rather than a mathematical expectation, whether moral or hedonistic or economics' (Keynes 1936, p. 161). In times of low confidence in expectations, however, there is no urge for action, and liquidity preference is high.

These two factors, the psychological expectation of yield on capital assets and the psychological attitude to liquidity, are two of the three 'ultimate psychological factors' which underpinned his macroeconomic theory (the third being the marginal propensity to consume) (Keynes 1936, pp. 246–7). Further, Keynes (1937) later suggested some heuristics to guide expectations formation, and thus behavior, under uncertainty: assume the present to be a guide to the future, assume current prices to be a correct valuation of assets, and adopt conventional judgements (conforming to the majority or average). These heuristics embody an emotional trust which may well prove to be disastrously wrong.

Keynes's realization that emotion and reason play interdependent parts is most explicit in his essay 'My Early Beliefs' (Keynes 1938 [1972]). His understanding of rationality is made clear by comparing Chapters 11 and 12 of the *General Theory*, as accounts of the investment decision. Under uncertainty it would never be rational, in the standard economic sense, to invest; a rational calculation could not be made. The investment decision requires the emotional urge to act in spite of uncertainty; this is potentially reasonable behavior, not irrational behavior. But of course in euphoric conditions, the urge to act may not be reasonable in retrospect, when asset prices fail to meet expectations.

Keynes put great emphasis on the 'psychology of the market' as determining opinion about the valuation of assets, and the confidence held in that valuation. While Keynes has been criticized (for example, Pixley 2004) as offering too individualistic an account of psychology, his theory of expectations emphasized the social dimension, in his 'beauty contest' example where individual expectations focus on the expectation of market expectations, or in his emphasis more generally on social convention (Davis 1994). Goodhart (2008) similarly criticizes Shackle's related ideas about expectations under uncertainty, in the context of financial market instability, as being unduly individualistic. We will explore the application of social, rather than individual, psychology to financial instability in the following section, as an approach which seems consistent with Minsky's structural approach.

Minsky (1975) was clearly inspired by Keynes. Indeed Chick (2001, p. 36) describes him as 'perhaps the earliest of the retrievers of Keynes's *Treatise on Probability*'. Minsky's epistemology, and thus methodology, were heavily influenced by Keynes. While he used formal representations as partial arguments, Minsky explicitly chose not to present his theory as a general formal model; the emphasis was on structural change and evolution (Foley 2001). Thus Minsky developed Keynes's ideas further, providing a systemic account of financial instability. His interest in Schumpeter is revived in Leather and Raines's (2004) analysis of financial cycles fueled by financial innovation. In what follows, we explore the field of emotional finance which likewise focuses on innovation as providing the psychological drive for financial instability.

Emotional finance
Within the modern finance literature there is renewed attention to the notion of the psychology of the market as the primary force behind financial instability, where emotion or sentiment is integrated with reason. The first field we will consider is emotional finance, associated with the work of Tuckett and Taffler (2008) which draws on Freud, and focuses on the role of novelty as an emotional spur. We will then consider a study by Pixley (2004) entitled *Emotions in Finance* which takes a more social psychology approach.

Freudian psychoanalysis sought a rational (in the broad sense) explanation for apparently irrational behavior, emphasizing the scope for beliefs, intents, desires, and knowledge to be unconscious as well as conscious. He focused on biologically induced emotions as physical and mental internal states (see further Wollheim 1999). The implication was that behavior was the outcome of reason, however defective might be the content of the reasoning (Simon 1986, p. 5209), but that reasoning could be unconscious. While Freud began from neuroscience, his later methods verged on the literary, weaving narratives around a small number of cases. While the content of much of his theory and methods have now been discredited in some circles, there seems to be a revival of interest in his more general approach.

According to Tuckett and Taffler's interpretation of Freud's psychoanalysis, behavior is driven by emotion and unconscious fantasy, and (in tune with both Adam Smith and the neuroscience literature) the subconscious search for a settled mind and the avoidance of anxiety. The starting-point is uncertainty and the sense of emotional conflict that creates. The argument is then developed that decisions made under uncertainty must be ambivalent, in particular between fantasy and reality-based thinking. Fantasy, or unrealistic wishes, corresponds to the wishful thinking Smith identified in the poor man's son. Financial instability can then be analyzed as a sequence whereby the tension between reality-based thought and fantasy is resolved as fantasy takes over.

Bubbles start with some novelty which causes excitement. Not only is the excitement of a euphoric state a response to a novel stimulus, but, as Scitovsky (1981) argues, we may actively crave novel stimuli. And yet the excitement itself alters judgement (Kaish 1986; see further Earl 1990, Chapter 12). Tuckett and Taffler (2008) use the dotcom bubble as an example, although we could consider structured debt instruments as the novelty which arose in the run-up to the current crisis (Chick 2008). Bubbles then follow an emotional sequence: patchy excitement turns into growing excitement and in turn manic/euphoric excitement. There is normally some conflict between emotion (wishful thinking) and normal asset valuation (reality-based cognition). This conflict increases as asset valuation diverges more and more from a reality-based valuation, causing anxiety. Market players avoid this anxiety by increasingly ignoring reality as the euphoria builds up. Indeed the market tends to be dominated by those who are willing to act, that is, those who resolve the tension by privileging fantasy; those who continue to retain reality-based thinking will drop out of the market as the euphoria is perceived to be excessive.

It is only when reality breaks through in some form that fantasy is challenged and the bubble bursts, and panic ensues. But the continuing dominance of wishful thinking is evident in the prevalence of blame rather than guilt when the bubble bursts; guilt would require acknowledgement that there had been a major departure from reality-based thinking.

This analysis treats emotion or sentiment as integral to market behavior, given rein by uncertainty compounded by the tensions in attitudes to asset valuation. It therefore has the potential to flesh out a Minskyan account of the psychology of the market. The notion of reality-based thought may be taken to imply some notion of objective valuation as a benchmark. For Minsky, as for Keynes, asset valuation is not an objective process, since it is conducted under uncertainty. Nevertheless, if we consider Keynes's notion of weight of argument, we can consider degrees of uncertainty, or conversely degrees of confidence, with respect to expectations, on the basis of experience, or evidence. Reality-based thinking therefore draws more on evidence than wishful thinking, which involves self-deception.

Tuckett and Taffler share with all the other approaches which aim to integrate emotion and reason a reliance on the inductive method, drawing evidence from surveying market players, while employing provisional theoretical principles which Freud had previously drawn from case study evidence. Just like Simon, Keynes and Minsky, they make no attempt to model behavior in any deterministic way. If knowledge is held with uncertainty, the switch from euphoric market behavior to panic becomes a potential as the bubble gains force and the structure of the financial system becomes more fragile, but the nature and timing of the events which provoke the onset of panic cannot be predicted. This 'potential' corresponds to the critical realist notion of 'tendency' as an underlying causal force which may or may not be in operation at any time (Lawson 1997).

Interviewing key players is also the approach of Pixley (2004), but the provisional principles on which she draws are those of Keynes and Minsky. The emotions on which Pixley focuses are trust and distrust, where these are understood in social terms, that is, trust and distrust in institutions. Starting with a Keynesian analysis of uncertainty, she explains the importance of the institutions of money and banking which help us cope with uncertainty. On the other hand these institutions rely on our confidence – if that is challenged (when there is a bank run, for example), then panic ensues and trust is destroyed. The source of this challenge, for Pixley as for Minsky, is not events as such, but the financial structure which has built up over the boom period. Her interviews add valuable, up-to-date evidence in support of the Minsky approach, but with an explicit focus on emotions as integral to decision-making under uncertainty. Further, her approach to uncertainty and to emotion is itself consistent with Minsky's structural approach, being understood at the level of social structures and institutions rather than isolated individuals.

Conclusion

We have seen in this chapter that the key to drawing on psychology in economics lies in epistemology. If, as in the benchmark mainstream model, knowledge is held with certainty, or certainty-equivalence, or with clearly specified imperfections, there is only room for risk, not uncertainty. Without uncertainty, psychology does not enter into knowledge. Further, if behavior is expressed as being goal-oriented, on the basis of this certain knowledge, then rational behavior can be clearly specified, and anything else is by definition irrational. The verbal behavioral economics literature suggests a much richer notion of psychology in relation to cognition and emotion, but the methodological requirements of the optimizing modeling approach impose severe limitations on what can be incorporated. The notion of rationality is constrained by the framework.

But if we depart from the formal requirements of models of optimisation subject to constraints, then a richer notion of psychology, and an integration of cognitive and emotional factors, are possible. Rationality, or reasonableness, inevitably combines reason with emotion. In particular, if knowledge (including the knowledge of economists) is seen as being in general held with uncertainty, then psychological factors are necessary to underpin knowledge, and indeed all activity. Rather than being separable in the form of preferences or information imperfections of some sort, psychology becomes integrated with reason and experience in the building up of knowledge as the basis for action.

There is a growing literature on which to draw, in finance, in economics and in psychology, and a growing body of evidence from a variety of sources. And this includes a fruitful set of ideas and experimental evidence in behavioral finance. But it is only when uncertainty is foundational to theory, rather than an imperfection relative to a perfect benchmark, and when behavior is understood as more complex than optimizing with respect to given psychological goals, that these ideas can actually bear fruit. It is only by paying attention to Minsky's uncertainty-based epistemology, and his corresponding methodology, that we will be able to take advantage of what psychology has to offer economics in aiming to understand financial instability.

Note

* This chapter has benefited from comments following presentations at Radboud University Nijmegen, the University of Stirling, and the 'John Maynard Keynes, 125 Years – What Have We Learned?' Conference at the University of Roskilde. The chapter has also benefited from comments from Peter Earl, Tatiana Kornienko and David Tuckett.

References

Altman, M. (2004), 'The Nobel Prize in behavioral and experimental economics: a contextual and critical appraisal of the contributions of Daniel Kahneman and Vernon Smith', *Review of Political Economy*, **16**(1), 3–41.
Ashraf, N., C.F. Camerer, and G. Lowenstein (2005), 'Adam Smith, behavioral economist', *Journal of Economic Perspectives*, **19**(3).
Baker, M. and J. Wurgler (2007), 'Investor sentiment in the stock market', *Journal of Economic Perspectives*, **21**(2), 129–51.
Berezin, M. (2005), 'Emotions and the economy', in N.J. Smelser and R. Swedberg (eds), *Handbook of Economic Sociology*, 2nd edition, New York and Princeton: Russell Sage Foundation and Princeton University Press.
Bikhchandani, S. and S. Sharma (2001), 'Herd behavior in financial markets', *IMF Staff Papers*, **47**(3), 279–310.
Bruni, L. and R. Sugden (2007), 'The road not taken: how psychology was removed from economics and how it might be brought back', *Economic Journal*, 117 (January), 146–73.
Camerer, C., G. Loewenstein and D. Prelec (2005), 'Neuroeconomics: how neuroscience can inform economics', *Journal of Economic Literature*, **153**(1), 9–64.
Chick, V. (2001), 'Cassandra as optimist', in R. Bellofiore and P. Ferri (eds), *Financial Keynesianism and Market Instability,* Cheltenham, UK and Northampton, MA, USA: Edward Elgar, pp. 35–46.
Chick, V. (2008), 'Could the crisis at Northern Rock have been predicted? An evolutionary approach', *Contributions to Political Economy*, **27**(1), 115–124.
Comim, F. (2006), 'Adam Smith: common sense and aesthetics in the age of experiments', in A. Dow and S. Dow (eds), *A History of Scottish Economic Thought*, London: Routledge.
Damasio, A.R. (1994), *Descartes' Error: Emotion, Reason, and the Human Brain*, New York: Avon Books.
Davis, J.B. (1994), *Keynes's Philosophical Development*, Cambridge: Cambridge University Press.
De Grauwe, P. (2007), 'The scientific foundation of DGSE models', ECB Working Paper (December).
Dopfer, K. and J. Potts (2008), *The General Theory of Economic Evolution*, London: Routledge.
Dow, S.C. (1990), 'Beyond dualism', *Cambridge Journal of Economics*, **14**(2), 143–58.
Dow, S.C. (forthcoming), 'Framing financial markets: a methodological approach', in P. Keizer (eds), *The Political Economy of Financial Markets*, Cheltenham, UK and Northampton, MA, USA: Edward Elgar.
Earl, P. (1990), *Monetary Scenarios,* Aldershot, UK and Brookfield, USA: Edward Elgar.
Earl, P.E., T.C. Peng and J. Potts (2007), 'Decision-rule cascades and the dynamics of speculative bubbles', *Journal of Economic Psychology*, **28**(3), 351–64.
Foley, D. (2001), 'Hyman Minsky and the dilemmas of contemporary economic method', in R. Bellofiore and P. Ferri (eds), *Financial Keynesianism and Market Instability*, Cheltenham, UK and Northampton, MA, USA: Edward Elgar, pp. 45–59.
Foucault, M. (1972), *The Archaeology of Knowledge*, translated by A.M. Sheridan, London: Routledge.
Gerhard, R. (2003), *From the Perspective of the Brain*, Frankfurt: Suhrkamp.
Gigerenzer, G. (2000), *Adaptive Thinking: Rationality in the Real World*, Oxford: Oxford University Press.
Gigerenzer, G. (2007), *Gut Feelings: The Intelligence of the Unconscious*, New York: Viking Press.
Gigerenzer, G. and T. Selten (2001), *Bounded Rationality*, Cambridge, MA: MIT Press.
Gigerenzer, G., Z. Swijtink, T. Porter, L. Daston, J. Beatty and L. Kruger (1989), *The Empire of Chance: How Probability Changed Science and Everyday Life*, Cambridge: Cambridge University Press.
Goodhart, C.A.E. (2008), 'Risk, uncertainty and financial stability', G.L.S. Shackle Memorial Lecture, St. Edmunds College, Cambridge (March).

Hausman, D.M. (1992), *The Inexact and Separate Science of Economics*, Cambridge: Cambridge University Press.

Hong, H. and J.C. Stein (2007), 'Disagreement and the stock market', *Journal of Economic Perspectives*, **21**(2), 109–28.

Hume, D. (1739–40 [1978]), *A Treatise of Human Nature*, Oxford: Clarendon.

Kahneman, D. (2003), 'Maps of bounded rationality: psychology for behavioral economics', *American Economic Review*, **93**(5), 1449–75.

Kahneman, D. and A. Tversky (1974), 'Judgment under uncertainty: heuristics and biases', *Science*, 185, 1124–31.

Kahneman, D. and A. Tversky (1979), 'Prospect theory: an analysis of decision under risk', *Econometrica*, **47**(2), 263–91.

Kaish, S. (1986), 'Behavioral economics in the theory of the business cycle', in B. Gilad and S. Kaish (eds), *Handbook of Behavioral Economics*, vol. B, Greenwich, CT: JAI Press.

Kelly, George A. (1963), *A Theory of Personality*, New York: W.W. Norton.

Keynes, J.M. (1921 [1973]), *A Treatise on Probability: Collected Writings of John Maynard Keynes*, vol. VIII, London: Macmillan.

Keynes, J.M. (1936 [1973]), *The General Theory of Employment, Interest and Money: Collected Writings of John Maynard Keynes*, vol. VII, London: Macmillan.

Keynes, J.M. (1937 [1973]), 'The General Theory of Employment', *Quarterly Journal of Economics*, reprinted in *The General Theory and After Part II: Defence and Development: Collected Writings of John Maynard Keynes*, vol. XIV, London: Macmillan, pp. 109–23.

Keynes, J.M. (1938 [1972]), 'My early beliefs', *Essays in Biography: Collected Writings of John Maynard Keynes*, vol. IX, London: Macmillan.

Klein, H.E. and M. d'Esposito (2007), 'Neurocognitive inefficacy of the strategy process', *Annals of the New York Academy of Sciences*, **1118**(1), 163–85.

Lawson, T. (1997), *Economics and Reality*, London: Routledge.

Leather, C.G. and J.P. Raines (2004), 'The Schumpeterian role of financial innovations in the new economy's business cycle', *Cambridge Journal of Economics*, 28, 667–81.

Loasby, B.J. (2009), 'The social science of economics', in R. Arena, S.C. Dow and M. Klaes (eds), *Open Economics: Economics in Relation to Other Disciplines*, London: Routledge, forthcoming.

Martins, N. (2008), 'Dispositions, motivations and the somatic marker hypothesis: an ontological perspective', paper presented to the Cambridge Critical Realist Workshop.

Minsky, H.P. (1975), *John Maynard Keynes*, London: Macmillan.

Minsky, H.P. (1982), *Inflation, Recession and Economic Policy*, Brighton: Wheatsheaf.

Minsky, M. (2006), *The Emotion Machine*, New York: Simon & Schuster.

Montes, L. (2004), *Adam Smith in Context*, Cambridge: Cambridge University Press.

Pixley, J. (2004), *Emotions in Finance: Distrust and Uncertainty in Global Markets*, Cambridge: Cambridge University Press.

Scitovsky, T. (1981), 'The desire for excitement in modern society', *Kyklos*, **34**(1), 3–13.

Sent, E.-M. (2004), 'Behavioral economics: how psychology made its (limited) way back into economics', *History of Political Economy*, **36**(4), 735–60.

Shiller, R.J. (2005), *Irrational Exuberance*, second edition, Princeton: Princeton University Press.

Simon, H. (1955), 'A behavioral model of rational choice', *Quarterly Journal of Economics*, **69**(1), 99–118.

Simon, H. (1986), 'Rationality and psychology in economics', *Journal of Business*, **59**(4:2), S209–24.

Smith, A. (1759 [1976]), *The Theory of Moral Sentiments*, D.D. Raphael and A.L. Macfie (eds), Oxford: Clarendon.

Smith, A. (1795 [1980]), 'The principles which lead and direct philosophical enquires: illustrated by the history of astronomy', in *Essays on Philosophical Subjects*, W.P.D. Wightman, J.C. Bryce and I.S. Ross (eds), Oxford: Clarendon.

Tuckett, D. and R. Taffler (2008), 'Phantastic objects and the financial market's sense of reality: a psychoanalytic contribution to the understanding of stock market instability', *International Journal of Psychoanalysis*, **89**(2), 389–412.

Whalen, C.J. (2007), 'The US credit crunch of 2007: a Minsky moment', Public Policy Brief No. 92, Levy Economics Institute of Bard College, Annandale-on-Hudson, New York.

Winslow, T. (1995), 'Uncertainty and liquidity-preference', in S.C. Dow and J. Hillard (eds), *Keynes, Knowledge and Uncertainty*, Aldershot, UK and Brookfield, USA: Edward Elgar.

Wollheim, R. (1999), *On the Emotions*, New Haven and London: Yale University Press.

14 The generalized 'Minsky Moment'
James K. Galbraith and Daniel Munevar Sastre

The concept of *systemic instability* is the cornerstone of Hyman Minsky's work. Minsky argued that system dynamics inherent to capitalism foster fragility, as stability spurs risky behavior, and risky behavior leads to crisis. As he put it, most succinctly: 'stability is destabilizing' (Minsky 1985).

This key notion is based on a clear and detailed analysis of modern financial capitalism, but it is also rooted in human psychology and behavior. There is nothing that restricts the application of Minsky's insight to the pecuniary realm. It is therefore astonishing how little has been done to extend the basic conceptual framework to other areas of social science.

This chapter is a first effort: we attempt here to take Minsky's theory of financial fragility into the realm of international relations. Our modest objective is to sketch an analytical framework that may help describe the economic, political and military interactions of nation states, in the light of Minsky's famous analytical distinction between hedge, speculative and Ponzi finance.

The chapter is presented in two sections. The first section outlines the theory. The second section presents a brief overview of modern history, using the terminology developed in the first section. The section also shows the connection between cycles of international relations and the evolution of the international monetary system. Thus it will develop that in this sphere, deterioration of the risk environment in politico-military terms usually has a counterpart in pecuniary relations after all.

A Minskyan approach to international relations theory

In Minsky's financial analysis, the unit of observation – the behavioral entity – is the firm. In our Minskyan theory of international relations, the unit of analysis is the nation-state. In this respect, we follow the conventional rational-actor paradigm of the standard realist model. However, we are not wedded to that interpretation. In a model of bureaucracy or politics, risky behavior for the conglomerate entity can emerge from stable environments in consequence of the actions of individual players, who become emboldened to test the limits traditionally placed on their behavior by convention, ethics, regulation or law. This is similar to the way in which firms can be endangered by risky behavior emanating from the CEO, from the ranks of management, or through a failure of labor-management relations.

Just as all firms do not possess the same relationship to the market, nation states do not enjoy symmetric relations within the global system. Rather, international relations exhibit an intricate and dynamic hierarchical structure. The central position is occupied by a hegemon, the preeminent power within a given sphere of influence. A second tier is composed of allies: countries that benefit from the established system but do not control it, whose economic and technological development put them in a position from which they may eventually move into control, should the hegemon falter. A third tier is composed of peripheral countries – the exploited – which provide commodities, labor, human capital and export markets to the hegemonic powers of the system. In former times peripheral regions were usually colonies. Today they may still be governed by agents of the hegemonic powers, directly or indirectly; their sovereignty and access to credit remain limited and their currencies, typically, are soft.

There may, of course, be several hegemonic systems in the world at any given time.

The degree of influence that each nation-state has within the international system thus varies according to its status. As in the case of market power – which determines the ability of firms to set mark ups and earn profits – the status of a nation-state determines the share of benefits that it receives from the hegemonic system of which it forms a part. In international relations as in economics, market power and (analogously) status determine only the distribution of profits, not total income or system welfare. The latter depends on macroeconomic conditions (Minsky 1986, p. 143), a product of collective endeavor.

We will focus here on the interaction of the countries belonging to the first two tiers of the system, that is, the hegemon and its allies. Within each system, each member faces the eternal trade-off between self-interest and collective interest, between actions aimed to increase its power at others' expense and actions to improve the collective welfare. Total welfare depends on progressive development, which requires peace, good governance and good order, at least between the hegemon and its allies. Violence toward the periphery or toward other hegemonic systems is a separate matter, since both the hegemon and its allies can benefit from it under certain material conditions. But it is risky.

Firms in a modern financial economy gain market power initially by production of something for sale, on an exclusive or semi-exclusive basis. Firms go on to exercise power, however, not only through price mark ups, but also through portfolio transactions – through borrowing and lending in the capital markets. In this way they can consolidate power, by acquiring and eliminating rivals. But generally a firm cannot obtain finance, and therefore its ability to produce is limited, unless it has market power in the first place (Papadimitriou and Wray 1999).

Similar exclusive or semi-exclusive control over key production processes typifies the political hegemon and its allies in the global system, and this is necessarily connected to a privileged financial position. A country cannot develop effective military capability unless it holds significant technical advantages, and it cannot finance the development and maintenance of state power unless those advantages are recognized by financial markets. Hence, the eternal importance of bankers to princes.

For this reason, even a hegemon faces certain limits on its power. It depends, for the continuity of its status, on the forbearance of its allies and, to a degree, also that of the peripheral countries within its sphere. It must borrow from the former, in order to sustain its technical and military advantages over them. As for the latter, their resistance and resentment cannot be so great, as to force the hegemon into an exhausting struggle to maintain its position.

In the international system, economic and technological development play the role of cash-flow-generating activities: they are the ongoing bread-and-butter of a power position. Military power and the financial arrangements required to support it, on the other hand, play the role of portfolio transactions: they are devices to project power beyond what can be justified by economic and technical supremacy alone. The game of maximizing status can be played through either channel, and great hegemons invariably play it through a combination of both.

For any firm, there will always be uncertainty about the match between cash-flow generating activities and portfolio transactions. The former are based on assumptions about future market conditions, the latter are given by contract and therefore known, at least to within the contingencies specified in the contract (Minsky 1986, p. 205). Thus the first question facing the hegemonic firm is whether the underlying basis of its market power – a superior product at a price not challenged by effective competition – will continue to generate profits sufficient to cover financial commitments.

In the case of the nation-state, the costs of peacetime military power are in the public budget and therefore known, while in most of modern history the financial obligations of the state are also disciplined by knowledge of – or at least a convinced belief in – the limitations imposed by financial markets. On the other hand, technological and therefore actual military superiority, in trade during peacetime and in the event of war, are always uncertain, because they always depend on the prospects of future competition. They depend, that is, on a match-up in the marketplace or on the battlefront that has not yet occurred, that may never occur, and whose outcome if it does occur cannot be entirely predicted. Great powers are driven by anxiety about their actual and potential rivals, of whom their knowledge of conduct and performance is 'based on conjectures and therefore uncertain by nature' (Minsky 1986, p.205).

Like firms in a market economy, countries seeking to project and defend their power must innovate, experiment and improvise. The competition is always in mind; 'objects in the mirror' often appear closer than they are. Like firms, countries 'operate on the basis of trial and error; if a behavior is rewarded, it will be repeated. Thus, stable periods naturally lead to optimism, to booms and to increasing fragility' (Papadimitrou and Wray 1999).

For Minsky, financial instability is linked to the relative importance of the different sources of revenue. Three basic profiles describe the reliance of firms on the different types of income: the hedge, speculative and Ponzi profiles. Firms engaging in hedge finance rely mainly on income cash flow to fulfill their obligations, whereas speculative and Ponzi schemes rely increasingly on portfolio transactions. The former face ordinary market uncertainties; any crisis they face is of ordinary competitive performance and market conditions, given the financial commitments.

This is not so for those engaging in speculative finance. Firms in a speculative position have taken on financial obligations for which expected cash flow is not expected to be fully sufficient. They must therefore not only maintain cash flow but also refinance their positions periodically. A speculative position may be refinanced if market conditions do not change, but it is vulnerable to unforeseen changes. If a firm in such a position cannot successfully refinance, the speculative position may simply collapse. But it also may become a Ponzi position, still afloat for the moment but inherently unsustainable, once its nature is recognized by the world.

The extension of these ideas to international relations is straightforward. Countries contesting for economic and technological advantage in a stable world environment are the analogs of hedge players: they are relying on future cash flow to assure their prosperity and progress, and to meet their commitments. Their financial capacity reflects an acknowledgment of economic and technological power, but it may go unused – as in the cases of modern Japan and China, a hedge player may be content to run a cash surplus. If they are financed, it is because their market position is expected to be sustained. The uncertainties they face are those of their own material capacities and competitive conditions.

A speculative profile would occur when a hegemonic power uses its power – particularly the threat of military action – to project influence in a way that is hostile or challenging toward other powers, or when an allied country decides to challenge the hegemon within its own system. The problem is that the position provokes the reaction of another strong player, and therefore comes under challenge. While the commitments of the speculative position are known, it must nevertheless be 'refinanced' periodically, under conditions whose character cannot be known in advance. The position may be tenable, or it may not be. If it is not tenable, the speculative player has two options: he can fold his hand, or he can double down and hope for the best.

As in finance, the transition from a speculative to a Ponzi profile is not fully under a country's control. It depends on whether the speculative position can be refinanced – whether (say) a provocative confrontation is resolved without escalation in the form of an arms race or outbreak of violence, either of which may have dire financial implications, and whether those implications can be handled by the hegemon's bankers. Once open conflict starts, it generally requires more economic resources than were provided for in the advance planning, and a process of accelerated depletion may begin. If what was initially considered as a limited engagement transforms into a military quagmire or explodes into total war, a vicious cycle gets under way that often ends with the collapse of the regime.

It is worthwhile to specify how national positions are affected by the evolution of the system and vice versa. A country in a hedge position maintains its status mainly through the development of economic and political influence. It relies on the mechanisms of collective security; if it is an ally it does not challenge the leadership of the hegemon and if it is the hegemon itself, it does not overreach and provoke revolt or passive resistance among its allies. On the other hand, abuse of the periphery is routine for both parties. But the periphery is, as a rule, so weak that it cannot effectively fight back, consequently the benefits of such abuse routinely exceed the costs.

The shift from a hedge to a speculative profile is typically a product of the success of this system. A hegemon at the peak of a well-functioning alliance and with a dependent periphery well under control, may decide to challenge other hegemonic powers. Indeed, in the extreme case of a globally preeminent hegemon, the very existence of spheres of influence outside direct control may seem intolerable. Needless to say, success against one rival hegemonic system is likely to breed extreme confidence that others are equally open to attack.

An allied state, weary of lending to its own hegemon, may come to feel that the security provided by membership in the hegemonic system is not worth the economic cost of the tribute required to sustain it. The relationship between the two always has both predatory and protective elements, and the former may come to outweigh the latter in the eyes of the lesser state. While direct conflict between a hegemon and its allied powers is rare, this challenge can take a more subtle form. Specifically, it can consist of denying easy credit, and therefore undermining the hegemon's chances of prevailing in a contest with third parties.

Once in the speculative position, countries are exposed not only to commercial, technological, economic and political risks – which is also true of hedge countries – but they also become vulnerable on the military and financial fronts. Bad things can then happen, and sometimes they do. When speculative positions must be financed, the terms on which they are refinanced may be unsustainable, in the sense of being incompatible with national success over time. But it is still better to refinance, and defer the day of reckoning, than to admit defeat. Thus, as with a firm, once a speculative position has been taken, the shift to a Ponzi position is largely outside national control. When it happens, it renders the national position, and that of the system as a whole, critically unstable (Minsky 1986, pp. 208-9); collapse is inevitable in due course.

Consequently, for countries as for firms, the movement toward the generalized Minsky Moment comes in two phases. 'The shift toward speculative positions, or fragility, occurs intentionally (and more-or-less inevitably because of the way in which expectations are affected by success), while the shift from speculative toward a Ponzi scheme is mainly unintentional' (Papadimitrou and Wray 1999).

There is an additional significant difference in the way speculative and Ponzi actors behave, as noted by Kregel (2004). The main objective of a speculative actor in international relations is to secure or expand economic and political advantages. The speculative actor relies in certain periods on military threat, but avoids open confrontation. When the situation transitions to the Ponzi phase, there is an inversion between means and objectives. Economic and political influence cease to matter except as they can help to sustain the active projection of military power and the financial backing it requires. The scheme is sustainable only so long as military and financial power can keep adding to economic and political assets. When they can no longer do this, the system crashes. This is because both the economy and the political system, already under severe stress in various ways, are unable to cope with the material, human and financial losses associated with the active projection of power against equally active opposition.

Once a Ponzi position exists, no shock is needed to generate a crisis. As Tymoigne (2006) explains, 'the immediate cause of a crisis does not matter. The forces at work that led to the crisis started to operate a long time before the factors triggering the occurrence of the crisis'.

Minsky and modern history

So: stability is destabilizing. If this were all there were to it, one might expect, as a logical outcome, a constant stream of wars between hegemonic powers. Similarly in the case of the financial system, one might expect a constant and recurring condition of crisis. But, as a matter of history, neither is the case. Confrontation, crisis and collapse have all happened, with bruising frequency, in the historical record. But hedge positions have also held for a long time, most notably in living memory.

From the end of the Napoleonic Wars until the outbreak of World War I Europe enjoyed comparative peace, interrupted more frequently by revolution than by war. Wars were of course continuous throughout this period, but in remote regions: across Africa, in India, in China, in the Crimea, between Japan and Russia, and inside the United States. Wars on European soil were rare, the notable exception being the quick Prussian victory over France in 1870. Why?

We believe the broad answer lies in the development of the national army, following the French Revolution and the consolidation of Germany and Italy into nation-states. In the context of the industrial revolution, the rise of the railroad, and the possibility of full-scale mobilizations, the national army was a new and quite terrifying development. It greatly raised the uncertainty associated with the prospect of military conflict close to home, and so induced hedging behavior. Competition now focused on obtaining economic and demographic supremacy, alongside the largest possible dependent empire. Bismarck, in particular, was a consummate hedge player, never going outside the power structures justified by Germany's rising industrial capacity.

Three elements were key in the processes of nineteenth-century colonization. The first was the overall supremacy of Britain, especially on the high seas, which promoted caution among those powers who might consider themselves her rivals (Block 1977, p. 12). The second element was the use of military means to establish free trade: 'the free movement of goods, people and money that developed under British hegemony between 1870 and 1913, was made possible, in large part, by military might, rather than market forces' (Chang 2008, p. 24). The third was the development of advanced technologies and weaponry, giving European countries a decisive advantage over peripheral regions, which made imperial expansion a cheap enterprise (McNeill 1982, p. 258). As Churchill wrote of the breech-loading rifle in Afghanistan, 'the respect which the Pathan tribesmen entertained for Christian civilization was vastly enhanced' (Churchill 1958, p. 135). Empires developed but those of France, Germany and Austria-Hungary were distinctly second-class.

By the early twentieth century, the project of empire building had reached geographic limits, while for each major European power the successes of the late nineteenth century bred a surpassing confidence in their military capacities. What remained was to tread on each other's toes, while engaging in a broad arms race. Hedge behavior became speculative, and crises between competing empires started to erupt, revealing among other things the weakness of the Russian empire (1905) and (at Tangier) the diplomatic isolation of the Germans. The Kaiser was emboldened by the first and enraged by the second; both moved him along the path of further speculative bets. It did not take much, in August 1914, for the speculative position to be transformed into a Ponzi profile by the assassination of Archduke Ferdinand at Sarajevo, the subsequent mobilizations and the outbreak of war. Once war started, there was nothing to do except double down, repeatedly, until by 1918 all the major European powers were bled dry and exhausted.

In the inter-war period the cycle repeated, in part because efforts to restore a stable hedge position were crippled from the beginning by the peace imposed at Versailles and by the defective design of the League of Nations. With the Great Depression, any prospect for a collaborative path toward economic development collapsed, and Germany launched on its well-known strategy of speculative confrontation with Britain and France.

The historian Adam Tooze (2007) has rewritten the economic history of World War II, to emphasize that German strategy, including the genocide, was substantially driven by a lust for land; without *lebensraum* and the agricultural terrain it would bring into German hands the Nazi leadership believed that Germany would be permanently reduced to the status of a second-rate power. For Germany, therefore, the hedge behavior compatible with sustained peace was never an option. Hitler chose to gamble, and initially, in Austria, Czechoslovakia, Poland, Belgium, Holland and France, his speculations paid off. In each case aggression provided a reward vastly greater than its cost. This led, in classic Minsky fashion, to overconfidence and willingness to increase the bet, until in May of 1941 Germany challenged the Soviet Union.

From that point forward, Germany's industrial and military capacities were limited quite severely by its finances. To pay for critical supplies from neutrals such as Sweden and Switzerland, equally critical materials including coal and steel had to be exported. Populations that had been overrun had to be looted, starved, even murdered: a costly and inefficient process. Petroleum could not be bought and had to be seized instead. Labor could not be paid, so slaves were imported and worked to death. Tooze makes clear, in particular, that the 'armaments miracle' which brought German war production to a peak at the end of 1944 (in despite of the strategic bombing campaign against it) would have ended quite soon. Japan's financial situation was, if anything, even more extreme, and Japanese policies in Manchuria and in occupied regions of the Pacific basin reflected this. Both systems were unsustainable, and if the war had gone on long enough both countries would have collapsed even if they had not been overrun.

In the cases of Britain and the Soviet Union, the situation was quite different as these countries were bound to each other and to the United States and the larger world by a functioning financial network. This permitted recognition of the Ponzi character of the British commitment, in particular, to be deferred until after the war was over. Britain borrowed heavily from the United States but also from its Empire, including India; these debts could be settled in part by granting independence after the war. But the result was in many ways effectively the same in the aftermath: Britain no less than Germany was to be reduced to second-tier status by the consequences – in her case financial rather than material – of World War II. The Soviet Union would escape this fate – for 45 years anyway – only by hanging on to an empire won on the ground. And only the United States, as the surviving hegemon of the world system, would have the luxury of writing new rules for the period to follow.

They were, by and large, enlightened rules. The end result of World War II was the construction of a world financial and political system that enforced hedging behavior on the major players for about twenty years. Each aspect of the system: the United Nations Security Council, North Atlantic Treaty Organization (NATO), the International Monetary Fund, the World Bank and each major program, from the Marshall Plan through the development of the European Economic Community, worked on the basis of mutual obligation and restraint. This was buttressed, in relations between the great powers, by the doctrines of deterrence and containment and by the deterrent power of the nuclear bomb. This period thus made possible the larger accomplishment of rapid economic recovery and sustained development – albeit based, as we now realize, on accelerated depletion of the world's natural resources and its environmental capacity to absorb the waste products of industrialization.

For Minsky, the apparent stability of the post-war economy was founded on the combined impact of strong regulation enforced by strong institutions, and the policies of Big Banks and Big Government effectively implemented from the onset of the New Deal. This stabilizing framework precluded excessive risk-taking and blocked the movement of financial players from hedge to speculative positions. Those movements that did occur could be managed; if the overall system was stable, the instability of small elements within it could be largely offset when difficulties arose. Likewise the international political system.

Yet as Minsky's thesis would predict, it did not last. The Cold War fostered hedging behavior by the hegemonic powers and their allies, but it also channeled outbreaks of actual violence away from the center and into the peripheral countries. The periphery was therefore wracked by violence. And some of that violence placed the two world systems in conflict, initiating the step-up process from hedge to speculative conflict.

The United States, in response to revolutionary initiatives – a form of what it perceived to be speculative behavior from the communist camp – moved to a speculative position of its own in Vietnam in the mid-1960s. Ultimately the US lost militarily, but this came at a moment after détente had been reached with China, and the loss was therefore not of strategic importance. What bothered US hegemony more in this period was the unsupportive financial behavior of its allies. Well before the defeat, the stalemate in Vietnam led to an unraveling of the favored position of the US at the heart of the Bretton Woods system – forcing the US off the gold-exchange standard in 1971 and moving to a system of flexible exchange rates in 1973. It has often been argued that a more restrictive fiscal policy in the late 1960s would have preserved the old system, but Eisner (1968) persuasively refutes this view. Given the unwillingness of the world to write blank checks, the only thing that could have saved the economy, as Eisner wrote, was not to get involved in the war in the first place.

The United States ultimately recovered from its Vietnam-engendered financial troubles. It did so by launching another major aggression against the periphery, this time financial: it took the form of the debt crisis, for which the groundwork was laid by the oil boom in the 1970s, and which was then precipitated by tight monetary policies in the early 1980s. The dollar was restored as the reserve currency for the entire world, and the basis laid for American economic expansion to resume into the 1990s. Unlike military adventurism, financial aggression paid.

Meanwhile, much of the world continued to feel a need to finance the military superiority of the United States, and success emboldened, as it always does. The economic decline of the Soviet empire made challenges to that empire's position, as in Afghanistan after 1979 or by Star Wars, highly effective in relation to their cost. And China, in addition to Japan, emerged as a power willing to support the US financial position, in return for secure access to US markets and also secure access to the raw materials and food of the Western hemisphere and the energy of the Middle East.

The peaceful end of the Cold War was expected by many to augur 'the end of history' (Fukuyama 2002). But the Minskyan logic dictated a different result. The end of the Cold War brought the prevailing structures of deterrence at least partially to an end, while fostering a sense of triumphalism in the surviving hegemon, the United States. It therefore encouraged elements within the US to enter once again what could be identified as the speculative phase of the cycle. As Madeleine Albright famously remarked to Colin Powell, 'What's the point of having this superb military you're always talking about, if we can't use it?'

With the first Gulf War, the United States 'kicked the Vietnam Syndrome for good' (the phrase was that of the first President Bush), greatly encouraging the architects of military power to brave its actual use. Through the 1990s, even though the US remained cautious, largely multi-lateral, and restrained in the ways military power was deployed, the ulti-mate successes of interventions in Bosnia and Kosovo reinforced the view that US military power could not be effectively challenged. This increas-ing confidence would lead to the taking of new speculative positions in the period immediately following September 11, 2001. A seemingly easy victory in Afghanistan – at least at first – would then increase the boldness with which policymakers were willing to approach other problems and other goals and objectives. But then came Iraq.

The Iraq war confronts American leadership, for the first time since Vietnam, with a speculative bet gone bad. The idea was that the war would be brief, successful, and that it would cost practically nothing. Had that been the case, then of course the architects of the war would have gone on to bigger things. They miscalculated. Why?

The principal reason now appears clearly. Iraq was not, as the war planners supposed, an isolated peripheral country like any other. It was, rather, a country well within the geopolitical reach of a neighboring (albeit regional) hegemon – a country outside the US sphere of control – that was, because of its minor place on the world stage, not clearly recognized as such at the time. This is Iran. Yet Iran has proved very capable of pro-jecting power into the Iraqi vacuum. American leaders thought they were knocking over a minor adversary, and ended up empowering a much more significant one.

And so after five years American leaders find themselves with no path to victory, with declining credit and no plausible way, consistent with their own goals and reputations, to engineer a return to the hedge system of mutual stabilization. To return to a hedge position is possible, but it would require leaving Iran in charge in Iraq. That is, of course, a possibility and it could be the prudent exit strategy.[1] Otherwise, the inexorable Minsky logic suggests that at some point the only way to refinance the power debts of the Iraqi debacle will be to incur new ones, for instance by taking on the rival hegemon directly.

The United States military cannot be defeated in Iraq, as it was in Vietnam. But that is not the issue. Rather, the American position depends on a willingness, by the world, to finance it. And that willingness depends, in turn, on three conditions. First, it depends on a continuing conviction by some countries – ostensibly allies – that the costs of failing to support the American global position outweigh the costs of maintaining that support. Second, it depends on a belief in other countries – in the periphery and among rival powers – that American military power cannot be successfully defied. The war in Iraq has gravely undermined both propositions. An attack on Iran would, without doubt, undermine them even more – particularly if it endangers the access of Europe, China and Japan to Middle Eastern oil.

The third condition is that the financial system of the United States remain second to none as a safe-haven for the maintenance of liquidity and investment value. The sub-prime crisis, the freeze-up of interbank borrowing, and the generally skittish and unreassuring behavior of the US financial authorities have all worked to undermine this third condition, even though at each turn financial problems in Europe have so far continued to keep the dollar one step ahead.

The situation thus poses the question: at what point does a speculative bet gone bad turn into a Ponzi profile? At what point does the financial position of a great power become irretrievable? How much pummeling can the technological, military and political reputation of the United States take? It is surely impossible for the US to return to a pure hedge position, with balanced external accounts and an isolationist foreign stance. It would be very difficult – though it may ultimately prove necessary – to reconstruct a formal world order with the expected stability of the Bretton Woods system. But, short of this, can the country find its way back toward the margin between hedge and speculation, so that doubts about its future stability begin to fade?

That question remains unresolved. It is an uncomfortable position, particularly when one recognizes that the potential for doubling down, for raising the speculative bet, remains very much alive, and will so long as the forces that pushed our luck remain in power.

Note

1. As this chapter goes to press, it appears that this is the exit strategy.

References

Andreassen, P. (1993), 'The psychology of risk: a brief primer', Working Paper No. 87, Levy Economics Institute of Bard College, Annandale-on-Hudson, New York.
Block, F. (1977), *The Origins of International Economic Disorder: A Study of United States International Monetary Policy from World War II to the Present*, London: University of California Press.
Chang, H. (2008), *Bad Samaritans: The Myth of Free Trade and the Secret History of Capitalism*, New York: Bloomsbury Press.

Churchill, W. (1958), *My Early Life: A Roving Commission*, New York: Charles Scribners' Sons.
Davidson, P. (2008), 'Is the current distress caused by the sub-prime mortgage crisis a Minsky Moment? or is it the result of attempting to securitize illiquid non-commercial mortgage loans', mimeo.
Eisner, R. (1968), 'War and taxes: the role of the economist in politics', *Bulletin of the Atomic Scientists*, (June), 13–18.
Fukuyama, F. (2002), *The End of History and the Last Man*, New York: Perennial.
Kregel, J. (2004), 'External financing for development and international financial stability', G-24 Discussion Paper Series, No. 32, United Nations Conference on Trade and Development.
McNeill, W. (1982), *The Pursuit of Power: Technology, Armed Forces and Society, Since A.D. 1000*, Chicago: University of Chicago Press.
Minsky, H.P. (1985), 'The legacy of Keynes', *Journal of Economic Education*, **16**(1), 5–15.
Minsky, H.P. (1986), *Stabilizing an Unstable Economy*, New Haven: Yale University Press.
Papadimitriou, D.B. and L.R. Wray (1999), 'Minsky's analysis of financial capitalism', Working Paper No. 275, Levy Economics Institute of Bard College, Annandale-on-Hudson, New York.
Tooze, A. (2007), *Wages of Destruction: The Making and Breaking of the Nazi Economy*, New York: Viking.
Tymoigne, E. (2006), 'The Minskyan system, part I: properties of the Minskyan analysis and how to theorize and model a monetary production economy', Working Paper No. 452, Levy Economics Institute of Bard College, Annandale-on-Hudson, New York.

Index